Østrup Press, LLC

Contracts, Commercial Law and Business Organizations

For Georgia Paralegals

Third Edition

****

Celia L. Murray, J.D.

Permissions
Østrup Press, LLC
535 South Main Street
Madison, Georgia 30650

To contact customer care or order copies of this book, please e-mail us at ostruppress@gmail.com or mail correspondence to:

Orders
Østrup Press, LLC
535 South Main Street
Madison, Georgia 30650

or visit our website at www.ostruppress.com.

Printed in the United States of America

ISBN: 978-0-9838031-2-6

Contracts, Commercial Law and Business Organizations

For Georgia Paralegals

Third Edition

A guide to the study of the law of contracts, commercial transactions and business organizations for the paralegal student with an emphasis on the law of the State of Georgia

Celia L. Murray, J.D.

Editorial Advisors:

Celia L. Murray, J.D.
Georgia Piedmont Technical College

Judge J. Virgil Costley (Retired)
Director, Paralegal Studies Program
Georgia Piedmont Technical College

Kye W. Haymore, J.D.
Instructor, Paralegal Studies
Georgia Piedmont Technical College

Karen L. Still, J.D.
Vice President, MDI Telecom Corp.

Dylan S. Pettis, Member
Member, Pettis Investment Properties, LLC

Alvah A. Shelton
Paralegal

Melissa Hardman
Georgia Piedmont Technical College

CONTRACTS, COMMERCIAL LAW AND BUSINESS ORGANIZATIONS

Table of Contents

PART I - Federal Authority

Chapter 1 Constitutional Law and Business

Chapter 2 The Employment Relationship and its Regulation

PART II - Contracts and the Contractual Relationship

Chapter 3 The Contractual Agreement and Consideration

Chapter 4 Legality, Capacity and Contractual Intent

Chapter 5 Classifications of Contracts and the Statute of Frauds

Chapter 6 Proper Form of a Contract

PART III - Business Organizations

Chapter 10 Franchises, Sole Proprietorships and General Partnerships

Chapter 11 Limited Partnerships, Limited Liability Companies And Professional Corporations

PREFACE

Commercial transactions, including contracts, surround us all. They permeate our lives and affect us in many different ways. We may have a mortgage on our home or a car loan, both of which are examples of contracts that involve promises to pay back a certain sum of money. We may have a lease agreement with our landlord. Our relationship with our employer is a contractual one, even though it may not be in writing. Each time we make a purchase in a store or go into a restaurant and order a meal, we enter into a contractual relationship.

Contract law is one of the most consistent areas of law. While other areas of law, such as criminal law, tort law and family law, have changed dramatically over the years, contract law is little altered from its common law origins. As you might imagine, most of the evolution in contract law has been in response to changes in technology and means of communication.

The same cannot be said with regard to the area of business organizations. Some business entities, such as sole proprietorships and partnerships, have existed for hundreds of years, while many others are quite new, having been created in recent decades to meet the demands of a changing economy.

Businesses, from the very small to the largest international conglomerate, are all required to follow various laws in connection with the operation of the business enterprise. Some of us may elect to work for others, and thus, avoid the perils of ownership. If we so chose, we avoid the risks of operating our own business, but, in trade, give up the potential for great rewards. Others of us are entrepreneurs who open and operate a business enterprise and who must decide what form of business organization to use and must also understand the many laws and regulations to which we are subject.

Given the pervasive nature of the topics, a fundamental understanding of contracts, commercial transactions, and business organizations is crucial for any paralegal, regardless of the area of concentration in which he or she is ultimately employed.

This text does not attempt, as many do, to provide an extensive appendix of sample contract clauses or examples of the documents required to establish various business organizations. Many such forms are available online and all paralegals are encouraged to avail themselves of the vast resources of the World Wide Web. For the Georgia paralegal in the area of business organizations, I recommend an excellent resource book, *Kaplan's Nadler Georgia Corporations, Limited Partnerships and Limited Liability Companies with Forms* by Jerome L. Kaplan. John K. Larkins, Jr.'s *Georgia Contracts: Law and Litigation* is a valuable treatise on general contract law and includes examples of typical clauses for use in standard contracts.

Part I - Federal Authority

Chapter 1 Constitutional Law and Business

OUTLINE

1.1 The Supremacy Clause and Federal Preemption
1.2 The Commerce Clause
1.3 State Police Power
1.4 The First Amendment and Business
Free Speech
Religion
1.5 The Equal Protection Clause
1.6 The Due Process Clause
1.7 Relations Among the States
The Privileges and Immunities Clause
The Full Faith and Credit Clause

Review Questions and Exercises
Practical Applications

The U.S. Constitution, sometimes referred to as the federal constitution, establishes our federal form of government in which sovereign power is shared by the national government and the states. The Constitution provides rights and protections not only to individuals, but also to businesses. To understand laws pertaining to business and contracts, one must also be familiar with several concepts of constitutional law.

1.1 The Supremacy Clause and Federal Preemption

> U.S. Constitution - Article VI (in part)
>
> This Constitution, and the Laws of the United States which shall be made in Pursuance thereof; and all Treaties made, or which shall be made, under the Authority of the United States, shall be the supreme Law of the Land; and the Judges in every State shall be bound thereby, any Thing in the Constitution or Laws of any State to the Contrary not withstanding.

The Constitution of the United States contains, in Article VI, the *Supremacy Clause*. This important provision establishes that the federal Constitution, federal laws, and federal regulations are the supreme law of the land. Any time there is a direct conflict between a federal law and a state or local law, the state or local law is invalid.

Congress may provide that a particular statute which it has passed exclusively regulates a specific area or activity. If so, then no state or local law which purports to regulate that area or activity is valid. More often, though, federal statutes do not expressly provide for exclusive jurisdiction. In these cases, state and local governments have *concurrent jurisdiction* to regulate the area or activity and may pass laws concerning that same area.

Preemption occurs when Congress chooses to act in an area in which the federal government and the states have concurrent powers and the acts of Congress expressly cover the subject area completely. In such a situation, a valid federal statute or regulation will take precedence over any conflicting state or local law or regulation on the same general subject. Any state or local law that "directly and substantially conflicts" with valid federal law is preempted under the Supremacy Clause. Often, however, it is not clear whether Congress, in passing a law, intended to preempt an entire subject area against state regulation. In these situations, it is left to the courts to determine whether Congress intended to exercise exclusive power over a given area, or whether the states may also legislate in that area.

1.2 *The Commerce Clause*

For many years, the *commerce clause* has had a greater impact on business that any other provision in the Constitution.

> U.S. Constitution - Article I, Section 8
> (in part)
>
> The Congress shall have the Power ... To regulate Commerce with foreign Nations, and among the several States, and with the Indian Tribes;

The commerce clause, which specifically authorizes the federal government to regulate commerce, promotes the development of national markets and free trade among the states. It also prevents states from establishing laws and regulations that would interfere with trade and commerce by favoring local goods or services over those from other states.

Geier v. American Honda Motor Company, Inc.
120 S.Ct. 1913 (2000)
Supreme Court of the United States

Facts: The United States Department of Transportation adopted a Federal Motor Vehicle Safety Standard that required automobile manufacturers to equip 10% of their 1987 vehicles with passive restraints including automatic seat belts or airbags. In 1992, Alex Geier, driving a 1987 Honda Accord in Washington, D.C., collided with a tree and was seriously injured. The car was equipped with seat belts, but not air bags. Geier sued the car's manufacturer, Honda, alleging that the company had negligently and defectively designed the car because it lacked a driver's side airbag in violation of the District of Columbia's tort law. The Court dismissed Geier's lawsuit, finding that the District of Columbia's tort law conflicted with the federal passive restraint safety standard and was therefore preempted under the Supremacy Clause of the U.S. Constitution. The Court of Appeals affirmed and Geier appealed to the U.S. Supreme Court.

Issue: Does the federal passive restraint safety standard, which has the force of law, preempt an action brought under the District of Columbia's common law tort law?

Holding: Geier's lawsuit depends upon his claim that the manufacturer had a duty to install an airbag when it manufactured the 1987 Honda Accord. Such a state law (a rule of state tort law imposing such a duty) would have required manufacturers of all similar cars to install airbags in the entire District of Columbia related portion of their 1987 new car fleet even though the federal safety standard at that time required only that 10% of a manufacturer's nationwide fleet be equipped with passive restraint systems.

The language of the federal passive restraint standard is clear. It sought a gradually developing mix of alternative passive restraint devices. The rule of state tort law for which petitioner

Geier argues would stand as an obstacle to the accomplishment of that objective. Ordinary principles of preemption apply and preclude Geier's action.

The commerce clause gives the federal government the authority to regulate interstate commerce. Pursuant to this clause, Congress has the authority to regulate the channels of interstate commerce and the instrumentalities of interstate commerce, that is, the people and things that move in interstate commerce. Because the federal government is, in theory, a limited one, it does not have authority to regulate intrastate commerce, being commerce that is completely internal to a given state.

While originally the courts interpreted the commerce clause more narrowly, the modern rule allows the federal government to regulate activities that *affect* interstate commerce. Under the *effects on interstate commerce* test, the regulated activity does not itself have to be in interstate commerce. Using this approach, the fact that a business may have an economic impact on the nation, regardless of whether it otherwise appears to be intrastate in nature, creates federal jurisdiction. In other words, any local (intrastate) activity that has an effect on interstate commerce is subject to federal regulation. Thus, this test subjects a substantial amount of business activity in the United States to federal regulation.

Consider, for example, the 1942 case of *Wickard, Secretary of Agriculture v. Filburn* which dealt with a federal statute that set a quota on wheat production and limited the amount of wheat a farmer could plant and harvest for home consumption. Mr. Filburn, a farmer, violated the law and, when penalized, argued that the statute was overly broad and that his was a purely local activity not subject to federal regulation. The U.S. Supreme Court upheld the statute on the grounds that it prevented nationwide surpluses and shortages of wheat. The Court reasoned that wheat grown for home consumption would affect the supply of wheat available in interstate commerce.

Heart of Atlanta Motel v. United States
379 U.S. 241 (1964)
Supreme Court of the United States

Facts: In the 1960's the Heart of Atlanta Motel was a large downtown motel operated in Atlanta two blocks from Peachtree Street. The motel was an independent business, locally owned by a Georgia resident, and not affiliated with any other motel or motel chain. The Heart of Atlanta Motel had 216 rooms available to guests and was readily accessible to interstate highways 75 and 85 and several major state highways. The Heart of Atlanta Motel had a long established practice of refusing to rent rooms to blacks.

The Civil Rights Act of 1964 made it illegal for public accommodations to discriminate against guests based on their race. After the act was passed, the owner of the motel declared his intention to continue his policy of refusing to rent rooms to blacks. The owner of the Heart of Atlanta Motel brought an action to have the Civil Rights Act of 1964 declared unconstitutional, asserting that Congress had no authority to regulate the activities of a locally owned business.

Issue: Did Congress, in passing the Civil Rights Act of 1964, exceed its constitutional powers to regulate commerce under the Commerce Clause?

Holding: The evidence clearly shows that the Heart of Atlanta Motel solicits patronage from outside the State of Georgia through various national advertising media, including magazines of national circulation, and that it maintains more than 50 billboards and highway signs. Approximately 75% of the motel's registered guests are from out of state. The interstate movement of persons is "commerce" which concerns more than one state.

Clearly, protection of interstate commerce is within the regulatory power of Congress under the Commerce Clause of the United States Constitution. Congress has the power to enact appropriate legislation with regard to a place of public accommodation, such as the Heart of Atlanta Motel, even if it is assumed to be of a purely "local" character since Congress' power over interstate commerce extends to the regulation of local incidents which might have a substantial and harmful effect upon interstate commerce.

Throughout much of the twentieth century, congressional authority grew significantly, virtually unchecked by the judiciary. During this time, the power of Congress to regulate activities extended to areas once thought to be exclusively the domain of the states including regulations for the general welfare of the people. Examples include:

- The criminalization of various acts including the interstate movement of women for immoral purposes, flight from one state to another to avoid prosecution, car-jacking, and many others;
- The Consumer Credit Protection Act;
- Anti-discrimination laws;
- Child labor laws; and
- Occupational safety regulations.

While, as is obvious from the *Heart of Atlanta Motel* case, the power of the federal government is extremely broad under the commerce clause and, at least theoretically, extends to the regulation of all commercial enterprises in the United States, this power is not completely unlimited. In several recent cases the U.S. Supreme Court has held that Congress enacted statutes beyond its powers under the interstate commerce clause. In these cases, the Court noted that the commerce clause specifically applies to "commerce" and found that there was no commercial activity being regulated by the challenged statutes.

United States v. Lopez
115 S.Ct. 1624 (1995)
Supreme Court of the United States

Facts: In 1990, Congress enacted the Gun-Free School Zone Act, a federal statute which made it a federal crime to possess a firearm in a school zone. On March 10, 1992, Alfonso Lopez, Jr., a 12th grader, arrived at Edison High School in San Antonio, Texas, carrying a concealed .38 handgun. After being caught, he was arrested and charged with violating the act. Lopez challenged the constitutionality of the statute.

Issue: Is the possession of a gun in a local school zone a commercial activity that substantially affects interstate commerce, thus authorizing the statute?

Holding: The Gun-Free School Zone Act, as passed by Congress, does not regulate commercial activity. Furthermore, this legislation does not require that the possession of a firearm covered by the act be connected in any way to interstate commerce.

In the past, the Court has permitted expanded congressional power under the Commerce Clause, but in this case the federal government has exceeded the outer limits of its power. The activity of carrying a gun in a local school zone does not involve a channel or instrumentality of interstate commerce nor does it have a substantial effect on interstate commerce.

As both the nation and the world "shrink" and as people and businesses become more and more closely connected and intertwined, particularly economically, it is inevitable that more and more activities will become subject to federal regulation. However, as the Supreme Court clearly indicated in the *Lopez* case, a true nexus between commerce and a regulated activity must exist. If an activity is not commercial in nature, its regulation belongs entirely to the states. Additionally, if an activity is entirely intrastate in character and does not involve a commercial activity which may affect interstate commerce, then the regulation of that activity belongs to the states.

United States v. Morrison
529 U.S. 598, 120 S.Ct. 1740 (2000)
Supreme Court of the United States

Facts: The plaintiff, Ms. Morrison, who had been a student at a Virginia university, was raped by two individuals while she was attending the university. She filed suit against her attackers in the United States District Court alleging that her attack violated 42 USCS 13981 which provided a federal civil remedy for the victims of gender-motivated violence.

Ms. Morrison's attackers alleged that 42 USCS 13981 was unconstitutional. The United States intervened in the case to defend the validity of the statute.

Issue: Did Congress have the authority under the commerce clause to enact a statute which provided a federal remedy for the victims of gender-motivated violence?

Holding: Under the Commerce Clause Congress had no authority to enact 42 USCS 13981 because gender-motivated crimes of violence are not, in any sense of the phrase, economic activity. Furthermore, the Constitution requires that a distinction be made between what is truly national and what is truly local. There is no better example of state police power than the suppression of violent crime and the vindication of victims.

Justice Breyer, joined by Stevens, Souter and Ginsburg, JJ. dissents, expressing the view that virtually every kind of activity in the nation – due to centuries of scientific, technological, commercial and environmental change – could affect commerce outside a specific state.

One should note that even commercial activity which is illegal is subject to federal regulation. In 2005, the Supreme Court considered whether the use of medical marijuana, which was authorized by California's Compassionate Use Act, was exempt from criminal prosecution for violation of the federal Controlled Substances Act (CSA).[1] The Court cited case law, including *Wickard*, which firmly establishes Congress' power to regulate purely local activities that are part of an economic "class of activities" that

[1] *Gonzales v. Raich*, 545 U.S. 1 (2005), United States Supreme Court

have a substantial effect on interstate commerce. The Court specifically noted that *Wickard* establishes Congress' power to regulate purely intrastate activity that is not itself "commercial," in that it concerns a product that is not produced for sale, if it concludes that failure to regulate that class of activity would undercut the regulation of the interstate market in that commodity. The Court noted that, like the farmer in *Wickard,* at issue was the cultivation for home consumption of a fungible commodity for which there is an established (albeit with marijuana, illegal) interstate market. The Court concluded that, just like the Agricultural Adjustment Act was designed "to control the volume (of wheat) moving in interstate and foreign commerce in order to avoid surpluses," a primary purpose of the Controlled Substances Act is to control the supply and demand of controlled substances. The Court found that it need only determine whether a "rational basis" exists for concluding that respondents' activities affect interstate commerce and concluded that, given the enforcement difficulties that attend distinguishing between marijuana cultivated locally and marijuana grown elsewhere and concerns about diversion into illicit channels, Congress had a rational basis for believing that failure to regulate the intrastate manufacture and possession of marijuana would leave a gaping hole in the CSA.

1.3 State Police Power

The federal government is not the only governmental entity with the authority to regulate business activities. As part of their inherent sovereignty, state governments have the authority to regulate affairs within their borders. This authority is derived in part from the Tenth Amendment to the Constitution which reserves all powers not delegated to the national government to the states or to the people. Thus, the states retain the power to regulate *intrastate* activity. Additionally, they also have the power to regulate much of the interstate business activity that occurs within the states' borders. State regulatory authority is commonly referred to as the states' *police powers.* The term does not refer solely to criminal law enforcement, but also includes the broad right of state government to regulate activities to protect or promote the public order, health, safety, morals, and general welfare. This includes the authority to enact laws that regulate the conduct of business activities. Examples of such laws include zoning ordinances, fire and building codes, state environmental laws, corporation and partnership laws, and property laws.

As indicated by the types of regulations that fall under the police powers, local governments, including cities, also exercise police powers. Cities derive their authority to regulate their communities from the state because they are creatures of the state. In other words, they cannot come into existence unless authorized by the state to do so. Generally, state and local laws enacted pursuant to a state's police powers carry a strong presumption of validity.

Fort Gratiot Sanitary Landfill, Inc. v. Michigan Department of Natural Resources
112 S.Ct. 2019, 119 L.Ed.2d 139 (1992)
Supreme Court of the United States

Facts: In 1988, the State of Michigan added restrictions to its Solid Waste Management Act which prohibited privately owned landfills in the state from accepting solid waste (garbage) from any source outside the county in which the landfill was located unless the county expressly permitted it. Fort Gratiot submitted an application to the county government seeking permission to accept out-of-state waste. The county rejected the application. Fort Gratiot sued alleging that the restrictions violated the Commerce Clause.

Issue: Do Michigan's Waste Import Restrictions violate the interstate commerce clause?

Holding: Solid waste, even if it has no value, is an article of commerce. The "negative" or "dormant" aspect of the Commerce Clause prohibits states from advancing their own commercial interests by curtailing the movement of articles of commerce, either into or out of the state. A state statute that clearly discriminates against interstate commerce is, therefore, unconstitutional unless the discrimination is demonstrably justified by a valid factor which is unrelated to economic protectionism.

In the instant case, the State of Michigan asserts that the restrictions are necessary because they enable counties to make adequate plans for the safe disposal of future waste. While accurate forecasts may be an indispensable part of comprehensive waste disposal plans, Michigan could attain that objective without discriminating between in- and out-of-state wastes. Michigan could, for example, have limited the amount of waste that landfill operators could accept each year.

While they can regulate, state and local laws cannot unduly burden interstate commerce. If legislation passed by a state or local government is found to impose a substantial burden on interstate commerce, the legislation will be held to be an unconstitutional violation of the commerce clause. This is true even if the federal government has chosen not to regulate in an area that it has the power to regulate. Under the principle known as the *dormant commerce clause*, state action is precluded in some circumstances even in the absence of federal legislation. The courts will balance the state's interest in regulating a certain matter against the burden that the state's regulation place on interstate commerce. If a state does regulate in an area in which the Congress has been silent, the state law still can, under no circumstances, unduly burden interstate commerce.

1.4 The First Amendment and Business

The first ten amendments to the U.S. Constitution, known as the *Bill of Rights*, provide certain freedoms and protections to individuals against various types of interference or intrusion by the federal government. The Bill of Rights also has a significant impact on business activities.

As originally intended, the Bill of Rights limited only the powers of the federal government and did not restrain the actions of state government. Eventually, the United States Supreme Court "incorporated" most of these rights into the protections which were afforded to citizens by the Fourteenth Amendment to the Constitution. Today, most of the rights and liberties set forth in the Bill of Rights apply to state governments as well as to the federal government. In other words, neither the national government nor state governments can deprive citizens of those protected rights and liberties.

Free Speech

One of the most honored freedoms guaranteed by the Bill of Rights is the First Amendment's *freedom of speech*. The founding fathers believed the people must be able to freely voice their political opinions and to criticize both the acts and policies of the government. Note that the First Amendment protects only speech and not conduct although "symbolic speech" is also protected. Symbolic speech includes gestures, movements, articles of clothing, and other forms of expressive conduct.

When discussing freedom of speech, it is critical to recognize that not all speech is protected. The Supreme Court divides speech into three categories: (1) *fully protected speech*, (2) speech which enjoys *limited protection*, and (3) *unprotected speech*.

Fully protected speech is that which the government cannot prohibit or regulate in any manner. The best example of such speech is political speech. As an example, the government cannot enact a law that forbids citizens from criticizing the policies of the political party in power in the Congress or currently holding the presidency. Fully protected speech can take the form of oral, written, or symbolic speech. As seen in the cases summarized below, corporations "speak" through their spending whether that spending is in the form of flyers or television advertising.

In January, 2010, a bitterly divided Supreme Court, in a 5-4 decision, held that the government may not limit corporate funding of independent political broadcasts in candidate elections. Note that this case did not involve the federal ban on direct contributions from corporations or unions to candidate campaigns or political parties.[2]

Citizens United v. Federal Election Commission
558 U.S. 310, 130 S.Ct. 876, 175 L.Ed.2d 753 (2010)
Supreme Court of the United States

<u>*Facts*</u>: In January 2008, Citizens United, a nonprofit corporation, released a 90 minute documentary entitled *Hillary: The Movie*. The movie expressed opinions about whether then-senator Hillary Clinton, a candidate for the Democratic presidential nomination, was fit for the presidency. Citizens United distributed the movie in theaters and on DVD, but also wanted to make it available through video-on-demand. It produced advertisements promoting the film and wanted to show them on broadcast and cable television. To pay for the video-on-demand distribution and the advertisements, Citizens United planned to use its general treasury funds.

The Bipartisan Campaign Reform Act of 2002 (BCRA) is a federal law which prohibits corporations and unions from spending their general treasury funds on "electioneering communications" or for speech that expressly advocates the election or defeat of a candidate. An "electioneering communication" is any broadcast, cable, or satellite communication that (1) refers to a clearly identified candidate for federal office, (2) is made within 30 days of a primary election or 60 days of a general election, and (3) is publicly distributed.

Citizens United sought an injunction against the Federal Elections Commission arguing that certain sections of the BCRA are unconstitutional as applied to *Hillary*. The district court denied this motion and granted summary judgment to the FEC. Citizens United appealed to the U.S. Supreme Court.

<u>*Issue:*</u> As applied to *Hillary: The Movie,* is the BCRA's prohibition on corporate independent election expenditures constitutional?

<u>*Holding:*</u> Justice Kennedy delivered the majority opinion.

The proper standard of review is strict scrutiny; thus, the government must demonstrate that the statute serves a compelling interest and was narrowly tailored to meet that interest. Corporations and unions have the same political speech rights as individuals under the First

---

[2] In addition to addressing the issue of speech, the Court in *Citizens United* also considered disclosure requirements contained in McCain-Feingold. The BCRA requires that for all electioneering communications expenditures of more than $10,000 disclosure statements must be filed identifying the person making the expenditure, the amount, the election to which the communication was directed, and the names of certain contributors. The Court considered whether the BCRA's disclaimer, disclosure, and reporting requirements are constitutional, and by and 8-1 vote, upheld BCRA's disclosure provisions.

Amendment. There is no compelling government interest for prohibiting corporations and unions from using their general treasury funds to make election-related independent expenditures.

A ban on independent expenditures is a ban on speech. There is no such thing as too much speech. If the First Amendment has any force, it prohibits Congress from fining or jailing citizens, or associations of citizens, for simply engaging in political speech. The provisions of the BCRA cannot be upheld without chilling political speech. The government may not suppress political speech on the basis of the speaker's corporate identity. No sufficient governmental interest justifies limits on the political speech of nonprofit or for-profit corporations.

Differential treatment of corporations cannot be squared with the First Amendment. The First Amendment protects the "open marketplace" of ideas and there is no support for the view that the First Amendment's original meaning would permit suppressing corporations' free speech.

The government argues that the provisions of BCRA are necessary to prevent corruption. However, independent expenditures do not give rise to corruption or the appearance of corruption. Furthermore, the governmental interest in preventing corruption or the appearance of corruption is limited to *quid pro quo* corruption.

Dissent: Justice Stevens, joined by Justice Ginsburg, Justice Breyer, and Justice Sotomayor, dissented.

The Court's ruling threatens to undermine the integrity of elected institutions across the Nation. The path it has taken to reach its outcome will, I fear, do damage to this institution. A democracy cannot function effectively when its constituent members believe laws are being bought and sold. The majority fails to recognize the possibility for corruption outside of strict *quid pro quo* exchanges and does not place enough emphasis on the need to prevent the "appearance of corruption" in elections.

The unique qualities of corporations and other artificial legal entities make them dangerous to democratic elections. These legal entities have perpetual life, the ability to amass large sums of money, limited liability, no ability to vote, no morality, no purpose outside of profit-making, and no loyalty. Therefore, the courts should permit legislatures to regulate corporate participation in the political process. Corporations "unfairly influence" the electoral process with vast sums of money that few individuals can match, which distorts the public debate.

Legal entities are not "We the People" for whom our Constitution was established. Therefore, they should not be given speech protections under the First Amendment.

At bottom, the Court's opinion is thus a rejection of the common sense of the American people, who have recognized a need to prevent corporations from undermining self government since the founding, and who have fought against the distinctive corrupting potential of corporate electioneering since the days of Theodore Roosevelt. It is a strange time to repudiate that common sense. While American democracy is imperfect, few outside the majority of this Court would have thought its flaws included a dearth of corporate money in politics.

While political speech enjoys absolute protection, certain other types of speech may be banned outright while still others enjoy only limited protection. If speech enjoys limited protection, the government cannot forbid it, but can subject it to time, place and manner restrictions. This type of speech generally falls into one of two categories:

•

- Commercial speech – advertising and marketing speech. For example, a city may limit the use of billboards, such as one advertising a nude dancing establishment, within its city limits for safety and aesthetic reasons so long as other forms of advertising such as print media are available.

- Offensive speech – speech that offends many members of society. (Note that this is not the same as obscene speech discussed below). For example, the FCC (Federal Communications Commission) can regulate the use of offensive language (what might be called 'adult' content) on television by limiting such language to time periods when children would be unlikely to be watching.

Federal Communications Commission v. Pacifica Foundation
438 U.S. 726, 98 S.Ct. 3026 (1978)
Supreme Court of the United States

Facts: Satiric humorist George Carlin recorded a twelve minute monologue entitled "Filthy Words" before a live audience in a California theater. He began referring to "the words you couldn't say on the public airways – the ones you definitely couldn't say, ever." He proceeded to list those words and to repeat them over and over again in a variety of colloquialisms.

At about 2:00, p.m., on October 30, 1973, a New York radio station owned by Pacifica Foundation broadcast the "Filthy Words" monologue. A man who heard the broadcast while driving with his young son complained to the FCC, the federal administrative agency in charge of granting radio licenses and regulating radio broadcasts. The FCC administers a statute that forbids the use of any offensive language on the radio. The FCC found that Carlin's monologue violated this law and censured the Pacifica Foundation for playing the monologue.

Issue: Can the FCC prohibit Pacifica Foundation from playing the Carlin monologue?

Holding: The Carlin monologue is not obscene speech, but does constitute offensive speech. As such, it is subject to governmental regulation. The government can impose time, place and manner restrictions to offensive speech, but it cannot totally forbid the same. The FCC can limit such language to time periods when children would be unlikely to be listening or watching, e.g., late at night.

Unprotected speech is that which is not protected and may be totally forbidden by the government. This category includes:

- dangerous speech – for instance, yelling "fire" in a crowded theater when there is no fire;
- speech that violates criminal laws – making threats against another person, for example;
- speech that incites the violent or revolutionary overthrow of the government;
- defamatory language;
- child pornography;
- obscene speech – according to the Supreme Court, speech is obscene when:
  - (a) the average person finds the speech or work violates contemporary community standards;
  - (b) the speech or work appeals to the prurient interest in sex;
  - (c) the work depicts or describes in a patently offensive way, sexual conduct; and

(d) the work, taken as a whole, lacks serious literary, artistic, political or scientific value.

Because the Supreme Court uses "community standards" to define obscenity, states are free to define what constitutes obscene speech in the local community. Thus, movie theaters, magazine publishers, record stores and others may be subject to legal challenges that the materials they display or sell are obscene and, therefore, are not protected by the First Amendment. For example, in the early 1990's a Florida judge issued an order finding that the album *As Nasty as They Wanna Be* by the rap group 2 Live Crew was obscene. The judge's order read, in part:

> "This is a case between two ancient enemies: Anything Goes and Enough Already. Justice Oliver Wendell Holmes, Jr., observed in *Schenck v. United States,* 249 U.S. 47 (1919), that the First Amendment is not absolute and that it does not permit one to yell 'Fire' in a crowded theater. Today, this court decides whether the First Amendment absolutely permits one to yell another 'F' word anywhere in the community when combined with graphic sexual descriptions."

The judge's decision was reversed on appeal.

Religion

The fundamental human right to religious liberty is enshrined in the First Amenment to the Constitution which declares that "Congress shall make no law respecting an establishment of religion, or prohibiting the free exercise thereof ..." The latter half of this declaration is known as the *free exercise clause* and it prevents the government from interfering with an individual's or group's religious beliefs. It has long been established that the First Amendment applies to goups as well as to individuals. For example, churches and charities can claim the protections of the free exercise clause. Furthermore, this freedom has been recognized as the freedom to the free exercise of one's religion in all aspects of life so long as public order or safety weren't compromised.

Regulations promulgated by the federal government as pursuant to the Affordable Care Act (Obamacare) require that employer provided health insurance include contraceptives. Some religious groups and employers have challenged the mandate asserting that its enforcement violates their religious liberty.

The notion that for-proft businesses could assert religious freedoms struck many as far-fetched. However, the Supreme Court, in a 5-4 decision, recognized "corporate free exercise rights."

Burwell v. Hobby Lobby Stores, Inc.
2014 U.S. LEXIS 4505 (June 30, 2014)

Facts: The Religious Freedom Restoration Act of 1993 prohibits the government from substantially burdening a person's exercise of religion even if the burden results from a rule of general applicability unless the Government demonstrates that application of the burden to the person—(1) is in furtherance of a compelling governmental interest; and (2) is the least restrictive means of furthering that compelling governmental interest.

The Department of Health and Human Services (HHS) promulgated regulations under the Patient Protection and Affordable Care Act of 2010 (ACA), which require specified employers' group health plans to furnish "preventive care and screenings" for women without "any cost sharing requirements." Congress did not specify what types of preventive care must be covered; it authorized the Health Resources and Services Administration, a component of HHS, to decide. Nonexempt employers are generally required to provide coverage for the 20 contraceptive methods approved by the Food and Drug Administration. Religious employers, such as churches, are exempt from this contraceptive mandate. HHS has also effectively exempted religious nonprofit organizations with religious objections to providing coverage for contraceptive services. Under this accommodation, the insurance issuer must exclude contraceptive coverage from the employer's plan and provide plan participants with separate payments for contraceptive services without imposing any cost-sharing requirements on the employer, its insurance plan, or its employee beneficiaries.

The owners of Hobby Lobby, a closely held for-profit corporation, have sincere Christian beliefs that life begins at conception and that it would violate their religion to facilitate access to contraceptive drugs or devices that operate after that point. They sued HHS under RFRA and the Free Exercise Clause, seeking to enjoin application of the contraceptive mandate insofar as it requires them to provide health coverage for four objectionable contraceptives.

Issue: Does the company, Hobby Lobby Stores, Inc., have a religious freedom right infringed upon by the ACA contraception provisions?

Holding: Justice Alito delivered the opinion of the Court.

HHS argues that the Hobby Lobby cannot sue because it is a for-profit corporation, and that the owners cannot sue because the regulations apply only to companies, but that would leave merchants with a difficult choice: give up the right to seek judicial protection of their religious liberty or forgo the benefits of operating as corporations. The text of the Religious Freedom Restoration Act (RFRA) shows that Congress designed the statute to provide very broad protection for religious liberty and did not intend to put merchants to such a choice. It employed the familiar legal fiction of including corporations within RFRA's definition of "persons," but the purpose of extending rights to corporations is to protect the rights of people associated with the corporation, including shareholders, officers, and employees. Protecting the free-exercise rights of closely held corporations thus protects the religious liberty of the humans who own and control them. A corporation is simply a form of organization used by human beings to achieve desired ends. When rights, whether constitutional or statutory, are extended to corporations, the purpose is to protect the rights of these people.

Business practices compelled or limited by the tenets of a religious doctrine fall comfortably within the understanding of the "exercise of religion" that this Court has previously set out. Any suggestion that for-profit corporations are incapable of exercising religion because their purpose is simply to make money flies in the face of modern corporate law. States, including those in which the plaintiff corporations were incorporated, authorize corporations to pursue any lawful purpose or business, including the pursuit of profit in conformity with the owners' religious principles.

Requiring family-owned corporations to pay for insurance coverage for contraception under the Affordable Care Act violates the RFRA. Imposing a requirement that the company provide contraception coverage imposes a substantial burden on the religious liberty of the Hobby Lobby since it could face annual fines of $475 million if the company failed to comply.

The Court accepts for the sake of argument that the government has a compelling interest in making sure women have access to contraception. But there were ways of doing that without violating the companies' religious rights. The government could pay for the coverage or it could employ the accommodation already in use for certain nonprofit religious organizations, one requiring insurance companies to provide the coverage.

<u>Dissent</u>: Justice Ginsburg dissented.

The majority's opinion is one of startling breadth. The court has for the first time extended religious-freedom protections to the commercial, profit-making world. The court's expansive notion of corporate personhood invites for-profit entities to seek religion-based exemptions from regulations they deem offensive to their faiths. The situation presented here is very different from that presented by religious organizations seeking exemptions. The commercial nature of for-profit corporations makes the difference. Religious organizations exist to serve a community of believers. For-profit corporations do not fit that bill. Although the court attempts to cabin its language to closely held corporations, its logic extends to corporations of any size, public or private.

1.5 The Equal Protection Clause

The Fourteenth Amendment, added in 1868, was designed to prohibit discriminatory and unfair action by government. Several provisions of this Amendment have important implications for business activities, particularly the *Equal Protection Clause* which provides that a state cannot "deny to any person within its jurisdiction the equal protection of the laws." While this clause expressly applies to state and local governments, the Supreme Court has held that it also applies to the federal government.

The equal protection clause prohibits governments, whether state, local or federal, from enacting laws that classify and treat "similarly situated" persons differently. In other words, equal protection means that the government must treat persons in similar situations in a similar manner. Corporations, which are considered artificial persons under the law, are also protected. It is important to note that this clause does not make the classifications of individuals unlawful per se; rather it is designed to prohibit invidious discrimination.

The Supreme Court has adopted three different standards for reviewing equal protection cases, with the standard used in a given case being determined on the basis for the distinction or classification. These standards are as follows:

- Strict Scrutiny Test – Any government activity or regulation that prohibits some persons from exercising a fundamental right or classifies persons based on a *suspect class* (race) is reviewed using this test. In order to be valid, the classification must be necessary to promote a "compelling state interest." Compelling state interests include remedying past unconstitutional or illegal discrimination. This is not the same as correcting the general effects of "society's" discrimination. Using this standard, most government classifications of persons based on race are found to be unconstitutional. Example: A government rule that permitted persons of one race, but not of another race, to receive government benefits would violate this test.

- Intermediate Scrutiny Test – This is the standard of review for any government classification based on *protected classes* (sex or age for example). The courts must determine whether the government classification is "substantially related" to a legitimate governmental purpose. Example: A law that punishes men but not women for statutory rape may be upheld if the important government objective is preventing illegitimate teenage pregnancy, but a rule prohibiting persons over a certain age from acting as government accountants would not be.

- Rational Basis Test – The lawfulness of all government classifications that do not involve suspect or protected classes is determined using this test. The courts will uphold government regulation so long as there is any rational or justifiable reason for the law. Example: A rule providing government subsidies for farmers but not for attorneys is permissible.

Village of Willowbrook v. Olech
528 U.S. 562, 120 S.Ct. 1073, 145 L.Ed.2d 1060 (2000)
United States Supreme Court

Facts: The Olechs asked the Village of Willowbrook to connect their property to the municipal water supply. The Village agreed on condition that the Olechs grant to the Village a 33 foot easement. The Village had required only a 15 foot easement from other property owners who sought access to the water supply.

Mrs. Olech, whose husband had died before the filing of the lawsuit, contended that the 33-foot easement demand was an "irrational and wholly arbitrary" demand and was motivated by ill will resulting from the couple's previous filing of an unrelated lawsuit against the Village. Mrs. Olech brought suit against the Village alleging that the Village's demand of an additional 18-foot easement, over and above what had been required of other homeowners, violated the equal protection clause of the Federal Constitution's Fourteenth Amendment.

Issue: Did Mrs. Olech's suit state a cognizable claim under the equal protection clause?

Holding: Mrs. Olech's complaint can fairly be construed as alleging that the Village intentionally had demanded a 33-foot easement as a condition of connecting her property to the municipal water supply while requiring only a 15-foot easement from other similarly situated property owners. Her allegations that the Village's action was motivated by spite and was irrational and wholly arbitrary are sufficient to state a claim for relief as a "class of one" under traditional equal protection analysis.

1.6 The Due Process Clause

Due process clauses are found in both the Fifth and Fourteenth Amendments to the Constitution. The due process clause of the Fifth Amendment applies to federal government action while the due process clause of the Fourteenth Amendment applies to state and local government action. Both provide that no person shall be deprived of "life, liberty or property" without due process of the law. Of course, the government is not prohibited from taking a person's life, liberty or property. For instance, people who violate the criminal laws may be incarcerated and, thus, deprived of liberty. Rather, the government must follow due process when depriving persons of these rights.

There are two categories of due process, one focused on substance and the other on form:

- Substantive Due Process – As the name implies, this form of due process focuses on the substance, or content, of the law in question. It generally requires that the government have an appropriate goal in enacting the law and that the law, as applied, sufficiently furthers that goal. It also requires that statutes, regulations, and other laws be clear on their face and not be overly broad so that a reasonable person is able to understand the law and to comply with it. Laws that do not meet this test are unenforceable, being declared *void for vagueness*. Example: A city ordinance that requires persons to wear "age appropriate clothes" would be held unconstitutional because a reasonable person could not clearly determine whether his or her conduct violated the law.

- Procedural Due Process – This form of due process is concerned with the form or procedure of any taking and requires that any government action to take one's life, liberty or property must be made equitably or fairly using fair procedures. For instance, the government must give a person proper *notice* and an *opportunity to be heard*. Before a person is deprived of his life, liberty or property, he must be given an opportunity to object to a proposed taking before an impartial, neutral decision maker. Example: If the government wants to take a person's land by eminent domain to build a government building, the government must give the landowner reasonable notice of its intent to take the property and provide the land owner with a hearing. Under the *Just Compensation Clause* the government must pay the landowner the fair value of the property.

1.7 *Relations Among the States*

The Constitution includes several provisions concerning relations among the states. Two of these, the Privileges and Immunities Clause and the Full Faith and Credit Clause, are of particular importance.

The Privileges and Immunities Clause

Article IV of the Constitution contains the *Privileges and Immunities Clause* that prohibits states from enacting laws that unduly discriminate in favor of their residents. The Fourteenth Amendment also contains similar language.

Hicklin et al. v. Orbeck, Commissioner, Department of Labor of Alaska
437 U.S. 518, 98 S.Ct. 2482, 57 L.Ed.2d 397 (1978)
United States Supreme Court

Facts: The State of Alaska enacted a statute requiring all Alaskan oil and gas leases, easements, or right-of-way permits for oil and gas pipelines to contain a requirement that qualified residents of Alaska be hired in preference to nonresidents of the state. The statute defined a "resident" as one who had lived in the state for a minimum of at least one-year. Plaintiffs, who were unable to obtain jobs as a result of the statute, challenged the law, alleging that it violated both the privileges and immunities clause of the U.S. Constitution and the equal protection clause of the Fourteenth Amendment.

Issue: Did the Alaska statute violate the privileges and immunities clause?

Holding: The Court, in a unanimous decision, found that the statute violated the privileges and immunities clause, even granting the dubious assumption that a state could validly attempt to alleviate its unemployment problem by requiring private employers within the state to discriminate against nonresidents since (1) no showing was made that nonresidents were a peculiar source of the evil the statute was enacted to remedy, namely the state's uniquely high unemployment, (2) even assuming that nonresidents were shown to be a peculiar source of the evil, the discrimination the statute worked against nonresidents did not bear a substantial relationship to the particular evil they were said to present, and (3) ownership by the state of the oil and gas that were the subject of the statute was not sufficient justification for the state's discrimination to take the statute from the scope of the privileges and immunities clause.

The purpose of such clauses is to promote nationalism. It is important to note that only invidious discrimination is prohibited. When a citizen of one state engages in basic and essential activities in another state (the foreign state), the foreign state must have a *substantial r*eason for treating the nonresident differently from its own residents. The idea is to generally prevent any state from discriminating against citizens of other states in favor of its own. Thus, while a state cannot enact a law that prevents residents of other states from owning property or businesses in that state, it can charge out-of-state residents higher tuition than in-state residents at its state universities since the state universities are funded, in part, by state tax dollars.

It is important to note that the privileges and immunities clauses apply only to persons, and do not protect corporations.

The Full Faith and Credit Clause

The *Full Faith and Credit Clause* of the Constitution applies only to civil matters, and ensures that rights established under deeds, wills, contracts and the like of one state will be honored by other states. It also ensures that any judicial decision with respect to property rights will be honored and enforced in all states. It is yet to be determined by the Supreme Court whether those rights include the recognition of same-sex marriages. Congress, in section 2 of the Defense of Marriage Act, has said that no state is required to recognize a same-sex marriage as valid in that state even though the marriage was legal in the state where it was performed. The Supreme Court has not issued an opinion with regard to the constitutionality of this provision.

The Full Faith and Credit Clause has contributed to the unity of American citizens because it protects the legal rights of citizens as they move about the country and from state to state. It also protects the rights of those to whom obligations are owed. For example, a person who is awarded money damages by a court in one state is assured that his judgment will be recognized by other states. This does not, of course, guarantee that he will be able to actually collect on the judgment. For these reasons, the Full Faith and Credit Clause is extremely important to the conduct of business in a country with a very mobile citizenry.

Review Questions and Exercises

1. Assume that there is a direct conflict between a decision by the United States Environmental Protection Agency and the Environmental Protection Department of the State of Georgia. Which law would a Georgia business follow and why?

2. A Georgia corporation, Peach State Produce, Inc., ships its products all across the nation. The State of Alabama, in an effort to protect local companies, has passed a law creating a two-tier fee structure for its toll roads. Trucks with out-of-state registration are charged a toll that is twice that charged to trucks with Alabama registration. Is the Alabama law constitutional? Discuss.

3. Explain the "effect on interstate commerce" test that is used to determine whether Congress has the power to pass a particular statute. What is the result of that test? What are the limits of Congressional authority? What is left to the states to regulate?

4. Explain the difference between substantive due process and procedural due process.

5. Assume that members of the city council of Conservative City have become concerned about under-age alcohol consumption and, in response, have passed an ordinance that prohibits any advertising by any restaurant, bar, club or other entity which includes any mention of any alcoholic beverage or drink service. If Joe's Bar challenges the constitutionality of the ordinance, what is the likely result and why?

6. Assume that the State of Georgia, acting through its Insurance Commissioner, required automobile insurers within the state grant female drivers aged 17-25 a discount on their insurance premiums of 25% as compared to the rates charged to males in that same age group. The Insurance Commissioner based his ruling on studies indicating that young male drivers are more likely to be involved in accidents than young female drivers. If the constitutionality of this rule were challenged, a court deciding the case would apply what standard? Why?

7. What types of speech enjoy "limited protection?" Give examples.

8. What are "police powers?" Give examples.

Practical Applications

1. State motor vehicle departments (DMVs) register automobiles and issue driver's licenses. These state agencies require auto owners and drivers to provide personal information, including name, address, telephone number, vehicle description, Social Security number, certain medical information and a photograph, as a condition for registering an auto or obtaining a driver's license. Many state DMVs sold this personal information to individuals, advertisers, and businesses, generating significant revenues for the states.

After receiving thousands of complaints, Congress passed the Driver's Privacy Protection Act of 1994 (DPPA) which prohibited states from selling the personal information of a person unless that state first obtained that person's affirmative consent to do so. The State of South Carolina sued the United States, seeking to have the DPPA declared unconstitutional.

Consider:
(a) Do the activities of the South Carolina DMV have an effect on interstate commerce?
(b) Did Congress, in passing the act, exceed its powers to regulate commerce under the Commerce Clause?

See - *Reno, Attorney General of the United States v. Condon, Attorney General of South Carolina,* United States Supreme Court, 120 S.Ct. 666 (2000).

2. Carl and Elaine Miles are an unemployed, married couple living in Augusta, Georgia. The Miles own "Blackie, the Talking Cat." Trained by Carl Miles, Blackie is, allegedly, able to speak several words and phrases. The Miles make their living by exploiting Blackie's talents. In addition to having contracts with several talent agents, the Miles accept contributions from pedestrians in the downtown Augusta area who want to hear the cat speak.

Under its charter, the City of Augusta is empowered to impose license taxes. The business license ordinance enacted by the City exhaustively lists the trades, businesses, and occupations subject to the ordinance and the amount of tax to be paid. Although the ordinance does not provide for the licensing of a talking cat, section 2 of the ordinance does require that any "... Agent or Agency not specifically mentioned ..." pay a $50.00 tax.

When the Miles were required by the City to obtain a business license, they challenged the constitutionality of the ordinance.

Consider:

(a) Did the City of Augusta have the power to levy an occupation tax?
(b) Was the business license ordinance enacted by the City of Augusta unconstitutionally vague and overbroad in contravention of the due process clause of the Fourteenth Amendment?

See – *Carl Miles, et al., v. City Council of Augusta, Georgia*, United States District Court for the Southern District of Georgia, 551 F. Supp. 349 (1982).

Editor's Note: Judge Dudley Bowen, in his opinion in the *Miles* case, demonstrates that lawyers, even federal judges, are possessed of a sense of humor. In footnotes to his opinion, Judge Bowen recites, in colorful detail, his personal encounter with Blackie on the streets of Augusta. Judge Bowen also makes mention of many famous cats of both contemporary culture and nursery rhyme fame including, but not limited to, Garfield, Felix, Sylvester, the Cat in the Hat, the Calico Cat who ate the Gingham Dog, and the Cat who went to London to see the Queen.

Judge Bowen's decision in the case was appealed to the United States Circuit Court of Appeals for the Eleventh Circuit. That court, in a per curiam opinion, was not to be outdone by the lower court and used virtually every word possible beginning with the letters c-a-t, referring to Blackie being "catapulted into public prominence," and "Blackie's cataclysmic rise to fame." Finally, the appellate court, in a footnote, added, "This court will not hear a claim that Blackie's right to free speech has been infringed. First, although Blackie arguably possesses a very unusual ability, he cannot be considered a 'person' and is therefore not protected by the Bill of Rights. Second, even if Black had such a right, we see no need for appellants to assert his right *jus tertii*. Blackie can clearly speak for himself."

Chapter 2 The Employment Relationship and its Regulation

OUTLINE

Traditionally, the employment relationship was governed by common law principles of agency and contract law. While these doctrines still play a major role in many areas of employment law, today's workplace is regulated extensively by federal and state statutes. This chapter will examine both the common law doctrines as well as prominent statutory law pertaining to the work environment.

2.1 Types of Employment Relationships

Under the common law, an employee is an individual who performs services for another person in exchange for compensation. This is, of course, not a precise definition. In fact, there are three different kinds of employment relationships and businesses frequently employ all three types of employees. They are:

- *Employee* – An employer-employee relationship exists when the employer hires an employee, a worker, to perform some kind of service. For example, the worker on an assembly line in a factory is an employee of his employer, the factory. An employee is not an agent of the employer unless the employer specifically authorizes the employee to enter into contracts on behalf of the principal employer.

- *Agent* – A principal-agent relationship is formed when an employer hires an employee and gives that employee authority to act on behalf of the employer and to enter into contracts on his or her behalf. An example of this type of relationship would be the manufacturing company who hires a purchasing agent to procure raw materials. Agency relationships are discussed at some length in Section 2.2 below.

- *Independent Contractor* – A principal-independent contractor relationship is formed when an employer hires an outsider to perform a specific task generally unrelated to the principle type of business of the employer. For example, the roofer hired by an attorney to replace the law office building roof is not an employee of the attorney, but, rather, is an independent contractor. The critical factor in determining whether someone is an employee or an independent contractor is the degree of control that the employer exercises. An independent contractor may or may not be an agent of the employer.

In determining independent contractor status, several factors are considered:

- whether the worker is engaged in a distinct occupation from that of the employer or works at an independently established business;
- the length of time that the worker has been employed by the employer;
- the number of hours that the worker works for the employer;
- whether the employee supplies his own tools and equipment;
- the method of payment the worker receives – whether he is paid by the job or by the number of hours worked;
- the degree of skill the worker must possess to complete the task;
- whether the worker hires others to assist him; and
- whether the employer has the right to control the manner and means of completing the task.

Whether or not one is an employee or an independent contractor determines important tax and benefit issues for both the worker and the employer. Employers are not required to deduct from the worker's paycheck or pay over to the government income, Social Security, and unemployment taxes for independent contractors. The independent contractor bears the responsibility to pay his or her own self-employment taxes (that portion of the Social Security tax normally paid by the employer) as well as his income taxes. Additionally, independent contractors are generally not eligible for the same fringe benefits (such as medical insurance and 401k retirement plans) received by employees. Because of these differences, an employer may be able to hire an independent contractor for less money than it would cost to hire an employee to do the same work. However, as seen from the *Vizcaino* case below, simply labeling a worker an "independent contractor" doesn't relieve the employer of his tax and benefit obligations.

Vizcaino v. Microsoft Corp.

97 F.3d 1187 (1996)

United States Court of Appeals for the Ninth Circuit

<u>*Facts*</u>: Microsoft employs a core staff of permanent employees and offers them a wide variety of benefits including paid vacation, sick leave, holidays, group health and life insurance, pensions, participation in the 401k retirement plan, and participation in the employee stock-purchase plan. Microsoft also employed a number of freelancers when it needed to expand its workforce to meet the demands of new product schedules. Many of the freelancers worked for Microsoft for months or even years. The company did not provide the freelancers with any of the employee benefits that its regular employees received.

The named plaintiffs were all hired to work on specific projects. All of them were told when they were hired that, as freelancers, they would not be eligible for benefits. All but one of the freelancers had worked for a minimum of two years prior to the time their action was filed. The plaintiffs were fully integrated into the Microsoft workforce. They often worked on teams with regular employees, sharing the same supervisors, performing identical functions, and working the same hours. They were required to work on site and received admittance key cards, office equipment, and supplies from the company.

In 1989 and 1990, the Internal Revenue Service (IRS) examined Microsoft's employment records and concluded that the freelancers were not independent contractors, but instead were actually Microsoft employees for withholding and employment-tax purposes. After learning of the IRS ruling, the plaintiffs sought employee benefits which had been denied to them as freelancers.

Issue: Were the freelancers independent contractors, and, thus, not eligible to participate in the employee benefits packages?

Holding: The employment status of an individual is not determined by the label used in the contract between the parties. If individuals, as here, are treated in virtually every respect as employees, the mere fact that they are designated independent contractors will not establish that status. In order to establish independent contractor status, employers must show that the workers have the right to control the manner and means by which they perform their work. This can include setting their own hours, the right to refuse assignments, the right to subcontract work, or the right to work for other companies.

Generally, the employer is not liable for any torts committed by an independent contractor during the time that contractor is engaged in work for the employer. Of course, an independent contractor, like everyone else, is personally liable for his or her own torts. With regard to contract liability, while an independent contractor is not automatically an agent of the employer, the employer can specifically authorize an independent contractor to enter into contracts on the principal's behalf. In such a case, liability is governed by the law of agency, discussed in Section 2.2 below.

As seen in the following case, sometimes, the employer may be liable for acts of the person working for him, whether he considers the worker to be an employee or an independent contractor.

Underberg v. Southern Alarm, Inc.
284 Ga.App. 08 (2007)
Court of Appeals of Georgia

Facts: Southern Alarm, Inc., is an authorized dealer for ADT Security Services and uses promotions representatives to sell its product. Promotions representatives are part-time employees who work on commission. Southern Alarm considered promotions representatives to be independent contractors. Promotions representatives were given two days training, provided a script to read to potential customers, given yard signs, t-shirts, and contracts and transported by Southern Alarm to large neighborhoods where they conducted door-to-door sales of ADT security systems. When Southern Alarm first opened in Savannah background checks were conducted on promotions representatives, but that practice was discontinued due to the high turnover rate among the representatives.

Southern Alarm hired Bert Fields as a promotions representative. No background check was performed. Had there been one, Southern Alarm would have learned that Fields had been convicted of burglary and kidnapping in South Carolina in 1979, sentenced to life in prison, and paroled in 1995.

On two occasions in November and December 2001, Fields knocked on the door of Kelly Underberg and asked to come in to speak with her about an ADT system. She declined both times. On February 6, 2002, Underberg parked in her garage and entered her home through an unlocked door, leaving the garage door up. Shortly thereafter, she saw Fields standing in her bedroom doorway. Fields pulled a gun and pointed it at Underberg. He asked whether she recognized him and identified himself as the "ADT salesman." Fields bound Underberg with duct tape, placed her in her own car and took her to South Carolina. After Underberg promised to give him $6,000, Fields drove her to back to Georgia.

Issue: Was Southern Alarm negligent in the hiring of Fields and did that negligence proximately cause the injury to Underberg?

Holding: The appropriate standard of care is whether the employer knew or should have known that the employee was not suited for the particular employment. The jury was entitled to find that Southern Alarm owed a heightened duty to ascertain whether individuals it hired to enter the homes of unsuspecting persons for the purpose of selling security systems were suited for this purpose.

As to the second issue, the causation element requires showing that, given the employee's dangerous propensities, the victim's injuries should have been foreseen as the natural and probable consequence of hiring the employee. In this case, Southern Alarm argued that, since the kidnapping occurred after the termination of Fields' employment with the company, the company was not the proximate cause of Ms. Underberg's injuries. However, we find that there can be a causal connection between an employment-related contact with the victim in her home by an unfit or dangerous employee and an injury inflicted on that occupant during a later, non-employment related entry into the home. In so holding, we consider favorably an Arizona case in which the defendant employee who installed the plaintiff's burglar alarm system had a history of criminal activity. After the employee's job was terminated, he returned to the plaintiff's home, disconnected the alarm and burgled the home. It matters not that ADT considered Fields an independent contractor.

Traditionally, the common law doctrine of *employment at will* has governed employment relationships. Under the employment at will doctrine the employee works at the pleasure of the employer. Thus, either party, the employer or the employee, may terminate an employment relationship at any time, and for any reason (except an illegal reason), unless an employment contract between the two parties specifically provides otherwise. An employer may, of course, discharge an employee for cause (for example, embezzlement), or for a business reason (for example, falling revenues require a reduction in the work force), or for no reason. However, an employer is not permitted to fire an employee for an illegal reason. For example, discharging an employee would be illegal if the firing would violate a federal or state employment statute such as one prohibiting employment termination for discriminatory reasons. Anti-discrimination laws, or equal opportunity in employment, are discussed at greater length in Section 2.8 in this chapter.

An employee who has an employment contract specifying his employment for a certain period of time cannot be terminated by his employer in violation of the terms of that contract. If the employer terminates the employment relationship without cause and before the end of the contract term, the employer subjects himself to a suit for breach of contract. If the employee violates the terms of the contract, he is in breach of the contract and the employer may terminate the contract, thereby ending the employment relationship.

2.2 Agency

Agency relationships are pervasive. This is obvious when one considers that many employees are also considered agents for their employers. In the simplest terms, an *agent* is someone who agrees to enter into contracts on behalf of, to act for, or to represent another party, called the *principal.*

> O.C.G.A. § 10-6-1
>
> The relation of principal and agent arises wherever one person, expressly or by implication, authorizes another to act for him or in his behalf.

An agency relationship itself is a contractual relationship and is quite common in many business settings. The employee who sells goods in a store does so as the agent of the store owner. A partner who signs a lease on behalf of the partnership binds the partnership in agency Law, and the purchasing agent who buys raw materials for the manufacturing plant does so as an agent of the corporation.

Creation of Agency Relationships

Agency relationships may be formed or may come about in any of several ways.

- *Express Agency* – This is the most common form of agency. The agent has the authority to enter into contracts or perform other acts on the principal's behalf based upon the express terms of the agency agreement. Express agency agreements can be either written or oral although in some circumstances the Statute of Frauds (discussed in Part II of this text) dictates that they must be written. For example, in most states a real estate broker's contract to sell real estate must be in writing.

  Express agency agreements may be exclusive meaning that the principal cannot employ any agent other than the exclusive agent.

  A power of attorney is one of the most formal types of express agency agreements. In a power of attorney the agent is called an attorney-in-fact, but does not have to be a lawyer.

- *Implied Agency* – This agency relationship is implied from the conduct of the parties as opposed from being expressly stated. In these agencies the extent of the agent's authority is determined from the particular factual situation. Implied authority can be conferred by industry custom, the prior relationship between the parties, the agent's position, and other factors. For instance, a shop clerk is unlikely to have a written agreement, yet his acts in selling merchandise, accepting returns, etc., will bind the employer (who is the principal).

- *Apparent Agency* – Sometimes called an agency by estoppel, an apparent agency relationship comes into existence when the principal creates the appearance of an agency that, in fact, does not exist.

  Example 2a:

  > Joe is being interviewed for a job, and accompanies his prospective employer to lunch as a part of the interview. When Joe and the employer encounter a business associate, the employer introduces Joe saying, "I wish I had more employees like Joe." Joe is not hired. Later, Joe enters into a contract with the business associate he met at lunch. If the employer has not corrected the misrepresentation he created, the employer is liable on Joe's contract. (The employer's remedy is to then sue Joe.)

- *Agency by Ratification* – An agency relationship can be created by ratification or acceptance of an agent's acts by the principal.

Example 2b:

Bill knows his friend Susan is looking for a new house. Bill sees a house he thinks Susan would like. Bill enters into a contract with the seller, signing the contract, "Bill as agent for Susan." Bill has no authority to enter into a contract to purchase a house for Susan. However, if Susan likes the house and agrees to purchase the house, there is an agency by ratification.

Circle Y Construction v. WRH Realty Services and WRH Hidden Colony
427 Fed.Appx. 772, 2011 U.S.App. LEXIS 10629 (2011)
United States Court of Appeals for the Eleventh Circuit

Facts: Circle Y Construction, Inc., entered into a contract with WRH Realty for the renovation of some housing units. WRH Realty was acting as the agent for Hidden Colony, a limited liability limited partnership, but did not disclose that fact to Circle Y. Grahame Brown, the vice-president of construction services at WRH Realty, was designated by Hidden Colony as its agent in administering the contract. Shortly after the contract was signed, Brown asked Circle Y to perform work outside the scope of the contract. Thereafter, Brown placed Waldy Sanchez in charge of supervising Circle Y's work. Sanchez also made additional work requests, outside of the scope of the original contract. In addition, Sanchez authorized two other WRH employees to make additional work requests, and Circle Y performed this work as well.

Sanchez kept Brown informed of the work requests mady by himself and the other two WRH Realty employees. Brown did nothing to stop the additional work, nor did he tell his subordinates to stop requesting additional work. Hidden Colony then refused to pay for work outside the scope of the original contract.

Issue: Was Hidden Colony obligated to pay for the work done by Circle Y that was outside the scope of the original contract?

Holding: This Court finds that, acting within his actual authority, Brown ratified and authorized the actions of those WRH Realty employees who requested that Circle Y perform extra work. By his ratification of their actions, Brown made those employees his agents. Brown had actual authority to act on behalf of Hidden Colony, and thus, Hidden Colony is liable for the costs of the extra work performed by Circle Y.

Duties of Principals and Agents

Agency relationships are *fiduciary* relationships. This means that they are relationships of trust. Thus, once the agency relationship has been established, the agents and principals both owe fiduciary duties to each other – duties of utmost loyalty, good faith, candor, and fair dealing. If one is a fiduciary, one should do everything for the benefit of, and nothing to the detriment of, the other party.

Generally, an agent owes the following duties to the principal:

- Duty of Performance - An agent who enters into a contract with a principal must perform the lawful duties he has agreed to perform as expressed in the contract and he must meet all standards of reasonable care, skill, and diligence while doing so.

- Duty of Notification - The agent must keep the principal advised of all information he learns from third parties or other sources which may be important to the principal.

- Duty of Loyalty - The agent must not act adversely to the interests of the principal. The agent must not engage in self-dealing (undisclosed dealing with the principal), must not usurp opportunities of the principal, must not compete with the principal, and must not misuse confidential information.

  Example 2c:

  MegaStore hires Watson to locate a suitable tract of property for a new warehouse. During the search, Watson finds a tract of land for sale by an elderly farmer at an extremely low price. The property is ideally suited for Megastore's needs, but Watson, knowing the true value of the property, does not tell Megastore about the land. Instead, Watson buys the land for himself so that he can later resell it and make a profit. Watson has usurped an opportunity of his principal in violation of his duty of loyalty.

- Duty of Accountability - The agent owes a duty to maintain an accurate accounting of all transactions which the agent undertakes on the principal's behalf and must keep accurate records of all property and money which he receives and/or expends while carrying out his duties.

Just as the agent owes certain duties to the principal, likewise the principal owes certain duties to the agent. These include:

- Duty of Compensation - Principals must pay agents for their services. Usually, the agency contract specifies the amount of compensation. If there is no express agreement, the law will imply a promise that the principal will pay the agent the customary fee paid in the industry or the reasonable value of the agent's services. If the agency is a gratuitous agency, there is no duty of compensation.

- Duty of Reimbursement and Indemnification - The principal must reimburse the agent for all expenses incurred by the agent on the principal's behalf. The principal also owes the agent the duty to indemnify (repay) the agent for any losses the agent suffers because of the principal.

- Duty of Cooperation - The principal must cooperate with the agent and must provide the agent with items necessary to perform her duties. For instance, a homeowner who employs a real estate agent owes a duty to allow the agent to show the property at all reasonable times and upon reasonable notice.

Liability of Principals and Agents

An agent, like everyone else, is personally liable for his own torts or civil wrongs. Likewise, a principal is personally liable for the torts he commits. In addition, the principal is also liable for the tortious conduct of an agent who is acting within the scope of his authority when the tort is committed. Liability of principals for the negligent conduct of their agents acting within the scope of their employment is based on the common law doctrine of *respondeat superior* (let the master answer) which, in turn, is based on the legal theory of *vicarious liability* (liability for the actions of another because of the relationship between the two parties). In other words, the principal is liable because of his or her employment contract with the negligent agent, not because the principal was personally at fault.

Edgewater Motels, Inc., v. Gatzke and Walgreen Co.
277 N.W.2d 11 (1979)
Supreme Court of Minnesota

Facts: Arlen Gatzke was a district manager for Walgreen Co. He was sent to Duluth, Minnesota, to supervise the opening of a new store. While in Duluth, Gatzke stayed at the Edgewater Motel. Gatzke was "on call" 24 hours a day. About midnight on the evening of August 23, 1979, Gatzke, after working 17 hours, went with several other Walgreen employees to a restaurant and bar. Within an hour's time, Gatzke consumed three "doubles" and one single brandy Manhattan. About 1:30, a.m., he went back to the Edgewater Motel and filled out his expense report. Soon thereafter, a fire broke out in Gatzke's room. Gatzke escaped, but the fire spread and caused extensive damage to the motel. The parties stipulated the damages to be $330,360.00.

Evidence showed Gatzke was a heavy smoker. An expert fire reconstruction witness testified that the fire started from a lit cigarette in or next to the wastepaper basket in Gatzke's room.

Issue: Was Gatzke's act of smoking within his "scope of employment" making his principal, the Walgreen Company, vicariously liable for his negligence?

Holding: An employee does not abandon his employment as a matter of law while temporarily acting for his personal comfort when such activities involve only slight deviations from work that are reasonable in the circumstances. An employer can be vicariously liable for his employee's negligent smoking of a cigarette if he was otherwise acting in the scope of his employment at the time of the negligent act. Here, the record contains evidence that Gatzke was involved in serving his employer's interests while at the bar since he was discussing the operation of the newly opened Walgreen's store with other Walgreen employees. Further, even if he was outside the scope of his employment while at the bar, he resumed his employment activities after he returned to his room and filled out the expense report. This is supported by the fact that Gatzke was a 24-hour-a-day man, and the motel room was his "office away from home."

Of course, an injured party is always anxious to have the principal held liable for the tort of the agent. The principal may have a considerably "deeper pocket" than the agent, meaning that the principal is likely to have a greater ability to pay a sizeable judgment than the agent has. For instance, a pedestrian who is injured when a delivery truck driver runs a stop sign and hits him may be more likely to collect a judgment against the driver's company, who is almost certainly insured, than he is to collect a judgment against the driver personally. Even if this is not the case, liability on the part of the principal increases the likelihood that the injured party will be able to collect a judgment in his favor since he has two potential sources of payment, the agent and the principal.

The agent is only liable for the tortious conduct of the principal if he or she directly or indirectly participates in, or aids, and abets the principal's conduct.

There are several rules related to a principal's liability which are important to recognize:

- *Frolic and Detour* – Agents sometimes do things during the course of their employment to further their own interests rather than that of the principal. For example, an agent might take a detour to run a personal errand while on an assignment for the principal. Principals are generally relieved of liability if the agent's frolic and detour is substantial, but, if the deviation is minor, the principal is liable for the injuries caused by the agent's tortious conduct.

- *Coming and Going* – A principal generally is not liable for injuries caused by its agents and employees while they are on their way to work or on their way home from work.

- *Dual-Purpose Mission* – Sometimes, principals request that agents run errands or conduct other acts on their behalf while the agent or employee is on personal business. In most jurisdictions, agents who commit torts while on such dual purpose missions create liability for both themselves and their principals.

With regard to contract liability, a principal who authorizes an agent to enter into a contract with a third party is liable on the contract. The third party can bring suit against the principal to enforce the contract and can recover damages if the principal fails to perform as he is obligated to perform under the terms of the contract.

In certain circumstances, the agent can also be held liable on the contract. Imposition of such liability depends upon whether the agent's status is:

- *Fully Disclosed* – In a fully disclosed contract, the third party entering into the contract knows that the agent is acting as an agent for a principal and also knows the actual identity of the principal. In such cases, the agent is not liable on the contract because the third party relied on the principal's reputation and credit when the contract was made.

- *Partially Disclosed* – If the agent discloses his status as an agent for another but does not reveal the principal's identity, a partially disclosed agency exists. Both the principal and the agent are liable on a contract with a third party. This is because the third party must rely on the agent's reputation, integrity and credit since the principal is unidentified.

- *Undisclosed* – In an undisclosed agency, the third party is unaware of either the existence of an agency relationship or, obviously, of the principal's identity. Such agencies are lawful and are often used when the principal feels that the terms of the contract would be changed if the identity of the principal were known. Both the principal and the agent are liable on the contract with the third party.

You'll See Seafoods, Inc., v. Gravois

520 So.2d 461 (1988)

Court of Appeals of Louisiana

<u>*Facts:*</u> James Gravois purchased a restaurant and named it "The Captain's Raft." While Gravois ran the restaurant, he did not, in fact, own it. The restaurant was actually owned by Computer Tax Services of La., Inc., a corporation which was, in turn, owned by Gravois.

Gravois did not inform the managers, employees or suppliers that the restaurant was owned by a corporation. The menus were printed with the name "The Captain's Raft" with no indication it was a corporate entity. Supplies for the restaurant were paid for with checks signed by Gravois with no indication of his agency capacity. You'll See Seafoods supplied fresh seafood to the restaurant and was paid with checks signed by Gravois.

You'll See Seafoods filed suit against Gravois doing business as (d/b/a) "The Captain's Raft" to recover unpaid invoices. Gravois responded by saying that he was merely acting as an agent for a corporate principal. The corporation was in bankruptcy and You'll See Seafoods was unable to recover what was owed to it from the corporation. You'll See Seafoods then attempted to collect the debt from Gravois personally.

Issue: Was Gravois liable on the debt owed to You'll See Seafoods, Inc.?

Holding: While Gravois is undoubtedly an agent of the corporation, an agent is liable to those with whom he contracts on behalf of his principal when he has bound himself personally. An agent so binds himself by entering into an agreement without disclosing the existence of or identity of his principal. Here, Gravois dealt with You'll See Seafoods as though he were the owner of the restaurant. Since You'll See Seafoods was unaware that an agency relationship existed between Gravois and the corporation, and since Gravois failed to disclose the agency relationship, he is individually liable for all debts incurred.

Circle Y Construction v. WRH Realty Services and WRH Hidden Colony
427 Fed.Appx. 772, 2011 U.S.App. LEXIS 10629 (2011)
United States Court of Appeals for the Eleventh Circuit

Facts: *Recall this case from the earlier discussion about creation of an agency by ratification. The relevant facts with regard to the issue of undisclosed agency, are these:* Circle Y Construction, Inc., entered into a contract with WRH Realty for the renovation of some housing units. WRH Realty was acting as the agent for Hidden Colony, a limited liability limited partnership, but did not disclose that fact to Circle Y. Beginning shortly after the contract was signed, Brown, who was designated by Hidden Colony as its agent, and agents of Brown asked Circle Y to perform work outside the scope of the contract. These requests were made on several different occasions and each time Circle Y performed the work.

Issue: Was Hidden Colony obligated to pay for the work done by Circle Y that was outside the scope of the original contract?

Holding: The Georgia agency statute provides as follows: "If an agent shall fail to disclose his principal, when discovered, the person dealing with the agent may go directly upon the principal under the contract..."

The Georgia Court of Appeals has explained this statute by saying, "Similar to the principle that a person may become liable as an ostensible partner is the principle that an agent who makes a contract without disclosing that he is acting as an agent or without identifying his principle, or an agent who makes a contract with the express or implied understanding with the other party that he is binding himself individually, will become individually liable on the contract." This Court finds that, to avoid personal liability, WRH Realty had the duty to disclose that it was acting solely as Hidden Colony's agent in making the oral contracts for additional work. Since the agency was not disclosed, Hidden Colony is liable for the work.

2.3 *Labor Unions*

Prior to the Industrial Revolution, the doctrine of *laissez-faire* controlled the employment relationship. After the Industrial Revolution large corporations enjoyed a tremendous advantage over their workers who were powerless in their ability to negotiate individually with employers. The emergence of this unequal bargaining position, coupled with concerns over the use of child labor and unsafe working conditions, brought about considerable changes and the enactment of federal legislation. However, as Georgia is a right-to-work state, discussed below, this text contains an abbreviated discussion of labor unions.

The National Labor Relations Act (NRLA) was passed by Congress to establish a system of free *collective bargaining* by workers. The Act defines the basic rights of employees which include:

- The right to form, join and assist unions;
- The right to bargain collectively through unions freely chosen by them;
- The right to engage in concerted activities with others in furtherance of collective bargaining or for their mutual aid and protection; and
- The right to refrain from any or all of these activities.

The National Labor Relations Board (NLRB) is the administrative body created by the NLRA. The board oversees union elections, prevents employers and unions from engaging in unfair or illegal labor practices, and enforces and interprets many federal labor laws. It is an *unfair labor practice* for an employer to "interfere with, coerce, or restrain" employees from exercising their right to form or join unions. An employer cannot threaten employees with retaliation in an effort to influence the employees' voting with regard to a union, nor is the employer permitted to promise employees some reward, such as a one-time pay bonus, to achieve that end.

Once a union has been elected, the employer and the union engage in the process of *collective bargaining*, or the discussion of the terms of employment of union members. The employer and the union attempt to negotiate a contract between the two parties. Wages, work hours and other conditions of employment must be covered by the collective bargaining agreement. Fringe benefits, health care plans and retirement plans may also be covered, but there is no requirement that these items be included. Additionally, many labor contracts contain arbitration provisions requiring this method of resolving disputes be used if disagreements arise under the labor contract.

If a collective bargaining agreement cannot be reached, union management has the right, under the NLRA, to recommend that the union call a *strike*. Strikes must be approved by the union members and, before there can be a strike, a majority of the union's members must vote in favor of it. An employer who anticipates a strike may engage in an *employer lockout* and prevent those employees from entering the work place or premises.

If a strike is voted for by the union, individual workers of the union do not have to honor the strike. Instead, they may choose (1) not to strike or (2) to return to work after joining the strikers for a time. These are called *crossover workers*.

Certain types of strikes are not legal and are not protected by federal labor law:

- Violent Strikes – If striking workers cause substantial damage to the property of the employer, a court may find the entire strike to be illegal;
- Sit-Down Strike – Striking employees continue to occupy the employer's premises;
- Partial or Intermittent Strikes – Workers strike part of the work day or work week;

- Wildcat Strikes – A wildcat strike lacks proper authorization from the union;
- Strikes During the Cooling Off Period – The NLRB can implement a mandatory cooling off period to give both sides time to negotiate and avoid a strike. A strike during this cooling-off period is illegal;
- Strikes in Violation of a No-Strike Clause – The collective bargaining agreement may contain a no-strike clause in exchange for increased economic benefits;

Striking union members may engage in *picketing*. Picketing is the act of standing or parading near the employer's business usually with signs of protest or worker's claims in the labor disputes. Picketing is lawful unless it is accompanied by violence, obstructs customers from entering the employer's premises, prevents non-striking employees from entering the employer's premises, or prevents pick-ups and deliveries at the employer's premises.

States seeking to attract industry and business may pass *right-to-work* laws. These measures outlaw union shops which mandate that a worker must become a union member within a specified time after he begins employment. In other words, in a state with a right-to-work law, an individual employee cannot be forced to join a union or pay union dues and fees even though a union has been elected by other employees. Thus, union membership cannot be required for obtaining or retaining employment with a given employer. Right-to-work states are often attractive to businesses and industries seeking to lower their labor costs, and the Chamber of Commerce, on behalf of business, has lobbied extensively for right-to-work laws. These laws are vehemently opposed by unions because they substantially erode the power of the unions leading, according to the unions, to lower wages and less safe working conditions. Georgia is a right-to-work state.

2.4 *Workers' Compensation Acts*

At common law, an employee who was injured on the job could file suit against his or her employer for negligence; however, such an action often took months or years to resolve and placed the employee at odds with his employer. The injured worker was also not guaranteed any recovery or compensation for his injury. In response, state *workers' compensation acts* were enacted which created an administrative procedure to assure that injured workers would receive compensation.

Most workers' compensation statutes are similar, and no state covers all employees. Typically excluded are domestic workers, agricultural workers, and temporary employees. Usually, the statutes allow employers to purchase insurance, either from a private insurer or a state fund, to cover the costs of the worker's benefits in the event of a claim. In order to receive compensation, a worker who is injured in an employment related incident must first file a claim with the appropriate state agency. Next, that agency will determine the legitimacy of the claim. A worker who disagrees with the determination of the state agency may appeal through the state court system.

Workers' compensation benefits are paid in accordance with preset limits established by statute. In exchange for preset compensation limits, workers are guaranteed benefits without the burden of having to prove fault. In other words, a worker injured on the job is guaranteed payment for his injuries, regardless of how the injury occurred or who was at fault. The trade off is that the level of payment is limited.

To receive compensation, the injured worker must prove that the injury arose "out of and in the course of his employment." An accident that occurs while the employee is actively working at his job is clearly covered. Accidents that occur while the employee is on the employer's premises are covered, regardless of whether or not the employee's own negligence caused or contributed to the accident. This is true even in cases where the employee fails to abide by posted safety precautions and the accident is clearly the employee's fault.

Example 2d:

Sasha works at Fresh Breads Bakery. While at work, Sasha is injured when she turns on a commercial mixer and receives an electric shock. Sasha can collect workers' compensation even though she had been aware of the short in the mixer switch prior to her injury and had been told by her supervisor not to use the mixer until it was repaired.

The simple fact that the employee is injured on the employer's premise makes the accident one that occurs "in the course of employment," even though the employee may not have been engaged in a purely work activity at the time. For instance, accidents that occur at the company cafeteria or in the employee break room are covered. Also covered would be the accident that occurs while the employee is away from the employer's premises but conducting the business of his employer. For example, an accident that occurs while the employee is on a business lunch with his employer's customer would be covered. However, an accident that occurs during the work day but while the employee is off-premises during his personal lunch hour is not covered.

An intentionally inflicted self-injury would not be covered by worker's compensation. An injury that occurs while the employee is traveling to or from work covered also not covered.

Much of the litigation in the area of workers' compensation law is over the issue of whether or not an employee's injury arose "out of and in the course of employment." While, at first glance, this may seem obvious, the case below illustrates the difficulty of making this determination in cases in which the accident occurs at some location other than the employer's premises.

Smith v. Workers' Compensation Appeals Board
191 Cal.App.3d 154 (1987)
Court of Appeals of California

Facts: Ronald Wayne Smith was employed by Modesto High School in Modesto, California, as a temporary math instructor with a one year contract which could be renewed the following year. In addition to teaching math, he coached the girls' baseball and basketball teams. The contract under which Smith was employed stated that he "may be required to devote a reasonable amount of time to other duties" in addition to his instructional duties. The teachers in the school system were evaluated once a year regarding both instructional duties and non-instructional duties including "sponsorship or the supervision of out-of-classroom student activities." The evaluation was particularly important to Smith as he was hired for only one year at a time.

Modesto High School's math club held an annual end-of-the-year outing. At the end of the school year in June, 1984, the club scheduled a picnic at the Modesto Reservoir as its annual event, with the picnic food being paid for out of the math club members' dues. The students invited all of their math teachers to attend. Smith, his wife, and their three children attended the picnic. One of the students brought along a windsurfer, and Smith watched the students use it before and after the picnic. When Smith tried to use the windsurfer, he fell, was seriously injured, and died a short time later. Smith's wife filed a claim for workers' compensation benefits. The employer objected, alleging that Smith was not acting in the course of his employment at the time of his accident.

Issue: Was Smith engaged in an employment related activity at the time of the accident?

Holding: Smith was a temporary math teacher. As such he was more vulnerable to pressure or suggestion that he participate in extracurricular activities to better his chances of being re-hired for the following school year. The math club was an official school club, and notices of meetings to plan the end-of-the-year outing appeared in the school bulletin. Clearly, the picnic was not an impromptu or informal gathering. Students were required to submit permission slips to the school and the food was paid for with math club funds. Thus, the school was more than minimally involved in the picnic. Teachers were encouraged to involve themselves in extracurricular activities of the school, thus conferring the benefit of better teacher-student relationships. More importantly, teachers were evaluated on whether they shared equally in the sponsorship or the supervision of out-of-classroom student activities.

The school argues that even if Smith's attendance at the picnic was required by his employment, his activities in using the windsurfer were outside the course and scope of his employment. An injury is deemed to have arisen out of one's employment if there is an incidental or causal connection between the employment and the accident. Because attendance at the picnic was an implied requirement of Smith's employment, his accident that resulted from his engaging in the recreational activities which were part and parcel of the picnic's "entertainment" is causally connected to his employment.

Workers' compensation is an exclusive remedy. This means that an injured worker cannot sue her employer in court for damages, regardless of how negligent the employer may have been. The injured worker can only look to workers' compensation for payment for her injuries. The only exception to this rule is if the employer *intentionally* injures the worker. In that case, the worker can collect both workers' compensation benefits and can sue the employer for the intentional tort which resulted in the injury.

If a worker is injured through the negligence of a third party, however, the worker can collect both workers' compensation benefits, because the injury occurred on the job, and the injured worker can also sue the negligent third party in tort. For example, assume a purchasing agent is on a business lunch with a supplier and is injured when the supplier, who is driving, runs a traffic light and crashes. The injured purchasing agent can collect workers' compensation because he was acting in the course of his employment at the time of the injury. In addition, he may also sue the supplier, a third party, for negligence which resulted in the purchasing agent's injuries.

Example 2e:

Recall Sasha, the Fresh Breads Bakery worker from Example 2d above. If Sasha is injured by the shock she receives when she turns on a mixer manufactured by ABC, Corp., Sasha is entitled to receive workers' compensation benefits for her job related injury even though her injury was not the fault of her employer. Additionally, Sasha can also sue ABC, Corp., for her damages resulting from their defective manufacture of the mixer (although, given the facts of Example 2d, ABC, Corp., will likely assert as a defense Sasha's knowledge of the defect).

2.5 *Occupational Safety and Health Act*

In 1970, Congress enacted the Occupational Safety and Health Act to promote health and safety in the workplace. Since the act applies to all employers engaged in business that affects interstate commerce, virtually all private employers are within the scope of the act (government employers are exempt). The act is administered by a federal agency, the Occupational Safety and Health Administration (OSHA), and requires employers to keep comprehensive records on employee illnesses and injuries and to report workplace accidents. OSHA has the authority to promulgate standards, make inspections, and enforce the act. OSHA has adopted thousands of regulations to enforce the safety standards established by the act. In addition to General Duty Standards, which impose a general duty on the employer to provide a work environment "free from recognized hazards," OSHA enforces Specific Duty Standards to address safety problems of specific jobs or industries.

OSHA compliance officers may enter and inspect the facilities of any employer covered by the act and may investigate any accident or incident. Additionally, employees may file complaints of violations which may also be investigated by OSHA. Under the act, an employer cannot discharge an employee who files a complaint or who, in good faith, refuses to work in a high-risk area if bodily harm or death might result.

2.6 Wage and Hour Laws

The Fair Labor Standards Act, first passed by Congress in 1938, sought to address the problem of child labor and forbids the use of oppressive child labor through the following regulations:

- Children under the age of 14 cannot work except as newspaper deliverers;
- Children ages 14 and 15 may work a limited number of hours in nonhazardous jobs approved by the Department of Labor;
- Children ages 16 and 17 may work an unlimited number of hours in nonhazardous jobs;
- Persons age 18 and older may work at any job whether it is hazardous or not.

Today, we may tend to think of child labor as a problem existing only in other countries. However, for many years, the use of child labor was quite common in the U.S. For instance, in the early 1900s, it was not uncommon for children as young as six or seven to work in textile mills across the South.[3]

The FLSA further provides that a minimum wage of a specified amount must be paid to employees in covered industries. The current federal minimum wage is $7.25 per hour although many states, and some cities, have enacted local statutes providing for a higher minimum wage. Georgia is not among these.

Under the FLSA, any employee who agrees to work more than forty (40) hours per week must be paid no less than one-and-a-half times (150%) his or her regular pay for all hours over forty. However, certain employees are exempt from the overtime provisions of the act. These exemptions typically include employees whose jobs are categorized as professional, executive, or administrative. Also exempt are outside sales persons. However, an employer cannot deny overtime wages to an employee based only on the employee's job title. It is the nature of the employee's work, and not his title, which determines whether he is entitled to overtime pay. The exemptions to payment of overtime do not apply to manual laborers or other "blue-collar" workers who perform tasks involving repetitive operations with their hands. The exemptions also do not apply to police, firefighters, licensed nurses and other public safety workers.

---

[3] Child labor was prevalent in coal mines, textile mills and other factories. Young boys were frequently employed in coal mines as their small stature was well suited to the tight mine shafts. For an exposé about child labor in coal mines, see John Spago's *The Bitter Cry of the Children* (1906). *And the Dead Shall Rise* by Steve Oney chronicles the infamous murder of 13-year-old Mary Phagan at the National Pencil Company in Atlanta where she worked for ten cents per hour and the lynching of factory manager Leo Frank, accused of her murder.

2.7 *Equal Pay Act*

Between 1950 and 1960 women with full time jobs earned, on average, between 59 and 64 cents for every dollar their male counterparts earned in the same job. The Equal Pay Act, enacted in 1963, protects both men and women from pay discrimination and prohibits disparity in pay for jobs that require equal skill, equal responsibility, and similar working conditions. Note that not all pay disparities are illegal. The Equal Pay Act expressly provides that differentials in wages based upon seniority, merit and quantity or quality of production are permissible.

While disparities in pay between men and women have decreased, they have not been erased and continue to be addressed by official action. In response to the Supreme Court's decision in *Ledbetter v. Goodyear Tire & Rubber Co., Inc.*, 127 S.Ct. 2162 (2007), Congress passed the Lily Ledbetter Fair Pay Restoration Act which allows victims of pay discrimination to file a complaint with the government against their employer within 180 days of their last paycheck. To further address the issue, in April, 2014, President Obama signed two executive orders to help eliminate wage disparities among federal contract workers. One order bans federal contractors from punishing workers for discussing salaries with co-workers, and the other calls on the Labor Department to create rules that require federal contractors to submit salary information broken down by race and gender. To date, Congress has failed to pass the Paycheck Fairness Act which would impose these measures on the entire American workforce.

2.8 *Equal Opportunity in Employment*

At common law, employers were free to hire and promote anyone they chose and could terminate an employee at any time and for whatever reason. The 1960's civil rights movement to end racial discrimination gave rise to a body of law protecting employees against discrimination in the workplace. This legislation was designed to afford workers with equal opportunity in employment and acted to erode the employment-at-will doctrine.

Title VII of the Civil Rights Act of 1964 (commonly referred to as Title VII), prohibits job discrimination against employees, applicants, and union members. Title VII does not and was not intended to eliminate all discrimination, but rather targeted job discrimination based upon the following *protected classes*:

- Race – refers to broad categories such as Black, Asian, Caucasian;
- Color – refers to the color of a person's skin;
- Religion;
- Sex; and
- National Origin – refers to the country of a person's ancestors or cultural characteristics.

Title VII applies to employers with 15 or more employees and to most federal, state and local governments. Title VII prohibits discrimination not just in hiring decisions but also in decisions regarding promotion or demotion, the payment of compensation, and any other "term, condition or privilege" of employment based upon a person's membership in one of the five protected classes. Bear in mind that Title VII does not prohibit all discrimination, just discrimination based upon membership in a protected class. So long as the employer's decision is not based upon the employee's membership in a protected class, an employer may make an employment decision for a good reason, a bad reason, or for no reason at all; he just cannot make it for an illegal reason. Thus, the real question to be decided in cases brought under Title VII is often the employer's motivation in making the employment decision. Was the employer basing his decision on the employee's membership in a protected class?

Title VII protects against two distinct types of discrimination:

- *Disparate Treatment Discrimination* – This type of discrimination occurs when an employer discriminates against a specific individual because of that individual's membership in one of the protected classes. For example, an employer firing a Muslim employee because the employer developed strong anti-Muslim feelings as a result of the war in Iraq would violate Title VII.

- *Disparate Impact Discrimination* – Disparate impact discrimination occurs when an employer discriminates against an entire protected class. These cases are often proven through statistical data about the employer's employment practices and often arise when the employer adopts a work rule that is neutral on its face but is shown to have an adverse impact on a protected class.

NAACP v. Town of Harrison, New Jersey
907 F.2d 1408 (1990)
United States Court of Appeals, Third Circuit

__Facts:__ The town of Harrison, New Jersey, followed a policy of hiring only town residents as employees of the city. Such a policy was specifically sanctioned by New Jersey state law.

Harrison is a small, industrial city located in Hudson County, but it is clearly aligned with Essex County to the west and is considered an extension of the city of Newark which it abuts. Adjacent counties are within an easy commute of Harrison. Only 0.2 percent of Harrison's population is black. None of its police officers, fire fighters, or non-uniformed employees are black. Several blacks who were members of the NAACP applied for employment with Harrison but were rejected because they did not meet the residency requirement. The NAACP then sued for employment discrimination.

__Issue:__ Does the residency requirement of the town of Harrison violate Title VII of the Civil Rights Act of 1964?

__Holding:__ The geographical area from which Harrison draws employees includes its own county of Hudson as well as Bergen, Union and Essex, where Newark is located. By reason of geographic location and transportation facilities, Harrison could reasonably be viewed as functionally a component of the city of Newark and a part of Essex County.

Newark's population is 60% black. Essex County's civilian labor force is 33.3% black. Harrison has no black employees, and, for all pracitical purposes, Harrison has no black residents. It would be hard to conclude that among the very substantial number of black workers in the four-county labor market, there are not large numbers of persons qualified to serve as police officers, firefighters, clerk typists, and laborers.

The evidence compels the conclusion that the residency requirements are the cause of at least a substantial part of the disparity. Thus, to limit employment or applications for employment to residents effectively excludes blacks from employment by the municipality. There is strong evidence that, if the residency requirement were removed, qualified black persons would seek positions with Harrison's municipal government. Thus, Harrison's facially neutral residency requirements have been shown to have a disproportionate impact on black persons.

The Equal Employment Opportunity Commission (EEOC) is the federal agency charged with responsibility for enforcing most federal anti-discrimination laws. To bring an action under Title VII, a complainant alleging discrimination must first file a complaint with the EEOC. After an investigation, assuming the EEOC finds a basis for alleging discrimination, the EEOC may choose to sue the employer on the complainant's behalf. Alternatively, the agency may choose to issue a *right to sue letter* to the complainant giving him or her the right to sue the employer. A plaintiff who is successful in his or her suit under Title VII can recover up to two years' back pay and reasonable attorney's fees.

The prohibition against discrimination based on sex applies equally to men and to women, although the overwhelming majority of cases are brought by women.

Sexual harassment is a form of discrimination prohibited by Title VII. Sexual harassment can be as obvious as refusing to hire or promote someone unless he or she has sex with the manager. More often, sexual harassment is evidenced by other forms of conduct such as lewd remarks, touching, intimidation, or verbal conduct of a sexual nature. Such conduct can create a *hostile work environment* and is a violation of Title VII. The Courts, in determining whether a hostile work environment exists, will consider the frequency of the discriminatory conduct, its severity, whether it is physically threatening or humiliating, and whether it unreasonably interferes with the employee's work performance.

In most situations, for example tort cases, courts use a "reasonable person" standard to determine whether conduct violates the norms of society by considering what the fictitious reasonable person would do in like circumstances. In sexual harassment cases where the victim is a woman, many courts apply the "reasonable woman standard," and analyze harassment from the victim's perspective.

The Supreme Court has held that same-sex sexual harassment is actionable under Title VII.

Harris v. Forklift Systems, Inc.
114 S.Ct. 367 (1993)
United States Supreme Court

<u>*Facts:*</u> Teresa Harris worked as a manager at Forklift Systems, Inc., an equipment rental company, for two years. Hardy was Forklift's president, and Harris had frequent contact with Hardy in the course of her employment. Throughout Harris's time at Forklift, Hardy often insulted her because of her gender and made her the target of unwanted sexual innuendos. Hardy told Harris on several occasions, in the presence of other employees, "You're a woman, what do you know," and "We need a man as the rental manager." At least once, he told her she was "a dumb ass woman." In front of others, he suggested the two of them "go to the Holiday Inn to negotiate (Harris's) raise." He occasionally asked Harris and other female employees to get coins from his front pants pocket. He threw objects on the ground in front of Harris and other women and asked them to pick the objects up. He made sexual innuendos about Harris's, and other women's, clothing.

Harris complained to Hardy about his conduct. He said he was surprised that Harris was offended, claimed he was only joking, and apologized. He also promised that he would stop. A few weeks later, Hardy's behavior resumed. While Harris was arranging a deal with one of Forklift's customers, Hardy asked her, in front of other employees, "What did you do, promise the guy some sex Saturday night?" Harris quit. Harris then sued Forklift claiming that Hardy's conduct had created an abusive work environment for her because of her gender. The district court held that because Harris had not suffered severe psychological injury she could not recover. Harris appealed.

Issue: Must conduct, to be actionable as abusive work environment harassment, seriously affect the victim's psychological well-being?

Holding: When the workplace is permeated with discriminatory intimidation, ridicule, and insults that are sufficiently severe or pervasive to alter the conditions of the victim's employment and create an abusive working environment, Title VII is violated. A discriminatorily abusive work environment, even one that does not seriously affect an employee's psychological well-being, can, and often will, detract from the employee's job performance, discourage employees from remaining on the job or keep them from advancing in their careers. Moreover, even without regard to these tangible effects, the very fact that the discriminatory conduct was so severe or pervasive that it created a work environment abusive to employees because of their race, gender, religion or national origin offends Title VII's broad rule of workplace equality.

Certainly Title VII bars conduct that would seriously affect a reasonable person's psychological well-being, but the statute is not limited to such conduct. So long as the environment would reasonably be perceived, and is perceived, as hostile or abusive, there is no need for it to be psychologically injurious.

Discrimination based upon a person's religion is prohibited by Title VII. Many religious discrimination cases involve a conflict between an employer's work rule and an employee's religious beliefs. For instance, an employee may object when he is required to work on his religious holiday. Such conflicts do not necessarily constitute religious discrimination because the right of the employee to practice his religion is not absolute. Under Title VII, an employer must *reasonably accommodate* the religious observances and practices of the employee, but only if that accommodation does not cause an undue hardship on the employer. In determining undue hardship, the courts will consider the size of the employer, the importance of the employee's position, and whether alternative workers are available.

Some religious discrimination is actually sanctioned by Title VII. Specifically, Title VII expressly permits religious organizations to give preference in employment to individuals of that same particular religion. For example, if it wishes to do so, a Catholic school may impose a rule under which it will hire only Catholic teachers.

It is important to remember that not all discrimination is illegal. In making employment decisions, such as the hiring or promotion of an employee, an employer may select or promote an employee based on merit. Merit can include such factors as educational experience, work history, and professionally developed ability tests. Employers may also lawfully reward long-time employees through the use of seniority systems.

Discrimination based on protected classes other than race or color is permitted so long as the employer can show there is a *bona fide occupational qualification (BFOQ)* that is both job related and a business necessity. For example, a department store's decision to hire only women to fit bras in the store's lingerie department is a valid and lawful BFOQ.

The Pregnancy Discrimination Act forbids employment discrimination because of pregnancy, child-birth, or related medical conditions.

The Age Discrimination in Employment Act prohibits employment discrimination against persons ages 40 and older. The act provides for EEOC enforcement and prohibits almost all mandatory retirement. It is important to note that persons under the age of 40 are not covered and so an employer can maintain an employment practice of hiring only workers who are 40 years of age or older. This federal statute also recognizes that, in some instances, age can be a bona fide occupational qualification. For example, police officers, firefighters, and airline pilots are not protected under the ADEA since their job performance may be hampered by age.

2.9 *Health Insurance*

The nexus between the workplace and health insurance is extremely important in the United States. The United States is the only large, industrialized nation that does not offer universal health care to its citizens. Instead, health care in the U.S. is dependent upon coverage provided by private, for profit, insurance companies. This system developed when the shortage of labor during World War II encouraged employers to offer health insurance as an added benefit to the employment package. Since health insurance coverage was not considered "income" by the Internal Revenue Service, this proved very popular with employees, and it was soon commonplace for employers to provide health insurance to their employees. Today, more than half of all Americans have health insurance coverage through an employer, including nearly two-thirds of adult workers who are too young to qualify for Medicare, the government provided healthcare coverage for seniors.

This system is not, however, without serious problems. Healthcare costs, including the premiums associated with employee healthcare insurance, have risen faster than the general rate of inflation, leading some businesses to cut back on the coverage they offer to employees. Often, small businesses do not offer health insurance at all. Additionally, day laborers, the unemployed, and the self-employed frequently have no health coverage unless they purchase health insurance policies in the private market. Furthermore, since health insurance companies are for-profit businesses who naturally want to maximize profits, the insurers have an incentive to provide coverage for the healthiest people and avoiding providing coverage for sicker people.

As a result, health care coverage and the costs of that care began to reach a crisis level a few years ago. In 2010, 45.7 million Americans, or 16% of the population, were without health insurance. Those without health care coverage often used hospital emergency rooms for primary care, driving up costs across the board. Those relying solely on emergency room care often faced crippling financial obligations in the event of a serious accident or illness.

In 2010, Congress passed and President Barack Obama signed into law, the Patient Protection and Affordable Care Act, commonly referred to as the Affordable Care Act (ACA) or Obamacare. The ACA was designed to increase the quality, accessibility and affordability of health insurance. It eliminates pre-existing conditions as a bar to insurance coverage, expands free preventative services, and prevents insurance companies from dropping insured persons when they become sick. It also requires most Americans to obtain health coverage by 2014 or pay a monthly fee, and, for individuals who must buy health insurance in the individual marketplace, the law provides subsidies to make insurance more affordable.

The ACA seeks to expand the number of employers who provide health coverage for their employees. To accomplish this, the law includes an employer mandate requiring that all businesses with over 50 full-time equivalent (FTE) employees[4] provide health insurance for their full-time workers or pay a per month "Employer Shared Responsibility Payment" on their federal tax return. Small

---

[4] To determine the number of full-time equivalent (FTE) employees an employer has, divide the average number of hours worked by part-time employees in a week by 30. Then add this number to the total number of full-time employees.

businesses with 50-99 full-time equivalent employees must being providing insurance to their workers by 2016. Those with 100 or more FTEs must provide health benefits to at least 70% of their workers by 2015 and to at least 95% by 2016.

The ACA also establishes minimum standards for employer-provided health coverage. In order to avoid the "employer shared responsibility payment," the coverage must be affordable. If an employee's share of the premium costs for the employee's coverage (coverage for the individual employee, not his entire family) is more than 9.5% of the employee's income, the coverage is not considered affordable.

Employer-provided health insurance must also provide a certain level of value. This means that certain services must be provided by the coverage and that the plan must pay a minimum level of benefit. In simple terms, a health plan meets minimum value if the plan provides the required services and its share of the total costs of all covered services is at least 60%.

While Obamacare continues to be an extremely controversial topic which has deepened the political divide in this country, implementation of the law is well underway and represents the first significant overhaul of the American healthcare system since the introduction of Medicare and Meidcaid in the 1960s.

2.10 Americans with Disabilities Act

The Americans with Disabilities Act, enacted in 1990, imposes obligations on employers and providers of public transportation, telecommunications, and public accommodations to accommodate individuals with disabilities. The act covers employers with 15 or more employees, and requires employers to make *reasonable accommodations* to individuals with disabilities, provided that doing so does not cause undue hardship to the employer.

Reasonable accommodations may include making facilities readily accessible to the disabled, providing part-time or modified work schedules, acquiring equipment or devices to assist the employee, and modifying training materials. Employers are not required to provide accommodations that would impose an undue burden on the employer, i.e., ones that involve significant difficulty or expense. In determining whether an accommodation would result in an undue hardship, the courts will consider factors such as the nature and costs of the accommodation and the financial resources of the employer. Additionally, the employer's type of operation is taken into consideration.

An individual with a disability is a person who, with or without reasonable accommodation, can perform the essential functions of the job that the person desires or holds. Under the act, a disabled person is defined as someone who (1) has a physical or mental impairment that substantially limits one or more of his or her major life activities, (2) has a record of such impairment, or (3) is regarded as having such impairment. Persons with HIV, mental retardation, schizophrenia, epilepsy, diabetes, and other diseases are covered by the ADA as are recovering alcoholics and drug addicts.

2.11 Employee Privacy Rights

Many employees have concerns about their privacy rights in the workplace while, at the same time, their employers are concerned about the productivity of the employees. Perhaps the greatest concern in today's workplace has to do with electronic monitoring.

Electronic Communications

According to a recent survey by an association of managers, more than two-thirds of employers engage in some form of electronic monitoring of their employees. This monitoring can take any of several forms including reviewing employees' e-mail and computer files, video recording of employee job performance, and recording and reviewing telephone conversations and voice mail.

Software manufacturers have responded to the demand of employers by creating a variety of products which have made it easier for an employer to track employees' internet use. Using such software, an employer can track virtually every move made by the employee while the employee is using the internet, including the specific web sites visited and the time spent surfing the web. Filtering software can also be used to prevent access to certain web sites, such as sites containing pornographic or sexually explicit images.

The Electronic Communications Privacy Act of 1986 prohibits the intentional interception of any wire or electronic communication or the intentional disclosure or use of the information obtained by the interception. However, specifically excluded are any electronic communications made through devices that are "furnished to the subscriber or user by a provider of wire or electronic communication service" and that are being used by the subscriber or user, or by the provider of the service "in the ordinary course of its business." Simply stated, this "business extension exception" to the ECPA permits an employer to monitor the electronic communications made by his employee in the ordinary course of business. Since the exception applies only to communications made in the course of business, the employer is still not permitted, under the act, to monitor employees' personal communications. However, the employer can engage in such monitoring if his employees consent to it. Thus, many employers now require employees, as a condition of employment, to sign consent forms indicating that they agree to submit to such monitoring.

Lie Detector Tests

In addition to monitoring their employees' online activities, employers also engage in other types of employee screening and monitoring practices. The Employee Polygraph Protection Act generally prohibits employers from requiring or causing employees or job applicants to take lie-detector tests or suggesting or requesting that they do so. This legislation also prohibits employers, in many circumstances, from taking or threatening negative employment-related action against employees or applicants based on the results of lie-detector tests or on the employee's or applicant's refusal to take the tests.

There are, however, a number of employers which are not covered by the act. Federal, state and local government employers are not covered. Also exempt are certain security service firms and companies manufacturing and distributing controlled substances. Additionally, other employers may lawfully use polygraph tests when investigating theft, embezzlement, or the theft of trade secrets.

Drug Testing

Many employers, including the government in some instances, require employees and prospective employees to submit to drug testing. By doing so, employers hope to promote safety in the work place and to reduce costs associated with workplace incidents including workers' compensation insurance premiums. Often, the question of whether an employer's drug testing policy is permissible hinges on whether the testing is reasonable. Quite naturally, many employees consider drug testing an invasion of their privacy. Furthermore, employees may be protected against drug testing by their union's collective bargaining agreements.

Laws vary from state to state concerning the privacy rights of employees and the appropriateness of drug testing by private-sector employers. Georgia's scheme is fairly typical of many states and requires employers who want to drug test their employees to furnish to both employees and job applicants a written policy statement on employee substance abuse which identifies the types of testing an employee may be required to submit to as well as the actions the employer may take against an employee or job applicant on the basis of a positive, confirmed test result. Some states, including Georgia, provide that an employer who requires job applicants to submit to a substance abuse test qualifies for a discount on the employer's workers' compensation insurance premium.

Government employers are subject to more constraints with regard to drug testing. The Fourth Amendment of the United States Constitution prohibits unreasonable searches and seizures by the government, and a drug test by a government employer constitutes a search of the employee. Remember, however, that the Fourth Amendment does not apply to drug testing conducted by private employers, so the constraints of the Fourth Amendment are applicable only to government employers.

There are, of course, exceptions. Even government employees are subject to drug testing when there is a reasonable basis for suspecting the employee of using drugs, or when drug use in a particular job could threaten public safety. For instance, employees of the Drug Enforcement Agency, who regularly come into contact with controlled substances, may be subjected to drug tests along with Customs officials and Border Patrol agents. However, the exceptions have limits as illustrated by the following case.

Chandler v. Miller
520 U.S. 305 (1997)
United States Supreme Court

<u>Facts</u>: In 1990, the State of Georgia enacted a statute which required that each candidate seeking to qualify for nomination or election to designated state offices certify that (1) the candidate, within 30 days prior to qualifying, had submitted to a urinalysis test for marijuana, cocaine, opiates, amphetamines, and phencyclidines, and (2) the results of such test were negative. The candidate could provide the test specimen at a laboratory approved by the state or at the office of the candidate's personal physician. Once a urine sample was obtained, a state-approved laboratory tested for the specified illegal drugs and prepared a certificate reporting the test results to the candidate.

In 1994, three candidates for state offices which were covered by the statute filed an action in federal court requesting declaratory and injunctive relief barring enforcement of the statute, alleging that the drug tests required by the statute violated their rights under the Fourth Amendment to the Constitution.

<u>Issue</u>: Does mandatory drug testing by the State of Georgia as a condition of holding elective office violate the Fourth Amendment of the Constitution?

<u>Holding</u>: It is uncontested that Georgia's drug-testing requirement, imposed by law and enforced by state officials, affects a search within the meaning of the Fourth Amendment. The statute's drug-testing requirement does not fit within the closely guarded category of constitutionally permissible suspicionless searches under the Fourth Amendment where: (1) the statute plainly was not tied to individualized suspicion of wrongdoing; (2) no Supreme Court precedent suggested that a state's power under the Tenth Amendment to establish qualifications for state offices diminished the constraints on state action imposed by the Fourth Amendment; (3) although the testing method which the statute

described was relatively noninvasive, the state had failed to show a special need which was substantial; and (4) the Fourth Amendment shielded society against state action which diminished personal privacy for a symbol's sake.

Respondents contend that unlawful drug use is incompatible with holding high state office because such drug use draws into question an official's judgment and integrity; jeopardizes the discharge of public functions; and undermines public confidence in elected officials. Notably lacking is any indication of a concrete danger demanding departure from the Fourth Amendment's main rule. The statute was not enacted in response to any fear or suspicion of drug use by state officials. A demonstrated problem of drug abuse, while not always necessary to the validity of a testing regime, would shore up an assertion of special need for a suspicionless general search program. In contrast to the effective testing regimes upheld in certain previous cases (sustaining drug-testing for Customs Service officers prior to promotion or transfer to certain high-risk positions and sustaining drug testing for student athletes), Georgia's certification requirement is not well designed to identify candidates who violate anti-drug laws and is not a credible means to deter illicit drug users from seeking state office. The test date is selected by the candidate, and, thus, all but the prohibitively addicted could abstain for a pretest period sufficient to avoid detection.

Hardly a decision opening broad vistas for suspicionless searches, *Von Raab* (the Customs Officers case) must be read in its unique context. The court noted that drug interdiction had become the agency's primary enforcement mission. The covered posts directly involved drug interdiction, and the employees would have access to vast sources of valuable contraband. Officers had been targets of, and some had succumbed to, bribery by drug smugglers. Moreover, it was not feasible to subject the Customs Service employees to the kind of day-to-day scrutiny that is the norm in more traditional office environments.

In telling contrast, the day-to-day conduct of candidates for public office attracts attention notably beyond the norm in ordinary work environments. What is left, after close review, is that the State seeks to display its commitment to the struggle against drug abuse. But Georgia asserts no evidence of a drug problem among the State's elected officials and those officials typically do not perform high-risk, safety-sensitive tasks. The need revealed is symbolic, not "special." The Georgia statute requiring candidates for elected office to be drug tested is an unconstitutional violation of the Fourth Amendment.

HIV/AIDS and Genetic Testing

Obvious safety concerns have prompted a number of employers in certain fields to test their workers for acquired immune deficiency syndrome (AIDS). A cynic might also suspect that some employers desire such testing of job applicants in order to avoid the high costs of providing health insurance for infected employees. Federal statutes offer some protection to employees or job applicants who have AIDS or have tested positive for the HIV virus. The general rule is that, although the law may not prohibit AIDS testing, it may prohibit the discharge of an employee based on the results of the test. Furthermore, the employer is also prohibited from disclosing the test results to unauthorized parties.

In an attempt to cut costs, some employers in recent years began conducting genetic testing of employees or prospective employees in an effort to identify individuals who might develop significant health problems in the future. By avoiding the employment of such individuals, employers hoped to reduce their costs for employee sick days in addition to saving on health insurance and disability premiums.

In one such case, a California laboratory began screening prospective employees for the gene that causes sickle-cell anemia. The applicants were not informed of the testing. When the prospective employees filed suit for violation of their privacy rights, the federal court held that they had a cause of action, and the case was settled for $2.2 million.[5] In another case, the EEOC (Equal Employment Opportunity Commission) brought an action against a railroad company that had genetically tested its employees. The EEOC contended that the genetic testing violated the Americans with Disabilities Act. In 2002, this case was settled out of court, also for $2.2 million.[6]

The Genetic Information Non-Discrimination Act of 2008 made it unlawful for employers with 15 or more employees, employment agencies, labor organizations, and insurance carriers to discriminate against persons based upon genetic information. The law also prohibits employers and other covered entities from requesting or requiring genetic information of employees or their family members.

2.12 Employer Recommendations

In years past, when an employee left a job, he or she frequently asked the former employer for a letter of recommendation. This assumes, of course, that the former employee left on good terms and could expect a favorable recommendation. In more recent years, however, employers around the country have begun instituting policies against providing reference information about former employees to prospective employers, opting instead to provide only confirmation of employment and basic information regarding start and end dates of employment. The reason for this change in policy is the employers' growing concern about lawsuits resulting from undisclosed facts in letters of recommendation.

Randi W. v. Muroc Joint Unified School District, et al.
929 P.2d 582 (1997)
Supreme Court of California

Facts: Randi W., a thirteen-year-old female student at Livingston Middle School, was sexually molested by Livingston Vice Principal Robert Gadams. The school system hired Gadams on the recommendations of three school districts that had previously employed him. Gadams had been accused of sexual misconduct with female students at each of his former schools and, at two of them, had been forced to resign because of the allegations.

The officials at Gadams's previous employers who wrote the letters of recommendation for Gadams were aware of his history, but, nevertheless, each provided a "detailed recommendation" that glowingly reviewed Gadams's work. One letter concluded, "I wouldn't hesitate to recommend Mr. Gadams for any position." Another stated he "would recommend Gadams for almost any administrative position." The third recommended Gadams "for an assistant principalship or equivalent position without reservation." None of the letters of recommendation made any reference to the prior allegations of Gadams's misconduct.

---

[5] See *Norman-Bloodsaw v. Lawrence Berkeley Laboratory,* 135 F.3d 1260 (9th Cir. 1998).
[6] The case, Equal Employment Opportunity Commission v. Burlington Northern Santa Fe Railway, United States District Court for the Northern District of Iowa, Western Division, Case No. C01-4013MWB, is discussed in *The National Law Journal,* May 13, 2002, p. A22.

Randi W. contended that the letters constituted negligent misrepresentations which the letter writers should have foreseen would cause injury to children at public schools. She argued that the letter writers owed a duty not only to the recipients of the letters (the schools themselves) but also to the children at those public schools who were injured as a result of the misrepresentations which led to Gadams being hired.

Issue: Did the writers of the letters of recommendations breach a duty which they owed to Randi W.?

Holding: The question of duty must be addressed by looking at foreseeability. We conclude that, while the chain of causation leading from the defendants' statements and omissions to the alleged sexual assault on Randi is somewhat attenuated, the assault was reasonably foreseeable. We also consider the availability of alternative courses of action and the balance of public policies. With regard to alternatives, the defendants could have just as easily written "full disclosure" letters which revealed all relevant facts about Gadams's employment or "no comment" letters which simply verified basic employment dates. The ruling of this Court may discourage employers from writing full disclosure letters for fear of tort liability, but it is the belief of this court that this effect is outweighed by the high priority society places on protecting children from sexual abuse.

The defendants' assertions that their letters represented "mere nondisclosures" and not "misleading misrepresentations" are rejected. Once the defendants undertook to provide some information about Gadams's ability and character, they were obligated to disclose all other facts that would materially qualify the facts disclosed. The letters written by the defendants were "misleading half-truths" for which they should be liable.

Review Questions and Exercises

1. Assume John wants to sell his home and enters into a contract with Susan, a realtor. Susan agrees to act as the selling agent and the parties agree to an exclusive listing agreement for a period of 90 days. On day 30 of the contract period, and after Susan has shown the house to a potential buyer, John unexpectedly notifies Susan that he is terminating the contract. Does John have the power to terminate his contract with Susan? Does he have the legal right to do so? Discuss.

2. Assume the following facts: Home DIY, Inc., is a home improvement store carrying a wide variety of building materials. Because most of the customers at Home DIY are men, the company has a policy of hiring only male sales persons to work the sales floor of its stores. Is the company policy a violation of Title VII? Discuss.

3. Assume the following facts: Liberty Films, Inc., is making a movie based on the life of South African leader Nelson Mandela. The movie will be filmed in Georgia and will employ local citizens as extras. Liberty Films advertises the "extra" positions on several Georgia radio stations, but notes in the ads that only African Americans will be hired. Has Title VII been violated? Discuss.

4. Jack is injured at work when scaffolding erected by Jack's co-worker, Mark, collapses. Who are the parties against whom Jack might assert a claim and what is the nature of each claim?

5. Explain disparate impact discrimination.

6. If, simply stated, an employer can fire an employee for a good reason, or for a bad reason, or for no reason at all, but cannot fire an employee for an illegal reason, what constitutes an illegal reason?

7. Assume the following facts: The employees of HeavyLift, Inc., are contemplating the formation of a union. The plant manager calls a meeting of all employees and tells the workers that if they vote against the union, he will authorize each worker voting against the union an extra paid holiday on his or her birthday. Has there been a violation of the labor laws? Explain.

8. Frank, a transplanted New Yorker and lifelong fan of the New York Mets baseball team, works for an Atlanta based company. Frank's boss and company manager is a lifelong Braves fan. On the morning after a particularly bitter loss by the Braves to the Mets, Frank walks into work wearing a Mets ball cap. His boss, in a foul mood over the loss, berates Frank for wearing the cap and fires him. Does Frank have a claim for discrimination under Title VII? Discuss.

Practical Applications

1. Manuel Fragante was born in the Philippines and lived there for the first 60 years of his life when he moved to Hawaii. Fragante applied for a job with the City of Honolulu's Division of Motor Vehicles and Licensing. The job was a clerk's position which required constant oral communication with members of the public, both at the information counter and on the telephone.

Applicants were required to take a written examination that tested word usage, grammar and spelling. Fragante scored the highest of the 731 test takers. Fragante and other candidates were then interviewed by two civil service employees who were familiar with the requirements of the position. Both found that Fragante's accent made it difficult to understand him. Frangante was not hired.

Consider:
(a) Was Fragante the victim of national origin discrimination in violation of Title VII?
(b) What defense(s), if any, could be raised by the City of Honolulu to such a charge?

See - *Fragante v. City and County of Honolulu,* United States Court of Appeals for the Ninth Circuit, 888 F.2d. 591 (1989).

2. Wright & Lopez, Inc., employed a group of workers. As a part of the contract of employment one of the employees would use his automobile for transporting fellow workers to and from work. In exchange, the worker was paid an additional $15 per week and furnished seven (7) gallons of gasoline per day.

On the day in question, the workers did not go straight home after work, but instead detoured to a liquor store where they made purchases. Several of the workers were drinking, including the driver, who turned the car over to a sober employee so that the sober employee could drive home. The new driver was driving the automobile and had returned to the regular route that was traveled each day by the group when the car of workers was involved in a collision. Two of the workers were killed in the collision and the other three injured. The injured workers and the estates of the deceased workers all filed workers' compensation claims.

Consider:
(a) Were the workers acting within the scope of their employment when the collision occurred?

(b) Would it make a difference if the collision had occurred while the workers were on the way to the liquor store instead of returning home after going there?
(c) Does the fact that the employees had returned to the usual route prior to the collision matter?
(d) Would it make a difference if the driver of the car had not been sober?
(e) What difference does it make that the owner of the automobile was not driving?

See – *Adams v. U.S. Fidelity & Guaranty Company*, 125 Ga.App. 232, 186 S.E.2d 784 (1971), Court of Appeals of Georgia.

PART II - Contracts and the Contractual Relationship

Chapter 3 The Contractual Agreement and Consideration

OUTLINE

The purpose of this chapter is to provide an understanding of the basic elements of a valid contract. A contract, in its simplest form, is an agreement.

People enter into agreements with one another every day. However, in the law, there are specific requirements with regard to the terms of the agreement which are necessary in order to create a contract. Thus, the parties may enter in an agreement, but, because that agreement does not meet the requirements of law, the agreement may not be enforceable in a court of law.

3.1 Definition of a Contract and Basic Requirements

We all enter into contracts regularly in the course of our daily lives, although we seldom think of ourselves as doing so. Some contracts are quite formal, for instance entering into a contract to purchase a home, while most are quite informal. We often engage in everyday activities which have a contractual component without ever recognizing the legal aspect of the transaction. For example, by ordering a meal in a restaurant or purchasing a DVD, we are entering into a contract.

Contract law deals with the formation and enforcement of agreements between parties. It focuses on the promises that are exchanged between the parties which create obligations on the part of the parties and on the enforcement of those obligations.

> OCGA § 13-1-1
>
> A contract is an agreement between two or more parties for the doing or not doing of some specified thing.

Contract law is designed to ensure the compliance of the parties with regard to the promises they made or, alternatively, to entitle the innocent party to some form of relief in the event of a breach of the contract by the other party.

A contract is really nothing more than an agreement - a legally enforceable agreement. The Restatement (Second) of Contracts defines a contract as "a promise or set of promises for the breach of which the law gives a remedy, or the performance of which the law in some way recognizes a duty."

> OCGA § 13-3-1
>
> To constitute a valid contract, there must be parties able to contract, a consideration moving to the contract, the assent of the parties to the terms of the contract, and a subject matter upon which the contract can operate.

Simply put, a contract is a legally binding agreement between two or more parties who agree to perform some act or to refrain from performing some act, either now or in the future.

In determining whether a contract has been formed, the element of intent is of the utmost importance. A party's intention to enter into a legally binding agreement, or contract, is judged by the outward, objective facts as interpreted by a *reasonable person* rather than by the party's own secret, subjective intentions.

To be legally enforceable every contract - from the most formal to the most informal - must have the same basic elements:

(1) an offer – the proposal by one party to another to enter into an agreement;
(2) an acceptance - the acceptance of the offer must mirror the offer. In other words, the terms of the offer and the acceptance must be identical;
(3) consideration - the thing of value for which the parties have bargained;
(4) legality of the subject matter - the purpose of the contract must be legal in order for the contract to be enforceable; and
(5) contractual capacity - the parties to the contract must have the legal capacity to enter into a contract.

Additionally, there must be mutual assent to the terms of the contract by the parties. This means that all parties to the contract must have contractual intent. They must actually intend to enter into the contract and must freely and voluntarily agree to all of the essential terms of the contract. If there is no mutual assent to the terms of the agreement there is no valid contract.

Every contract must have all of the essential elements in order to be legally enforceable.

3.2 *The Agreement – Offer and Acceptance*

A contract is the meeting of two minds for one purpose. That is, for a contract to be deemed valid, the parties to the contract must manifest to each other their mutual assent – they must agree - to the same exact same terms at the same time. It is that agreement between the parties which is the basis of the contract.

Offer Defined

Recall from the earlier discussion that at least two parties are required in order to have a contract. The *offeror* is the party who initiates the contract by making the offer or proposal to another party, and the *offeree* is the party to whom the offer or proposal is made. In other words, the *offer* is the proposal by the offeror to the offeree to enter into a contract.

An offer is a promise or commitment to do a certain thing in the future or, in some cases, to refrain from doing some specified thing which one has a legal right to do in the future. In other, simpler language, an offer is:

- A promise to do something for someone else provided that he or she promises to do something for you; or
- A promise to do something if the other person agrees not to do something that he or she has a right to do and might do otherwise; or
- A promise to do something for someone else if the other person simply does what you ask of him.

The offeror, by his offer, determines all of the relevant provisions of the contract. The offer defines the subject matter of the contract, sets the consideration, dictates the time for performance, and specifies any other conditions. Be mindful, however, that while it is the offeror who initiates the contract, it is the offeree who has the power to create the contract. He does so simply by accepting the offer.

Not all proposals constitute legal offers. For example, if you offer to sell your car to a classmate but do not mention a price you have not made a valid offer.

To be a valid contractual offer, the law requires three conditions be met:

- The offeror must manifest a *present contractual intent*. It must appear to a reasonable, objective person that the offeror actually intended to make an offer. The law does not permit a contract to be thrust upon an unsuspecting person. The offeror must be serious. A joking offer to sell a house for a dime will not constitute an offer.

- The offer must be *communicated* to the offeree. Since a contract can only be formed if the offer is accepted, it is necessary that the offer be communicated to the offeree. The exact method of communication is left to the offeror and any means is sufficient so long as the communication is effective in actually conveying the offer to the offeree. Oral communications, in person or by telephone, written communications, and mechanical or electronic communications are all legally sufficient.

- The offer must be *certain and definite* in its terms. The more certain and definite the terms of the proposal, the more likely it is that the proposal constitutes an offer to create a contract. Because the parties are required to demonstrate mutual assent, it would be impossible to have the assent if the parties did not know or were uncertain as to what they were agreeing. The essential elements which must be included are the price, the subject matter of the contract, identification of the parties, and the time of performance for fulfilling the contract.

The concept of *contractual intent* as it relates to the wording of an offer can be clarified through an examination of the types of expressions and statements that are not offers.

Hunt v. McIlroy Bank & Trust
616 S.W.2d 759 (1981)
Arkansas Court of Appeals

Facts: Ben Hunt and several others operated a farm under the name S.B.H. Farms. Hunt went to McIlroy Bank & Trust and requested a loan to build hog houses, buy livestock, and expand the farming operation. The bank agreed to loan S.B.H. Farms $175,000 on a short-term basis. Hunt and the other owners of S.B.H. Farms signed short-term promissory notes.

At the time the short-term loan was procured, oral discussions were held with the bank officer regarding long-term financing of S.B.H.'s farming operations. However, no dollar amount, interest rate, or repayment terms were discussed. When the owners of S.B.H. Farms defaulted on the short-term promissory notes, the bank filed for foreclosure on the farm and other collateral. S.B.H. Farms counterclaimed for $750,000 damages, alleging that the bank breached its oral contract for long-term financing.

Issue: Was there a contract for long-term financing?

Holding: There was no oral contract for long-term financing. Where the officer of the bank and the borrower discussed financing the expansion of the farm operation, but never decided on the total amount of the loan, interest rate, or repayment terms, the essential terms were too ambiguous to allow the court to enforce an oral contract.

An expression of *opinion* is not an offer. For instance, expressing an opinion as to what may or may not happen at some time in the future is not an expression of intent to enter into a binding agreement regarding that future event.

Example 3a:

An air conditioning repairman tells Maggie that if she makes certain repairs to her home's system, she will probably be able to go five more years without having to replace it. Maggie hires the repairman to do the suggested work. When the system fails two years later, Maggie does not have a breach of contract claim against the repairman. He had merely expressed his opinion as to how long the repaired system would last, not entered into a contract to guarantee it.

A statement of *future intent* is not an offer. If you state that you *plan* to sell your car stereo for $200, your friend who hears the statement cannot "accept" the "offer" and tender $200 in exchange for the stereo system. You have merely expressed your intention to take a certain action in the future. A reasonable person would conclude that you were only *considering* the sale of the stereo, not *promising* to sell it.

A request or *invitation to negotiate* is not an offer. It only expresses a willingness to discuss the possibility of entering into a contract. Asking a question such as "Will you sell the family farm?" is not an offer since a reasonable person would not conclude that this statement evidenced an intention to enter into a binding obligation. This is just an inquiry and, perhaps, the start of negotiations.

Some proposals, which may sound like offers, are generally not considered to be offers. These include requests for bids, social invitations, and brochures.

Example 3b:

The State of Georgia invites contractors to submit bids for the construction of a new state office building. This invitation to submit bids is not an offer and a contractor does not bind the government by submitting a bid. The bid that the contractor submits is, however, an offer, and the government can bind the contractor by accepting the bid.

Generally, *advertisements* are generally treated not as offers to contract but merely as invitations to negotiate. This also applies to price lists. However, an advertisement which makes an offer that is very specific to an identified or identifiable person or group and is clearly intended to be binding on the offeror may be treated as an offer. Compare and contrast the following examples and the case which follows with regard to the treatment of advertisements.

Example 3c:

A mattress store places an ad in the local newspaper that reads: "The first customer in the store on Valentine's Day will receive $100 toward the purchase of any mattress set." This advertisement would likely be held to be an offer because it is addressed to a specific person - the first customer on Valentine's Day - and not to the general public. The specific person need not be identified by name, but need only be a readily identifiable individual.

Example 3d:

Hunter Manufacturing Company advertises a used forklift for sale. An advertising flyer is mailed to dozens of warehouses and manufacturing facilities and reads, "Used forklift for sale. Only used 500 hours. Used exclusively indoors, never exposed to outdoor weather. Price: $10,500." When Clarke Warehouse calls and says, "We accept your offer," no contract is formed. A reasonable person would conclude that Hunter was only soliciting offers to buy the machine. If such an ad was held to constitute a legal offer, and ten people accepted the offer, there would be no way for Hunter to perform all ten of the resulting contracts as Hunter only has one forklift for sale.

Lefkowitz v. Great Minneapolis Surplus Store
86 N.W.2d 689 (1957)
Minnesota Court of Appeals

<u>*Facts:*</u> The Great Minneapolis Surplus Store published the following advertisement in a Minneapolis newspaper:

Saturday 9 A.M.
2 Brand New Pastel Mink 3-Skin Scarves, Selling for $89.50
Out they go Saturday, Each $1.00
1 Black Lapin Stole, Beautiful, worth $139.50 .... $1.00
First Come, First Served

Lefkowitz was the first to present himself on Saturday and demanded the Lapin stole for one dollar. The store refused to sell to him because of a "house rule" that the offer was intended for women only. Lefkowitz sued.

Issue: Did the advertisement constitute a valid offer?

Holding: On the facts before us we are concerned with whether the advertisement constituted an offer, and, if so, whether the plaintiff's conduct constituted an acceptance. There are numerous authorities which hold that a particular advertisement in a newspaper or circular relating to the sale of articles may, in some circumstances, be construed as constituting an offer, acceptance of which would complete a contract. The test of whether a binding obligation may originate in advertisements addressed to the general public is whether the offer is clear, definite, and explicit, and leaves nothing open for negotiation. Whether in any individual instance a newspaper advertisement is an offer rather than an invitation to make an offer depends on the legal intention of the parties and the surrounding circumstances. We are of the view on the facts before us that the offer by the defendant of the sale of the Lapin fur was clear, definite, and explicit, and left nothing open for negotiation.

The defendant contends that the offer was modified by a "house rule" to the effect that only women were qualified to receive the bargains advertised. The advertisement contained no such restriction. While an advertiser has the right at any time before acceptance to modify his offer, he does not have the right, after acceptance, to impose new or arbitrary conditions not contained in the published offer.

Compare and contrast the above case with the *PepsiCo, Inc.*, case below with regard to the treatment of advertisements as offers. These two cases illustrate the specificity of terms which are required in order for an advertisement to be deemed an offer.

Leonard v. PepsiCo, Inc.

210 F.3d 88 (2000)

United States Court of Appeals for the Second Circuit

Facts: In the 1990's Pepsi conducted a promotional campaign entitled "Pepsi Stuff" which encouraged consumers to collect "Pepsi Points" from specially marked packages. Consumers could then redeem these points for merchandise featuring the Pepsi logo.

John Leonard saw the Pepsi Stuff commercial which featured a teenage boy leaving for school. When the boy appeared on screen wearing a tee-shirt with a Pepsi logo, the sub-title "T-SHIRT 75 PEPSI POINTS" scrolled across the screen. When the boy appeared wearing a leather jacket, the sub-title "LEATHER JACKET 1450 PEPSI POINTS" scrolled across the screen. As the boy stepped outside and put on a pair of sunglasses, the sub-title "SHADES 175 PEPSI POINTS" appeared. The scene shifted to a school where a Harrier jet landed next to a bike rack, the cockpit opened, and the teenager can be seen, holding a Pepsi. The sub-title "HARRIER FIGHTER 7,000,000 PEPSI POINTS" appeared. An additional subtitle referred customers to the "Pepsi Stuff Catalog" for details.

Inspired by the commercial, the plaintiff set out to obtain a Harrier Jet. He consulted the Pepsi Stuff Catalog which did not contain any description of the Harrier Jet. He did find, however, a notation that in the event a consumer lacked enough Pepsi Points to obtain a desired item, additional Pepsi Points could be purchased for ten cents each. Plaintiff then raised about $700,000 through acquaintances, and submitted a Pepsi Stuff Order Form, on which he had written in the item column "1 Harrier Jet," together with fifteen original Pepsi Points and a check for $700,008.50. Pepsi's fulfillment house rejected John's submission and returned the check, advising that the item requested was not part of the Pepsi Stuff collection.

Issue: Was an offer made by the advertisement which was subsequently accepted by John, forming an enforceable contract?

Holding: The general rule is that an advertisement does not constitute an offer; rather an advertisement is understood to be a mere request to consider, examine and negotiate. Furthermore, an advertisement is not transformed into an enforceable offer merely by a potential offeree's expression of willingness to accept the offer through, among other means, completion of an order form.

The exception to this rule that advertisements do not create any power of acceptance in potential offerees is where the advertisement is "clear, definite, and explicit, and leaves nothing open for negotiation." This present case does not fall into the exception because it specifically reserved the details of the offer to a separate writing, the Catalog.

In sum, there are three reasons why plaintiff's demand could not prevail as a matter of law. First, the commercial was merely an advertisement, not a unilateral offer. Second, the tongue-in-cheek attitude of the commercial would not cause a reasonable person to conclude that a soft drink company would be giving away fighter planes as part of a promotion. Third, there is no writing between the parties sufficient to satisfy the Statute of Frauds.

Essential Terms of the Offer

Recall that an offer is a promise or commitment to do some specified thing or, alternatively, to refrain from doing some specified thing in the future. To constitute an offer to enter into a binding contractual agreement, the offer must have terms that are reasonably definite so that if the offer is accepted and a contract is formed, a court can determine if a breach of the contract has occurred and can provide an appropriate remedy.

While the specific terms required to constitute a valid offer depend on the type of contract, generally, an offer to enter into a contract must include certain terms essential terms. These essential terms are the parties to the agreement, price, the subject matter, and the time of performance.

- *Price* of the contract – The price is the consideration to be paid including the amount of money and method of payment such as cash, check, etc.;

- *Subject matter* of the contract – The subject matter of the contract must be identified in such a manner that both parties, and later the court if necessary, understand exactly the item that has been bargained for. For example, a 1999 Honda Accord, VIN # xxxxxx, as opposed to "car" if the offeror has more than one car;

- *Parties* to the contract - Depending on the circumstances, the offer can be made to one individual (an offer to hire a particular actor for a role in a movie), to any member of a class of persons (an offer to hire a bonded, insured tree surgeon) or to anyone at all (offer to sell a used car). The language identifying the parties will reflect to whom or the class of persons to whom the offer is made; and

- *Time of performance* - How critical the time of performance is depends on the circumstances, but offers are not meant to be indefinite (an offer to a roofer to replace the roof on a house may not need to be performed by 2:00, p.m., tomorrow, but the home owner also doesn't want to wait until March, two years from now).

Cobaugh v. Klick-Lewis, Inc
561 A2d 1248 (1988)
Superior Court of Pennsylvania

Facts: On May 17, 1978, Amos Cobaugh was playing in the East End Open Golf Tournament on the Fairview Gold Course in Lebanon, Pennsylvania. When he arrived at the ninth tee, he found a new Chevrolet Berretta, together with signs which proclaimed "HOLE-IN-ONE Wins this 1978 Chevrolet Beretta GT Courtesy of KLICK-LEWIS Buick Chevy Pontiac."

Cobaugh hit a hole-in-one and attempted to claim his prize. Klick-Lewis, however, refused to deliver the car, explaining that it had offered the car as a prize for a charity golf tournament played two days earlier and that it had neglected to remove the car and the posted signs prior to Cobaugh's hole-in-one.

Issue: Was there a valid offer which was accepted?

Holding: An offer is a manifestation of willingness to enter into a bargain, so made as to justify another person in understanding that his assent to that bargain is invited and will conclude it. Prize-winning contests are offers to award a prize which result in enforceable contracts if the offer is properly accepted by the rendition of the requested performance prior to revocation. The offer of Klick-Lewis specified the performance which was the consideration or price to be given. A person reading the sign would reasonably understand that he or she could accept the offer and win the car by performing the feat of shooting a hole-in-one on the ninth hole. The posted signs did not reveal any intent by Klick-Lewis that the automobile be a prize only for an earlier tournament. Further, there is no evidence that Cobaugh had knowledge greater than that acquired by reading the sign.

It is the manifested intent of the offeror and not his subjective intent which determines the persons having the power to accept the offer. In this case, the offeror's manifested intent, as it appeared from the posted signs, was that a hole-in-one would win the car. The offer was not limited to any prior tournament.

(This defense of mistake as raised by the dealership is considered in Chapter 4).

Acceptance Defined

Acceptance is the second essential element of a valid contract. Acceptance is a voluntary act (either words or conduct) by the offeree that shows assent to the terms of the offer. It is the acceptance of the offer which actually creates the contract. The acceptance by the offeree must be unequivocal and unqualified and must be conveyed to the offeror in the manner requested or authorized by the offeror.

If the offeree makes any change in the terms of the offer, he has made a *counter-offer*. In effect, the offeree has now rejected the original offer and proposed a new offer. He has now terminated his ability to accept the original offer, and he is now the offeror of the new offer.

The acceptance of the offer must be the *mirror image* of the offer. This means that all essential terms must be exactly the same. A variance of any term creates a counter-offer which may then be either accepted or rejected by the original offeror, now the offeree of the counter-offer. Furthermore, an offer may or may not specify the person who can accept the offer. If the offer is made to a group of persons, any one of them may accept.

Roth v. Malson
67 Cal. App.4th 552, 79 Cal. Rptr.2d 226 (1998)
California Court of Appeals

Facts: George Malson owned a 23 acre parcel of real estate in Sutter County, California. In July, 1995, he offered it for sale through Stromer Realty at a $47,600 asking price. On October 25, 1995, John Roth made an offer to purchase the property for $41,600. The offer was made on Stromer Realty's "SALES AGREEMENT AND DEPOSIT RECEIPT FORM," a standard form used by realtors. On November 2, 1995, Malson executed and delivered a counteroffer to Roth to sell the property at $44,000. The counteroffer was made on a standard real estate form titled "COUNTEROFFER." On November 6, 1995, Roth did not sign the portion of this document called "ACCEPTANCE," but instead signed and dated the portion of the document labeled "COUNTER TO COUNTEROFFER" and wrote by hand the words, "Price to be $44,000 as above. Escrow to close on or before December 6, 1995. All cash."

Subsequent analysis showed that Roth's handwritten terms were not different from the terms of Malson's counteroffer. Malson rejected Roth's counteroffer and took the property off the market. Roth sued Malson to specifically perform the alleged contract. Malson defended, arguing that Roth had not accepted his counteroffer and therefore no contract existed.

Issue: Did Roth's signature on Malson's "COUNTEROFFER" constitute acceptance creating a contract?

Holding: No binding contract had been formed because there was no valid unqualified acceptance of Malson's counteroffer. A general rule of contract law is that an acceptance must be absolute and unqualified, and a qualified acceptance is, in reality, a counteroffer - a new proposal. Contract formation is governed by objective manifestations, not subjective intent of any individual involved. The test is what the outward manifestations of intent would lead a reasonable person to believe.

Here, Roth's signing of the clear, easy-to-read form in the area labeled "COUNTER TO COUNTEROFFER" and addition of handwritten terms indicated his intent to make a counteroffer and not his intent to accept the terms offered by Malson. The buyer here, having deliberately or unintentionally, signed the form in the wrong place, and now seeks to enforce the "agreement." Can any reasonable person ignore the possibility that a plaintiff who seeks to enforce such an "agreement" in his favor would not use his actions to avoid the purchase if it were not in his favor? This potential for game-playing must be avoided at all costs. The form was clear. The facts are clear. Plaintiff Roth did not absolutely and clearly accept Malson's counteroffer.

Normally, the offeree must affirmatively accept the terms of the offer. Silence will not suffice. There are two exceptions to this rule - first, if the offer was solicited by the offeree, silence may constitute an acceptance. Secondly, if the contract is implied in fact, silence may constitute an acceptance.

Method of Acceptance

Acceptance of a bilateral contract (promise for a promise) is complete when the offeree gives the promise requested of him. The *mailbox rule* provides that the acceptance is effective – and, thus, the contract created – when the acceptance is properly dispatched by an authorized means of communication. Thus, under this common law rule, a contract may be actually formed before the offeror even knows of the acceptance.

OCGA § 13-3-3

If an offer is made by letter, an acceptance by written reply takes effect from the time it is sent and not from the time it is received; hence, withdrawal of the offer by the offeror after that time is ineffective. If an offer contains alternative propositions, the party receiving the offer may elect between the alternative propositions.

More troubling, since the acceptance is effective when it is dispatched, a contract may be formed even though the acceptance is lost in transmission.

The problem of the lost acceptance can be minimized by expressing an alternative to the mailbox rule in the offer. The offeror can do this very simply by stating in the offer that acceptance is effective only upon actual receipt of the acceptance.

Soldau v. Organon, Inc.
860 F.2d 355 (1988)
Ninth Circuit Court of Appeals

Facts: John Soldau was discharged by his employer, Organon, Inc. He received a letter from Organon offering to pay him double the normal severance pay in exchange for a release by Soldau of all claims against Organon regarding the discharge. Soldau signed and dated the release and deposited it in a mailbox outside of a post office. When he returned home, he found he had received a check from Organon for the increased severance pay. Soldau returned to the post office, persuaded a postal employee to open the mailbox, and retrieved the release. He cashed the severance check and then brought an action against Organon alleging a violation of the Age Discrimination in Employment Act.

Issue: Did Soldau accept the release contract?

Holding: We apply the "mailbox rule," and find that the acceptance was effective when Soldau first deposited the signed release in the mailbox outside the post office. Soldau's later retrieval of the release did not undo his acceptance. His acceptance was effective when it was mailed. The "mailbox rule" is almost universally accepted in the common law world.

A unilateral contract (a promise for an act) may be accepted only by the offeree actually performing the act requested. The offeror is not looking for a promise that the offeree will do something in the future – he is looking for performance of the requested act.

Termination of the Ability to Accept

The offeree may accept the offer, and thereby create a contract, only for so long as the offer remains open. If the offeree has rejected the offer, either by simply declining the offer outright or by making a counter-offer, then the offer is no longer on the table. The offeree may not go back and accept later an offer which he has previously rejected. His ability to accept the offer has been terminated.

Other actions or circumstances may also terminate the ability of an offeree to accept an offer. The offeror may revoke, or withdraw, the offer at any time prior to acceptance except in limited circumstances such as when an option contract exists. Additionally, an offer may also be terminated by operation law after which time, it can no longer be accepted.

There are four events that terminate offers by operation of law:

- Lapse of time – Offers are not kept open indefinitely, although how long will be considered a reasonable amount of time will vary depending on the circumstances. For instance, an offer to sell stock at a given price is very time sensitive, and the offer will not be open long while the offer to sell a house will be open much longer.

- The death or destruction of the subject matter – It is impossible to sell a house that has burned and so the offer is considered terminated. Likewise, if one has offered to purchase a race horse and the horse dies before the offer is accepted, the offer will be considered terminated.

- The death or insanity of the offeror or offeree – Obiously, living persons are necessary to a contract. Issues of capacity are discussed later in the next chapter.

- Supervening illegality – If the offer which was made involved the performance of a legal act when the offer was extended, but that act has now been made illegal, the offer is terminated. For example, if an offer is made to loan money at a certain interest rate, but before the loan is completed, the state legislature changes the law so that the interest rate offered now violates state usury laws, the offer is terminated.

An *option* contract also serves to limit the ability of the offeror to terminate an offer. An option contract creates an irrevocable offer. An offeree can prevent the offeror from revoking his or her offer by paying the offeror compensation to keep the offer open for an agreed-upon period of time. In other words, the offeror agrees to keep the offer open for a specified period of time during which he or she has no power to revoke the offer. The offeror also agrees not to sell the property to anyone else but the offeree during the option period.

Example 3e:

Martin offers to sell a piece of property to Ansley Development Corp. for $750,000. Ansley wants some time to respond so that it can make an informed decision about the purchase. Specifically, Ansley wants to investigate zoning requirements, utility installation, and other matters. Ansley pays Martin $15,000 to keep his offer open for 90 days. During that 90 day period, Martin cannot sell the property to another purchaser. At any time during that period, Ansley may exercise the option and pay Martin the $750,000 purchase price. The offer to sell the property to Ansley for $750,000 is irrevocable during that 90 day period. If Ansley lets the option expire, however, Martin gets to keep the $15,000 and is free to sell the property to someone else.

3.3 Consideration

Consideration is the bargain that supports the entire contractual relationship. Without consideration, no contract can exist. Consideration is the subject matter of the agreement over which the parties have bargained; that is, consideration is the "price" of a promise in a bargained-for exchange. It is the aspect of a contract that induces a party to enter into the agreement in the first place.

Consideration is something of legally sufficient value given in return for a promise or in return for a performance. Consideration must be both given and received by both parties to the contract (with only very limited exceptions which will be discussed in future chapters). In other words, consideratio is based on the idea of *quid pro quo*, or "something for something," being exchanged between the parties.

Consideration can come in many forms, and can be either a benefit received or a detriment incurred. An affirmative benefit is most easy to understand. It is the good or service purchased or the money received in exchange for the sale of an item. However, a detriment may also be consideration. For a detriment to qualify as consideration, the person incurring the detriment must be giving up a legal right at the request of the other party in exchange for something of legal value. That is, the person is agreeing not to do something that he has a legal right to do. A very common example of a detriment as consideration is the release which an injured party executes giving up the right to sue the tortfeasor who caused his injuries. The release is consideration given in exchange for payment of an amount of money in compensation for the injuries.

Example 3f:

Jennifer is injured when Brandon negligently runs a red light and his car collides with Jennifer's car. Jennifer has a legal right to sue Brandon to recover damages as compensation for her injuries. If Jennifer and Brandon (or more likely, Jennifer and Brandon's insurance company) are able to agree on an amount of damges, Jennifer will sign a release giving up her legal right to bring suit, therey incurring a detriment, in exchange for payment of the settlement amount.

OCGA § 13-3-42

(a) To constitute consideration, a performance or a return promise must be bargained for by the parties to a contract.

(b) A performance or return promise is bargained for if it is sought by the promisor in exchange for his promise and is given by the promisee in exchange for that promise.

(c) The performance may consist of:
(1) an act other than a promise;
(2) a forbearance; or
(3) the creation, modification or destruction of a legal relation

Adequacy of Consideration

Consideration is something of legal value which is exchanged to form the basis of the contract. There should be a quid pro quo, or "something for something," exchange in a contract. *Legal sufficiency* of consideration involves the requirement that consideration be something of legally sufficient value in the eyes of the law. However, legal value and monetary value are not the same. In fact, there is a very distinct difference between the two. Legal value involves questions of "any" value recognized by the law – that it, an objectively determinable benefit that is recognized by the courts. *Adequacy* of consideration involves questions of "how much" consideration is given – that is, whether the exchanges are fair and reasonable as a result of equal bargaining for things of approximately equal value.

OCGA § 13-3-46

Mere inadequacy of consideration alone will not void a contract. If the inadequacy is great, it is a strong circumstance to evidence fraud; and, in an action for damages for breach of a contract, the inadequacy of consideration will always enter as an element in estimating the damages.

While at first glance, one might conclude that fairness would or should be an issue when the items exchanged are of unequal value, in general, the law is not concerned with the monetary value of the consideration, unless it is so low as to "shock the conscience." Thus, the general rule is that a court will not question the adequacy of consideration if the consideration is legally sufficient. The law does not protect people from entering into transactions in which they come out on the short end of the deal. This happens regularly – many a purchaser has regretted his decision to pay what he later considered to be too much for a new house or car. The law applies the doctrines of *caveat emptor* (let the buyer beware) and *caveat venditor* (let the seller beware). The law is only concerned with whether there was legal consideration for the transaction, not whether the consideration was adequate.

Hamer v. Sidway
124 N.Y. 538 (1891)
Court of Appeals of New York

<u>*Facts:*</u> William E. Story, Sr., was the uncle of William E. Story, II. In the presence of others, the uncle promised to pay his nephew $5,000 if the nephew would refrain from drinking, using tobacco, swearing, and playing cards or billiards for money (all of which were legal at the time) until the nephew was twenty-one years of age. The nephew agreed and fully performed his part of the contract.

When he reached twenty-one, the nephew wrote his uncle, advising the uncle that he had fulfilled the bargain and was entitled to $5,000. The uncle responded that he was pleased with the nephew and said, "... you shall have five thousand dollars, as I promised you. I had the money in the bank the day you was twenty-one years old that I intend for you, and you shall have the money certain... P.S. You can consider this money on interest." The nephew received his uncle's letter and agreed that the money should remain with his uncle according to the terms and conditions of the letter.

The uncle died twelve years later without having paid any portion of the $5,000 to the nephew. The plaintiff, Hamer, a third party to whom the nephew had transferred his rights in the note, sought to enforce the agreement. The executor of the uncle's estate (the defendant, Sidway) claimed that there had been no valid consideration for the promise and refused to pay.

<u>*Issue*</u>: Had the nephew given valid consideration under the law?

<u>*Holding*</u>: Courts will not ask whether the thing that forms the consideration is of any substantial value to anyone. It is enough that something is promised, done, forborne, or suffered by the party to who the promise is made as consideration for the promise made to him. In general, a waiver of any legal right at the request of another party is sufficient consideration for a promise. Any forbearance of a right will be sufficient consideration for a promise.

In the case before us, the nephew, before the uncle's request of him, occasionally drank liquor and used tobacco, and he had a legal right to do so. That right he abandoned for a period of years upon the strength of the promise of his uncle. We need not speculate on the effort which may have been required of him to give up the use of those stimulants. It is sufficient that he restricted his lawful freedom of action within certain prescribed limits upon the faith of his uncle's agreement. Therefore, the nephew, or in this case, his assignee, is entitled to payment.

However, *nominal consideration*, or consideration that has such an obviously small monetary value relative to the consideration for which it is exchanged, may be considered suspect by the law. Even though the monetary value is not a prime concern of the law, and the courts usually leave the parties to their own devices when it comes to bargaining powers, the law does want to make sure that a bargain actually exists. Thus, the courts will usually inquire into the surrounding circumstances if the bargain, on its face, appears to be dramatically one-sided.

O'Neill v. DeLaney
415 N.E.2d 1260 (1980)
Illinois Court of Appeals

Facts: Mr. and Mrs. DeLaney were married in 1953, and a few years later acquired a painting, allegedly the work of Peter Paul Rubins, titled "Hunting of the Caledonian Boar." In 1966, the DeLaneys moved into an apartment building and became friends with the O'Neills. Mr. DeLaney and Mr. O'Neill became very good friends.

On August 18, 1970, Mr. DeLaney purportedly sold the painting to Mr. O'Neill for $10 and "other good and valuable consideration." A written contract embodying the terms of the agreement was prepared and signed by Mr. DeLaney and Mr. O'Neill. Mrs. DeLaney was not informed of the sale and knew nothing about it. The painting, at that time, was worth at least $100,000. Despite the sale, the painting remained with the DeLaneys.

In 1974, Mrs. DeLaney instituted a divorce action against her husband. At that time, she learned for the first time of the purported sale of the painting to O'Neill which had occurred years earlier. Mrs. DeLaney claimed an interest in the painting as marital property, and instituted an action regarding title to the painting.

Issue: Was the sale valid?

Holding: This Court finds that the consideration paid by Mr. O'Neill for the painting "shocks the conscience of the court." The transfer is, therefore, void. According to the testimony, the "other good and valuable consideration" was the "love and affection" Mr. DeLaney had for Mr. O'Neill, but that is not legal consideration in Illinois. Therefore, the only consideration in the contract is $10, and a purchase price of $10 for such a valuable work of art is so grossly inadequate consideration as to shock the conscience of the court.

Agreements that Lack Consideration

There are some things which, at first glance, appear to be things of legal value but which are not, in fact, consideration. In such an agreement, the courts will find consideration to be lacking. These include the following:

- Past Consideration

A *gift given formerly or in the past* or consideration in a past contract cannot form the basis of a new contract. A promise that is based on a party's past consideration lacks current consideration. Promises made in return for actions or events that have already taken place are unenforceable. In other words, one can bargain for something to take place now or in the future but not for something that has already taken place.

Example 3g:

Two years ago, Mr. Waters, an extremely demanding boss, gave his secretary a diamond watch. Last year, he gave her two weeks paid stay at a luxury spa. Now, he tells the secretary that he wants to use these items as consideration for her current services. Mr. Waters' past generosity with his secretary cannot form the basis of a current contract. He must provide new consideration.

Whitmire v. Watkins
267 S.E.2d 6 (1980)
Georgia Supreme Court

Facts: A.J. Whitmire and R. Lee Whitmire were brothers. From 1923 until 1929, A.J. lived with his brother and his brother's wife, Lillie Mae. During this period, A.J. performed various services for his brother and sister-in-law. In 1925, R. Lee and Lillie Mae purchased some land. A.J. ceased to live with his brother and Lillie Mae in 1929, and he did not do any work for R. Lee or Lillie Mae after 1929, and none was expected of him after that date.

In 1944, in the presence of Lillie Mae, R. Lee told A.J., "When we're gone, this land is yours." On May 26, 1977, after both R. Lee and Lillie Mae had died, A.J. filed a claim with the estate of Lillie Mae seeking specific performance of the 1944 promise.

Issue: Did A.J. provide sufficient consideration for a contract?

Holding: The Court finds that in this case the only consideration for a promise made in 1944 to devise land was past consideration which was not sufficient to convert a promise into a contract.

- Moral Consideration

A sense of *moral obligation* does not form contractual consideration unless the parties can demonstrate that they bargained with one another. A moral obligation has no legal substance. Simply because someone feels morally obligated to another person, it does not follow that the moral obligation is sufficient to form the consideration of a contract. Thus, while an aging uncle may feel a moral obligation to make provision in his will for the niece who has cared for him during his old age, he has no legal obligation to do so. Of course, if the niece can demonstrate that she bargained with her uncle to provide services, they may have a contractual relationship. Also included in this category are agreements to pay the obligations of others or to care for relatives. Likewise, "love and affection" will not support a contract, although it may be of the highest moral order.

- Gifts

A *gift* is not consideration because there is no quid pro quo - nothing flows back to the giver. No contract is formed if it can be shown that the true intent of the parties was to confer a gift. The courts will review all of the surrounding circumstances to ascertain that all of the elements of a contract, including the intent to bargain, exist.

Alden v. Presley
637 S.W.2d 862 (1982)
Supreme Court of Tennessee

Facts: Elvis Presley, a singer of great renown and a man of substantial wealth, became engaged to Ginger Alden. Presley was generous with the Alden family, paying for landscaping the lawn at the Alden home, installing a swimming pool, and making other gifts to family members. When Ginger's mother, Jo Laverne Alden, sought to divorce her husband, Presley promised to pay off the remaining mortgage indebtedness on the Alden home which Mrs. Alden was to receive in the divorce settlement. On August 16, 1977, Presley died suddenly, leaving Mrs. Alden's mortgage unpaid. When the legal representative of Presley's estate refused to pay the $39,587 mortgage, Mrs. Alden brought an action to enforce Presley's promise.

Issue: Was the promise to pay the mortgage an enforceable promise?

Holding: Presley's promise was a gratuitous executory promise that was not supported by consideration, and, as such, it was not enforceable against Presley's estate. Mrs. Alden had not given any consideration in exchange for Presley's promise.

Example 3h:

Mr. and Mrs. Murphy offer to sell their house, valued at $250,000, to Ms. Jenkins for $150,000 and Ms. Jenkins agrees. Whether or not there is a contract would depend on the circumstances. If the Murphys are the well-to-do parents of Ms. Jenkins, who is recently divorced and suffering financial difficulties, it would appear that a gift of $100,000 was intended. If, however, the parties are strangers to each other, but the Murphys need a quick sale in order to relocate to another state for a job promotion, and the employer has agreed to compensate them for any loss, a contract has been created.

- Pre-existing Duty

If one is already obligated to perform a given act, that person's promise to do that which he is already legally bound to do cannot form the basis of a contract. One is not giving anything new if he is under a *pre-existing duty* to perform, either because of a contractual or other obligation; thus, a promise to fulfill that existing obligation is insufficient consideration for a new contract. An agreement to do one's duty is not consideration.

Example 3i:

Fireman Watkins arrives at the White home to find it ablaze. He promises Mr. White that he will put out the fire if Mr. White agrees to pay him $300. There is no valid contract since the fireman is already obligated, by virtue of his employment, to extinguish the fire. Fireman Watkins cannot use the courts to enforce Mr. White's agreement to pay him $300.

However, under certain circumstances, what appears to be a pre-existing duty may be consideration for a new agreement if:

- new or different consideration is given; or
- the purpose is to ratify a voidable obligation; or
- the duty is owed to a third person, not the promise; or
- unforeseen circumstances make the duty more difficult to perform.

Every contract must be individually supported by consideration, and any modification to an existing contract must be supported by additional consideration.

Example 3j:

Katherine owes Lois $200. When the debt comes due, Katherine asks Lois to accept $100 now and $110 next month. Lois agrees to modify the existing contract. This amended agreement would be valid and enforceable because Lois will receive something of value ($10) in addition to what she was already owed.

Chuckrow Construction v. Gough
159 S.E.2d 469 (1968)
Georgia Court of Appeals

Facts: Robert Chuckrow Construction Company was employed as the general contractor to build a Kinney Shoe Store. Chuckrow employed Ralph Gough to perform the carpentry work on the store. Chuckrow's contract with Gough stipulated that Gough was to provide all labor, materials, tools, equipment, scaffolding, and other items necessary to complete the carpentry work.

On May 15, 1965, Gough's employees erected 38 trusses at the job site. The next day, 32 of the trusses fell off the building. The reason for the falling of the trusses was unexplained, and evidence showed that it was not Chuckrow's fault or due to any deficiency in the building plans. Chuckrow told Gough that he would pay him to re-erect the trusses and continue work on the project. When the job was complete, Chuckrow paid Gough the original contract price, but refused to pay him for the additional cost of re-erecting the trusses. Gough sued Chuckrow for this expense.

Issue: Was there any consideration for the second agreement such that Gough can recover for the erection of the trusses the second time?

Holding: The Court finds that Gough had a duty to construct the trusses under his original contract. Since this duty was pre-existing at the time Chuckrow promised additional compensation, Gough could not get paid for the additional cost for re-erecting the trusses. There was no new consideration to support the agreement to pay the builder to rebuild the trusses which he was already obligated to erect.

- Illusory Promises

When one party has subjective, discretionary control over the terms, there is no contract. Even if words of consideration are used, the "consideration" is legally inadequate because an objective determination cannot be made as to what is to be given.

Only if the consideration cannot be objectively determined is a contract *illusory*. If the consideration can be objectively quantified, it is not illusory. For instance, an offer to buy stock for the market price at the close of business on a given date in the future can be determined with certainty on that date. Thus, it is objectively quantifiable.

Example 3k:

Attorney Smith hires Robert as a paralegal and agrees to pay Robert what Attorney Smith thinks he is worth. The promise is illusory because there is no determinable consideration, and therefore, no valid offer or contract exists.

Special Agreements

There are several special agreements that ordinarily would fail as valid contracts for lack of consideration. However, due to public policy concerns, the law recognizes these special agreements as enforceable obligations.

- Charitable Subscriptions

A *charitable subscription* is a pledge made to a charitable organization. It is actually a gift to the charity for which the giver receives no consideration. However as a matter of public policy, the law has mandated that these pledges are enforceable by the charities, especially if reliance on the pledge was reasonable. In reality, however, those who do not fulfill their pledges are rarely taken to court because there is usually not enough money involved to make it worthwhile to the charity.

- Debtor's Promises

A person can be legally relieved from paying his debt by going through a bankruptcy proceeding and being discharged or because the statute of limitations on the claim has expired. If a debtor, in one of these circumstances, voluntarily agrees to pay the debt, this gratuitous promise is enforceable against him or her even though the promise is not supported by consideration. Again, public policy is the reason – it is beneficial to encourage people to repay their debts.

If the debt is barred by the statute of limitations, the promise alone is generally considered sufficient to make the contract enforceable. If, on the other hand, the debt has been deemed unenforceable due to bankruptcy, the Bankruptcy Act imposes certain additional requirements to make the promise enforceable. The act requires the debtor to reaffirm the promise prior to final discharge by the court and to receive the court's consent.

- Guarantees

A *guarantee* is a written promise to answer for the debts of another person. A guarantee is enforceable against the *guarantor*, the person making the guarantee. Under general contract principles, it would appear that the guarantor is not legally bound because he or she has not received any benefit from the promise. However, in order to promote business and industry, public policy makes such agreements enforceable.

Example 3l:

Anthony has just graduated from college and obtained a job. He wants to buy a house, but doesn't have a sufficient credit history to obtain a mortgage. The bank agrees to give him a mortgage if his parents guarantee the loan. When Anthony takes out the mortgage, his parents sign the mortgage contract as Anthony's guarantors. The parents are agreeing to answer for Anthony's mortgage debt if Anthony does not pay.

Note that a guarantor is not the same thing as a *co-signer*. In a guarantee situation, the creditor can look to the guarantor for payment only after the obligor, the primary debtor, has failed to pay. Co-signers are persons who agree to be *equally* bound with the obligor, and the creditor can look to a co-signer for payment instead of the actual obligor because each is equally liable.

- Formal Contracts

A formal contract is a contract that meets special statutory requirements and, as such, is valid even though no consideration is mentioned. States which recognize formal contracts do so by statutory provision.

3.4 *Promissory Estoppel*

Courts of equity were designed around concepts of fairness. A court's equitable powers may provide a remedy to persons when the legal result appears unjust or unfair. If a person reasonably believes that he has entered into a contract, even though no contract actually exists, and, relying on his belief, he has materially changed his position in reliance on the promise made to him, the law will not allow him to suffer. Where a defect in formation would ordinarily render the agreement unenforceable under traditional contract principles, the court can look to the precepts of fairness and rely on the doctrine of *promissory estoppel*. In this way, equity balances the harsh consequences of contract law.

Royal Associates v. Concannon
490 A.2d 357 (1985)
Superior Court of New Jersey, Appellate Division

Facts: The Concannons, leased an apartment from Royal Associates. The initial two year written lease contained a provision prohibiting pets on the premises. During that first two year lease period, the Concannons noticed other tenants had acquired dogs. Mr. Concannon telephoned the owner of the complex and requested permission to purchase a dog. Permission was granted so long as the Concannons "maintained" their pet. All lease renewals contained the "no pets" provision although no action was taken to enforce it, and the Concannons were not required to pay any further deposit or additional rent as consideration for permission to keep the dog. For more than ten years, the defendants had their dog with no complaints from management or from any other tenant. The landlord agreed that the Concannons fully complied with his conditions regarding ownership of the dog.

Almost eleven years after obtaining their pet, the Concannons received a letter addressed to all tenants in the apartment complex indicating that there was a problem with dogs in the complex. The letter went on to say that all tenants would be required to get rid of their dogs. When the Concannons questioned the owner, he indicated that the "no pets" provision was in their current lease and would be enforced. The owner then moved to evict the Concannons when they refused to get rid of their dog.

Issue: Does the doctrine of promissory estoppel apply?

Holding: The defendants spent money to buy and maintain the dog. Further, in reliance on the landlord's initial permission, the defendant's affection for their pet was permitted to grow over an eleven year period during which they gave no cause for the landlord's or another tenant's complaint.

The doctrine of promissory estoppel will apply where: (1) there is a clear and definite promise; (2) made with the expectation that the promisee will rely on it; (3) the promisee does in fact reasonably rely on the promise; and (4) detriment of a substantial nature is incurred in reliance on the promise. Whatever may be the landlord's rights with respect to another tenant, in the status defendants occupy, they have the right to enforce their separate agreement.

Note that there are two specific requirements before a party can receive relief on equitable principles. The party seeking relief must show that (1) there was a promise upon which he *reasonably* relied; and (2) he has *materially* changed his position in *reasonable reliance* upon the promise. Merely beginning performance is not enough. There must be a significant reliance upon the promise to the detriment of the promisee.

Review Questions and Exercises

1. Describe the essential elements of every valid contract.

2. Write an offer to sell a piece of your own property.

3. What terms are generally considered essential to a valid offer? Why?

4. Explain the mirror image rule and its purpose.

5. Give two examples in which the actions of the offeree reject a written offer.

6. Discuss the circumstances that would terminate a person's ability to accept a valid offer. Give an example of each.

7. Explain the mailbox rule.

8. Explain how a detriment incurred can serve as the consideration for a contract. Give an example of a detriment incurred as consideration.

9. In each of the following examples, examine the consideration given:

   a) A budding sculptor, seeking public exposure for her work, promises to lend a large sculpture to First Bank if First Bank will promise to exhibit it in its foyer for one year. What is the consideration for the sculptor's promise? Is it valid consideration? Explain.

   b) At his granddaughter's graduation, Granddad promises to pay her $5,000 because she graduating with honors. What is the consideration for Granddad's promise? Is it valid consideration? Explain.

   c) Several months after Harry was injured in an automobile accident, Harry learned that Nurse Julie had rendered first aid and that Nurse Julie's quick action probably saved his life. Acting upon this information, Harry promised to pay Julie $2,000 for saving his life. What is the consideration for Harry's promise? Is it valid consideration? Explain.

   d) Maria's mother is worried about Maria's smoking, a habit Maria picked up in college. Mom offers Maria $1,000 if Maria quits smoking for a year. What consideration is Maria offering? Is it valid consideration? Explain.

   e) Tom's mother is worried about Tom's marijuana use. Mom offers Tom $1,000 if Tom quits using marijuana for a year. What consideration is Tom offering? Is it valid consideration? Explain.

10. Under what circumstances would a person argue the doctrine of promissory estoppel? What must a party show before receiving relief under this doctrine?

11. Explain the difference between legal sufficiency of consideration and adequacy of consideration.

Practical Applications

1. Davis was a real estate developer who conducted business through a corporation. Davis and McCurry had been personal friends for several years. Davis suggested to McCurry that they form a limited partnership for the purpose of investing in various endeavors, and the partnership was formed between McCurry and Davis' corporation, GGI, with McCurry investing $152,500 and GGI making no capital contribution. The partnership lost considerable monies.

Davis agreed to purchase McCurry's interest in the partnership for $75,000 and signed a note for that amount. McCurry executed a release contemporaneously with the note, which released Davis individually, along with all entities through which he was conducting business, for all claims associated with the partnership.

Davis later refused to pay the note, alleging that the contract was not valid because of a lack of consideration.

Consider:
(a) Did McCurry give any valid consideration for the execution of the note?
(b) Did Davis receive any benefit from the contract?

See – *Davis v. McCurry*, 2000 Tex.App. LEXIS 2918 (2000), Texas Court of Appeals.

2. Logan Ranch is a partnership that owned farmland. The Farm Credit Bank of Omaha (FCB) made a loan to Logan and took back a mortgage on the farmland to secure the loan. When Logan ran into financial difficulties, it deeded the land to FCB in lieu of foreclosure.

Gene Welsh offered to purchase the land from FCB. Pursuant to the federal Agricultural Credit Act, FCB had to offer the previous owner, Logan, the opportunity to purchase the land (re-acquire it) before it could be sold to anyone else. To comply with this requirement, FCB made an offer on March 15, to sell the land to Logan for $988,500 with the purchase price to be paid when the deed was delivered at closing. The offer provided that acceptance of the offer would require that the closing be held on or before April 15. On April 15th, Logan returned FCB's offer. Logan had altered the language of the offer by adding the following terms and conditions:

(a) $150,000 to be paid when deed is delivered;
(b) Conditional upon Logan's ability to obtain a loan in the amount of at least $739,650 from NorWest Trust; and
(c) Loan to be obtained within 60 days.

FCB rejected those terms and made arrangements to sell the land to Welsh. Logan sued for specific performance of its agreement with FCB for the purchase of the land.

Consider:
(a) Was there a valid acceptance by Logan of the offer made by FCB?
(b) Why or why not?

See - *Logan Ranch, Karg Partnership v. Farm Credit Bank of Omaha*, Supreme Court of Nebraska, 472 N.W.2d 704 (1991).

3. James Reindel had extensive media contacts in the sports field. Reindel was contacted by his childhood friend, George Weasel, with an idea for a business to create and distribute audio and video sports information. The two met several times over the next three months, and Reindel arranged a meeting with the head of CNN.com.

Weasel then sent Reindel an email asking Reindel what Reindel wanted to earn and what he thought was fair. This started a series of back and forth emails between the two in an attempt to settle on a compensation package for Reindel with Weasel's company. Eventually, Weasel emailed Reindel offering Reindel one of two compensation packages, Plan A, a fixed salary and stock, or Plan B, stock and a percentage of the net dollars on deals Reindel introduced to the company. Reindel responded, "Let's consider me as you put in Plan B, a deal maker." In his email, Reindel states that he would like a "commitment" from Weasel regarding the CNN relationship already arranged by Reindel and asked Weasel to "write back asap to confirm and commit this part of [their] relationship."

Consider:

(a) Was there a valid employment contract between Reindel and Weasel's company?
(b) Did Reindel's email's constitute an unconditional acceptance of Weasel's offer?

See – *Reindel v. Mobile Content Network Company, LLC, and Weasel*, 652 F.Supp. 2d 1278 (2009), United States District Court for the Northern District of Georgia.

Chapter 4 Legality, Capacity and Contractual Intent

OUTLINE

In addition to an agreement between the parties supported by consideration, a valid contract must also be made for a legal purpose and by parties who have the legal capacity to enter into the contract. Additionally, the parties must have contractual intent, freely entering into the agreement.

4.1 Legality of Subject Matter

While the offer, acceptance, and consideration elements of a contract focus on the actual terms of the agreement itself, the legality of the subject matter and the ability of the parties to enter into an enforceable contract are concerned with the circumstances surrounding the agreement. While there may have been a perfectly valid offer that set forth clearly all terms of the offer, an unequivocal acceptance of the same, and valid consideration supporting the agreement, if the act which is to be performed is an illegal one, this fact alone will render the contract void.

> OCGA § 13-3-5
>
> Impossible, immoral and illegal conditions are void and are binding upon no one.

For a contract to be valid and enforceable the contract must have been formed for a lawful purpose. Thus, a contract that is entered into for an illegal purpose is void from its inception.

The law recognizes two categories of illegality in contract law much as it does in the context of criminal prosecutions (felonies and misdemeanors).

Malum In Se

The more serious of these two categories is the one that is concerned with those crimes that are considered evils to society as a whole. Contracts that violate public policy are called *malum in se* - evil in and of themselves. Malum in se crimes are those acts which are universally recognized as immoral and repugnant including murder, rape, arson, and most other felonies.

An agreement which calls for the performance of such an act is absolutely unenforceable because the purpose is inherently bad. The courts will never find any justification whatsoever for this type of "contract." The courts will not aid either party when the contract is malum in se, regardless of whether the contract has been performed by either party. Very simply, the court will not participate in any manner in an illegal contract and will never assist either party in obtaining compliance with the terms of the contract. Nor will the courts ever award damages in such cases, but will, instead, leave both of the parties where they find themselves.

Maner v. Chatham County
246 Ga. App. 265; 540 S.E.2d 248 (2000)
Court of Appeals of Georgia

Facts: In December 1996, Charles Maner was a Chatham County police officer. Chatham was the subject of an Internal Affairs Division investigation after pointing his service firearm at other police officers. After the investigation, the chief terminated Maner's employment. Maner obtained counsel who investigated a possible appeal of his termination and/or ways to help Maner keep his Police Office Standards and Training (POST) certification. Counsel spoke with the police chief and the human resources director for the county.

After these discussions, Maner's counsel made an offer to the human resources director that, "rather than go forward with the appeal, we would withdraw the appeal, submit our resignation for Mr. Maner, if they would give him the help, whatever medical, psychological help he might need, clean up his disciplinary jacket, and allow him to keep his [POST] certification." Maner's counsel informed the police chief of these negotiations, reached an agreement on those terms with the human resources director, and sent a letter confirming their agreement. However, the records of the disciplinary proceeding were not removed from Maner's file and his resignation was reported to the POST council which suspended Maner's certification for two years.

The POST council was established by the Georgia legislature to regulate various aspects of law enforcement statewide. Local police departments are required by statute to maintain duplicate records on all peace officers or candidates covered by the Act and to forward one copy to the council. Finally, council regulations state that any local department receiving a resignation in lieu of termination "shall inform the Council in writing within ten (10) days of such action and records concerning the disciplinary action shall be made available to an investigator with POST Council."

Issue: Is the agreement between Maner's counsel and the human resources director enforceable?

Holding: A contract to do an immoral or illegal thing is void, and parties cannot circumvent law by settlement agreement. The purported agreement to "remove any and all disciplinary materials from Mr. Maner's employee file . . . to preserve his [POST] certification and show a continuity in his employment record," violates both the letter and the spirit of the applicable law. Failing to report Maner's resignation and "sanitizing" Maner's records would have violated not only the council's regulations but also the record-keeping requirements of Georgia statute and the prohibition of law against knowingly making "misleading, deceptive, untrue, or fraudulent representations in the practice of being a peace officer or in any document connected therewith."

Flood v. Fidelity & Guaranty Life Insurance Co.
394 So.2d 1311 (1981)
Court of Appeals of Louisiana

<u>*Facts*</u>: Ellen and Richard Flood, who were married, lived in Louisiana. Richard worked as a maintenance man and Ellen was employed at an insurance agency. Evidence indicated that Ellen was unhappy with her marriage. Ellen took out a life insurance policy on the life of her husband and named herself as beneficiary. The policy was issued by Fidelity & Guaranty Life Insurance Co.

Richard became unexpectedly ill. He was taken to the hospital where his condition improved. After a visit at the hospital from his wife, Richard died. Ellen was criminally charged with the murder of her husband by poisoning. Evidence showed that six medicine bottles at the couple's home, including Tylenol and paregoric bottles, contained arsenic. The court found that Ellen had fed Richard ice cubes laced with arsenic at the hospital. Ellen was tried and convicted of the murder.

Ellen, as beneficiary of Richard's life insurance policy, requested that Fidelity pay her the benefit. Fidelity refused, and, instead, returned all premiums paid on the policy. Ellen sued.

<u>*Issue*</u>: Was the life insurance policy an illegal contract that is void?

<u>*Holding*</u>: The Court finds that the life insurance policy Ellen Flood took out on the life of her husband is void based on public policy. A beneficiary named in a life insurance policy is not entitled to the proceeds of the insurance if the beneficiary feloniously kills the insured. Our law does not and cannot sanction any scheme which has as its purpose the certain infliction of death for financial gain through receipt of the proceeds of life insurance. To sanction this policy in any way would surely shackle the spirit of the letter and life of our laws.

In such a contract, there can never be any "innocent" party to whom damages may be awarded in equity. For example, Tony Soprano cannot sue to enforce his contract for a mob "hit" to eliminate a competitor if the hit man fails to knock off the mobster's rival. "Murder for hire" contracts are per se invalid and illegal. Of course, this is the extreme example, and one cannot imagine that a party to a contract murder would actually seek enforcement of the contract in the courts. As is obvious, most malum in se "contracts" which are declared void and, therefore, unenforceable, involve lesser crimes.

Malum Prohibitum

Sometimes the subject matter of the contract involves a minor violation of the law or a *malum prohibitum* - a prohibited wrong. The purpose of a contract malum prohibitum is not morally reprehensible, but, rather, is merely prohibited as a violation of the law. Certain acts are not allowed in order to maintain a harmonious and fair society. Although these contracts are also unenforceable – again, the court will not become the paymaster for an illegal contract – in some instances, some quasi-contractual relief may be available to a party who can show that to deny him any relief would unjustly enrich the other party to the agreement.

One example of these types of laws are usury laws which prohibit "loan sharking." These law are designed to prevent lenders from taking unfair advantage of people in need of money. State legislatures set the legal limit on what rate of interest can be charged on contracts for loans. If the contract is found to be usurious, requiring an exorbitant amount of interest well above the limits set by statute, the court can either reduce the rate to the legal limit or void the contract altogether. Malum prohibitum subject matters also include gambling statutes and licensing statutes

Ryno v. Tyra
752 S.W.2d 148 (1988)
Court of Appeals of Texas

Facts: R.D. Ryno, Jr., owned Bavarian Motors, an automobile dealership in Fort Worth, Texas. On March 5, 1981, Lee Tyra discussed purchasing a 1980 BMW M-1 from Ryno for $125,000. When the parties were unable to agree on terms, Ryno suggested a double-or-nothing coin flip. Tyra agreed. When Tyra won the coin flip, Ryno said, "It's yours," and handed Tyra the keys and title to the car. Tyra drove away in the car. Ryno then sued to recover ownership of the car.

Issue: Who owns the car?

Holding: Tyra, the patron at the car dealership who won the coin toss, owns the car. There was sufficient evidence to sustain the jury finding that Ryno intended to transfer to Tyra his ownership interest in the BMW at the time he delivered the documents, keys, and possession of the car to Tyra. A gambling contract is an illegal contract, and, therefore, unenforceable. Thus, the court could not have compelled Ryno to honor his wager with Tyra; however, since the contract was illegal, the court will leave the parties where it finds them - with Tyra in possession of the car.

The Statute of Frauds, discussed in detail in Chapter 5, is a law that requires certain types of contracts to be in writing in order to be enforceable. Even though it is a violation of a statute for one of these types of contracts not be reduced to writing, if one of the parties has actually performed under the oral agreement, he may be entitled to some relief in equity. Thus, while these contracts are not legally enforceable, some remedies may still be available to a party to such an agreement.

Covenants Not to Compete

Generally speaking, public policy and fairness dictate that agreements restricting free trade, market competition, and a person's livelihood are invalid. The Sherman Act, which dates to 1890, provides that "every contract ... in restraint of trade or commerce ... is declared to be illegal." Today, however, only those restraints on trade that *unreasonably restrict* competition are prohibited. *Covenants not to compete* are often found in employment agreements and in contracts for the sale of businesses. These provisions have been determined by the courts to be legally permissible so long as they are reasonable.

In an employment contract, the employer may desire to attempt to control what an employee does after she leaves the employer's company. The employer may have a legitimate interest in protecting the time and expense expended on the employee's training, and/or ensuring that he is not grooming a potential competitor. The employer also has a legitimate interest in protecting his trade secrets, client lists, and the like. Thus, the employer may require the employee to sign an employment agreement which contains an ancillary agreement that attempts to prohibit the former employee from working for a competitor for a certain period of time.

Georgia's non-compete statute, found at O.C.G.A. §13-8-53, follows the most commonly accepted rules. While the courts may consider a covenant not to compete to be an illegal restraint on trade, such provisions will be enforced where the employer or the purchaser of the business can show that the provisions are reasonable with regard to:

- the scope of the restricted activity – the specific profession or type of business;
- the period of time for which activity is restricted – for example, 3 years; and
- the geographic area of the restriction – by miles or region.

Example 4a:

Susan owns a travel agency in a small town. When she decides to sell the business, the purchaser insists on a clause which provides that Susan will not start up or work for another travel agency within a thirty mile radius for a period of two years. This provision is likely to be upheld by the courts as being reasonable. However, if the provision provided that Susan would not work for any business for which any employee did any travel, or the geographic area included the entire state, or the duration was twenty years, the provision would be considered illegal and be unenforceable.

Lee v. Environmental Pest & Termite Control, Inc.
271 Ga. 371, 516 S.E.2d 76 (1999)
Supreme Court of Georgia

Facts: When Lee was hired as a branch manager of Environmental Pest & Termite Control, Inc., he signed an employment agreement. Lee agreed that he would not use confidential information obtained during his employment with Environmental Pest for a period of two years following the termination of his employment, The protected information included proposals, customer and client lists, and information relating to sales and processes.

Lee voluntarily terminated his employment with Environmental Pest and, shortly thereafter, he and a partner formed Future Pest Control, Inc. When Future Pest sought business with Environmental Pest customers, Environmental Pest brought suit against Lee, his partner, and Future Pest seeking injunctive relief and damages resulting from Lee's breach of the employment agreement.

Issue: Does Environment Pest have a binding covenant not to disclose agreement?

Holding: Covenants not to disclose and utilize confidential business information general covenants not to compete because of the similar employer interest in maintaining competitive advantage. Their reasonableness turns on factors of time and the nature of the business interest sought to be protected. In determining whether restraints on disclosure are reasonable, two factors are of importance: (1) whether the employer is attempting to protect confidential information relating to the business such as trade secrets, names of customers, personnel data and so on; and (2) whether the restraint is reasonably necessary to the protection of the information.

Since Lee's agreement with Environmental Pest sought to protect confidential business information and was reasonably related to the protection of that information, it cannot be said that the employment agreement is unreasonable.

The "goodwill" of a business is often an extremely valuable asset. Goodwill is the reputation and loyal clientele that the company has developed and built up over the years. This goodwill is often an important consideration in the negotiations for the sale of a business, with purchasers willing to pay substantial sums for the benefits associated with a well-established business. The purchaser who wants to protect this valuable asset will insist upon a non-compete clause in the sales contract.

Gann v. Morris
122 Ariz. 517, 596 P.2d 43 (1979)
Court of Appeals of Arizona

Facts: Morris owned a silk screening and lettering shop business which he sold to Mr. and Mrs. Gann. The sales agreement provided, in part, that Morris would not enter into a silk screening or letter shop business within a 100 mile geographic radius of the shop for a period of ten years after the sale. The agreement also provided that Morris would not compete with the Ganns in any manner whatsoever and, further, that he would refer all silk screening and lettering shop business to the Ganns.

Morris later entered into a competing business and argued that the 100 mile radius was unreasonably broad. The trial court found as a fact that Morris had "breached the contract in that he competed with the buyers and failed to refer all business under the terms of the contract."

Issue: Is the contract, including the covenant not to compete, unenforceable as a restraint on trade which violates public policy?

Holding: Covenants not to compete, although amounting to partial restraints of trade, will be enforced where they are ancillary to contracts for employment or the sale of a business and are reasonably limited as to time and territory. What is reasonable depends on the whole subject matter of the contract, the kind and character of the business, its location, the purpose to be accomplished by the restriction, and all the circumstances which show the intention of the parties. Where limited as to time and space, the covenant is ordinarily valid unless it is so broad as to require the seller to refrain from all business whatsoever.

The rationale for enforcing covenants not to compete is particularly valid in the case of a small business, operated by an individual who has developed a clientele and a reputation in a specialized business area. The sale of such a business necessarily includes the sale of goodwill and the purchaser has the right to assure himself, as best he can, of the transfer of good will. In this case, where one of the customers has offices extending beyond the 100 mile radius, it cannot be said that the scope of the covenant was unreasonable as broader than necessary to protect the interest of the buyers of a small business.

4.2 *Contractual Capacity*

The law has determined that certain parties are unable to make informed decisions regarding their potential contractual obligations. Such persons are said to be lacking *contractual capacity* and cannot enter into a binding contractual relationship.

Recall that, in order for a valid contract to exist, both parties to the agreement must have the legal ability to enter into a binding contract. This concept is based upon the law's concern that one party may take advantage of a person who is unable to protect his or her interests. The widely accepted rule is that minors, mentally handicapped persons, and insane persons lack the legal capacity to understand the nature and effect of an agreement. Thus, contracts entered into by these persons will not be enforced against them.

Age

As a general policy, contract law does not want to hold impetuous teenagers to potentially overwhelming contractual promises. Thus, a minor (in Georgia, anyone under the age of 18 years) lacks contractual capacity.

A contract entered into by a person under the age of majority is considered *voidable* at the election of the minor. The contract is not *per se* void. In other words, the contract is not invalid from its inception. Rather, a minor has the option, upon attaining the age of majority, of either ratifying the contract or avoiding it. If the minor chooses to ratify the contract, he validates it, acknowledging that the contract is valid and enforceable. It is as if the contract is newly entered into when the newly adult party confirms its validity. Ratification is not a formal process. The minor, upon reaching the age of majority, can simply continue to abide by the terms of the contract. This continued performance indicates that the former minor intends to honor the contract.

OCGA § 13-3-20(a)

Generally the contract of a minor is voidable. If in a contractual transaction a minor receives property or other valuable consideration and, after arrival at the age of 18, retains possession of such property or continues to enjoy the benefit of such other valuable consideration, the minor shall have thereby ratified or affirmed the contract and it shall be binding upon him or her. Such contractual transaction shall also be binding upon any minor who becomes emancipated by operation of law or pursuant to Article 6 of Chapter 11 of Title 15.

Bobby Floars Toyota, Inc. v. Smith
269 S.E.2d 320 (1980)
Court of Appeals of North Carolina

Facts: Charles Edward Smith, a minor who was 17 years old, purchased an automobile from Bobby Floars Toyota on August 15, 1973. Smith executed a security agreement to finance part of the balance due on the purchase price, agreeing to pay off the balance in 30 monthly installments. Just over a month later, on September 25, 1973, Smith turned 18, which was the age of majority. Smith made ten monthly payments after turning 18. He then decided to disaffirm the contract and stopped making the payments. Smith claims he may disaffirm the contract entered into when he was a minor. Bobby Floars Toyota claims that Smith had ratified the contract after attaining the age of majority.

Issue: Had Smith ratified the contract after attaining the age of majority?

Holding: The Court finds that Smith's acceptance of benefits and continued payment after he turned 18 constituted ratification of the contract. Smith cannot, at this late date, be allowed to disaffirm the contract.

With every general rule, there are exceptions. A minor cannot avoid responsibility for contracts for *necessities* - that is, things deemed essential to support life. If a minor enters into a contract for the acquisition of food, shelter, clothing, medical care, and the like, the minor is not permitted to disaffirm the contract. Public policy prefers that all citizens obtain the necessities of living, and the law protects the suppliers of these necessities by disallowing avoidance for them. This exception to the general rule applies only to items which are truly necessary and does not include things like automobiles or computers, even though many consider these essential.

Gastonia Personnel Corporation v. Rogers
172 S.E.2d 19 (1970)
Supreme Court of North Carolina

Facts: In May, 1969, Bobby Rogers was 19 years old. The age of majority at that time was 21. Rogers was an emancipated minor who had quit college and sought to go to work to support his wife and expected baby. Rogers had sought employment with at least two companies but was unable to find a job.

Rogers then contracted with Gastonia Personnel Corporation, an employment agency, agreeing to pay Gastonia a $295 fee if Gastonia found him employment with a starting salary above an agreed upon floor. Under the contract, Rogers was free to continue his own quest for employment. He was to become obligated to Gastonia only if he accepted employment from an employer to whom he was referred by Gastonia. Shortly thereafter, Rogers was employed by a company referred to him by Gastonia. The job paid above the specified minimum starting salary. However, Rogers refused to pay the contract fee of $295 and sought to disaffirm the contract with Gastonia.

Issue: Can the minor disaffirm his contract with the employment agency?

Holding: The purpose of the provision in the law which allows minors to disaffirm their contracts is to protect them from improvident or unfair contracts. However, the law should not deny minors the opportunity and right to obligate themselves for articles of property or services that are reasonably necessary to provide for themselves and their families. Thus, the minor should be held liable for the reasonable value of articles of property or services received pursuant to such contracts. Rogers employment is a necessity for him and his family, and he is bound by his contract.

When a minor disaffirms a contract, the minor will be restored to the position he or she was in before contracting. Prior to the time the minor disaffirms the contract and seeks restitution for the benefit he or she has conferred on the other contracting party, the minor may have used what the other contracting party provided to him in exchange for his promise and it may have depreciated. Should the minor compensate the other contracting party for the value of the use and/or the depreciation of what the minor received prior to the time of disaffirmance? Courts are divided on this issue. Some reason that the minor's right to disaffirm would no longer be absolute if the minor was required to compensate the other party for use and depreciation. Other courts reason that the minority doctrine should protect minors but not go so far as to give them a windfall.

Mental Capacity

A mentally deficient person also lacks contractual capacity. Mental incapacity may arise from of a variety of causes including mental illness, brain damage, mental retardation, senility, and the like.

The law draws a distinction between persons who have been declared legally insane by a court of competent jurisdiction and those who suffer from some mental impairment but have not been adjudged insane by a court.

A contract is *void* if a party to the contract has been adjudged by a court to be mentally incompetent or mentally impaired. If a court has previously determined that a person is mentally incompetent and has appointed a guardian to represent that individual, only the guardian can enter into binding legal obligations on the incompetent person's behalf.

If, however, no formal ruling on the issue of insanity has been made by a court, any contract entered into by a person who suffers from a mental impairment that makes him legally insane is *voidable* by the insane person as opposed to absolutely void.

The distinction between a void contract, which is void at its inception, and a voidable contract, which may be avoided by one of the parties, is discussed further in the next chapter.

OCGA § 13-3-24

(a) The contract of an insane, a mentally ill, a mentally retarded, or a mentally incompetent person who has never been adjudicated to be insane, mentally ill, mentally retarded, or mentally incompetent to the extent that he is incapable of managing his estate as prescribed by this Code is not absolutely void but only voidable, except that a contract made by such person during a lucid interval is valid without ratification.

(b) After the fact that a person is insane, mentally ill, mentally retarded, or mentally incompetent to the extent that he is incapable of managing his estate has been established by a court of competent jurisdiction in this state and the affairs of such person are vested in a guardian, the power of such person to contract, even though restored to sanity, shall be entirely gone; any contracts made by such person shall be absolutely void until the guardianship is dissolved. One may recover for necessaries furnished an insane person, a mentally ill person, a mentally retarded person, or a mentally incompetent person upon the same proof as if furnished to minors.

Alcohol and Drugs

Contracts that are entered into by persons who are intoxicated, either by drugs or alcohol, at the time of the contract are voidable by the intoxicated party. To affect a party's contractual capacity requires a very significant level of impairment. Many valid and enforceable contractual agreements have been finalized over a cocktail.

Generally, a party may avoid his contractual obligations on the basis of his intoxication only if, at the time he entered into the contract, the intoxicated person was so impaired that he was incapable of understanding or comprehending the nature of the transaction. In such a situation, the impaired person would have option of avoiding his contractual obligation.

OCGA § 13-3-25

A contract made by an intoxicated person is not void, though the intoxication is brought about by the other party, but is merely voidable at the election of the intoxicated person and may be ratified by him expressly or by conduct inconsistent with its rescission.

Whether an individual is so intoxicated as to be able to disaffirm a contract varies from case to case and must be determined based upon the particular facts and circumstances of the specific situation.

As one might imagine, it is not often that a contract is deemed voidable because of the voluntary intoxication of one of the parties.

4.3 Contractual Intent Defined

An examination of contractual intent looks at whether the parties actually intended to enter into a binding contract. Intent relates back to the concept of mutual assent. If the parties did not freely and voluntarily agree, there can be no valid contract. There must be a meeting of the minds before an agreement can be deemed to be a legally enforceable contract. Every binding contract requires genuineness of assent to the contract on the part of both parties. That is, the parties to the contract must actually intend to enter into a contract for the same bargain at the same time and the parties must have the same understanding of the contractual terms and of the consideration for the contract.

Of course, the only way to determine the mental state of a party, and therefore, whether that party had contractual intent, is to examine the words and actions of that party. This determination depends on an analysis of the subjective intent of the parties. Since they can't read minds, the only way courts can determine the subjective intent of a party is by examining the circumstances surrounding the parties' agreement together with the parties' words and actions. If it can be demonstrated that a contract was not intended by one, or both, of the parties, no contract can exist because there was no mutual assent or agreement. In other words, if it is determined that there are differing interpretations of the terms of the agreement or improper reasons for entering into the bargain, then the courts may allow the innocent party to avoid the contract.

Fraud and Misrepresentation

Genuineness of assent can be questioned in several different situations. The first of these involves allegations of *fraud.* If one party tricks another into entering into the agreement, there is no contract because the innocent party cannot be said to have voluntarily consented to the terms of the agreement. All five elements of fraud must be present.

Fraud is defined as:

- the misrepresentation
- of a material fact
- made with the intent to deceive
- relied upon by the innocent party
- which results injury to the innocent party or acts to his detriment.

> OCGA § 13-5-5
>
> Fraud renders contracts voidable at the election of the injured party.

If fraud is present, the innocent party has option of rescinding, or avoiding, the contract because of his lack of contractual intent. He may, alternatively, enforce the contract and seek damages for any injuries resulting from the fraud.

Example 4b:

> Mike offers to sell his used car to Melissa for $5,000, assuring Melissa that the car has been well cared for and has only 55,000 original miles on it. Mike is dishonest and paid his friend, a mechanic, to roll back the odometer from 138,000 to 55,000. Because the mileage on a used car is a material fact and Mike lied to Melissa to induce her buy the car, he has committed a fraud. Melissa has been injured since a car with 138,000 miles on it is not worth nearly as much as the same car with only 55,000 miles.

A fraudulent misrepresentation may involve either *fraud in the factum* (fraud in the essence) or *fraud in the inducement.*

Fraud in the inducement involves a misrepresentation that entices a party to accept an offer. This form of fraud is much more common. Whenever a party fraudulently induces another to enter into a transaction, the deceived party may disaffirm the contract and, in those cases where the defrauded party has conferred a benefit on the defrauding party, claim restitution. This power to disaffirm the contract protects innocent parties from deliberately dishonest statements. Both of the following cases involve fraud in the inducement.

Campbell v. McClure
357 Cal.App,3d 806 (1986)
California Court of Appeals

Facts: Robert McClure owned a vehicle salvage and rebuilding business. He listed the business for sale and had a brochure printed which described the business and stated that during 1981 the business grossed $581,117 and had a net profit of $142,727.

Fred Campbell saw the brochure and inquired about buying the business. Campbell hired a CPA to review the business records and tax returns, but the CPA could not reconcile these with the income claimed for the business in the brochure. When Campbell asked McClure about the discrepancy, McClure stated that the business records did accurately reflect the cash flow and profits of the business. He also acknowledged that the tax returns did not accurately reflect the profits of the business because it was such a high-cash operation and much of the cash was (illegally) not being reported to the IRS.

McClure signed a warranty in which he gave assurances that the true income of the business was as he had represented in the brochure and not as reflected on the tax returns. Campbell bought the business based on these representations. However, the business, although operated in substantially the same manner as when owned by McClure, failed to yield a net income similar to that warranted by McClure. Expert evidence showed that McClure's representations were substantially overstated.

Issue: May Campbell rescind the contract on the basis of fraud?

Holding: The elements of fraud in the inducement of the contract have been established in that there was substantial evidence both of the intentional misrepresentation on the part of the defendant seller and of the plaintiff buyer's justifiable reliance thereon. Therefore, the buyer is permitted to rescind the contract and recover the purchase price.

Wilson v. Western Nat'l Life Insurance Co.
235 Cal.App.3d 981, 1 Cal.Rptr.2d 157 (1991)
California Court of Appeals

Facts: Daniel and Doris Wilson were husband and wife. On August 13, 1985, Daniel became unconscious from a narcotics overdose and was rushed to the hospital. Doris accompanied him. Daniel responded to medication and recovered from his overdose. The emergency room physician noted that Daniel had probably suffered from a heroin overdose. The physician further noted that Daniel had multiple puncture sites on his arms.

On October 8, 1985, an agent for Western National Life Insurance Company met with the Wilsons in their home for the purpose of taking their application for life insurance. The agent asked questions and recorded the Wilsons' responses on a written application form. Daniel answered the following questions:

In the past 10 years, have you been treated or joined an organization for alcoholism or drug addiction? Yes ____ No _X_

In the past 5 years, have you consulted or been treated or examined by any physician or practitioner? Yes ____ No _X_

Both of the Wilsons signed the application form and paid the agent the first month's premium. The life insurance policy took effect immediately. Daniel Wilson died from a heroin overdose two days later. Western rescinded the policy and rejected Doris Wilson's claim to recover the policy's $50,000 death benefit, alleging the failure to disclose the August 13th incident. Doris sued to recover the benefits.

Issue: Was there a concealment of a material fact that justified Western's rescission of the life insurance policy?

Holding: There was a concealment by the Wilsons that warranted rescission of the policy. A material misrepresentation or concealment entitles the innocent party to rescind the contract. Here, evidence shows that the Wilsons made such a misrepresentation by concealment; that it was material; and that Western relied on it and was injured. The evidence showed that Western would not have issued the policy to Daniel Wilson if it had been informed of his prior drug overdose.

Fraud in the factum involves the very character of the proposed contract. If the deceived party neither knows nor has reason to know of the character of the proposed contract, the effect of the misrepresentation is that the parties never entered into a contract. Fraud in the factum is extremely rare and occurs when a legal instrument as actually executed differs from the one intended for execution by the parties. For instance, a blind person who signs a mortgage after being misleadingly told he's signing a letter is a victim of fraud in the factum.

Example 4c:

Sally visited Import Motors, Inc., a used car lot. Sally saw a sign indicating that Import Motors was giving a free trip to the Bahamas to the winner of a drawing. A salesperson encouraged Sally to sign her name to the entry form without reading the very fine print. Had she read it, she would have discovered she was purchasing a used BMW. Since Sally did not know that what she had signed was the acceptance of an Import Motors's offer, the effect of the fraud is that she never entered into a contract.

In order to rescind a contract due to fraud, the plaintiff must prove the defendant had the intent to deceive. In some cases where there is no intent to deceive, the innocent party may still be entitled to relief due to an innocent *misrepresentation*. Misrepresentation is closely related to fraud, but here the deception is innocent. Sometimes one may make a statement he believes to be true but which actually misrepresents the facts. If the misrepresentation is one of a material fact, the innocent party is entitled to the same relief - he can avoid the contract or elect to fulfill it.

Example 4d:

Ellen is selling her farm to Haley and tells Haley that the farm consists of 300 acres. The farm is actually only 270 acres. Ellen does not intend to give Haley false information but is mistaken. Haley is induced by the statement to enter into a contract to buy the farm. Even though the mistake was an innocent one, Haley can avoid the contract because the misrepresentation is material.

Duress

Intent can also be called into question if there are allegations of *duress*. Duress is some form of force or coercion exercised by one party over the other to induce that party to enter into a contract. Assent to the terms of a contract is not genuine if one of the parties is forced into the agreement.

Duress occurs when one party threatens to do some wrongful or illegal act unless the other party enters into a contract. Duress does not mean stress alone. Rather, it means that a party to the agreement really had no choice at all and was forced into the contract. If one party to a contract has been forced into making the contract, the assent is not voluntary, and the contract is not enforceable against the innocent party even though the contract may be valid in its form.

OCGA §13-5-6

Since the free assent of the parties is essential to a valid contract, duress, either by imprisonment, threats, or other acts, by which the free will of the party is restrained and his consent induced, renders the contract voidable at the election of the injured party. Legal imprisonment, if not used for illegal purposes, does not constitute duress.

Example 4e:

After several weeks of negotiating a settlement in their divorce action, Bob threatens to kill Betty unless Betty signs the latest version of the agreement. Since Bob has been violent towards Betty in the past, she believes she is in danger. She signs the agreement to protect herself from violence. Betty's consent has been obtained through duress.

Duress can take the form of physical duress, mental duress, or economic duress. However, in all cases, there must be an immediate force, such as the threat of physical harm. It is duress to threaten a party with some physical harm unless he executes a contract. Likewise, it is duress to threaten to bring (or not drop) a criminal lawsuit. Generally, for duress to occur the threatened act must be wrongful or illegal. Thus, a threat to bring a civil lawsuit does not constitute duress because the law recognizes that it is not duress to threaten to do what there is a legal right to do. Blackmail and extortion to induce consent to a contract also constitute duress.

In recent years, some courts have recognized economic duress as a legitimate claim. Economic need alone is not sufficient to constitute duress, and thus, it is not duress when one party demands a high price for something the other party needs. However, if the party exacting the high price also creates the need, economic duress may be found. Compare and contrast the two cases presented below. Consider whether the different results reflect the differences in California law and Georgia law or, perhaps, are based more on the parties' actions and positions.

R & W v. Ashton Development, Inc.
157 Cal.App.3d. 81154 (1984)
California Court of Appeals

Facts: Ashton hired Bob Britton, a general contractor, to build a development. Britton signed a contract with a subcontractor, R&W, to provide grading and excavation work for the project. The contract stated that "any rock encountered would be considered an extra at current rates" and expressly excluded blasting work. The contract price was $112,990.

When rock was encountered, a meeting was held among the parties, and Britton instructed R&W to go ahead with the rock work. Britton agreed to pay for the additional work. R&W proceeded with the excavation and rock removal which included some blasting work. During the course of the work, R&W was paid $109,000 in interim payments. After completing all of the required work, R&W submitted a final bill to Britton for $72,286 which was approximately $68,000 above the original contract price. Ashton and Britton refused to pay the final bill. R&W told Britton the company was a new one and that it would "go broke" if payment was not received. On July 10, 1981, Britton presented

R&W with an agreement whereby Britton would pay $25,000 upon the signing of the agreement and another $25,000 on August 10, 1981. When R&W complained of the financial bind it was in, Britton stated, "I have a check for you, and you just take it or leave it, this is all you get. If you don't take this check, you have got to sue me." After claiming it was "blackmail," R&W accepted the check. Britton did not pay the other $25,000 until August 20th after requiring R&W to sign a release of claims form.

In December, 1981, R&W sued Ashton and Britton for payment of the balance due. The defendants contended nothing further was owed to R&W and argued that the settlement agreement and release signed by R&W prevented it from collecting.

Issue: Was there economic duress which induced R&W to sign the July agreement?

Holding: The Court finds that Ashton and Britton had acted in bad faith when they refused to pay R&W's final billing and offered instead to pay a compromise amount of $50,000. At the time of their bad faith breach and settlement offer, Ashton and Britton knew R&W was a new company overextended to creditors and subcontractors and faced with imminent bankruptcy if not paid its final billing. Under these circumstances, the July 10th agreement and August 20th release were products of economic duress and are, therefore, unenforceable.

Abdullah v. Klosinski

898 F. Supp. 2d 148 (2012)

United States District Court for the Southern District of Georgia

Facts: Abdullah owned a sporting equipment store, incorporated as Sportsman's Link, Inc. When Sportsman's Link began losing money and was sued by its major supplier, Abdullah, acting on behalf of Sportsman's Link, employed Klosinski to file a Chapter 11 bankruptcy proceeding. The suit filed by the supplier was automatically stayed by the bankruptcy filing.

The supplier filed an application for the appointment of a trustee to take over the property of the Sportsman's Link, or, in the alternative, for a lifting of the bankruptcy stay. Appointment of a trustee would have ousted Abdullah from control of Sportsman's Link's operations and could have resulted in liquidation of the corporation's assets. Sportsman's Link owed the supplier more than $460,000. In order to induce the supplier to withdraw the Trustee Motion, Abdullah agreed to execute a personal guaranty of the Sportsman's Link's debt in favor of the supplier. One provision of the guaranty was a waiver of certain defenses should the supplier bring suit on the guaranty agreement. After the United States Trustee determined that Abdullah was stripping Sportsman's Link of the corporation's assets, including taking $440,000 in salary in one year, the U.S. Trustee converted Sportsman's Link Chapter 11 action to a Chapter 7 action. The supplier then sued Abdullah on his personal guaranty agreement, and a substantial judgment was entered in favor of the supplier. Abdullah, in turn, sued Klosinski for legal malpractice.

In a claim for legal malpractice, the plaintiff's proof of damages effectively requires proof that he would have prevailed in the original litigation but for the act of the attorney charged with malpractice. Abdullah contends he could have prevailed in the case filed by the supplier if he had been able to assert a defense of duress.

Issue: Did Abdullah enter into the guaranty agreement under duress, thereby making it void?

Holding: Since the free assent of the parties is essential to a valid contract, duress, either by imprisonment, threats, or other acts, by which the free will of the party is restrained and his consent induced, renders the contract voidable at the election of the injured party. The defense of duress sets a very high hurdle for those seeking its refuge - it requires no less than a showing of conduct "amounting to coercion, or tending to coerce the will of another, and actually inducing him to do an act contrary to his free will."

The duress in this case does not concern any physical harm or threats, consisting instead of what is commonly referred to as "economic duress." Business compulsion or economic duress involves the taking of undue or unjust advantage of a person's economic necessity or distress to coerce him into making a contract. Though recognized as a valid defense, Georgia courts are reluctant to void contracts, and there is no Georgia decision voiding a contract on the theory of economic duress. Hard bargaining by itself cannot support a duress defense. One may not void a contract on the grounds of duress merely because he entered into it with reluctance, the contract was very disadvantageous to him, the bargaining power of the parties was unequal, or there was some unfairness in the negotiations preceding the agreement. Counsel for the supplier may have been shrewd in filing the Trustee Motion and negotiating the terms of the Guaranty, but there is no foul in cunning. In any event, when the signer of an agreement is sophisticated in business matters and has access to and in fact obtains advice of counsel, the defense of duress is not available to void the contract. Because the facts presented fall squarely within parameters of this caveat, the purported defense of duress fails.

To be a valid claim of duress the duressed party must prove that he or she had no choice but to give in to the demands of the other party. Economic duress usually occurs when one party to a contract refuses to perform his or her contractual duties unless the other party pays an increased price or enters into a second contract.

A contract of adhesion falls under the category of duress. Here, one party has an unfair bargaining position, so superior that the other party's assent to the terms of the contract is suspect. An adhesion contract is written *exclusively* by one party (the dominant party, usually the seller or creditor) and presented to the other party (the adhering party, usually the buyer or borrower) on a take-it-or-leave-it basis. The adhering party has no opportunity to negotiate the terms of the contract.

Undue Influence

Closely related to duress is *undue influence*. The result is almost identical: a party enters into an agreement on terms that are not necessarily what would have been chosen if not for some sort of impermissible persuasion from the other party.

Undue influence occurs in close, *fiduciary relationships,* sometimes referred to as *confidential relationships*. Undue influence arises from these special kinds of relationships in which one party can greatly influence another party, thus overcoming that party's free will. One party dominates the other, unfairly influencing him or her. The greater degree of psychological control the dominating party exercises over the second party, the more likely it is that a court will find that the contract was induced by undue influence.

Minors and elderly people are often under the influence of guardians, people who are legally responsible for them. If a guardian induces a young person or elderly ward to enter into a contract that benefits the guardian, undue influence may have been exerted. Undue influence can arise from a number of confidential or fiduciary relationships: attorney-client, physician-patient, guardian-ward, parent-child, husband-wife, or trustee-beneficiary. The essential feature of undue influence is that the party being taken advantage of does not, in reality, exercise free will in entering into a contract. Instead, he simply acquiesces to the wishes of the other party.

Schaneman v. Schaneman
291 N.W.2d 412 (1980)
Supreme Court of Nebraska

Facts: Conrad Schaneman had eight children. He owned an 80 acre farm in Nebraska. Conrad was born in Russia and could not read or write English. Prior to 1974, Conrad had frequent contact with all of his children and all of them helped with his needs. In 1974, the oldest son, Lawrence, advised the other children that he would henceforth manage his father's business affairs.

After much urging by Lawrence, Conrad deeded the farm to Lawrence in exchange for $23,500. Evidence showed that at the time of the sale, the reasonable fair market value of the farm was between $145,000 and $160,000. At the time of the conveyance, Conrad was more than 80 years old and had suffered a serious deterioration in health, having heart problems, diabetes, high and uncontrollable blood sugar levels, and difficulty breathing. He could not walk more than 15 feet and had to have a jack hoist to lift him in and out of the bathtub. He was for all purposes an invalid, relying on Lawrence for most of his personal needs, transportation, banking, and other business matters. After Conrad's death, his estate brought an action to set aside the deed conveying the farm to Lawrence.

Issue: Was the execution of the deed the result of undue influence and fraud?

Holding: There existed a confidential relationship between Conrad and Lawrence. During the period when the deed was executed, Conrad had relied on Lawrence for advice in his business affairs. Conrad's mental acuity was impaired at times and he sometimes suffered from disorientation and lapse of memory. Conrad was subject to the influence of Lawrence. Lawrence had the opportunity to exercise undue influence, and the conveyance appears to be the effect of such influence.

Mistake

Yet another situation in which the parties' intent can be brought into question occurs when one party, or sometimes both, makes a mistake when entering into a contract. A mistake, of course, does not involve any evil intent or dishonesty. Since we all make mistakes, it is not surprising that mistakes are sometimes made by the parties when contracts are formed. A mistake concerning an incidental or insignificant detail will not affect the enforceability of an agreement. However, a *material* mistake, or mistake about a significant term, generally goes to the heart of the agreement. Thus, a mistake as to a material term of the agreement may result in the parties' agreement being unenforceable.

> OCGA § 13-5-4
>
> If the consideration upon which a contract is based was given as a result of a mutual mistake of fact or law, the contract cannot be enforced.

If a mistake concerns the future market value or quality of the subject of the contract, the mistake is one of value, and the other party can normally enforce the contract. When parties form a contract, their agreement establishes the value of the subject of their transaction. Each party is considered to have assumed the risk that the value will change in the future or prove to be different from what he or she thought it would be. Differing judgments and opinions about the bargain are present in practically all contracts and are considred incidental mistakes.

Without this rule, almost any party who did not receive what she or he considered to be a fair bargain could argue mistake. The courts would then be overwhelmed with litigants who didn't believe that they got the better end of the bargain.

Mutual Mistakes of Fact

Mistakes of fact can be either *mutual* or *unilateral.* In a mutual mistake, both parties to the contract are mistaken with regard to some underlying *material fact.* Recall that a material fact is one that is important to the subject matter of the contract. In a case of a mutual mistake, there is no contract because there is no meeting of the minds. Unilateral mistakes, in which only one party is mistaken about some fact, are discussed below.

The most notorious example of mutual mistake is the famous 1864 case of *Raffles v. Wichelhaus*, also known as the case of the good ship Peerless. The parties agreed on a sale of cotton that was to be delivered from Bombay by ship. However, unknown to either of the parties, there were two ships, both coincidentally named "Peerless." Each party, in agreeing to the sale, was referring to delivery by the ship "Peerless," but each was referring to a different ship since neither party knew of the existence of the other "Peerless." Because the sailing dates of the two ships were materially different, neither party was willing to agree to shipment by the other "Peerless." The court ruled that there was no binding contract because each party had a different ship in mind when the contract was entered into.

Beachcomber Coins v. Boskett
400 A.2d 78 (1979)
Superior Court of New Jersey, Appellate Division

Facts: Ron Boskett, a part-time coin dealer, purchased a dime purportedly minted in 1916 at the Denver Mint. Boskett paid $450.00 for the coin. The "D" on the coin signified Denver mintage and made the coin rare and valuable. Boskett sold the coin to Beachcomber Coins, Inc., for $500.00. A principal of Beachcomber examined the coin for between 15 and 45 minutes prior to its purchase.

A short time later, Beachcomber received an offer for the purchase of the coin for $700.00. The offer was conditioned upon certification of the coin's genuineness by the American Numismatic Society. When the ANS labeled the coin counterfeit, Beachcomber sued Boskett to rescind the purchase of the coin.

Issue: Can Beachcomber rescind the contract for the purchase of the coin based upon mistake?

Holding: The Court concludes that this was a case of mutual mistake and we rule that the contract can be rescinded. When both parties are mistaken about a fact that is the basis of the contract, it is voidable by either party if enforcement of it would be materially more onerous to the rescinding party than it would have been had the facts been as the parties believed them to be. Because both parties thought that the coin was of Denver mintage, the mistake was mutual, and Beachcomber has the right to rescind the contract.

Unilateral Mistakes of Fact

In a *unilateral mistake*, only one party to the contract is mistaken as to some fact underlying the agreement. The general rule is that a unilateral mistake does not afford the mistaken party any right to relief from the contract. For instance, if a party is mistaken because of some computation error on his part or because of his own poor judgment, the contract may still be enforced by the innocent party, that is, the party who neither caused the mistake nor knew that there was, in fact, a mistake. The basic philosophy behind this principle is simple – a party should not be allowed to benefit from his or her own ignorance or carelessness. When discussing mistakes, it is critical to remember that a mistake as to value will never suffice to permit relief. If one enters into a bad bargain, he or she must live with it.

Example 4f:

Sara offers to sell Lindsey a blue stone ring for $200. Sara believes the stone in the ring to be a blue quartz, but Lindsey thinks the stone is a more valuable sapphire. Lindsey agrees to the contract. Later, when Lindsey discovers that the stone is blue quartz and not a sapphire, she wants to back out of the agreement because she was mistaken as to the object of the contract. The contract is valid because the parties only contracted for the sale of a "blue stone ring." The fact that Lindsey was mistaken as to its value is irrelevant to the contract.

Example 4g:

Sara offers to sell Lindsey her blue quartz ring for $200, and Lindsey agrees. Both believe the ring to be a blue quartz. Later, when Lindsey discovers that the stone is a sapphire worth $2,500, Sara wants to back out of the contract. The contract is not valid. Sara sold a "blue quartz ring" and Lindsey agreed to buy a "blue quartz" ring. However, she received a sapphire. Since both were mistaken as to the object of the contract, the contract is not enforceable.

Cobaugh v. Klick-Lewis, Inc

561 A2d 1248 (1988)

Superior Court of Pennsylvania

<u>Facts</u>: *Recall this case from the discussion in Chapter 3 of acceptance of an offer. The relevant facts are these:* Cobaugh was playing golf when he saw a sign on the golf course advertising a new car to anyone who made a hole-in-one. Cobaugh hit a hole-in-one and then tried to claim the prize. The dealership that had advertised the prize refused, explaining that the car had been offered as a prize in a charity tournament played two days earlier but they had not yet removed the sign. Klick-Lewis maintained that even if a valid offer was made by the sign, the dealership was relieved of its obligations on the basis of mistake.

<u>Issue</u>: Was there a mistake which permitted Klick-Lewis to rescind its offer?

<u>Holding</u>: The posted signs did not reveal any intent by Klick-Lewis that the automobile be a prize only for an earlier tournament. Further, there is no evidence that Cobaugh had knowledge greater than that acquired by reading the sign.

Where the mistake is not mutual but is unilateral and is due to the negligence of the party seeking to rescind the contract, relief will not be granted. It is the manifested intent of the offeror rather than his subjective intent which determines the persons having the power to accept the offer. In this case, the offeror's manifested intent, as it appeared from the posted signs, was that a hole-in-one would win the car. Nothing in the offer indicated that it was limited to any prior tournament, nor did the offeror remove the signs in a timely manner. It is clear that the mistake was unilateral and was the product of the offeror's failure to exercise due care. Such a mistake does not permit the offeror to avoid the contract.

4.4 *Unconscionability*

An *unconscionable* contract is one that is so completely unreasonable and irrational that it shocks the conscience. The courts have generally failed to adequately define what constitutes unconscionable terms, instead relying on the theory (as espoused in another context) that they'll "know it when they see it."[7]

Unconscionability may be found where none of the other defects in formation apply, but the court cannot permit the oppressing party to escape some liability for taking unscrupulous advantage of another. Sometimes, superior knowledge and bargaining position put one party at such an advantage over the other that some protection must be afforded to the subjugated party.

Many standard-form contracts used by businesses contain fine-print provisions that shift a risk naturally borne by one party to the other. Examples include life insurance policies, loan agreements, and leases. To avoid enforcement of the contract or of a particular clause in the contract, the aggrieved party must show that the parties had substantially unequal bargaining positions and that enforcement of the contract would be manifestly unfair or oppressive. The terms of the contract do not have to be fair, but if they are outrageously prejudiced against one party, the court may come to the conclusion that there was no meaningful meeting of the minds.

Review Questions and Exercises

1. Explain the difference between misrepresentation and fraud. What, if any, are the differences in the relief a party may seek if he can prove fraud as opposed to misrepresentation?

2. Give an example of a contract induced by economic duress not discussed in the chapter.

3. Brad is shopping for an engagement ring. A salesman tells Brad that the diamond ring he wants to purchase is "the best quality diamond I have in the entire store and, in fact, the best diamond I have ever seen." After Brad buys the ring, he discovers that the diamond is a very low grade. Has he been defrauded? Why or why not?

4. Mary is 82 years old and frail. Her stepson, a real estate developer, convinces her to sell him her house by telling her that, because of her frail health, the state is going to take her house away and put her in a home. Mary signs a contract with her stepson for the sale of her house. Has Mary entered into a valid contract? What defenses does she have in the event she is sued for breach of contract when she refuses to attend the closing?

5. Explain the differences between contracts that are considered *malum in se* and those that are considered *malum prohibitum*.

6. What is the consideration for the promise in a unilateral contract?

7. Assume the following facts: Jennifer, aged sixteen, contracts to buy a gold pendant from Jim's Jewels for $500. She paid the purchase price and received the pendant.

---

[7] Justice Stewart, in *Jacobellis v. Ohio*, 378 U.S. 184 (1964), wrote: "I shall not today attempt further to define the kinds of material I understand to be embraced within that shorthand description; and perhaps I could never succeed in intelligibly doing so. But, I know it when I see it ..." Justice Stewart was referring to obscenity.

a) Over the next six months, the price of gold increases dramatically, and the pendant increases in value. Can Jim's Jewels disaffirm the contract, return Jennifer's $500, and get the pendant back?

b) Assume that in the six months after Jennifer bought the pendant, the price of gold decreases dramatically in value. Can Jennifer disaffirm the contract, return the pendant, and get her $500 back?

Practical Applications

1. Mrs. Chaney died leaving a house in Annapolis, Maryland. The representative of her estate listed the house for sale with a real estate broker, stating that the property was approximately 15,650 square feet. Drs. Steele and Faust made an offer of $300,000 for the property, which was accepted by the estate. A contract for the sale of the property was signed by all parties.

When a subsequent survey done before the deed was transferred showed that the property had an area of 22,047 square feet, the estate requested that the buyers pay more money for the property. The buyers declined. When the estate refused to transfer the property to the buyers, the buyers sued for specific performance.

Consider:
(a) Was there a mistake made that negates contractual intent?
(b) Can the estate rescind the contract based upon mistake?
(c) Why or why not is the contract enforceable?

See - *Steele v. Goettee*, Maryland Court of Appeals, 542 A.2d 847 (1988).

2. As a child, Martha Carr, a resident of New York, once visited her mother's 108 acre tract of unimproved land in South Carolina. Carr inherited the property upon her mother's death. Two years later, she contacted the Campbells, who had leased the property for thirty years, about selling the property to them. Carr asked Mrs. Campbell "how much the property went for," and Mrs. Campbell told her that the Tax Assessor's agricultural assessed value was $54,000. The Campbells knew at the time that the county had assessed the total property value at $103,700. Carr and Mr. Campbell entered into a written contract for the sale of the property for $54,000. An expert appraiser valued the property at $162,000. Carr did not attend the closing because she felt the sales price was unfair.

Carr had been diagnosed as having schizophrenia and depression more than a decade earlier. She was on multiple prescription drugs for the conditions and had been hospitalized five or six times for the illnesses. At the time of the contract, Carr had only been shortly released from a mental institution after some six or eight years of confinement.

Consider:
(a) Should the court enforce the contract between Carr and the Campbells?
(b) What bearing, if any, should the inadequacy of the consideration have on the court's decision?

See – *Campbell v. Carr, 361* S.C. 258, 603 S.E.2d 625 (2004), Court of Appeals of South Carolina.

Chapter 5 *Classifications of Contracts and the Statute of Frauds*

OUTLINE

The classification or type of a given contract depends on various factors including the manner in which the contract was formed, whether the parties have performed their obligations under the the contract, and whether the contract is legally enforceable under the law. This chapter also explores the Statute of Frauds which requires that certain contracts be in writing in order to be enforceable by the courts.

5.1 Classification of Contracts

Contracts can be categorized in several ways based on legal distinctions as to formation, performance, and enforceability.

Bilateral Contracts vs. Unilateral Contracts

Every contract involves at least two parties. The *offeror* is the party making the offer to enter into the contract while the *offeree* is the party to whom the offer is made. The offeror initiates the contractual relationship between the parties, but it is the offeree who has the power to create the contract. The offeree does this by his acceptance of the offeror's offer. It is the offeror who decides whether the contract will be bilateral or unilateral. He does this by the terms of his offer. Whether the contract is *bilateral* or *unilateral* depends on what the offeree must do to accept the offer and bind the offeror to a contract.

In a *bilateral* contract, the offeree must only promise to perform some act at some point in the future. Thus, a bilateral contract is a "promise for a promise." No performance, such as the payment of money or the delivery of goods, need take place at the moment the contract is formed. The contract comes into existence at the moment the promises are exchanged while the actual performance of the contract is carried out later.

Example 5a:

On Monday, Mark offers to buy Jan's iPod for $40. Mark tells Jan that he will give her the money for the iPod on Friday. Jan accepts Mark's offer and promises to deliver the iPod to him on Friday when he gives her the $40. Mark and Jan have formed a bilateral contract. The contract is formed on Monday when the parties exchange their promises although performance will not take place until Friday.

A *unilateral* contract is formed if the offer is phrased so that the offeree can accept the offer only by completing the contract performance. Hence, a unilateral contract is "a promise for an act." In other words, the time of contract formation in a unilateral contract is not at the moment when promises are exchanged (because there are no promises for future conduct), but when the contract is actually entered into and performed.

Example 5b:

Professor Jones says to Tom, "If you will pick up my package at the post office and deliver it to me at school, I will pay you $10." Only upon Tom's complete performance of the requested act - picking up the package and delivering it to Professor Jones at school - has Tom fully accepted Professor Jones's offer. It is at that time that the contract is formed. If Tom chooses not to undertake the errand, there are no legal consequences because there was no contract.

Contests, lotteries, and other such competitions involving prizes are examples of offers to form unilateral contracts. If one complies with the rules of the contest, such as by submitting the right lottery number at the right time and place, a unilateral contract is formed binding the organization offering the prize to a contract to perform as promised in the offer. Most contracts, however, are bilateral.

Ardito v. City of Providence

263 F.Supp.2d 358 (2003)

United States District Court, District of Rhode Island

Facts: In 2001, the city of Providence, Rhode Island, began hiring police officers to fill vacancies in the city's department. Because only individuals who had graduated from the Providence Police Academy were eligible to fill the vacancies, the city decided to conduct two training sessions. To be admitted, an applicant had to pass a series of tests and be deemed qualified after an interview by members of the department. On October 15th the applicants judged the most qualified were sent a letter informing them that they had been selected to attend the academy if they successfully completed a medical checkup and psychological exam. The letter stated that it was "a conditional offer of employment."

Meanwhile, the new Chief of Police decided to revise the selection process. As a result of the revisions, some of those who had received the "conditional offer of employment" letter were rejected. Derek Ardito and thirteen other newly rejected applicants, all of whom had completed the examinations, filed suit.

Issue: Do the plaintiffs have a valid breach of contract action?

Holding: The letter received by the plaintiffs is a classic example of an offer to enter into a unilateral contract. The letter expressly stated that it was a "conditional offer of employment," and the message conveyed was that the recipient would be admitted into the Academy if he or she successfully completed the medical and psychological examinations.

The October 15th letter was in marked contrast to the notices sent to the applicants at earlier stages of the selection process. The earlier notices merely informed applicants that they had completed a step in the process and remained eligible to be considered for admission into the academy.

The plaintiffs accepted the city's offer of admission into the academy by satisfying the specified conditions. Each of the plaintiffs submitted to and passed lengthy and intrusive medical and psychological examinations. The October 15th letter was a unilateral offer which the plaintiffs had accepted by passing the required exams, and the city is prohibited from conducting the police academy training unless the plaintiffs are included.

The classification of whether a contract is unilateral or bilateral can be critical since it determines the starting point of the contractual relationship. In a bilateral contract, the parties' binding contract comes into being upon the exchange of their promises, and thus, each side is entitled to contractual remedies if the other side fails to perform under the terms of the agreement. In a unilateral contract, however, the contract does not come into existence until one party actually performs the act requested of him. This means the other party cannot enforce the "contract" if the first party fails to perform because no contract ever existed. It was merely proposed.

Express vs. Implied-in-Fact Contracts

Another way in which contracts can be categorized is as express *or* implied by the conduct of the parties. This classification is based on the manner or method by which the contract was created.

In an *express* contract, the parties have stated, or spelled out in words, their assent to the terms of the contract. That is, the terms of the contract are fully and explicitly stated in words, either oral or written.

Example 5c:

Another student agrees to purchase your used textbook from last semester for $30. An express oral contract has been entered into.

In an implied, or *implied-in-fact* contract, the promises are inferred from the conduct of the parties. This type of contract differs from an express contract in that it is the conduct of the parties, rather than their words, which creates and defines the terms of the contract. Certain requirements must be met for an implied-in-fact contract to arise. Generally speaking, if the following conditions exist, a court will hold that an implied-in-fact contract was formed:

- The plaintiff furnished some service or property to the defendant;

- The plaintiff expected to be paid for that service or property, and the defendant knew or should have known that payment was expected; and
- The defendant had a chance to reject the services or property and did not do so.

Example 5d:

Aaron enters a restaurant, reviews the menu, and orders a meal. The waiter doesn't say to Aaron, "Do you promise to pay for this meal if I promise to serve it to you?" The promise of payment is inferred from Aaron's conduct in ordering the meal.

A contract may be a mixture of an express contract and an implied-in-fact contract. In other words, a contract may contain some express terms, while others are implied from the actions of the parties.

While not a true contract, another category of agreement, called *quasi-contracts* or *implied-in-law* contracts, are also recognized by the law. In such a situation, no real contract exists because one of the essential elements is missing. However, in certain cases, a court will use its equitable powers to provide a remedy because it would be too unfair to one of the parties not to do so. In these cases, the courts will treat the parties as if they did have a contract because equity, or fairness, demands it. If one party has unjustly benefited from the other party under circumstances in which a mutual benefit would have been expected, the court may find a quasi-contract. To do otherwise and deny any relief would simply be too unjust.

Executed vs. Executory Contracts

Contracts are also classified according to the degree to which they have been performed – that is, by whether or not both of the parties to the contract have fulfilled their respective obligations under the contract.

A contract that has been fully performed by both parties is called an *executed* contract. There is nothing else left to be done by either party. Each of the parties has done everything required of him or her under the contract and each has received all of the benefits due to him or her pursuant to the terms of the contract.

Example 5e:

Your classmate took tort law last semester and agreed to sell to you and you agreed to buy her used tort law textbook for use this semester. On the first day of class, you paid your classmate the agreed upon price for her used textbook and she delivered the book to you. Your contract is fully executed.

A contract that has not been fully performed by the parties is called an *executory* contract. In an executory contract, at least one party still has obligations yet to be performed under the terms of the agreement. In some cases, both parties have partially, but not fully, performed their obligations. Obviously, such a contract is considered executory. If one party has fully performed and the other has not, the contract is said to be executed on the one side and executory on the other, but the contract is still classified as executory.

Example 5f:

Kelly agrees to buy twelve plants for her garden from Mike's Garden Center. Mike agrees to deliver the specified plants to Kelly's house and to bill her for them at the end of the month. Mike delivers the plants, but Kelly has not yet paid for them. At this point, the contract is executed on the part of Mike and executory on the part of Kelly. The contract is considered to be executory. After Kelly pays Mike's bill, the contract will become an executed one.

Formal vs. Informal Contracts

Contracts can be classified as *formal* or *informal*. Only contracts which meet certain statutory requirements are considered formal contracts. These are contracts which require a special form or method of creation (formation) to be enforceable. One type of formal contract is the *contract under seal*, a formalized writing with a special seal attached. The seal may be an actual seal (one made of wax) or one impressed on the paper. It may also be indicated simply by the word "seal" or the letters "L.S." (Latin for locus sigilli, meaning "the place for the seal") at the end of the document.

The contract under seal has been almost entirely abolished under provisions of the Uniform Commercial Code, but it is still common to use a seal (or an acceptable substitute) in real estate sales contracts.

Informal contracts include all other contracts. Such contracts are also called *simple* contracts. No special form is required except that certain types of contracts must be in writing. These contracts will be discussed in detail later in this chapter.

5.2 *Contract Enforceability*

Enforceability is the classification which determines whether a party to a contract can have that agreement enforced in a court of law.

Valid Contracts

A *valid* contract is one which has all of the elements necessary to entitle at least one of the parties to enforce it in court. This means it is a contract in which a proper offer has been made and a proper acceptance, which mirrors the offer, given; valid consideration has been given and received by each of the parties; the parties each have the legal capacity to enter into a contract; the contract is one for a legal purpose; and the parties both genuinely intended to enter into contract. The contract is complete under the law. Generally speaking, either party can bring suit for the enforcement of a valid contract.

While the majority of contracts are valid, not all of them are enforceable under the law. In other words, situations can exists in which the parties have a completely valid contract, but for which the law will offer no recourse or remedy in the event of a breach. Such contracts are discussed in more detail later in this chapter.

Voidable Contracts

A *voidable* contract is a valid contract but one that can be avoided at the option of one or both of the parties. The party having the option can elect to either avoid any duty to perform under the contract or to ratify (make valid) the contract. In other words, a party to the agreement has the option of avoiding his legal obligation without any negative consequences, or he can, if he wishes to do so, affirm his obligation and thereby be contractually bound to perform his duties. If the contract is avoided, both parties are released from it. If the contract is ratified, then both parties must fully perform their respective legal obligations.

A contract entered into by a minor is an example of a voidable contract. Legally, a minor does not have contractual capacity, the legal ability to enter into a contract. Thus, he can avoid fulfilling contracts into which he has entered. A voidable contract may become valid and enforceable if the party under the disability, for example, the minor, later affirms his obligation when the disability is removed.

Example 5g:

Austin, who is sixteen, enters into a contract with Frank, an adult, to buy Frank's boat, agreeing to pay Frank for the boat on his eighteenth birthday. If Austin changes his mind, he can avoid the contract. However, if on Austin's eighteenth birthday, he affirms his promise by paying for the boat, the contract is totally enforceable. The option of avoidance is with Austin, who is under the disability, and not with Frank who is under no such disability.

Void Contracts

In reality a *void* contract is no contract at all. The terms "contract" and "void" are contradictory. A void contract produces no legal obligation on either of the parties. A contract may be void because one of the parties was adjudged by a court to be legally insane (and, thus, lacked the capacity to enter into a contract) or because the purpose of the contract was illegal. Recall that both capacity to enter into contracts and legality of purpose are necessary requirements in order for a valid contract to exist.

Unenforceable Contracts

An *unenforceable* contract is a valid contract for which the law offers no recourse or remedy if its obligations are not fulfilled. In other words, an unenforceable contract is one that cannot be enforced because of certain legal defenses against it. For instance, a contract may exist in which one party failed to meet her contractual obligation, but, by the time the aggrieved party decides to sue, the statute of limitations has run. Now the aggrieved party has no means of enforcing the otherwise valid contract.

A valid contract may not be enforceable for other reasons in addition to the running of the statute of limitations. The law may have changed after the contract was entered into but before performance such that the purpose for which the contract was formed cannot now be legally performed. Another instance in which a valid contract may be unenforceable concerns the Statute of Frauds. This law requires that contracts pertaining to certain subject matters be in writing in order to be enforceable. If such a contract is a verbal one, the contract is unenforceable. While all of the requirements of a valid contract may be satisfied, the contract will be unenforceable due to the lack of writing.

Example 5h:

Susan is looking to buy a home. Her co-worker, Albert, expresses an interest in selling his home. Susan and Albert discuss the matter and Susan looks at Albert's house. Liking it, she makes a verbal offer to purchase the house for $250,000 with the sale to close in 30 days. Albert agrees and the two shake hands but do not reduce their agreement to writing. When Albert telephones Susan the day before the scheduled closing and tells her that he has changed his mind about selling, Susan is without recourse as the statute of frauds requires that contracts for the sale of real property be in writing.

5.3 *The Statute of Frauds*

The law generally makes no distinction between contracts that are written and contracts that are oral. Each is given legal validity and can be enforced. However, almost every state, including Georgia, has a statute modeled after a seventeenth century English law which stipulates that certain types of contracts must be in writing in order to be enforced by a court. These statutes are collectively referred to as the *Statute of Frauds*.

The Statute of Frauds has its origins in an act passed by the English Parliament in 1677 known as "An Act for the Prevention of Frauds and Perjuries." The act established that certain types of contracts, in order to be enforceable in a court, had to be evidenced by a writing and signed by the person against whom enforcement was sought. Do not be misled by the name "Statute of Frauds." The "fraud" here is not the contractual concept of fraud previously discussed, but concerns preventing perjury and fraud with respect to proving contractual clauses. The Statute of Frauds denies *enforceability* to certain contracts which do not comply with its requirements. It is the courts' attempt to deny enforcement of dubious claims by providing some assurance that the contract in question does, in fact, exist.

Thus, in reality, the Statute of Frauds deals with the law of evidence and not the law of contracts. It is simply easier to demonstrate a contractual promise if the trier of fact can read the contract itself. If the terms of the contract have to be proven by oral testimony, there can be a conflict between what the parties to the agreement remember about the terms, putting an extra burden on the trier of fact.

OCGA § 13-5-30

To make the following obligations binding on the promisor, the promise must be in writing and signed by the party to be charged therewith or some person lawfully authorized by him:

(1) A promise by an executor, administrator, guardian, or trustee to answer damages out of his own estate;
(2) A promise to answer for the debt, fault, or miscarriage of another;
(3) Any agreement made upon consideration of marriage, except marriage articles as provided in Article 3 of Chapter 3 of Title 19;
(4) Any contract for the sale of lands, or any interest in, or concerning lands;
(5) Any agreement that is not to be performed within one year from the making thereof;
(6) Any promise to revive a debt barred by a statute of limitation; and
(7) Any commitment to lend money.

If parties enter into an agreement that would fall under the Statute of Frauds but the parties do not memorialize it in writing, the agreement is not automatically void. The parties are free to perform on their oral contract. The Statute of Frauds merely protects parties' interests once they are involved in litigating the contractual dispute. Parties are free to make any oral promise they want and to fully perform on it. Unless the court gets involved, there is no need for the formality of a writing. However, since parties to a lawsuit tend to recall events and agreements in a light most favorable to themselves and not necessarily reflecting the facts accurately, the Statute of Frauds helps the court avoid the "he said/she said" dilemma.

Example 5i:

Alan and his friend Betsy agree that Alan will purchase Betsy's house for $250,000 with the closing to take place in 30 days. They put nothing in writing, but rather simply shake hands to solemnize their agreement. The Statute of Frauds requires that contracts for the transfer of real property be in writing. Both do everything required of them by their agreement. Thirty days later Betsy executes a deed transferring ownership of the property to Alan who pays Betsy the agreed upon price. Their agreement is perfectly valid.

Example 5j:

Assume the same agreement between Alan and Betsy exists. Ten days after they shake hands to seal the deal, Betsy tells Alan that she has changed her mind and will not sell her house. Since the agreement is not in writing, it cannot be enforced against Betsy. Thus, Alan cannot sue Betsy for specific performance of the contract.

Under the *equal dignity rule*, if a contract is one that the Statute of Frauds requires to be in writing, and a agent has entered into the contract on behalf of a principal, then the agent's authority to enter into the contract must also be in writing.

Garrett v. Southern Health Corporation of Ellijay, Inc.
320 Ga.App. 176, 739 S.E.2d 661 (2013)
Court of Appeals of Georgia

Facts: Southern Health Corporation of Ellijay, Inc., entered into an option agreement to purchase land owned by Garrett and others for the development of a new hospital facility. The contract was executed by Sheila Brockman in her capacity as the Assistant Secretary of Southern Health. After Southern Health exercised its option to purchase the land but the sellers failed to close on the sale, Southern Health filed suit against the sellers seeking damages for breach of contract.

In defense of the lawsuit, Garrett asserted that the option contract had not been signed by an authorized representative of Southern Health and was unenforceable under the "equal dignity rule." Garrett asserted there was no competent evidence indicating that Southern Health's Board of Directors had, in writing, authorized their agent to sign the option contract.

Issue: Can the seller defend a breach of contract action on the basis that the buyer's agent lacked written authority to enter into the contract as required by the Statute of Frauds?

Holding: The Sellers' argument that the Option Agreement was unenforceable under the "equal dignity rule" is misplaced. Pursuant to that rule, "the authority of an agent to execute an instrument required by the Statute of Frauds to be in writing must also be in writing." Because the Statute of Frauds requires that an option contract for the purchase of land be in writing, the authority of an agent to execute such a contract likewise must be in writing. Nevertheless, even if Ms. Brockman's authority to sign the Option Agreement on behalf of Southern Health was given to her verbally rather than in writing, the Sellers are not the correct parties to challenge her authority under the "equal dignity rule." This Court has previously held that in cases where the equal dignity rule is invoked, the invoking party is the principal who is challenging the authority of its own alleged representative. Thus, the Sellers were not entitled to rely upon the "equal dignity rule."

5.4 *Contracts Covered by the Statute of Frauds*

As we have previously seen, the majority of contracts are oral ones. These simple, informal agreements are entered into many times each day and are seldom thought of as "contracts" by the parties who enter into them. We will now, however, the specific types of contracts which must be in writing in order to be enforceable in the courts.

Contracts for an Interest in Real Property

For centuries, land ownership has been regarded as one of the most important interests an individual can possess. Thus, to be enforceable, every contract conveying an interest in real property must be in writing. The requirement that deeds be in writing gives assurance that ownership of property can be traced conclusively and without the necessity of reliance upon the sometimes faulty memories of people. Furthermore, contractual terms can be proved, even if the persons involved in the agreement have died and are, therefore, unavailable to testify about the contract.

The Statute of Frauds applies to contracts conveying "an interest in real property." Real property means the land itself and anything permanently affixed to it. The most obvious inclusion in this category is a contract for the actual sale of a piece of real estate. Compare that to a contract for the sale of the fruits of the land such as crops. This is not a contract for the transfer of an interest in land because, at the time the performance is due under the contract, taking the crop or other product from the land separates the interest from the land. Likewise a contract for putting something on the land is not included; thus, a contract to build a house on a piece of land is not a contract tied to land and is, therefore, outside of the Statute of Frauds. If the contract does not concern the land itself, but rather concerns something that is separate and apart from the land, the contract does fall within the provisions of the statute and may be enforceable even if it is oral.

Note, however, that there are other interests in real property that qualify for inclusion under the Statute of Frauds aside from contracts for the sale of real property. Mortgages, easements, leases, and liens on property as security for obligations are all included. The underlying reason for this are contract law's love of certainty and the long held belief that land rights are considered too important to be left to faulty memories.

Most writings relating to real property interests are recorded in a clerk's office so that the interests in the real estate are matters of public record. Requiring a writing under the Statute of Frauds also protects this governmental interest and assures certainty and security.

Example 5k:

Jose signs a contract for the purchase of a retail property in connection with his plan to open a sporting goods store. The contract conveys "an interest in real property" to Jose. Jose's contract must be in writing to satisfy the Statute of Frauds. However, Jose's contract with the contractor he hires to make improvements to the store property need not be in writing in order to be enforceable.

Contracts in Consideration of Marriage

In medieval times, women were at significant disadvantages in many ways, and a marriage was more a matter of property rights than the union of lovers. The husband was entitled to a dowry (money or property paid to the husband in consideration of the marriage) from the wife's family. If the wife's family did not pay the dowry specified in the agreement, the husband could sue to force the payment. Today, dowries are virtually extinct, at least in western cultures, but the concept that a promise given in consideration of marriage must be in writing continues.

The Statute of Frauds does not apply to the mutual promise to actually marry the other person, but it does apply to all other arrangements and/or conditions attached to that agreement. This is most often recognized as a *prenuptial agreement* wherein both parties make certain decisions regarding the allocation of assets and other consideration should the marriage fail. A prenuptial agreement can be likened to writing the divorce settlement before the marriage ceremony even takes place. The contract must contain conditions attached to the actual agreement to become married, not just incidental to it. The end to be attained must be the marriage and by the contract the conditions are set forth.

Example 5l:

Bill and Mollie are planning to marry. The marriage is a second marriage for both and both have children from their first marriages. Bill and Mollie are professionals who have accumulated significant assets. They want to avoid any disputes between themselves in the event the marriage doesn't work out or between their children in the event that one of them dies. They agree upon each party's property rights in the event of divorce or death. This contract must be in writing to be enforceable.

While some courts have become more willing to recognize similar agreements between unmarried couples, because there is no actual marriage in these cases, such agreements are enforceable without a writing (if they are enforceable at all). The Statute of Frauds stays traditional and requires the actual marriage to be part of the consideration to support the contract.

Contracts Not to be Performed Within One Year

Time has a tendency to cloud one's recall of the particulars of an agreement. Therefore, the Statute of Frauds requires contracts to be in writing where the performance under the contract could not take place within one year.

For purposes of determining the applicability of the statute, the one year time period starts from the day of the agreement, the formation of the contract, and not the date on which performance is to start. In other words, it is the amount of time that lapses between the acceptance of the contract and performance of the terms of the contract that determines whether the contract falls under the Statute of Frauds.

Slater v. Jackson, et al.
163 Ga.App. 342, 294 S.E.2d 557 (1982)
Court of Appeals of Georgia

Facts: Jackson made an oral offer of employment to Slater to commence on January 22, 1979, and to run for one year. The offer was made on January 14, 1979, and accepted on January 15th. When Slater was terminated, he sued, alleging breach of contract.

Issue: Did Slater have an enforceable employment contract with Jackson?

Holding: The Georgia Statute of Frauds provides that a contract that is not to be performed within one year from the making thereof falls within the Statute of Frauds and must be in writing in order to be enforceable in the courts. The contract between Slater and Jackson was formed on January 15, 1979, and was, by its terms, not to be fully performed until January 21, 1980. This contract is one that could not to be performed within one year from the date of its formation. Therefore, although legal in every respect, since the contract was oral and not written, it cannot be enforced against Jackson by the court.

This provision of the Statute of Frauds is concerned with situations in which it is *impossible* for the performance to be completed within one year. If, under any conceivable circumstance, the performance could be completed within one year, the contract does not fall within the statute. The probability that the contract will be fully performed within one year is irrelevant. If there is a remote possibility that the contract could be performed within one year, the statute does not apply.

Example 5m:

Frances hires Stan, a contractor, to construct a new home. The contract provides that construction will be complete not later than fourteen months after the execution of the contract. This contract is not within the Statute of Frauds. If Stan is a good contractor and luck favors him (no unexpected delays, good weather, etc.), he may complete the house in seven or eight months. Since the possibility exists that the contract could be completed before one year has passed, the contract does not fall within the Statute of Frauds.

Example 5n:

Lee agrees to lease his tractor to Farmer Jones for eighteen months. Farmer Jones agrees to pay Lee $200 per month for the term of the lease. To be enforceable under the Statute of Frauds, the contract must be in writing since performance of the contractual obligations will take more than one year.

Additionally, if the performance is conditioned upon some future uncertain event, the contract does not fall within the statute. Because any uncertain event *may,* but may not, occur in less than one year, the statute does not apply.

As we saw in the *Slater* case, employment contracts for more than one year and covenants not to compete for more than one year after termination of employment are within the Statute of Frauds. An employee cannot fully perform an employment contract that requires him/her to work for the employer for more than one year since it is impossible to compress time.

Guarantees

Recall from Chapter 3 that, in some situations, one person, a *guarantor*, may agree to pay for the debts of another party even though there is no legal obligation requiring him to do so. Where the promise to pay for the debt of another is unrelated to and without gain to the promisor/guarantor, there is, in fact, no consideration for the promise. However, the law recognizes that such contracts have a value to society as a whole, and thus, will enforce such contracts, despite the lack of consideration.

Such an agreement falls within the Statute of Frauds and must be in writing in order to be enforced.

Note that a guarantor is different from a co-signor. A guarantor is only liable for payment after the default of the primary debtor. Conversely, both co-signors of a loan are held equally responsible for the payments from the outset. Co-signors both received consideration in exchange for their promises to repay the loan. Thus, there is no need to wait until one defaults to collect from the other.

Example 50:

Beth has a note at First National Bank. Beth and her husband, Ben, have been paying the monthly payments on the note out of their joint income. When Ben moves out, telling Beth that he wants a divorce, and refuses to make any further contribution towards payment of the note, Beth is unable to pay it in a timely manner. Her parents agree to help her out by promising the bank to pay the note if Beth finds herself unable to do so. The parents have become guarantors and their promise to the bank must be in writing to be enforceable.

Windham & Windham, Inc., et al. v. Suntrust Bank

313 Ga. App. 841, 723 S.E.2d 70 (2012)

Court of Appeals of Georgia

<u>Facts</u>: In 2007, SunTrust Bank extended a line of credit to Windham and Windham, Inc., and also gave the company a commercial loan. Jeffrey and Robyn Windham, the owners of the company, executed unconditional guarantee agreements with regard to both loans, personally guaranteeing the debts. In 2010, the Bank sued the company and both the Windhams individually, alleging that the company had failed since July 2008 to make any payments under the note and also had failed to make required payments on the line of credit. The bank asserted that Ms. and Mrs. Windham were liable to it pursuant to the guaranee agreements.

The Windhams claimed that they signed the guarantee agreements only as officers of Windham and Windham, Inc., and not in their personal capacities. Additionally, Robyn Windham claimed she had been concerned about personal liability, and, specifically, about her home; that she had discussed this matter with a bank officer; and that the bank had assured her she would have no personal liability for the debts of the company.

Issue: Are Jeffrey and Robyn Windham personally liable for the debts of Windham and Windham, Inc."

Holding: The guarantee provisions of the line of credit agreement and the unconditional guarantees executed by the Windhams are unambiguous. They appear on their face to be a complete statement of the agreement between the parties about the obligation of the Windhams to ensure the repayment of the indebtedness that the Windham company owed the Bank. The Windham company being in default, the Windhams are personally liable.

Executor's Promise to Pay Decedent's Debts

Closely related in theory to guarantee agreements are agreements of an executor to pay the debts of the deceased out of the executor's own pocket. These must also be in writing in order to be enforceable and for the same reason – there is no consideration paid to the executor in such an agreement. The obligations of a deceased person are obligations of the estate of the deceased and are not personal to the executor who merely administers the estate. It is not unusual for the estate of a deceased person to lack sufficient funds or assets to pay all of the debts of the estate. When an executor, for whatever reason, agrees to pay some debt of the estate out of his own (the executor's) personal assets, then that agreement must be in writing to be enforceable.

Example 5p:

Annie is the executor of her grandmother's estate. The estate has no assets, but Annie agrees to pay her grandmother's doctor's bills out of her own funds. Annie believes that the doctor did his best to make Grandmother comfortable during her final illness and wants to see him compensated. Annie's promise, as a *surety*, to pay the doctor would have to be in writing if the doctor sought collection of the bill in court.

Contracts for the Sale of Goods

The Uniform Commercial Code will be discussed at some length in Chapter 7 later in this text, but, for the sake of a complete discussion of the Statute of Frauds, one requirement is mentioned here. Historically, contracts for the sale of goods valued above a specified amount had to be in writing to be enforceable. Personal property was not considered as valuable as real property until a certain value was reached, but at some monetary point, the property became sufficiently important for the law to require a writing to protect the parties. Obviously, the dollar amount of that specified amount has increased over the years.

The UCC, a version of which has been adopted by every state, provides that any contract for the sale of goods for a *price* over $500.00 is required to be memorialized in some written form. Note that it is the price of the goods, and not their value, which is important. Price is the amount of money that the seller will accept to transfer the item to the buyer. The *value* of the item may be completely different, either higher or lower, and can be subjective.

Example 5q:

Patty collects antique pottery. Roy owns an antique shop and has for sale a bowl priced at $450.00. Patty considers this a bargain and agrees to purchase the bowl. Patty would have been willing to pay up to $700 for the bowl because she believes that to be its true value. Under the Statute of Frauds and the UCC, this transaction would not have to be in writing because the price is $450. If the value of the piece were the measure of determining whether the agreement fell under the Statute of Frauds, whose standards of valuation would apply – the seller's or the buyer's? This is why the UCC references the price of the goods, not the value.

The UCC's requirements for merchants also allow for some leeway in the form the writing takes. There only needs to be "some writing sufficient to indicate that a contract for sale has been made ..." Thus, a receipt printed by a cash register will suffice to satisfy the requirement that a writing memorialize the transaction. Today's modern electronic registers which read the bar codes printed on merchandise provide a record of details about the item sold including the date and location of the sale and the manner of payment (cash, credit card, etc.) in addition to the price paid for the merchandise.

5.5 *The Writing – Satisfying the Statute of Frauds*

While a written contract may be an extensive, full-blown formal document enumerating all of the terms and conditions of the agreement, such a writing is not necessary to satisfy the Statute of Frauds. So long as all the requisites of an agreement can be established by the writing, the Statute of Frauds is satisfied. The essentials which must be included in the writing include the identity of the parties, the price and subject matter of the contract, and the time for performance. A memo written on a scrap of paper torn from an envelope or scribbled by the parties on a paper napkin may be enough to satisfy the Statute of Frauds so long as it is clear from the memo that the parties did assent to the terms contained therein.

It is also possible to read several writings together to form one whole which satisfies the Statute of Frauds. It is not uncommon for a contract to consist of not just one writing, but of a series of writings. The parties may have exchanged several communications such as letters or faxed memos as they worked to arrive at the terms of their agreement. More commonly today, the series of communications will be a chain of emails. Regardless of the form the communications take, so long as the series of communications, when all read together, spell out all of the essential terms of the parties' agreement, a written contract has been entered into.

The simple act of writing out the terms of a contract requires the parties to carefully think about the terms they are agreeing upon. Thus, a written contract may be more definite, complete, and refined than an oral contract. In addition, of course, the writing acts to provide the parties with documentation of the terms of their agreement rather than relying on memory alone.

The Restatement (Second) of Contracts provides that a contract within the Statute of Frauds is enforceable if it is evidenced by any writing, signed by or on behalf of the party to be charged, which:

(a) reasonably identifies the subject matter of the contract;
(b) is sufficient to indicate that a contract with respect thereto has been made between the parties or offered by the signor to the other party; and
(c) states with reasonable certainty the essential terms of the unperformed promises in the contract.

Stated more simply, what is required is a writing that states all of the essential terms of the agreement with reasonable certainty. The writing should indicate the identity of the parties, the subject matter of the agreement, the material terms, including the price or consideration given, and include the signature of the parties to be bound under the contract.

Complying with the Statute of Frauds creates another requirement for the enforceability of contracts. Although the Statute of Frauds is not an element of a valid oral contract, it does raise a barrier to the enforcement of a seemingly valid contract. It is necessary to understand the extent of a writing required to satisfy the Statute of Frauds.

Identity of the Parties

The parties to the contract must be identified by the writing. This does not mean that the full, legal names of the parties must be set out in the writing. The identity of the parties must, however, be clearly indicated by the writing. While this sounds quite basic, it can be of significance with some individuals, such as fathers and sons with the same name, as well as with some business entities. For example, in Georgia there are two limited liability companies registered with the Secretary of State's office - Dublin Nephrology Associates, LLC, and Dublin Nephrology Care, LLC. A contract which identified one of the parties as "Dublin Nephrology" would be insufficient to indicate the identify of the contracting party. If any doubt arises as to the identity of the parties, it is highly unlikely the writing requirement has been met.

Subject Matter of the Contract

The writing cannot leave any question as to the subject matter of the contract. The subject matter must be identified in such a manner that no question can arise between the parties who have entered into the agreement. It is important that the subject matter be identified in specific terms and in a manner that is clear to both parties.

Example 5r:

Over drinks at a tavern, Mark offers to sell Max his automobile. Mark takes a paper napkin from the bar and writes on it: "Mark Jones and Max Wilson hereby agree that Max will buy Mark's 2011 Nissan 350Z for $28,500. Payment in cash and delivery on April 2, 2014." Mark signs his name. Max reads and signs the napkin. It is not necessary to provide the vehicle identification number in the writing in order to sufficiently identify the car. If, however, the writing had simply stated, "The parties agree that Max will buy Mark's car for $28,500," and Mark owned more than one car, then the writing would not sufficiently identify the consideration and would not be enforceable.

Powell v. Adderholdt, et al.
230 Ga. 211, 196 S.E.2d 420 (1973)
Supreme Court of Georgia

Facts: Albert Poole agreed to buy a tract of real property containing approximately 18 acres from W.T. Campbell. Poole agreed to pay $4,250 for the property, paying $300 to Mr. Campbell at the time the parties reached their agreement, and, thereafter, making additional payments totaling $1,650. Mr. Campbell died before Poole finished paying for the land and before Campbell executed a deed to Poole. J.D. Adderholdt was the executor of the estate of Campbell. Poole tendered to the estate the balance due on the land and requested a deed from Adderholdt. Campbell's daughter, Mrs. Powell, objected, asserting that if the contract was made, it was not in writing and was unenforceable, being in violation of the Statute of Frauds.

The only written evidence produced by Poole was a small account book and a rough drawing, both found in the possession of the deceased, in a desk drawer with other papers. The account book had the notation on one page "17 or 18 acres." On another page it had "land book" and then "Albert E. Poole bought land from Mr. W.T. Campbell August 14, 1965 and this book will show payments." Then followed dates and amounts of payments which totaled $1,950. The rough drawing had, at the top, the words "Albert Poole land mark," and at the bottom, "Bought August 14, 1965 from W.T. Campbell." The drawing was an irregular rectangle and around the sides were the notations: "Road 2600 feet – 225 ft. – 2600 feet – Gulley 481 ft." No other descriptive words were given.

Issue: Were the writings of Mr. Campbell sufficient to constitute a written contract for the sale of land?

Holding: Where writings are relied on to take a transaction out of the Statute of Frauds, they "must (a) identify the buyer and seller, (b) describe the subject matter of the contract, and (c) name the consideration." In this case, no particular land was described and the terms of the sale were not given. Although Poole had partially paid for the land prior to Campbell's death, partial payment of the purchase money alone, when not accompanied with possession of the property, is not such part performance of the contract as will compel performance. The evidence in this case did not show possession by Albert Poole. The land was in timber, and Poole testified that he had not done anything to the land – he had not occupied it; had not cut timber on it; had not farmed it; had not planted a garden on it; and had not paid the taxes on it.

Poole had made payments under the invalid oral contract of sale. The estate of the deceased is not entitled to retain these payments, and Poole is entitled to have judgment for this amount, but the estate is entitled to retain the land.

In some states, if the subject matter of the contract is real property, a legal description must be given; however, in other states, it is sufficient if the description of the property is given as a specific street address. As seen from the above case, in Georgia, a street address is not sufficient. The land must be identified with reasonable definiteness by describing the particular tract by legal description or by reference to a plat of survey.

Consideration and Other Material Terms

Obviously a material term which is essential to satisfy the Statute of Frauds is the price to be paid or the consideration exchanged by the parties. Therefore, the amount and terms of payment should be clearly stated in the contract.

Any and all other material terms must be set out in the writing. A material term is any important term which goes to the heart of the contract and without which the contract would not have been entered into by the parties.

The items which are considered material terms vary from contract to contract. Therefore, there is no specific formula for determining what additional items must be included in any given contract. Each party must understand the substance of the contract, and the writing must set out all terms that caused either party to be induced to enter into the contract. Terms such as the delivery date of goods, warranties given with regard to goods, and the size or color of a product may all be considered material terms. Ultimately, whether this requirement has been fulfilled - that all material terms be set out in writing – will be determined on a case by case basis.

Signature

If a contract is to satisfy the Statute of Frauds, the party against whom enforcement of the contract is being sought must have signed the writing. While it is not necessary that the writing contain the signatures of both or all parties to the agreement, it must contain a signature, or other indication of assent such as initials, of the party to be charged. If such a writing contains only the signature of one party, then that party is the only one against whom a court of competent jurisdiction can enforce the contract. The contract cannot be enforced against a party who did not sign it.

The signature requriement does not mean that the party must sign his or her full legal name. A party's initials can constitute a signature that is sufficient as can a party's mark. In the days when large segments of the population were illiterate, a party's mark was commonly an "X" made by a party who was illiterate, indicating his assent to a contract. Today, a typewritten name or electronic signature is sufficient to satisfy the Statute of Frauds and is often used when the parties exchange documents electronically.

One must always bear in mind that the Statute of Frauds is concerned only with the enforceability of a contract, and not with the validity of the contract terms. Enforceability concerns only whether the contract can be given force in a court of law.

5.6 *Circumventing the Statute of Frauds*

With every rule, there are exceptions. Occasionally, a situation may arise in which a court may not require a contract that falls under the Statute of Frauds to be in writing in order to give an injured party some relief. Exercising its equitable powers, a court may enforce such a contract without a complete written document.

Equitable remedies are designed to prevent unfairness and unjust enrichment. In equity, the court may fashion a remedy as it sees fit under the particular circumstances of the case before it. The purpose of allowing these exceptions is to prevent fraud or unfairness. One will not be allowed to hide behind the rules of the Statute of Frauds when his own actions indicate some type of bad faith. Likewise, the court may enforce such a contract when to refuse to do so would result in fundamental unfairness.

Part Performance

Even if the Statute of Frauds does apply and the writing requirement is not met, the court may still give the aggrieved party who is not at fault a remedy to prevent injustice. If a party has begun to perform on an oral contract that should be in writing, that party, by this *part performance*, may have preserved his or her right to enforce the terms of the contract. In such cases, reliance on the agreement may be a way to circumvent the lack of a writing as required by the Statute of Frauds.

Recall that it is not illegal, or even a bad thing, to perform on a promise even when that promise does not conform to the Statute of Frauds. The Statute of Frauds relates solely to enforceability of the contract, not to its validity. Thus, a contract which should be in writing, but which is, instead, oral may be perfectly valid. That contract would simply be unenforceable in a court should one party decide not to abide by his promise, but nothing prevents the parties from honoring their agreement.

OCGA § 13-5-31

The provisions of Code Section 13-5-30 do not extend to the following cases:

(1) When the contract has been fully executed;
(2) Where there has been performance on one side, accepted by the other in accordance with the contract;
(3) Where there has been such part performance of the contract as would render it a fraud of the refusing to comply if the court did not compel a performance.

Note that, in order for the doctrine of part performance apply, the part performance must be substantial and essential to the contract.

Sutton v. Warner
California Court of Appeals
12 Cal.App.4th 415, 15 Cal.Rptr.2d 632 (1993)

<u>Facts</u>: In 1983, Arlene and Donald Warner inherited a one-third interest in a home at 101 Molimo Street in San Francisco. The Warners bought out the other heirs and obtained a $170,000 loan on the property. Donald Warner and Kenneth Sutton were friends. In January, 1984, Donald Warner proposed that Sutton and his wife purchase the residence. His proposal included a $15,000 down payment towards a purchase price of $185,000. The Suttons were to pay all mortgage payments and real estate taxes on the property for five years, and, at any time during this five-year period, they could purchase the house. All of this was agreed to orally.

The Suttons paid the down payment and for four-and-one-half years paid cash payments equal to the monthly mortgage payments of $1,881 to the Warners. They paid the annual property taxes on the house. The Suttons also made improvements to the property. In July 1988, the Warners reneged on the sales/option agreement. At that time, the value of the house had risen to between $250,000 and $320,000. The Suttons sued for specific performance of the sales agreement. The Warners defended, alleging the oral promise to sell real estate had to be in writing under the Statute of Frauds and was, therefore, unenforceable.

<u>Issue</u>: Does the equitable doctrine of part performance take this oral contract for the sale of real property out of the Statute of Frauds?

<u>Holding</u>: Normally, a contract to purchase real property must be in writing to satisfy the Statute of Frauds. However, the part performance by the Suttons - making the down payment, paying the monthly mortgage payments and annual property taxes, and making improvements to the property - sufficed to remove the bar of the Statute of Frauds. Therefore, the specific performance of the oral contract to sell real estate is equitable.

Promissory Estoppel

Another possible manner in which the Statute of Frauds might be circumvented is by use of the doctrine of *promissory estoppel*. A court may apply this doctrine when one party to a contract has relied, to his detriment, on another's promise to do something and has changed his position in reliance on that promise. The actions taken by the promisee must unquestionably relate to the oral promise. There can be no other reason the promisee might have taken his actions.

If the reliance is substantial and detrimental to the innocent party, the court may use the doctrine of promissory estoppel to prevent the unjust enrichment of one of the parties. Of course, if the promise was not relied upon by the innocent party, then the innocent party has not been harmed and the court will not enforce the agreement.

This is a "but for" test: but for the existence of the oral agreement, the promisee would not have taken the action he took. The actions themselves explain the existence of the agreement, and, therefore, the court can consider this a reliable means of proving the existence of the contract. This is the reason for creating the Statute of Frauds in the first place – to ensure honesty on the part of the parties to the contract.

To circumvent the Statute of Frauds using this theory, the party seeking enforcement must establish the following:

(a) that a promise was made;
(b) that the promisor should have reasonably expected the promise to induce action or forebearance on the part of the promisee;
(c) that the promise did, in fact, induce such action or forebearance; and
(d) that injustice can be avoided only by enforcement of the promise nothwithstanding the Statute of Frauds.

Hemispherx Biopharma, Inc., v. Mid-South Capital, Inc.
690 F.3d 1216 (2012)
Unites States Court of Appeals for the Eleventh Circuit

Facts: Hemispherx is a medical research company. In August 2008, Hemispherx needed to raise between capital. To that end, Hemispherx's chief executive officer met with officials from Mid-South who had raised capital for Hemispherx in the past. The next month, Hemispherx asked for and received Mid-South's standard Engagement Letter. The Engagement Letter discounted Mid-South's usual brokerage fee because Hemispherx was a previous customer. The Engagement Letter additionally provided that Mid-South would act as Hemispherx's broker on a non-exclusive basis and that either party could terminate the agreement with thirty days' written notice to the other party. But even after the agreement terminated, Hemispherx would be obligated to pay Mid-South a commission for another two years on any transactions involving investors Mid-South had identified or introduced to Hemispherx during the term of the agreement. Although Hemispherx had requested the Engagement Letter, no one ever signed the Letter on Hemispherx's behalf. Once Hemispherx received the Mid-South Engagement Letter, however, the CEO authorized Mid-South to begin seeking investors for Hemispherx.

On May 8, 2009, Mid-South notified Hemispherx of offers from two investors to buy several million dollars worth of Hemispherix stock. Unbeknownst to Mid-South, however, Hemispherx was negotiating to retain another broker, and, on Sunday, May 10, Hemispherx signed an engagement letter with that broker making him its exclusive investment broker for thirty days. The new broker closed a sale of Hemispherx stock to the two investors Mid-South had proposed, one closing the next day, May 11, and the second, the following week.

When litigation ensued over Mid-South's commission fees, Hemispherx asserted that statute of frauds prevented Mid-South from enforcing the unsigned Engagement Letter.

Issue: Does the doctrine of promissory estoppel take the contract out of the Statute of Frauds?

Holding: Hemispherx argues that the Statute of Frauds bars Mid-South from enforcing the unsigned agreement against Hemispherx. Georgia's Statute of Frauds requires, in pertinent part, that "any agreement that is not to be performed within one year from [its] making" must be in writing and signed by the party against whom the agreement is to be enforced. This statute applies here because the Engagement Letter, by its terms, could not be performed within one year as it provided for commissions to be paid for two years after the termination of the letter agreement, if the deal involved investors Mid-South had identified or introduced to Hemispherx during the term of the agreement.

Under Georgia law, a party's conduct may bind him to the terms of a contract, even if he does not sign the agreement. Georgia law recognizes an exception to the Statute of Frauds "where there has been performance on one side, accepted by the other in accordance with the contract." Enforcing an unsigned agreement under this exception is premised on estoppel principles.

The circumstances presented here fall within this exception to the Statute of Frauds. After requesting and receiving the Engagement Letter, Hemispherx formally authorized Mid-South to begin seeking such investors. After sending Hemispherx the Engagement Letter and after Hemispherx authorized it to do so, Mid-South undertook efforts to identify potential investors for Hemispherx, present investment proposals to Hemispherx, and facilitate negotiations between the potential investors and Hemispherx. These allegations establish that Mid-South performed according to the terms of the Engagement Letter, and that Hemispherx accepted that performance, sufficient to invoke the doctrine of promissory estoppel.

Mid-South was relying on promises made primarily by Hemispherx's CEO. Additionally, the parties had an established a course of dealing with one another from their prior relationship. Given these facts, Mid-South reasonably relied on Hemispherx's promise to pay Mid-South a commission according to the terms of the unsigned Engagement Letter.

Review Questions and Exercises

1. When does a contract become executed?

2. What conditions must exist in order for there to be an enforceable implied-in-fact contract?

3. What is the difference between a contract that is void and one that is voidable?

4. What is the consideration for the promise in a unilateral contract?

5. Discuss whether the purchase of a bag of chips from a convenience store is a contract? If so, what type of contract is created by this transaction?

6. Explain the purpose behind the Statute of Frauds.

7. Identify which of the following contracts fall within the Statute of Frauds and specify which provision of the Statute controls:
   a) Premier Productions enters into a contract with Rock Band X to perform at a concert which is to take place on a specified date fourteen months after the date of the contract.
   b) Jack promises to marry Jill.
   c) Sam offers to sell his crop of apples to Pete's Produce for $800.
   d) Sam offers to sell his farm to Joe for $400 because he's sick of the all the work it takes and just wants to get rid of it.
   e) Joe offers to employ Rita for life on his new farm.
   f) The executor of Mr. Clark's estate promises the funeral home that the estate will pay the burial expenses.
   g) The executor of Mr. Clark's estate promises the funeral home that he, Mr. Clark, will pay the burial expenses from his own funds.

8. Give three examples of circumstances in which a valid contract would be unenforceable in a court of law.

9. Mr. Green agrees to sell his house at 123 Main Street to Mr. Brown for $150,000. They prepare a writing which reads, "I, A.B. Green, agree to sell my house to E.F. Brown." The paper is signed by Mr. Green. Is this an enforceable contract? Why or why not?

10. Explain the doctrine of part performance. Under what circumstances might this doctrine be invoked? What must a party seeking to enforce an agreement using this doctrine show to the court?

Practical Applications

1. Dr. Roberts, a dentist, hired Vera Sawyer as a dental hygienist. Sawyer prepared a written contract of employment for a three-year term. Both Roberts and Sawyer executed the agreement. The contract provided the terms of Sawyer's remuneration and that her work hours consisted of a "40 hours work week Monday thru Friday." The contract was silent as to the nature of the services to be rendered or the place of employment.

When Dr. Roberts terminated Sawyer's employment four months later, she filed suit.

Consider:
(a) Was the agreement one which the Statute of Frauds required to be in writing in order to be enforceable?
(b) Did the terms of the writing satisfy all of the requirements of the Statute of Frauds? If not, what necessary terms were missing?

See – *Sawyer v. Roberts,* Georgia Court of Appeals, 208 Ga.App. 870, 432 S.E.2d 610 (1993).

2. When DeKalb County's stormwater drainage system caused damage to their property, several property owners sued. The parties attempted to resolve the case through alternative dispute resolution. During this process the county submitted a concept plan to correct drainage issues and make repairs to the damaged property. An offer of settlement was made by the county. After a series of emails was exchanged between the attorney for the county and the attorney for the property owners, an agreement appeared to have been reached although there remained some reference to the property owners' desire for "adjustments" to the concept plan. The county attorney sought clarification. The property owners' attorney's last email stated that conditions contained in an earlier email were not part of the settlement agreement or were covered by the concept plan and confirmed that the owners were willing to accept the offer of damages and implementation of the concept plan.

DeKalb County began attempts to formalize a written settlement agreement, but the property owners' attorney refused, commenting that the concept plan final design did not incorporate his prior recommendations. DeKalb County filed a motion to enforce the agreement.

Consider:
(a) Were all essential terms addressed by the emails?
(b) Was there a writing sufficient to satisfy the Statute of Frauds?

See – Johnson et al. v. DeKalb County et al., Georgia Court of Appeals, 314 Ga.App. 790, 726 S.E.2d 102 (2012).

Chapter 6 Proper Form of a Contract

OUTLINE

Contracts contain two separate types of paragraphs, known as clauses. These clauses are referred to as covenants and conditions, and it is important to understand the differences between the two in order to properly interpret a contract. Additionally, rules of construction have been developed by the courts to assist them in interpreting and enforcing contracts.

When preparing to draft a contract, it is necessary to understand how the court will interpret the clauses as well what kinds of evidence the court will consider to prove them.

6.1 Covenants

Every contract contains provisions known as *covenants.* A *covenant* is defined as an unconditional, absolute promise to perform. It is the contractual promise to which no conditions are attached. In most contracts, the promises of the parties to perform their contractual obligations are not expressly conditioned or qualified in any way. Instead, they are absolute and must be performed. In such cases, if one of the parties, who has promised the performance of an act, fails to keep his promise and perform the promised act, that party will be in breach of the contract.

A covenant is the consideration that the party gives in order to induce the other side's promise. It is the price to be paid or the item to be purchased. Thus, it is the basis of the contractual agreement. If a person fails to perform on his covenant, the contract is breached, and the breaching party can then be sued. Furthermore, the other party (the non-breaching party) is relieved of all other performance promised under the contract.

Example 6a:

Kelly agrees to work as a paralegal for Jones & Jones, P.C. The agreed upon salary is $400 per week payable every two weeks. After two weeks, Kelly expects a paycheck. When the firm's managing partner says the firm cannot afford to pay her, the firm has breached the contract. Kelly is no longer obligated to work for the firm and can sue for back wages. In this contract, Kelly's covenant is to perform paralegal services and the firm's covenant is to pay Kelly's salary of $400 per week.

6.2 *Conditions*

The covenant is the basis of the contractual agreement. It is not, by itself, enough. As incident to every contractual covenant, the parties must also come to some agreement with respect to when the promises are to be performed. This timing element for performance of the covenant is known as a *condition*. In other words, a condition is a fact or an event, the happening or non-happening of which, creates or extinguishes an absolute promise to perform. More simply put, the covenant is *what* must be performed and the condition indicates *when* it must be performed. A condition, therefore, qualifies the contractual obligation, and acts as a trigger to the promises between the parties.

The Restatement (Second) of Contracts defines a condition as "an event, not certain to occur, which must occur, unless its non-occurrence is excused, before performance under a contract becomes due."

Conditions fall into two types. They can be categorized by *when* they create (or extinguish) a duty to perform under the contract. These include conditions precedent, conditions subsequent, and concurrent conditions. Conditions can also be categorized by *how* they were formed; that is, by how the parties arrived at them. Express conditions, implied-in-fact conditions, and implied-in-law conditions fall into this category.

Conditions Precedent

A *condition precedent* is a condition that qualifies the contractual obligation before it comes into existence. It is a condition that must occur *before* one party has an obligation to perform under a contract. Thus, the condition must be fulfilled before the contractual obligation actually comes into existence. A condition precedent is created by the use of words and phrases such as *when, if, before, after, on condition that, subject to, provided that*, and *so long as*. When words such as these are used in a contract, the contingency they provide for must be performed before the contractual obligation comes into existence. If the condition does not occur, then the parties have no obligation to perform any further actions contemplated by the contract.

Below is an example of an extremely common condition precedent often found in real estate contracts.

Example 6b:

Sasha contracts with Maria to purchase Maria's house for $250,000. Sasha inserts a clause in the contract which conditions the sale on her ability to obtain, within thirty days, financing of 80% of the contract price at an interest rate not exceeding 6%. This is a condition precedent. Should Sasha be unable to obtain the financing, she is not obligated to purchase the house. The financing is an external event that gives rise to her enforceable promise to purchase.

Yi v. Li
313 Ga.App. 273, 721 S.E.2d 144 (2011)
Court of Appeals of Georgia

Facts: Yi operated a Bruster's ice cream store that Li was interested in acquiring. Li submitted an application to Bruster's for the right to operate a franchise store and met multiple times with Bruster's vice president of sales. At a meeting on May 26, 2007, Li signed a franchise agreement although it was not signed by Bruster's.

Yi and Li entered into a purchase agreement for the sale of the ice cream store. The agreement provided that the closing of the deal was conditioned upon obtaining the Franchisor's (Bruster's) Consent; that the purchaser was responsible for obtaining that consent; and that the agreement could be terminated prior to the closing date by either party if the Franchisor's Consent could not be obtained.

Li knew that as of June 13, 2007, Bruster's had not yet consented to the transfer of the franchise. Nevertheless, on that date he executed the Agreement and paid the Seller $230,000 even though the closing was not scheduled until July 31. The very next day, June 14, 2007, Li took possession of the ice cream store and its operation. Bruster's never consented to the parties' proposed transfer of the Seller's franchise. On August 7, 2007, Bruster's memorialized in writing that it was withholding its consent of the transfer. In a letter dated September 13, 2007, Li formally notified the Seller that he, Li, was rescinding the Purchase Agreement and demanded that the Seller return all monies paid and take back possession of the ice cream store.

Issue: Could Li rescind the contract based on the failure of the condition precedent?

Holding: To justify rescission, there must be a material nonperformance or breach by the opposing party that is so substantial and fundamental as to defeat the object of the contract.

A condition precedent must be performed before the contract becomes absolute and obligatory upon the other party. The obtaining of Bruster's consent was a condition precedent and the failure to satisfy the condition precedent would have excused the parties' obligations and performance under the Purchase Agreement.

The Purchaser was the one who pursued and coordinated his efforts to obtain the required consent with Bruster's. Consequently, the failure to satisfy the condition did not constitute a breach by the Seller. Moreover, there is no evidence that the Seller did anything wrong or otherwise caused a breach of the Purchase Agreement provisions. Thus, while failure of the condition would have excused performance, it cannot be the basis for rescission of the contract after the fact.

Conditions Subsequent

A *condition subsequent* is a condition that triggers the contractual obligation after the contract comes into existence and relates to the performance of future contractual obligations. A condition subsequent usually acts to *extinguish* a previous absolute duty to perform. In other words, a condition subsequent is an act or event that could occur after the parties have agreed to a contract and which, if it occurs, will then trigger some obligation or relieve one of the parties from a duty.

This type of condition is not as common as conditions precedent, but is often found in insurance policies. For instance, most automobile insurance policies contain a provision which requires that the insured person notify the company within a specified number of days after an accident or loss. If the insured fails to give the insurance company the notice required by the policy, the company is relieved of its obligation to pay the claim. The failure of the insured to provide the company with the required notice acts to extinguish the insurance company's absolute duty to perform by paying claims pursuant to the policy.

Example 6c:

Dorothy and Walter were previously married but are now divorced. As part of the divorce settlement agreement (the contract entered into by the parties and approved by the court), Walter agreed to pay Dorothy alimony payments of $500 per month until such time Dorothy dies or remarries. Dorothy's potential remarriage is a condition subsequent – it may or may not occur, but if it does Walter will be relieved of his obligation. When Dorothy remarries two years after the divorce, Walter's obligation to make the monthly alimony payments is extinguished and he is relieved of his absolute duty to perform that term of the contract.

Conditions Concurrent

A *concurrent condition* is the most common form of condition and is found in most bilateral contracts. A condition concurrent occurs when the mutual performances of the parties are capable of *simultaneous* execution, and the parties expect the promise and the performance to occur at the same time. In other words, each party will perform his or her obligation under the contract and receive the consideration promised to him at the same time.

Example 6d:

Olivia agrees to sell, and Martin agrees to buy, Olivia's used textbook for $25. When Olivia gives the book to Martin, she expects to receive the money, and when Martin gives the money, he expects to receive the book. This is a condition concurrent.

Express Conditions

Thus far, we have been discussing categories of conditions that explain *when* they create or extinguish the duty to perform the covenant. Recall that conditions can also be categorized according to *how* the parties arrived at the condition. Here we are considering the manner in which the condition was created.

An *express* condition is a condition that has been specifically manifested in so many words by the parties themselves. It is one that is specifically stated in a contract. The parties have, by the words in their writing or by their oral expressions in a verbal contract, expressly set out the condition.

Example 6e:

Eli has a used car for sale. Joe examines the car and agrees to buy it for $3,500 provided that Eli has the broken rear-view mirror replaced first. Eli agrees. This is an example of an express condition, something specifically agreed to by the parties. It is also a condition precedent because Joe has no obligation to perform on his promise to buy the car until and unless Eli has the broken mirror repaired.

Implied-in-Fact Conditions

An *implied-in-fact condition* is what the parties would, in good faith, expect from each other. An implied-in-fact condition is not set out in specific words; rather, it is what the parties could reasonably expect under the circumstances. An implied-in-fact condition is inferred or presumed under the law. The parties would reasonably understand that the implied condition exists even though it, unlike an express condition, is not specifically stated in their contract. No words are used at all in the contract because none are necessary.

Example 6f:

When Joe agrees to buy Eli's used car, he conditions his offer upon the repair of the mirror. This is the express condition. Although he did not specifically state it, another condition is also implied in the transaction – it is reasonable that Joe would assume Eli has a transferable title to the car. If Eli does not, there is no contractual obligation on Joe's part to go through with the purchase of the car.

Implied-in-Law Conditions

An *implied-in-law condition*, also known as a *constructive condition,* is a condition that the law imposes in the interest of fairness. This category of conditions arises in situations where the parties have not specifically agreed to any definite timing element. A court will imply a condition, even though neither of the parties expressly agreed to it and it is not implied-in-fact, because the existence of the condition is implied in the parties' respective duties under the contract. The purpose of these implied-in-law conditions is to give each party to the agreement the same amount of time in which to perform. They are designed to impose an element of fairness with respect to the timing of the performances.

There are three general rules with respect to constructive conditions:

- When one party's performance requires time to complete, the other side may take the same amount of time.
- When a date is set for one party's performance, the other party is expected to perform on that same date.
- When the performances can be simultaneous, they will be simultaneous.

It is important to remember that the parties are free to establish any particular conditions they wish. However, if none have been expressed by the parties themselves and none are implied in fact, the law will give each side an equivalent amount of time to perform his or her obligations under a contract.

6.3 *Rules of Construction*

Generally speaking, the role of the courts is to uphold contracts, not to undo them. While courts do not want to rewrite contracts, in some cases the courts have no choice but to try to interpret what was really meant by the parties' agreement. To this end, the courts have fashioned several principles to assist them in interpreting and enforcing contract provisions. When drafting a contract, it is important to understand not just how the contract will be read and understood by the parties, but also how it might be interpreted by the court.

Rules of construction are the guidelines the courts use to interpret all contractual provisions. These are sometimes referred to as *rules of interpretation* for the obvious reason. The rules of construction are designed to allow the court, where possible, to uphold a contract as valid. The rules are also designed to help the courts arrive at a proper interpretation of the presumptive intent of the contracting parties.

Of course, the guiding principle of contract law is certainty. Contracts are interpreted, generally speaking, according to the same set of rules in order to avoid inconsistent application of the law.

The rules of construction are arranged hierachically. The hierarchy is based on the idea that, in the event of a dispute, the most certain evidence of the parties original agreement is considered first and the least reliable is considered last.

Some of the most common rules of construction are:

(1) Interpret a contract within its own pages;
(2) Give common words their plain meanings;
(3) Give technical words their technical meanings;
(4) Examine the contract as a whole;
(5) Negotiated provisions control over standardized ones;
(6) Consider the parties' course of dealing and business custom and trade usage; and
(7) Construe terms more strictly against the drafter.

OCGA § 13-2-2

The following rules, among others, shall be used in arriving at the true interpretation of contracts:

(1) Parol evidence is inadmissible to add to, take from, or vary a written contract. All the attendant and surrounding circumstances may be proved and, if there is an ambiguity, latent or patent, it may be explained; so, if only a part of a contract is reduced to writing (such as a note given in pursuance of a contract) and it is manifest that the writing was not intended to speak the whole contract, then parol evidence is admissible;
(2) Words generally bear their usual and common signification; but technical words, words of art, or words used in a particular trade or business will be construed, generally, to be used in reference to this peculiar meaning. The local usage or understanding of a word may be proved in order to arrive at the meaning intended by the parties;
(3) The custom of any business or trade shall be binding only when it is of such universal practice as to justify the conclusion that it became, by implication, a part of the contract, except in regard to those transactions covered by Title 11;
(4) The construction which will uphold a contract in whole and in every part is to be preferred, and the whole contract should be looked to in arriving at the construction of any part;
(5) If the construction is doubtful, that which goes most strongly against the party executing the instrument or undertaking the obligation is generally to be preferred;
(6) The rules of grammatical construction usually govern, but to effectuate the intention they may be disregarded; sentences and words may be transposed, and conjunctions substituted for each other. In extreme cases of ambiguity, where the instrument as it stands is without meaning, words may be supplied;
(7) When a contract is party printed and partly written, the latter part is entitled to most consideration;
(8) Estate and grants by implication are not favored;
(9) Time is not generally of the essence in a contract; but, by express stipulation or reasonable construction, it may become so.

Four Corners Doctrine

The most certain measure of the parties' intention is the written language of the contract. The principle rule of construction, sometimes called the *strict construction doctrine*, states that a contract should be interpreted within its own pages. When the intention of the parties is apparent from the words within the "four corners of the document," there is no need for judicial interpretation – the contract speaks for itself. Under the *four corners doctrine*, the court assumes that the words written within the four corners of the pages of the contract document are those that the parties chose, and chose for a reason, at the time of they entered into the contract.

> OCGA § 13-2-3
>
> The cardinal rule of construction is to ascertain the intention of the parties. If that intention is clear and it contravenes no rule of law and sufficient words are used to arrive at the intention, it shall be enforced irrespective of all technical or arbitrary rules of construction.

The court, with few exceptions, will enforce the contract by its own terms. This reflects the court's intention of enforcing the contract as the two parties intended when they created it, not after some time and difficulties have come to pass. Of course, there are problems with this kind of enforcement – it assumes that the contracting parties used precise language and that both parties subjectively understood the language in the same way.

McCollum v. O'Dell
241 Ga.App. 6, 525 S.E.2d 721 (1999)
Georgia Court of Appeals

Facts: O'Dell and Antonelli formed a partnership for the purpose of opening a restaurant. Although the two men intended to incorporate the restaurant, the paperwork was never completed. In December 1995, Antonelli and O'Dell executed what purports to be a contract with McCollum. The handwritten document, which was prepared by Antonelli in collaboration with McCollum, stated:

This agreement between Glenn McCollum and Antonelli's Restaurant Inc. is borrowing [sic] the sum of twenty five thousand dollars from Glenn McCollum.

Payment agreement between parties is monthly payment of 650.00 per month starting with the first payment due Jan. 1, 1996 for the total payments of 48 months for total amount of thirty one thousand and two hundred dollars.

Antonelli's Inc is giving a 6 month option for Glenn McCollum to come in as a full partner starting date Jan. 1, 1996 expiring July 1, 1996 for the total sum fee of one hundred and twenty five thousand dollars paid into Antonelli's corp. as Glenn McCollum options if during 6 month grace period expires Glenn McCollum has the option to refuse partnership and Antonelli will continue to make payments to 48 month contract.

Glenn McCollum [signature]
Bob O'Dell [signature]
Basile Antonelli [signature]

On the bottom right of the document was a corporate seal for Antonelli's, Inc.

The restaurant failed and McCollum was not repaid.

Issue: Does McCollum have an enforceable contract against O'Dell or against any other?

Holding: This case presents a perfect example of what happens when lay persons exercise their right to draft a legal document. An issue of contract construction is at the outset a question of law for the court. The first step is to look to the four corners of the instrument to determine the meaning of the agreement from the language employed. If the contract language is ambiguous, however, then the court must apply the applicable rules of construction. The cardinal rule of contract construction is to ascertain the intention of the parties. If, after applying the rules of construction, the language remains ambiguous, then the finder of fact must resolve the ambiguity. Here, the inexpertly drafted contract is ambiguous in at least two respects. First, the contract is ambiguous regarding the nature of the business entity. Although the contract refers to the entity as "Antonelli's Restaurant Inc.," "Antonelli's Inc.," and

"Antonelli's corp.," the contract also contains a clause granting McCollum an option to become a "full partner" and refers to the business as a "partnership."

Because the nature of the business entity is ambiguous, we turn to the rules of contract construction and attempt to ascertain the intention of the parties by reading the contract as a whole. But the contract in this case is so poorly worded that the rules of construction are not helpful in ascertaining the intent of the parties. Thus, we must look to parol evidence. According to O'Dell's uncontradicted testimony, the business was a partnership rather than a corporation when the contract was signed.

Equally ambiguous is to whom the loan was made. The first sentence of the purported contract states that the agreement is "between Glenn McCollum and Antonelli's Restaurant Inc.," which indicates that the loan was to a business. But the contract subsequently provides that, if McCollum does not exercise his option to join the business, "Antonelli will continue to make payments." This sentence may be read to mean that the loan was to Antonelli, individually, rather than to the business.

At trial, the parties offered widely differing accounts as to who was intended to be liable for repayment of the loan. If, as Antonelli and McCollum testified, the loan was a business loan, then O'Dell would be liable because the business was a partnership and "all partners are jointly and severally liable for all debts, obligations, and liabilities of the partnership." But if, as O'Dell testified, the parties intended that the loan was to Antonelli individually, then O'Dell would not be liable for repayment.

In its order, the trial court made no specific factual findings regarding the intent of the parties. Accordingly, the judgment of the trial court is reversed. On remand, the trial court, as the factfinder, must address whether the parties intended that the loan be made to the business or to Antonelli individually.

Plain Meaning

Words in a contract are to be construed according to their ordinary, or *plain,* meanings. Unless the parties stipulate otherwise, the words used in an offer or in a completed contract are given their generally accepted meaning or ordinary dictionary interpretation. That is, courts enforce terms as they are understood objectively by the majority of parties in similar circumstances.

The parties are always free to define any words as they wish in the contract itself, and the parties' specific definition, should they give one, will prevail. Thus, in drafting a contract, it is essential to define specifically any words to which the parties want to give a specialized meaning or that may create definitional problems at a later time; otherwise, that meaning might be lost in enforcement.

Hellenic Investment, Inc., and Pasadena Associates v. The Kroger Company
766 S.W.2d 861 (1989)
Texas Court of Appeals

<u>*Facts:*</u> Pasadena Associates owned a shopping center and leased space to Kroger for a grocery store. Under the terms of the lease, Pasadena agreed that it would not lease any other premises in the shopping center for use as a "bar," "night club" or "other business of like nature." Pasadena later leased space to Hellenic which opened an establishment called "Hallabaloo" after investing $150,000 in renovating the premises. Under the terms of Hellenic's lease, it was allowed to use the premises for a

"restaurant" or "dining facility… with the sale of alcoholic beverages, dancing, games and related facilities and activities."

Hellenic acknowledged that Kroger was the major anchor in the shopping center and that Kroger's lease prohibited Pasadena from leasing center premises to a "night club." Hellenic also warranted that it was not a "night club."

Hallabaloo was a great success, immediately attracting large crowds. As a result, the shopping center parking lot was often congested and Kroger customers sometimes could not find parking. Kroger complained of inordinate amounts of trash in the lot and of loud and boisterous crowds of undesirable persons in the lot when many of Kroger's customers were using its store.

Kroger sought and obtained a temporary injunction against Hellenic and Pasadena Associates which enjoined the continued operation of Hallabaloo as a "bar," "night club" or "other business of like nature." The trial court, after a bench trial, issued a permanent injunction, defining the term "night club" as an operation selling "alcoholic beverages while also, in combination, playing loud volume dance music, providing a space for dancing and allowing its patrons to dance, so long as its gross food sales make up less than 70% of its gross sales from all sources."

Issue: Was Hellenic operating a "night club" as that term was used in the lease provisions?

Holding: Each party presented the testimony of experts as to what constituted a "night club," and it is upon this definition that the case turns. The parties did not include any definition of this term in their contract, and under the law, evidence is permitted to explain ambiguous terms to ascertain the intent of the parties. Expert testimony indicated that the sale of alcoholic beverages, the use of strobe lights and special effects, and the loud dance music were indicia of a "night club." The Court noted that there is a "fine line" between operating a restaurant, which is permissible under the terms of the lease, and operating a "night club," which is not permitted by the lease. Based upon the expert testimony and the explanation of what the term "night club" meant, the court of appeals agreed that the lower court could have properly found that Hellenic was operating a night club facility as the term was used in Hellenic's lease.

The appellate court reversed the trial court, finding that the injunction could not be enforced as written since the court's decree made Hellenic's food/alcoholic beverage sales ratio the controlling factor in determining whether Hellenic was operating a "night club." The court remanded the case for further proceedings.

If technical words are used in the contract, they are construed in their technical sense. A term used in a specific industry may have a very specific meaning that differs from the usual or plain meaning of the term. In such cases, a court may look to an expert to interpret the technical words used and the meaning of such words in that specific industry.

Writing Viewed as a Whole

Lengthy communications are viewed as a whole and any inconsistent words are discarded. The courts will try to ascertain the intentions or purpose of the parties from the contract as a whole and not from isolated provisions or sections that may not reveal the parties' true meaning. The rule in contracts is to look at the "big picture," and the courts will try to harmonize the terms of the entire contract. Sometimes, however, this is not possible. Many contracts are formed only after lengthy negotiations, and, in the course of those negotiations, the parties may create inconsistent clauses.

Because the prime objective of the court is to salvage the contract, the court will examine the entire agreement. All parts of the contract, including all of the various clauses, paragraphs, sentences and specific words, will be considered in light of the entire document. The court will then discard any provisions that are inconsistent with the document as a whole and with the existence of a valid contract.

The court will attempt to arrive at a consistent interpretation of the contract provisions, and this doctrine of interpretation places a burden on the drafter of the contract. The fallback position of the court is to construe an ambiguous clause as *against the drafter* of the contract. The person who wrote that document was in the best position to avoid the confusion since he chose the wording and presumably knew what was intended. This rule of construction encourages drafting parties to strive for clarity since they will not be able to take advantage of purposeful ambiguities to gain an upper hand in the enforcement of the contract.

Last in Time

Negotiated terms prevail over standardized ones. Many contracts are entered into using standardized, pre-printed forms. Sometimes the parties will negotiate terms that differ from those contained in the pre-printed form. If there is an inconsistency with words that are printed, typed, or handwritten, the handwritten terms prevail over the typed terms, and typed terms prevail over any mechanical printing or printed form terms.

The purpose behind this rule of construction is to ascertain the exact intent of the parties at the moment of the signing of the contract. It is not uncommon to add handwritten notes or changes to a document right before signing to reflect last-minute negotiations or corrections. Handwriting done at the last moment before signing most clearly reflects the intent of the parties at the time the contract was entered into. Typing may also be inserted on a preprinted form to make changes or to insertion a term or clause, and so, again, the later addition to the printed form indicates the parties' intent close to the moment of contracting.

Example 6g:

Pine Valley Apartments uses a standardized lease which provides that 30 days notice will be given of a leasee's intent to vacate the premises. If the landlord and tenant negotiate and ultimately change this provision by striking through "30 days" and inserting the handwritten phrase "20 days," the negotiated provision will prevail over the standardized form.

These "last in time" terms are "first in right." This means that since the typed or handwritten terms were agreed to closest to the time of the execution of the contract, they will be enforced over any other inconsistent clauses in the printed contract form.

Course of Dealing and Business Custom and Usage

Special rules apply to dealings between *merchants* – persons or businesses who hold themselves out as having expertise peculiar to the goods in which they deal. The actions of parties who have dealt with one another in the past can play a part in contract interpretation as can the general customs in a particular community or trade. When interpreting contracts entered into between merchants, the courts can look to industry standards or customs to help determine the parties' intent. They can also examine any patterns or prior relationships between the parties to determine their intent.

Often the parties will have established a *course of dealing* with one another. A course of dealing is the private conduct or individualized method of transacting business with one another that the parties have established by their prior contracts and interactions.

Example 6h:

James and Melanie have dealt with one another for several years and have always conducted business by email. They make offers via email and communicate acceptances the same way. One day, James emails Melanie and offers to sell 100 units for $20 each. James waits two days and, when he has received no response, he sells the units to another buyer. Melanie, however, has accepted the offer by U.S. mail, but her acceptance does not reach James until three days later. Melanie sues since she cannot find the needed units at a price as good as that offered by James. The court would look to the parties' course of dealing with one another to establish whether a contract existed.

Where merchants express one intention in words and another in the way they act in carrying out their required performance under the contract, their actions will influence a court's interpretation of the contract more than the actual words or lack thereof. *Course of performance* refers to the pattern of performance the parties have established with regard to the existing contract. In this regard it is different from the course of dealing which focuses on the pattern established by the parties in prior contracts.

Example 6i:

Fred owns a fabric warehouse and Sally has agreed to purchase 20 bolts of silk fabric to be shipped in four batches of five bolts each. The contract calls for payment in cash at the time of delivery of each batch. For the first three shipments, Fred has accepted payment by personal check; however, on the last shipment, he insists on cash despite there having been no problem with negotiating Sally's previous checks. This is contrary to his prior course of performance on the contract.

6.4 *The Parol Evidence Rule*

Parol evidence is oral or verbal testimony offered as proof regarding the terms of a written contract. The *parol evidence rule* was created to prevent parties from attempting to change the provisions of a written agreement by offering verbal evidence to dispute the terms of their agreement. The basic rule states that once a contract has been reduced to writing, that writing is the final expression of the parties' agreement. The writing itself prevails and will not be varied, contradicted, or altered by any oral declarations made prior to or contemporaneously with the writing. Oral testimony will not be admitted to vary the terms of a written instrument because it is assumed that the writing will speak for itself. All previous oral agreements merge into the final written contract which will not be modified by parol evidence.

Including a *merger clause* may prevent a challenge to the final contract. A merger clause is a provision in a contract providing that all prior verbal or written agreements have been merged into the written contract and that the written document is the final expression of the parties' agreement. A merger clause creates a presumption that the contract is a totally integrated agreement. The presumption is that if any other terms or conditions were discussed, they were eliminated in preliminary discussions or drafts of the contract and, therefore, did not become a part of the final document. Through the use of a merger clause, the parties can, by their own terms, exclude parol evidence.

Windham & Windham, Inc., v. SunTrust Bank
313 Ga. App. 841, 723 S.E.2d 70 (2012)
Court of Appeals of Georgia

Facts: *Recall this case from the discussion in Chapter 3 of consideration and special agreements. The relevant facts are these:* In 2007, SunTrust Bank extended a line of credit to

Windham and Windham, Inc., and also gave the company a commercial loan. Jeffrey and Robyn Windham, the owners of the company, executed unconditional guarantee agreements with regard to both loans, personally guaranteeing the debts. In 2010, the Bank sued the company and both the Windhams individually, alleging that since July, 2008, the company had failed to make any payments under the note and also had failed to make required payments on the line of credit. The bank asserted that Ms. and Mrs. Windham were liable to it pursuant to the guarantee agreements.

The Windhams claimed they signed the guarantee agreements only as officers of Windham and Windham, Inc., and not in their personal capacities. Additionally, Robyn Windham claimed she had been concerned about personal liability and, specifically, about her home; that she had discussed this matter with a bank officer; and that the bank had assured her she would have no personal liability for the debts of the company.

Issue: Did Robyn Windham's discussion with a SunTrust Bank officer and his assurances regarding her personal liability relieve her of her obligations under the guarantee agreement?

Holding: Parol evidence is inadmissible to add to, take from, or vary a written contract. Here, the guarantee provisions of the line of credit agreement and the unconditional guarantees executed by both the Windhams are unambiguous. They appear on their face to be a complete statement of the agreement between the parties about the obligation of the Windhams to ensure the repayment of the indebtedness that the Windham company owed the Bank. Robyn Windham's parol evidence about an agreement to the contrary is insufficient to vary the terms of the written agreement.

Note that the parol evidence rule applies only to prior or contemporaneous agreements between the parties. Any *subsequent* agreement between the parties is completely outside of the scope of the rule against parol evidence.

While the courts look primarily within the four corners of the contract - at the language contained in the contract itself - to determine the agreement between the parties, there are instances in which the contract cannot speak for itself. Since the written agreement represents the final agreement between the parties, the courts do not want to hear oral explanations of "he said, she said" which actually contradict the terms of the written agreement. In some cases, however, there may be inconsistencies, illogical interpretations, or omissions in the written agreement. In such cases, the court may look to parol evidence to "speak" to the court as to the parties' true intentions and meanings.

Among the exceptions are:

- Evidence to show a failure of consideration - If there is a failure of consideration, the contract provisions are not being questioned. The contract recites what the consideration is, but it cannot, of course, speak to future events such as the failure of consideration. In such a case, oral testimony is permitted to show that the consideration given was not what was promised in the writing

Example 6j:

A written contract indicates that the buyer paid for the object of the sale by check, but parol evidence may be introduced to show that the check was dishonored.

- Evidence to show that the contract was induced by fraud, duress, or mistake – If there is a defect in the formation of the contract, testimony may be required to show that there was no meeting of the minds. Again, the provisions of the contract itself are not being questioned. Oral testimony is permitted to show that one party lacked the requisite intent to enter into the contractual relationship.

Smith v. Jones
154 Ga.App. 629, 269 S.E.2d 471 (1980)
Court of Appeals of Georgia

Facts: Smith, an investor, gave Jones $30,000 to invest in a mall property project. When the developer encountered financial difficulties and the project lost money, Smith filed suit seeking the return of his investment, alleging Jones had repeatedly told him that he would protect and guarantee the investment. Smith alleged that he was assured that leases had been obtained for space in the development that apparently had not been negotiated; that the financing was assured when it was not; and that things looked "real good" for making a real profit while, all the time, the real estate market was becoming increasing tight.

Issue: Is parol evidence of the assurances Smith received admissible in a suit for the return of the investment?

Holding: Given the facts of this case, it is clear that the investors, particularly Smith, were without particular skill, expertise, or experience in real estate development and, accordingly, looked to Jones to successfully invest their money. That this was the intent is manifested by the fact that Jones' consideration for his share of the investment appears to be, at least in some part, based upon his managerial skill. These facts indicate that Jones made misrepresentations as to the development of the property in order to induce Smith to enter into the enterprise in the first place. Where the alleged misrepresentations go to the inducement of the contract rather than a promise to perform under the contract, parol evidence is admissible to shows that the contract was procured by fraud.

- Evidence to prove the existence of a collateral oral agreement – In some cases, the written contract is not being questioned, but the existence of a second, oral contract is being proved so that both contracts may be considered. Recall that the parol evidence rule prohibits the admissibility of evidence of prior or contemporaneous agreements that contradict the terms of the contract. However, occasionally, the parties may enter into a *supplemental* agreement which does not contradict the contract, but deals with additional matters. In such cases, parol evidence may be admissible to explain the supplemental agreement.

Example 6k:

Claire agrees to buy Connie's gold bracelet for $300. After the contract is signed, Connie agrees to sell Claire her gold ring as well for a total price of $425 for both pieces. Oral testimony may be used to show the existence of the second agreement.

- Evidence to explain ambiguities in a written contract – Oral testimony may be used to explain, but not contradict, an ambiguous term in the written agreement.

Example 6l:

A contract provides for the sale of a house owned by Smith and located on Peachtree Street in Atlanta. In fact, there are two houses that could fit the description. Oral testimony may be used to show which house was intended by the parties. Recall, however, that if such a contract were challenged with regard to the sufficiency of the writing under the Statute of Frauds, such a vague description (house on Peachtree Street) would not be sufficient.

Tanner v. Tinsley
152 Ga.App. 330, 262 S.E.2d 602 (1979)
Georgia Court of Appeals

Facts: Tanner and Tinsley entered into an agreement to assume responsibility for payment of a note and share any money collected from a property leasehold venture. The agreement signed by the parties said they would "equally assume the responsibility of a certain note from Hugh and Marilyn H. Tanner to Dan McDougall dated 12-1-69." The agreement continued: "We further agree that we will share equally any money collected from tax escalation or past due rents and/or any responsibility which may arise from the said Northside Drive-Eleventh Street leasehold venture."

Tanner was sued on the notes referred to in the memorandum agreement and a judgment entered against him. Tinsley refused to pay a pro rata share. Tinsley alleged that the document was too vague and indefinite to be enforced as a contract.

Issue: Was the document entered into by the parties an enforceable contract?

Holding: Contracts may be partly oral and partly in writing. There is some "looseness" in the language of the document at issue here, including the identification of the note ("note from Hugh and Marilyn H. Tanner to Dan McDougall dated 12-1-69"), the subject matter ("Northside Drive-Eleventh Street leasehold venture"), and the duties to be performed ("we will share equally any money collected from tax escalation or past due rents, and any responsibility..."). Parol testimony may be admitted to explain ambiguous language, or to show a distinct collateral understanding, although it may not contradict or vary the writing itself. In this case, the language of the parties' agreement is subject to explanation and the surrounding circumstances are subject to explanation. It is elemental that between the parties the efficacy of an instrument is not controlled by irregularities in execution.

- Evidence to show that a condition precedent has not been met – Oral testimony may be used to show that certain events have not occurred which are a prerequisite to performance of the contract terms.

Example 6m:

Recall example 6b: Sasha contracts with Maria to purchase Maria's house for $250,000. Sasha inserts a clause in the contract which conditions the sale on her ability to obtain, within thirty days, financing of 80% of the contract price at an interest rate not exceeding 6%. This is a condition precedent. Parol evidence will be admissible to show that Sasha was unable to obtain the financing – that the condition precedent has not been met.

Note that while we speak of exceptions to the parol evidence rule, the word "exception" is somewhat inaccurate. More correctly stated, there are several instances in which parol evidence may be admitted to assist the court in interpreting a contract. In these cases, the parol evidence or oral testimony is not permitted to vary the written terms, but, rather, it is admitted to show something outside the writing that changes the meaning of the contract or explains what the parties intended by a confusing or ambiguious term.

6.5 *Drafting the Contract*

The ability to draft legal documents, including contracts, is essential to the effectiveness of paralegals. Initially these tasks can seem daunting. That said, it is extremely rare for an attorney or paralegal to draft a contract from scratch. When given a contract to prepare, use as a guide some of the many sources of sample contracts which are readily available. These are discussed below.

Regardless of the resources available, having a basic plan for drafting a contract is essential. Equally important is attention to detail.

Understanding the Client's Wishes

The initial consideration when drafting any contract is knowing what the client wants. Having a thorough understanding of the wishes and expectations of the client will minimize future problems. The drafter should take care to ensure that he or she has a clear understanding of the relationship the client desires to create and the purposes he wants to accomplish with the contract.

The paralegal should take comprehensive notes or have a written memorandum from the supervising attorney detailing the client's needs. Memories fade and comprehensive notes will help ensure a satisfied client.

Forms

Virtually all attorneys and paralegals use models or forms when drafting contracts. Be aware of and make use of some of the great variety of forms and reference materials which are available in both book and electronic form. Almost anyone, attorney or paralegal, setting out to draft a contract would be lost without forms or models to use as a guide.

An excellent beginning point for the paralegal tasked with drafting a contract is to locate models or samples which the supervising attorney, or another attorney in the firm, may have used in the past. These may be drawn from old client files. Many law offices compile form banks containing copies of different documents the firm has used in the past. These form files may be in electronic or hard copy format and are compiled for the express purpose of using these documents as guidelines for future work. Using materials from such files will save valuable time for the drafter. In addition to using the firm's form files, many paralegals have their own form files consisting of copies of documents they have accumulated through their experience.

Many law firms also have *templates* of standard documents. These generic forms usually contain blanks for the insertion of specific information. Filling in the blanks of the template based upon the client's terms may be a good beginning towards creating a specific document for the client.

Form books, either in hard-bound volumes or as electronic versions, are also valuable resources for both the attorney and the paralegal. Very similar to templates, these books contain sample documents containing what are considered to be standard provisions. As with templates, these forms often have blanks which must be filled in with information specific to the client's needs. Virtually all states have form books which reflect state law requirements. The better practice is to consult the state specific form books before going to the general form books since the general forms may not comply with the state's regulations for a specific transaction.

Whether using a template or form book, the paralegal should take care to tailor the language of the form or template to the needs of the firm's client. Forms were never intended to be used without modification but are designed only as a flexible guide. Where possible, look at multiple sample contracts or forms. Doing so allows one to compare and contrast the various clauses and to use wording from various forms to create a document which suits the client's specific needs. Forms should not be copied without careful adaptation to the specific facts and circumstances of the client's needs.

Developing an Outline

Preparing an outline of the contract to be prepared will help ensure all necessary topics are addressed and will minimize unintentional omissions and errors. The outline should begin with the basic necessary elements of all contracts. Thus, the outline should start with:

- Identification of the parties – include the legal names of all parties as well as the type of entity of the party where necessary (corporation, partnership, etc.);
- The subject matter of the contract – indicate consideration and include a description of what each party is giving and receiving;
- Effective date and termination – indicate the effective date of the contract (if it is different from the execution date), the termination date, and include any grounds for terminating the agreement prior to the intended termination date;
- Signatures – the parties' signatures, evidencing their assent to the terms of the contract, must be included.

In addition to the basics, the outline should include provisions specific to the client's particular situation. These might, but will not necessarily, include:

- Title – many contracts have a title other than simply "Contract;"
- Statement of purpose – often a contract will contain a clause which spells out the purpose underlying the parties' agreement;
- Definitions – many industries have their own terminology which may give words meaning different from the common meaning, and care must be taken to ensure that such words are defined within the contract;
- Special provisions such as risk of loss, waivers, assignments, or delegations;
- Security agreement, if any;
- Severability clauses, if any;
- Default provisions, if any.

Clauses

Every contract must contain certain clauses. Other clauses will be included depending upon the nature of the contract and the wishes of the client. Found below are explanations and examples of several commonly used contract clauses.

- Indentification of the Parties – The first clause of a contract identifies the parties and should do so by exact legal names. This clause often also indicates a nomenclature for each of the parties that is then used throughout the remainder of the agreement. This is done for simplicity's sake and may also indicate the roles the parties play in the agreement such as "Buyer" or "Seller."

Example 6n:

This agreement is made this 20th day of August, 2014, between Stuart Hudson Products, LLC, a Georgia limited liability company, hereinafter referred to as "Seller," and John McMasters, a resident of the State of Georgia, hereinafter referred to as "Buyer."

- Description of the Consideration – The consideration clause specifies what each party to the contract is giving and receiving and should address all issues related to the consideration including price, quantity, quality, and time of performance. This clause should also include any conditions the parties wish to attach to their performance.

    - Fully describe the consideration:
        - For money, indicate the exact amount, writing out dollar amounts as well as indicating them numerically to avoid confusion and mistakes;
        - For real property, give a complete legal description in addition to the street address;
        - For personal property, include serial numbers, or, if there are none, describe the items fully and completely;
        - For services, specify the services to be performed.
    - Indicate mutuality of consideration.
    - Indicate the time of performance of the contractual obligations.
    - Specify any conditions or timing elements that attach to the performance.

Example 6o:

In consideration of the sum of Eleven Thousand Five Hundred Dollars ($11,500.00), Seller agrees to sell to Buyer the following: one (1) model year 2011 Kubota L3430 Farm Tractor, serial number B85663X222. Said sum shall be paid in full by cashier's check or other certified funds at the time of delivery of the tractor. Delivery shall take place not later than August 30, 2014.

Example 6p:

In consideration of the sum of Eleven Thousand Five Hundred Dollars ($11,500.00), Seller agrees to sell to Buyer the following: one (1) model year 2011 Kubota L3430 Farm Tractor, serial number B85663X222. Buyer hereby agrees to pay to Seller the sum of Two Thousand Five Hundred Dollars ($2,500.00) upon delivery of the said tractor and not later than August 30, 2014, and thereafter to pay to Seller the sum of One Thousand Dollars ($1,000.00) on the first day of each consecutive month beginning October 1, 2014, until the full purchase price is paid. All payments shall be made by cashier's check or other certified funds. In the event of failure by the Buyer to make any installment payment as it becomes due, then the full outstanding balance shall immediately become due and payable.

- Security Agreement – If the parties desire to create a security interest in some property in the case of default, the contract should specify that a secured interest is being created.

Example 6q:

Buyer hereby grants to Seller a security interest in the said model year 2011 Kubota L3430 Farm Tractor, serial number B85663X222.

- Warranties – Recall that, if the contract is one for the sale of goods, certain implied warranties exist regardless of what the contract specifically says with regard to them. In addition, the parties may create express warranties if they intend that there be specific guarantees with respect to the goods.

Example 6r:

Seller hereby warrants that the said tractor is in good and merchantable condition and is free and clear of all liens, security interests and encumbrances. Seller further warrants that said tractor has less than six hundred (600) original hours use as of the date of this contract.

- Title – The contract should indicate the moment at which title is transferred from the seller to the buyer. Since title to property indicates ownership and the right to control, possess, insure, and transfer property, all buyers are interested in assuring that they have full title to the property they are purchasing. Unless otherwise stated, title is transferred simultaneously with receipt of payment.

Example 6s:

Title shall vest in the Buyer upon payment of all installments due under this contract, but until such time, title shall remain in the Seller.

- Assignments – Most contracts are assignable, but regardless of the parties' desires in this regard, most contracts contain clauses specifically covering the issue. Thus, contracts most often will state that the contract may not be assigned or, if it is assignable, indicating the method of effectuating the transfer of rights.

Example 6t:

This contract is not transferable or assignable.

Example 6u:

No assignment of this contract shall be effective unless executed in writing and signed by all parties.

- Choice of Law – A standard contract provision in today's economy is one declaring which state's law will govern any disputes that arise between the parties.

Example 6v:

This agreement shall be governed and construed in accordance with the laws of the State of Georgia.

Language in the Contract

Almost everyone is familiar with term "legalese" which refers to the complicated, confusing, and often unintelligible language of lawyers. While easy-to-understand contract language may be desirable, some technical language in contracts is unavoidable because some words or phrases are *terms of art*. "Terms of art" are words that have very specific meanings in the legal profession. Terms of art cannot be simplified without changing the meaning of the contract clause. For example, the word "domicile" has a very specific meaning within the law which is different from the common or ordinary meaning. The common meaning of "domicile" is simply a "place of abode or residence." A person who owns more than one house has more than one residence, but, under the law, a person can have only one domicile. A person's domicile can be critical in determining the proper venue for a lawsuit. Therefore, substituting the word "residence" for the word "domicile" in a contract would change the meaning of the clause.

When drafting a contract, or any legal document, keep in mind that often those reading the document may not have a legal background. Therefore, write in language that is understandable and straight-forward and try to avoid long, needlessly complex sentence structure. Do not hesitate, however, to use terms of art where appropriate. Striking the right balance between legalese and plain English is difficult but everyone in the legal profession should strive to attain it.

It is also important to avoid vague or unclear phrases in drafting legal documents. The use of words or phrases which create ambiguity in the document results in confusion. Ambiguity is created anytime the reader can interpret a sentence or phrase in more than one way. Precise writing is important, especially in legal documents.

Both run-on sentences and sentence fragments create ambiguity. Long, run-on sentences having many components are common in legal documents. They are a hazard many attorneys are unable to avoid. While a long sentence can be grammatically correct, it is often difficult to follow, making it difficult to understand. If a sentence goes on for several lines, breaking it into two sentences will make it easier to understand. Take care, however, not to create a sentence fragment, or incomplete sentence, in the process.

Commas are among the most common and important tools of punctuation. Commas are used to separate thoughts, set off parenthetical phrases, and set off transitional phrases. Some of the basic rules for comma usage are:

- Use a comma to separate the elements in a series of three or more – "Seller hereby conveys all right, title, and interest ..."

- Use a comma followed by a conjunction to connect two independent clauses – "Buyer shall pay to the Seller the sum of One Hundred Dollars, but Buyer shall have the right to inspect the goods prior to purchase."

- Use a comma to set off parenthetical phrases (added information which is not essential to the meaning of the sentence) – "Eleanor, a paralegal, has applied to law school."

- Use a comma to set off a transitional word or phrase such as *therefore, furthermore, however, consequently*, etc. – "Run-on sentences are confusing. Therefore, they should be avoided."

- Commas should precede and follow abbreviations such as *Esq., Jr.*, etc. – "This contract is made between John Smith, Jr., and ..."

- Use a comma preceding abbreviations such as *Co., Inc., Ltd.*, etc. – "This contract is made by Acme Holding, Corp., as 'Buyer,' and John Smith, as 'Seller.'"

Use commas with caution. There are many reasons for using commas in addition to the ones listed here, and, yet, overuse of commas is quite common. The better practice is to try not to use a comma unless you can apply a specific rule for doing so.

As you can see from the following article, the proper use of the comma can be critically important. Consulting a grammar book may be necessary, but in many cases, it may be easier to simply break up the long, comma-laden sentence into two or more shorter ones. Perhaps the real culprit in the following case situation was the drafter of the contract who tried to cram too much information into one sentence.

Drafting Errors: The Case of the Million Dollar Comma

Pace International Law Review Blog
Oct 13, 2011 By Peter LaGreca

Consider the following sentence: Woman without her man is lost. How would you punctuate the sentence to make its meaning clear? Would the meaning of the sentence change, depending on where you place the comma? Consider the following:

- Woman, without her man, is lost.
- Woman, without her, man is lost.

The result yields two completely different propositions - all dependent on the placement of a single comma!

Now consider the case of Rogers Communications, Inc., Canada's largest cable television provider. In 2002, Rogers Communications, Inc., entered into a contract with Bell Aliant, a telephone company in Atlantic Canada, in which Aliant agreed to string Rogers' cable lines across roughly 91,000 utility poles in the Maritimes for an annual fee of $9.60 per pole. In 2005, Aliant informed Rogers that it was terminating the contract and increasing its rates to $18.91 per pole. Rogers objected on the grounds that the contract couldn't be terminated until the spring of 2007. Aliant, on the other hand, was of the view that the agreement could be terminated at any time with only one year's notice. The disputed language is as follows:

Subject to the termination provisions of [the Agreement], [the Agreement] shall be effective from the date it is made, and shall continue in force for a period of five (5) years from the date it is made, and thereafter for successive five (5) year terms, unless and until terminated by one (1) year prior notice in writing by either party."

What do you think - can the contract be terminated by either party at any time after providing one year's notice (as Aliant argues)? Or, can the contract only be terminated at the end of a five year period (as Rogers argues)?

Well, the answer depends on whether the phrase, "unless and until terminated by one year prior notice in writing by either party" modifies both preceding clauses, or just the immediately preceding clause. In its 2006 ruling, the Canadian Radio Telecommunications Commission stated that, based on the rules of punctuation, the presence of the comma immediately before the word "unless" suggests that the closing modifier modifies both preceding clauses. Thus, Aliant could terminate the contract on one year's notice during the initial five year period.

What if the comma preceding the word "unless" wasn't there - would that change the interpretation of the contract? Clearly it would:

[the Agreement] shall be effective from the date it is made, and shall continue in force for a period of five (5) years from the date it is made, and thereafter for successive five (5) year terms unless and until terminated by one (1) year prior notice in writing by either party."

In this iteration, the phrase, "unless and until termination by one year prior notice," modifies only the immediately preceding clause pertaining to renewal of the contract. Thus, the contract as it appears here cannot be terminated until the end of five years.

On appeal, Rogers produced the French language version of the contract, absent from which is the errant comma. The Commission reversed its decision, reasoning that it was appropriate to review the French version of the contract because the Commission had approved the pole access rates and regulations in both English and French in 2000 when the rates and regulations were put in place. The Commission further reasons that between the two versions, it is appropriate to prefer the French language version as it has only one possible interpretation, and that interpretation is consistent with one of the two possible interpretations of the English language version.

A final but extremely important part of drafting any document is proofreading and editing. Begin by utilizing computerized spell and grammar check tools, but be aware that the software will not pick up everything. Because some errors are difficult to catch, it is important not to rely solely on the computer when reviewing documents. Note, also, that some spelling deviations, especially those found in the legal profession, are not found in a computer's dictionary. Thus, even when a word is indicated as being incorrect, it is necessary to carefully check the suggested correction.

Editing is a necessary element of drafting any document. Carefully evaluate the document in an effort to improve it. Cut out language that is unnecessary and double-check to ensure all necessary provisions are included. Consider whether the various sections flow logically. Look for substantive accuracy, but also proofread for errors in grammar, punctuation, spelling and sentence structure. Strive to make the document better through careful editing and re-writing where needed.

Review Questions and Exercises

1. Give an example of a condition precedent.

2. Give an example of a condition subsequent.

3. What is the purpose of the rules of construction and the hierarchy of these rules?

4. Assume the following facts: Rachel and Will enter into a real estate contract for the purchase of a house. The sales contract is the preprinted standard form the realtor uses. On the form, there are blank lines under "fixtures included" whereon the agent has typed in "living room drapes, washer and dryer, and mirror over den mantel." At closing, a computational error is found, the typed figure $289,500 is corrected by hand to read $289,900. Additionally, the washer and dryer have been taken away by the previous owners. Those items have been crossed out and initialed by hand.
   (a) Which fixtures are included in the sale? Explain.
   (b) What is the final contract price? Explain.

5. What is the parol evidence rule? List the exceptions to the parol evidence rule.

6. A promissory note reads: "Sixty (60) days after the date of this instrument, I, Sam Wilson, hereby promise to pay to First Bank the sum of One Thousand Dollars ($1,000), in consideration of value received." Does the note contain a covenant? If so, identify it. Does the note contain a condition? If so, identify it.

7. What are implied-in-fact conditions? Why do they exist? Give an example of such a condition.

8. Why do handwritten changes in a contract prevail over a printed form?

9. Maria agrees to purchase John's used car for $2,000 provided that her father will lend her the money for the car. Is there an express condition in this agreement? If so, what is that condition? Is there an implied condition in this agreement? If so, what is it?

10. James Williams buys and sells used lawn equipment such as tractors and mowers. He cleans the equipment and makes some minor repairs when necessary. He is concerned about being sued and wants to make sure buyers know that he sells all equipment "as is" with no warranties. James has hired your firm to draft a simple sales contract. Assume that your supervising

attorney has asked you to draft the contract. Locate a template using resources online or at the law library, and prepare a draft of a contract for James to use.

Practical Applications

1. Stephen Putnal is a nuclear pharmacist. He bought a disability insurance policy which provides benefits in the event the insured becomes "totally disabled." The policy defines that term to mean being "unable to perform the major duties" of the insured's occupation.

Dr. Putnal suffered a cerebrovascular stroke which caused extensive brain tissue death and left him significantly impaired. He has a loss of function and weakness on the left side of his body, does not have fine motor control of his left hand, and suffers from decreased balance, gait, coordination, and endurance. His stamina has also been significantly impaired.

Putnal applied for benefits under his disability policy. Guardian denied the claim, saying that the policy required that Putnal be unable to perform "all of the major duties" of his regular occupation.

Consider:
(a) What do the words "major" and "duties" mean in this context?
(b) How should the court interpret this language?

See - *Putnal v. The Guardian Life Insurance Company of America*, 2006 U.S. Dist. LEXIS 70931 (2006), United States District Court for the Middle District of Georgia.

2. American Cyanamid and Stafford Enterprises entered into a contract for steel, carpenter and millwright work to be performed by Stafford on the premises of American Cyanamid. The agreement included an indemnity clause in which Stafford agreed to hold American Cyanamid harmless for any claim resulting from Stafford's performance unless the damages were caused by the sole negligence of American Cyanamid. This contract expired by its own terms on June 30, 1975.

Sometime after July 1, 1975, Stafford sent American Cyanamid a printed contract "nearly identical" to the first with the exact same indemnity clause. The first sentence of the contract read, "This contract entered into as of __________." Typed in was the date "July 1, 1975." The last sentence of the contract read, "In witness whereof, the parties hereto have executed this contract as of the date and year first above written." No date appeared in the body of the contract. Stafford's agent executed the contract. Just under the agent's signature in the same handwriting appears the date "July 15, 1975."

On July 10, 1975, an employee of Stafford, Mr. Ring, fell from a scaffold and was killed. His widow brought a negligence action against American Cyanamid. American Cyanamid then brought in Stafford as a third party defendant under the indemnity clause of the July, 1975 contract.

Consider:
(a) Did Stafford's agent, by dating the contract "July 15, 1975" below his signature intend to make the contract effective as of that date? Explain the basis of your answer.
(b) Was the contract in effect on July 1, 1975? Why or why not?
(c) Is the contract ambiguous with regard to its effective date? Explain.
(d) May parol evidence be used to clarify the effective date of the contract? Explain your answer.

See – *American Cyanamid Company v. Ring*, 248 Ga. 673, 286 S.E.2d 1 (1978) Georgia Supreme Court.

Chapter 7 The Uniform Commercial Code

OUTLINE

As a result of the fast pace of economic development in the United States and around the world, the common law began to lag behind the needs of the commercial world. This led to the various states passing statutes for the purpose of regulating commercial transactions. It was not long, however, before the need for a uniform system of laws to govern such transactions was recognized. The Uniform Commercial Code is the major statutory basis of several important areas of contract law. It is important to note that the UCC is not a universally-applied federal statute, but rather is a *model act*. Each state has enacted some version of all or part of the UCC. Georgia's UCC is codified in Title 11 of the Official Code of Georgia, Annotated.

7.1 General Background of the UCC

The Uniform Commercial Code is the product of the efforts of two organizations of lawyers and legal scholars. The American Law Institute and the National Conference of Commissioners on Uniform State Law promulgated a model act which was designed to clarify and modernize laws governing commercial transactions and to attempt to make mercantile law uniform among all of the states. This model statute, known as the Uniform Commercial Code and promulgated in 1952, was the first major attempt to codify general contract law.

The UCC is a model act only, and, as such, had to be adopted by each state individually. Eventually, every jurisdiction adopted some version of the UCC, either in whole or in part. The state enactments of the UCC were, perhaps, not as uniform as the drafters had envisioned. Nevertheless, the UCC has been highly influential and its enactment has largely standardized the way commercial transactions are conducted in this country. However, it remains necessary to research each jurisdiction specifically to determine whether its version of the UCC differs from that of any other state involved in the transaction under consideration. Georgia's version of the UCC is found in Title 11 of the Code, and selected portions of it are found in Appendix II of this text.

The purpose of the UCC, as stated by its text, is "to ... simplify, clarify, and modernize the law governing commercial transactions" and "to make uniform the law among the various jurisdictions." The UCC was designed to promote interstate commerce and to facilitate the furthering of business interests. Consequently, the UCC forms a basic part of almost all business law. The Code generally only codifies the common law of contracts and was not intended or designed to create a radically new concept of contractual arrangements. Rather, it was intended to unify conflicting common law doctrines and to regularize existing commercial practices.

The UCC covers a wide spectrum of law, from sales to banking, to letters of credit and bulk transfers. The UCC is divided into nine major sections called Articles. Three of these Articles are directly concerned with contract law and will be discussed in this text.

As the world has become "smaller" in terms of communications and transportation, international transactions have become more prevalent, thus giving rise to the need for a body of laws concerned with international sales transactions. Such transactions are governed by the United Nations Convention on Contracts for the International Sale of Goods (CISG) which was first presented in 1980. Much like a model act, this agreement must be adopted by each country recognizing it. The United States and approximately seventy other countries have done so. Those countries which have adopted the CISG have agreed that the provisions of the agreement will apply to all international commercial sales transactions. The CISG does not apply to consumer transactions. While international sales transactions are beyond the scope of this text, it is important to note the existence and applicability of the CISG.

7.2 *Article I – General Provisions*

Article I, the General Provisions, establishes the form and operation of the UCC. Article I establishes the three basic guidelines to be used in applying the UCC:

- The law of the state applies unless otherwise superseded by the UCC. Each state, in adopting the UCC, specifically states in its statute its intent with regard to whether the UCC was to be the prevailing law in a given subject, thus superseding or replacing the prior existing state law. Thus, when drafting a commercial agreement, one must determine exactly what the law of a given state is and whether the UCC supersedes it. It cannot be assumed that a UCC provision of one state is applicable to another state. *See O.C.G.A. § 11-1-103.*

- The parties to a contract may, by their agreement, vary the provisions of the UCC. Since the purpose of the UCC is to facilitate commerce, and not to hinder it, the parties must be able to vary terms to suit their needs. Article I permits and encourages freedom of contract between the parties. However, in the event the agreement of the parties is silent with regard to a given subject, then the provisions of the UCC shall apply and the UCC will provide the legal standard to be applied to that provision. *See O.C.G.A. § 11-1-102(3).*

Example 7a:

GA, Inc., is a Georgia corporation, looking to expand its operations into the state of West Virginia. GA enters into a contract with The Blue Grass Company, a Kentucky corporation, for the purchase of real estate located in West Virginia. Since GA, Inc., is a Georgia corporation with Georgia attorneys, it prefers the law of Georgia to apply to the contract. Article I of the UCC permits the parties to agree to a contract term providing that the laws of the State of Georgia shall govern interpretation of the contract. If the parties do not specify which law is to govern a contract, the court will make the choice of law in the event a dispute arises concerning the contract.

- The UCC is to be liberally construed. Again, because the UCC is meant to promote business, and not hinder it, the UCC is to be applied in a manner which helps business. This may mean a liberal interpretation. This is quite different from most regulatory statutes which must be strictly complied with. Of course, this liberal construction must be reasonable and all interpretations must still be consistent with the Code as a whole. *See O.C.G.A. § 11-1-102(1).*

Article I of the UCC imposes three obligations on all parties whose transactions with one another are governed by the statute. These obligations are as follows:

- Parties are under an obligation to perform in *good faith*. This means all parties must deal with one another honestly. The UCC provides that "good faith" means honesty in fact in the conduct or transaction concerned. *See O.C.G.A. § 11-1-203.*

Example 7b:

Martin agrees to sell 50,000 component parts to Mitchell Manufacturing with delivery to be within ten (10) days. Martin knows he cannot make the ten (10) day delivery deadline, but believes he can deliver within two (2) weeks. Martin, in order to obtain the large order, is willing to pay some damages for the delay in delivery. Martin is entering into a contract he knows he cannot meet and is, therefore, violating the provisions of Article I of the UCC.

Crooks v. Chapman Company, Inc.
124 Ga.App. 178, 185 S.E.2d. 787 (1971)
Court of Appeals of Georgia

Facts: Buyer and Seller signed a contract for the sale of a radio station. A condition of the contract was that the Buyer would seek the FCC's consent to assignment of the station's license from Seller to Buyer. No time frame was stated in the contract for performance of this condition. The agreement further provided that the earnest money paid by the Buyer to an escrow agent would be considered liquidated damages in the event of a breach of contract by the Buyer. When six months passed without the Buyer taking action on the FCC license issue, the Seller requested that the escrow agent pay over the escrow funds as damages. The escrow agent did so, and the Buyer sued to recover his escrow money.

Issue: Did the Buyer act in good faith with regard to his contractual obligations?

Holding: Plaintiff Buyer contends his only contractual duty was diligence. This is without merit. Good faith is, if anything, a minimum standard of conduct in any contract. While this particular agreement does not come within the UCC, it is a commercial transaction in the broad sense and the legislature has specifically declared that good faith is a basic obligation in all such transactions. Georgia law calls for "substantial compliance with the spirit, and not the letter only, of the contract" in its performance. "Good faith" is merely a shorter way of saying the same thing.

- Parties are under an obligation to perform their contractual obligations in a *reasonable time*. What is "reasonable" in one case may be completely unreasonable in another. Thus, "reasonableness" is to be determined by the facts and circumstances of each situation. *See O.C.G.A. § 11-1-204.*

Example 7c:

Martin agrees to sell and deliver 50,000 component parts to Mitchell Manufacturing Company with delivery to take place within ten (10) days. Delivery is conditioned upon receipt of payment. The parts are not delivered within the ten (10) day period and Mitchell is forced to shut down its assembly line due to a lack of parts. The parts were delivered eight (8) days late. Mitchell asserts a failure on the part of Martin to deliver in a reasonable time. Martin is in breach of his contractual obligation and in violation of the UCC. If, however, Mitchell's payment for the parts was not received until a week after the scheduled time for delivery, then Martin's delivery was reasonable and there is no breach of contract or violation of the UCC.

Crooks v. Chapman Company, Inc.
124 Ga.App. 178, 185 S.E.2d. 787 (1971)
Court of Appeals of Georgia

Facts: *Recall the facts of the case above:* Buyer and seller signed a contract for the sale of a radio station. A condition of the contract was that the buyer would seek the FCC's consent to assignment of the station's license from seller to buyer. No time frame was stated in the contract for performance of this condition. The agreement further provided that the earnest money paid by the buyer to an escrow agent would be considered liquidated damages in the event of a breach of contract by the buyer. When six months passed without the buyer taking action on the FCC license issue, the seller requested that the escrow agent pay over the escrow funds as damages.

Issue: Was six months a "reasonable time" for performance of the condition?

Holding: Plaintiff contends the court injected an artificial time limit into a contract which specified no time limit and which was not warranted by the evidence. The contention is without merit. Where no time for performance is specified in a contract, there is a presumption that the parties intended it to be within a reasonable time; and what is reasonable is a question of fact for the jury. The contract also stated that time was of the essence. Defendant introduced evidence that a time frame of substantially less than six months was usual for the transfer of a license when pursued diligently. Plaintiff, therefore, had the burden of persuading the jury that six months or more was reasonable, under the circumstances, in order to recover the forfeited earnest money.

- Parties are under an obligation to perform according to *past business dealings and practices*, and in accordance with established *custom and usage*. Thus, it is necessary to determine the practices and terms which are peculiar to each industry, as well as those between particular merchants. These customary practices are then made a part of the contract itself. Because of this, definitions of particular terms will vary from industry to industry, and particular care must be taken when using "standard" contract provisions. In the event of a dispute between the parties, it may be necessary to prove the customs of the industry involved in the dispute or to prove the prior practices of the parties in dealing with one another. *See O.C.G.A. § 11-1-205.*

Example 7d:

Martin has been selling component parts to Mitchell Manufacturing Company for several years. Throughout their business relationship, Martin has billed Mitchell for the parts after delivery and Mitchell has paid for the parts within thirty (30) days of the billing. Suddenly, with no prior notice and with no change in Mitchell's payment practices, Martin demands payment immediately upon delivery. Because the parties have not agreed to payment upon delivery, they are still bound by their past practices and dealings and Mitchell has thirty (30) days to pay for the parts.

7.3 *Article II – Sales*

In many ways, Article II of the UCC codifies the common law of contracts. For instance, Article II reiterates the parol evidence rule, the rules of construction, and restates the Statute of Frauds with regard to contracts for the sale of goods valued at over $500. In addition, Article II also expands general law principles with regard to sales contracts. Generally, three types of contracts are regulated by Article II of the UCC. These are contracts for the sale of goods, contracts for the lease of goods, and contracts between merchants.

The UCC is designed to apply to all transactions that involve the buying and selling of goods and to apply to such transactions regardless of whether the parties are professionals or laypeople. Of course, professionals are usually more familiar with all aspects of these types of transactions than are laypeople. Furthermore, as discussed previously, professionals often follow industry practices that laypeople may be unfamiliar with. As with any profession or business, people who regularly deal in a particular kind of activity are likely to have more expertise with regard to their specialty than others might have. This concept applies to professionals who deal in a particular kind of goods – they will have more expertise than casual buyers and sellers of the same goods.

Article II of the UCC contains certain provisions, known as *merchant's provisions*, which apply only to experts in buying and selling goods and which are not applicable to casual buyers and sellers. Therefore, it is important to be aware of the identity of the parties to a contract for the sale of goods. Merchant's provisions will obviously apply to contracts in which both parties are "merchants," and will be inapplicable to contracts in which neither party is a "merchant." In contracts in which one party is a "merchant" and the other is not, the wording of the specific merchant provision will dictate whether or not that specific provision will apply.

In some instances it is readily apparent that one is a professional in the buying and selling of a particular kind of goods. In other cases, it may not be easy to distinguish between a merchant and a casual buyer. Fortunately, the UCC helps by providing a definition.

O.C.G.A. §11-2-104

(1) "Merchant" means a person who deals in goods of the kind or otherwise by his occupation holds himself out as having knowledge or skill peculiar to the practices or goods involved in the transaction or to whom such knowledge or skill may be attributed by his employment of an agent or broker or other intermediary who by his occupation holds himself out as having such knowledge or skill.

Goods

As stated, Article II concerns the sale of goods and requires that contracts for the sale of goods valued over $500 must be in writing. *Goods* are defined by the UCC as things that are existing and movable at the time the contract concerning them was made. Under this definition, goods include, in addition to the expected items, food or drink, crops, and growing timber. Also included is anything that can be removed from land without material harm to the land itself such as minerals, oil, or natural gas. Even electricity is included. In applying the UCC definition, a sales contract encompasses both present sales of goods already existing and present sales of goods that will exist in the future. Therefore, even contracts for the sale of the unborn young of animals are included.

Article II specifically excludes two common movable items from the definition of "goods" – money used as currency and investment securities. And so, with very limited exceptions, any agreement that relates to the sale/purchase of identifiable tangible, movable things that will change hands from merchant to buyer is covered by the provisions of Article II of the UCC.

The UCC imposes *strict liability* in contracts for the sale of goods; that is, in the event that a product proves to be defective, the seller is automatically held liable to the injured party regardless of how careful the manufacturer/seller may have been with respect to the manufacture of the product. The seller cannot be relieved from this liability by his attention to care, quality control standards and the like. If the product is defective, the seller is liable.

Example 7e:

Acrid Products, Inc., manufactures electrical supplies and contracted to sell to wiring, electrical boxes, and other materials necessary in the construction of an office building for Philip. After installation of Acrid's products, the building caught fire and burned to the ground as a result of faulty insulation on the wiring materials supplied by Acrid. Under the UCC, Acrid is strictly liable to Philip and it doesn't matter how careful Acrid was in the manufacture of the wiring materials. Because the wiring was defective, the manufacturer is liable.

Article II covers only transactions in goods. Contracts for the sale of services and employment contracts are not governed by the UCC. If the contract is for the provision of services, the contract is governed by common law principles. In these cases, there is no strict liability, and the provider of the services will be liable for injury to the other party only if the injured party can prove negligence.

Example 7f:

Glenn employs Max Connelly, Attorney at Law, to represent him in a tort suit arising out of injuries Glenn received in an automobile accident. Glenn's contract with Attorney Connelly for legal services is not covered by the UCC because it is a contract for services, not goods.

Interesting questions arise when the contract is a *hybrid sale,* or one that involves both goods and services. According to Article II, if the contract cannot be determined to be one either strictly of goods or strictly of services, the court will determine into which category the contract falls. Using this *predominant factor test*, the court must determine the predominant nuture of the contract. That determination will then control the standard for the entire contract and will determine whether a dispute which arises between the parties to the contract will be decided pursuant to the provisions of the UCC or pursuant to the common law. This analysis of the predominant category of a contract is not always an easy undertaking.

Example 7g:

Beverly contracts with Harriet's Housecleaners to provide cleaning services for her home on a weekly basis. Harriet's provides various supplies in connection with the cleaning services. This is a contract for services. Providing the cleaning supplies is incidental to the main, or predominant, purpose of the contract. This contract would be controlled by the common law.

Example 7h:

Karen contracts with Judd for the purchase and installation of a new water heater. Judd is strictly liable. Although services were involved (installation of the water heater), the predominant purpose of the contract was to provide Karen with a new water heater. This is a contract for the sale of goods.

Example 7i:

Aspen Corporation sells, installs, and services machinery used in the formation of plastic cups. This machinery requires servicing at regular and frequent intervals. Aspen sells machinery to All Cups, Inc.

Pursuant to the terms of the contract, Aspen will install the machinery and service it for the life of the machines. A court would more likely conclude this is a sale of goods as the machinery was movable at the time the contract was made. Alternatively, a court could conclude that the primary subject matter and purpose of the contract was the installation and servicing of the equipment.

Cleveland Lumber Company v. Proctor & Schwarzt, Inc.
397 F. Supp. 1088 (1975)
United States District Court for the Northern District of Georgia

Facts: Plaintiff lumber company bought a wood drying kiln from the defendant kiln company. The kiln was installed by the seller. When the kiln failed, litigation ensued. The kiln company asserted that the complaint was barred because it was outside the applicable statute of limitations of the Uniform Commercial Code (UCC). The lumber company claimed that the six-year limitation for written contracts was applicable.

Issue: Was the contract for the purchase and installation of the kiln a contract for the sale of goods governed by the UCC?

Holding: Plaintiff contends that the contract was not a contract for the sale of goods as defined by the UCC. In this case the services involved (installation of the kiln) were incidental to the basic purpose of this contract which was the sale of a drying kiln to plaintiff. It is difficult to conceive of a contract, in the proportions of the instant contract, that would not provide for incidental services in connection with the purchase. Services always play an important role in the use of goods, whether it is the service of transforming the raw material into some usable product or the service of distributing the usable product to a point where it can easily be obtained by the consumer. The fact that the contract involved substantial amounts of labor does not remove it from inclusion under the UCC.

The Court finds that, in this case, the essence of the contract was the sale of goods movable at the time of identification to the contract for sale. Other clauses in the contract, which may amount to services, are merely incidental to the main purpose of the contract and do not take it out of the sales provisions of the UCC. Accordingly, the UCC statute of limitations appears to apply rather than the general Georgia statute of limitations on contracts.

In cases in which a contract involves mixed subject matter and does not clearly fall under the UCC or common law, a court may examine any relevant factors and circumstances surrounding the contract. These include:

(a) the intentions of the parties as expressed by the parties themselves;
(b) how similar contracts have been treated by both these parties and others;
(c) industry practice;
(d) the type and duration of performance each party would provide under the contract;
(e) how the courts have dealt with other similar contracts.

Warranties

Both the UCC and the common law recognize a variety of warranties in contracts. Specifically, the UCC provides for certain warranties which attach to goods. A *warranty* is simply a guarantee that the seller makes with respect to the goods covered by the sale. These warranties may cause the manufacturer/seller of goods to be liable to the buyer and to the ultimate consumer as well.

Certain warranties are implied by law. Very simply, these warranties need not be spelled out by the seller because they arise out of the buyer/seller relationship and are the common-sense implications which spring from the reasonable expectations of the buyer. The UCC imposes those warranties which are commercially fair and reasonable to expect, and further, the UCC also delineates the method by which the seller can create or avoid other kinds of warranties.

First, and most basically, the UCC imposes a *warranty of title*. Very simply, the seller must actually own the goods he is selling. He must also have the right to pass ownership of the goods to the buyer free and clear of the interests of any other party. This means that when he sells the goods, the seller is not selling goods that are pledged to some third party as collateral or otherwise encumbered by any third-party interest. Certainly, no buyer wants to purchase something that the seller does not own or is not otherwise entitled to sell. *See O.C.G.A. § 11-2-312.*

The UCC further imposes two types of *implied warranties* which come about by operation of law:

- *warranty of merchantability* – The warranty of merchantability guarantees the buyer that the goods sold are in a fit condition for the ordinary purposes for which they were intended, or, alternatively, that they pass without objection in the trade under the contract description. This warranty is imposed only upon merchants and assures the buyer that the goods are of the same quality as the market requires and expects. *See O.C.G.A § 11-2-314.*

Example 7j:

If an average-sized man properly erects and climbs up a ladder to perform an overhead task, and the ladder collapses, injuring him, the ladder was not fit for the ordinary purpose for which it was intended. There has been a breach of the implied warranty of merchantability. If, however, the man is injured when he uses a table as a step ladder and the table collapses, there is no breach of warranty because the table was not being used for the ordinary purpose for which it was intended.

Paulk v. Thomasville Ford Lincoln Mercury, Inc.
317 Ga.App. 780, 732 S.E.2d 297 (2012)
Court of Appeals of Georgia

<u>*Facts:*</u> Thomasville Ford acquired a used Cadillac for $21,500 and performed an inspection without noting that the car had been in a collision. Six months later, the dealership sold the car to the Paulks for $24,876.98 (including tax, tag, and title). At the time of sale, the car had 10,420 miles on it and was still covered by the manufacturer's warranty. Prior to the sale, Mrs. Paulk asked if the car had been wrecked. The salesman responded that he wasn't sure.

Thereafter, the buyers complained of defects in the car – it stalled twice, had a leaky trunk and leaky sunroof. The trunk and sunroof were repaired under the manufacturer's warranty. After the Paulks learned that the car had been involved in a roll-over collision and repaired prior to the the time they bought it, they sued. By that time, they had put more than 24,000 miles on the car.

In the course of the suit which followed, the Paulks' expert testified that "any person in the used car business would have discovered the previous damage to [the Cadillac] from even a cursory inspection of the vehicle." The expert also reported that the Cadillac was worth $8,000 less than it would have been had it not been in the collision and repaired as it was.

<u>Issue</u>: Was there a breach of the implied warranty of merchantability?

<u>Holding</u>: Under Georgia's version of the Uniform Commercial Code, a warranty that the goods shall be merchantable is implied in a contract for their sale if the seller is a merchant with respect to goods of that kind. This warranty protects consumers from defects or conditions existing at the time of sale. To be merchantable, used cars must pass without objection in the trade under the contract description, and they must be fit for the ordinary purposes for which cars are used. Proof that a car was defective when sold is an essential element of this claim.

The Paulks have cited no authority for the proposition that the mere fact a car has been repaired after a collision would cause it not to "pass without objection in the trade." Here, for example, Thomasville paid $21,500 for the car shortly before selling it to the Paulks showing that it indeed passed without objection in the trade before being offered to a consumer for sale. Finally, the other defects of which the Paulks complained - a leaky trunk and sunroof, now repaired - do not amount to defects making the Cadillac unmerchantable, particularly in light of their use of the car for over 24,000 miles.

- *warranty of fitness for a particular purpose* - The warranty of fitness for a particular purpose guarantees the buyer that the goods are capable of performing any particular function the buyer has indicated he requires of the goods. For there to be a warranty of fitness for a particular purpose, the seller must know of the buyer's intended use of the goods and the buyer must be relying on the seller's expertise in supplying appropriate goods to meet that intended use. *See O.C.G.A § 11-2-314.*

Example 7k:

Sally wants a rug for her covered porch. She consults Michael at the floor covering store and explains to him that her porch, while covered, is exposed to outside temperatures, humidity, and sometimes gets wet when the rain is blowing. When Sally finds a rug she particularly likes, Michael assures her that her selection will work just fine on her porch. When the rug fades, mildews, and frays after a few weeks, there has been a breach of the warranty of fitness for a particular purpose.

Mack Massey Motors, Inc., v. Felicitas Garnica

814 S.W.2d 167 (1991)

Court of Appeals of Texas

<u>Facts</u>: Felicitas Garnica sought to purchase a vehicle capable of towing an Airstream trailer she had on order. She went to Massey Motors where a salesman referred her to the sales manager. The sales manager called the Airstream dealer concerning the specifications of the Airstream trailer Mrs. Garnica was purchasing. Mrs. Garnica testified that the purpose of the inquiry was to determine the specifications of the trailer and to advise her whether the Jeep Cherokee could do the job of pulling the 23-foot trailer. Massey Motors represented that the Jeep Cherokee was suitable to tow the Airstream, and Mrs. Garnica, relying on the recommendation of Massey Motors, purchased the Jeep Cherokee.

The purchase order Mrs. Garnica signed contained language on the back side which stated that the manufacturer made no warranties except the express written warranty furnished by Jeep

Eagle. No evidence was presented at trial that Mrs. Garnica had waived any warranty of fitness for a particular purpose.

After the purchase, the Garnicas experienced various problems in towing their Airstream and complained that the Jeep did not have sufficient power to pull the trailer. Mrs. Garnica had to repeatedly exercise her right under the vehicle warranty and return the Jeep to the dealer for repair. After returning to the dealer at least six times in five months, Mrs. Garnica was told by Massey Motors to take her Jeep Cherokee and "go elsewhere." Less than two weeks later, the drive shaft twisted apart. At that time, the vehicle had been driven 7,229 miles. Massey Motors refused to make a warranty repair, contending this breakdown was due to misuse.

Issue: Was a warranty of fitness for a particular purpose created by Massey Motors and, if so, was there a breach of this warranty?

Holding: Massey Motors was in a position of expertise in the sale of the Jeep Cherokee, and Mrs. Garnica relied on their superior knowledge regarding the vehicle's capabilities. The sales manager, after investigating the specifications of the Airstream trailer, represented to Mrs. Garnica that the Jeep Cherokee was suitable for the purpose intended, specificially towing of the Airstream trailer. When Massey Motors' sales manager undertook to determine the suitability of the Jeep Cherokee for the expressed intended purpose of towing the Airstream trailer and thereafter represented that the Jeep Cherokee was the proper vehicle for Mrs. Garnica to buy, he created a warranty of fitness for a particular purpose.

This warranty was not waived by virtue of the language printed on the back side of the purchase order. This language, designed to limit or exclude warranties other than the express written warranty made by the manufacturer, Jeep Eagle, was not conspicuous, and there was no evidence that Mrs. Garnica was aware of this disclaimer.

Expert testimony presented at trial showed that the Jeep Cherokee had a towing capacity of 5,000 pounds and that the Airstream trailer had a 5,800 pound gross vehicle weight rating. Evidence also showed that the Jeep Cherokee did not have a sufficiently large enough motor to pull the 23-foot trailer. Further, the use of the under-powered Jeep to pull the trailer could have overly stressed the vehicle causing the continual transmission and drive shaft problems which occurred. Expert testimony concluded that the Jeep Cherokee was an unsuitable vehicle to tow the Airstream, and the jury was entitled to find a breach of the warranty of fitness for a particular purpose.

Mrs. Garnica was awarded $124,217.75 in actual damages, $47,500.00 in attorney's fees, and $210,000.00 in punitive damages.

Warranties can also be created by the specific words of the seller as set out in the contract or by the conduct of the seller. These types of warranties, known as *express warranties,* may be created in any of three different ways. *See O.C.G.A § 11-2-313.*

An express warranty may be created by:

- The specific promise or affirmation of the seller appearing in the contract – For instance, if the seller promises in the contract that the goods being sold will not wear out or fail to perform for a period of at least one year, the seller has created an express warranty.

- A description that the seller uses in a catalog – If a seller, for example, describes his product, shirts, in a catalog as being made from 100% cotton, and the shirts are actually a polyester-cotton blend, the seller has breached the express warranty created by the catalog.

- A sample or model used by the seller to induce the sale – When a seller displays or provides to the buyer a sample of his goods or a model of his product, he is creating an express warranty that the sample or model is representative of the actual items being sold.

Example 7l:

Margaret owns a shoe store. Marvin, a salesman for Footsy Products, a shoe manufacturer, meets with Margaret and shows her several Footsy samples, all of which are made of high quality leather. Margaret orders several dozen pairs. When the shoes arrive, they are of the style Margaret ordered but are not made of leather as the samples were. Footsy has breached its express warranty.

Warranties are not created by "puffing," or sales talk. Talking up one's product in order to make a sale by the expression of the opinion of the seller is not considered a representation of fact and is not intended to create a guarantee of the seller's product. For instance, a used car salesman's representation that a car is "the best little used car I've ever had on the lot," is mere puffing and does not create any warranty with regard to the car. When a merchant is dealing with the public, the merchant must take care to make sure his sales talk is understood as just that – statements of opinion.

A merchant may limit or exclude any and all warranties. However, since the UCC prefers that warranties exist in order to protect buyers, the UCC requires any limitation or exclusion of warranties be conspicuous in order to ensure that buyers are aware of the exclusion or limitation. The simplest way for a seller to protect himself from a warranty obligation is by the use of words such as "as is," "with all faults," or "without warranty of any kind, whether express or implied." "As is" is a particularly simple and unambiguous statement which is most appropriate for the sale of used or second-hand merchandise. The words "as is" alone are sufficient to signal to the buyer that there may be some defects which the seller will not warrant. *See O.C.G.A § 11-2-316.*

To be effective, the seller must bring this limitation language to the buyer's attention in such a way that a reasonable person ought to notice it. This may be accomplished in any number of ways such as by using larger print or a contrasting color in the contract.

The UCC also provides that there is no warranty if the buyer, before entering into the contract, examined the goods or if the buyer refused to examine the goods when such an examination would have revealed the defect or flaw. *See O.C.G.A. § 11-2-316(3)(b).*

Risk of Loss

Prior to the enactment of the UCC, the *risk of loss* of goods – that is, who pays if the goods are damaged, destroyed or lost in shipping – was born by the party who had title at the time of the loss. The UCC provides rules with regard to the risk of loss which are not entirely dependent on title.

The parties may specifically contract to determine at what point the risk passes from the seller to the buyer, and they are free to provide whatever terms they desire in this regard. However, if there are no contract provisions, the general UCC principle is that the risk of loss is dependent on whether the contract of sale is a "shipment contract" or a "destination contract." The general rule is that the risk of loss of the goods falls on the person who has control over the goods. It is important to recognize that risk of loss is a different concept than title or ownership. *See O.C.G.A. § 11-2-319.*

Whichever party bears the risk of loss has the right to maintain an action (to file suit) for the damages caused in the event the goods are destroyed. It is also this party who has the right to insure the goods. If the goods are destroyed while the seller bears the risk, the seller must replace the goods at his own expense. However, if the goods are destroyed while the buyer bears the risk, the buyer is still obligated to pay the seller for the goods even though he now has no goods.

With a *shipment contract*, the risk of loss passes to the buyer when the seller delivers the goods to a carrier. If the contract does not require that the seller deliver the goods to a specified destination, then the carrier is considered an agent of the buyer. *See O.C.G.A. § 11-2-319.* Shipping contracts are frequently created by the use of the following terms:

- *FOB (place of shipment)* – The initials "FOB" stand for "free on board." The risk stays with the seller until he places the goods in the hands of the carrier. For example, if the contract provides "FOB Hartsfield Airport, Air Express," the seller would bear the risk of loss until he delivers the goods to the Air Express office at Hartsfield Airport.

- *FAS (vessel)* – These initials stand for "free alongside," and the seller retains the risk of loss until the goods are taken alongside the transportation vehicle. The seller is required to deliver the goods to the transportation vehicle at his expense. For example, "FAS, *Morning Star,* Port of Savannah" would require the seller to deliver the goods to the dock alongside the ship, *Morning Star,* at the Port of Savannah. The vessel could also be a plane, as in "FAS, Delta Flight 5603, Hartsfield Airport, Atlanta."

- *CIF* - The initials stand for "*cost, insurance and freight.*" The parties' contract may provide that the seller agrees to insure the goods during transportation even though the risk of loss has passed to the buyer who would normally pay the cost to insure the goods. The seller may provide insurance regardless of the type of shipment arrangement agreed upon by the parties. If the goods are lost, the buyer, who bears the risk, receives the insurance proceeds even though the seller paid for the insurance.

Note that in shipment contracts, it is the buyer who has the greater risk. These contracts occur most often when the seller is in a superior bargaining position to that of the buyer, for instance, if the seller has highly sought after goods which are in short supply.

A *destination contract* passes the risk of loss to the buyer when the goods are delivered to a specified destination. This a more common shipping arrangement between buyers and sellers.

- *FOB (place of destination)* - The risk passes to the buyer when the carrier delivers the goods to a general destination point. For example, "FOB Port of Savannah" means that the risk of loss would pass when the goods were delivered to the Port of Savannah as the destination point.

- *Ex-ship* – The risk and expense of loss are borne by the seller until the goods have actually been unloaded from the ship or other transportation mode. *See O.C.G.A. § 11-2-322.*

- *No arrival, no sale* – The risk of loss only transfers to the buyer when the goods have arrived at the destination point and have been tendered to the buyer. If the goods do not arrive, there is no contract. If the goods arrive damaged, the seller is responsible. See O.C.G.A. *§ 11-2-324.*

In a *conditional contract*, the sale is predicated upon certain conditions being met at the time of transferring the goods. There are four types of conditional contracts under the UCC:

- *Cost on delivery* - A COD provision means that the risk of loss of the goods remains with the seller until the goods have been delivered to and paid for by the buyer. The contract itself will indicate the place of delivery.

- *Sale on approval* - In a "sale on approval" contract, the seller retains the risk of loss until the goods have been delivered to the buyer and the buyer has indicated his approval of them. The approval may be express, implied or conveyed by silence after the passage of a contractually specified period of time. In this type of contract, the buyer has a right to inspect the goods so the risk is retained by the seller for a longer period than with a COD contract.

- *Sale or return* – In a "sale or return" contract, the risk of loss passes to the buyer on delivery. If the buyer does not approve of the goods, or if he chooses to return them, it is the buyer who bears the risk and the cost of returning the goods to the seller.

- *Consignment* – In a consignment, the buyer is receiving goods for resale. The risk of loss remains with the seller until the buyer resells the goods. The buyer never has a risk of loss.

Often, a seller will transfer goods to the buyer by means of an independent carrier such as the U.S. Postal Service, UPS, or Federal Express. In a general shipment contract, the contract merely requires the seller to send the goods to the buyer. Therefore, once the goods are shipped, the risk passes to the buyer. However, the parties may make special arrangements if they intend to transfer the goods by means of an independent carrier.

Recall that the UCC places a higher duty on merchants than on non-merchants. This is true with regard to the risk of loss provisions. The UCC provides that if the seller is a merchant, he or she bears the risk of loss until delivery of the goods to the buyer; however, if the seller is a non-merchant,the risk of loss passes to the buyer when the goods are tendered for delivery, that is, when they become available to the buyer.

Remedies

Both buyers and sellers have legal and equitable remedies available for breaches of contract. In addition to the same remedies permitted for all injured parties under general contract law, the UCC provides some unique remedies.

If the seller is the injured party, he has three additional methods, over and above his common law remedies, of addressing a breach of contract. *See O.C.G.A. § 11-2-702*. They are:

- *Withhold delivery* – the seller may withhold delivery of goods to the buyer under any of the following circumstances:
  - The buyer wrongfully rejects the goods.
  - The buyer fails to pay for the goods as required by the contract.
  - The buyer does not cooperate with the seller.
  - The buyer repudiates the contract.
  - The buyer becomes insolvent before delivery.

- *Stop delivery* – the seller may stop delivery of the goods in transit and resell them to another buyer if one of the following circumstances arises:
  - The buyer does not pay for the goods as required by the contract.
  - The buyer repudiates the contract.
  - The buyer becomes insolvent before delivery.

- *Reclaim goods from an insolvent buyer* – The UCC will not require a seller to become a creditor of an insolvent buyer. This remedy is available only in certain, limited circumstances. The seller is allowed to reclaim goods from the buyer after delivery if:
    - The goods are sold on credit; and
    - The buyer is insolvent; and
    - The seller makes her demand within ten days of the buyer's receipt of the goods.

If the buyer is the injured party, the UCC offers him four additional remedies over and above general contract remedies (*See O.C.G.A. § 11-2-711*). They are:

- Cover – The buyer is entitled to *cover* or purchase goods which substitute for those that are the subject of the breached contract. If the substituted goods cost more, the buyer can sue the seller for the difference.

- Replevin – If cover is not available, the buyer may replevy, or retake, the goods he had previously rejected from the seller. *Replevin* is an equitable remedy which is available when the buyer believes that non-conforming goods are better than none at all.

- Revocation – If the goods do not conform to the contract specifications, the buyer can revoke his acceptance with the result that no contract exists.

- Claim goods from insolvent seller – If the seller becomes insolvent, the buyer can claim the goods he has purchased from the seller provided the goods have been paid for. The UCC will not require a buyer who has paid for goods to become a creditor of an insolvent seller. Once paid for, the goods are the property of the buyer, and the seller's creditors have the purchase price the buyer has already given to divide up among themselves.

As we will see later in this text, the common law of contracts provides that substantial performance of a contract is considered "performance." However, the UCC imposes a different, and higher, standard with regard to the seller's obligation to tender, or make available, conforming goods. Under the *perfect tender rule,* the goods must be tendered strictly in conformity with the contract. In other words, the buyer is entitled to perfect performance of the contract and may reject goods that "fail in any way to conform with the contract."

Once the seller has made the goods available to the buyer, the buyer must tender payment before taking possession unless the parties have agreed otherwise in their contract.

Article 2A

In a *lease*, the owner of real or personal property, called the lessor, transfers the right of possession of the property to another, known as the lessee. The lessee then has the right to use the property for his or her own purposes for a period of time for an agreed-upon consideration, the rent. UCC Article 2A, first proposed in 1987, applies many of the general principles of the UCC, such as those pertaining to trade use and the course of dealings between the parties, to the leasing of goods. Note that Article 2A applies only to the lease of personal property and not to real estate.

Article 2A was necessary for several reasons. Primarily, it had become necessary to define the term "lease" because of the growing practice in the business community of leasing equipment as opposed to making an outright purchase. In a true lease, the item leased returns to the lessor at the termination of the lease period. Prior to the introduction of Article 2A, the name "lease" was often given to contracts which were more accurately contracts for the sale of goods with a hidden security agreement. In these agreements, at the conclusion of the lease period, the lessee has the right to purchase the leased property for a nominal fee because the useful life of the property has been exhausted during the lease period and the item leased has no real remaining value. Thus, the lessee is actually purchasing the goods over the course of the lease period, and the lessor is protected by his right to terminate the lease and reclaim the property if the lease payments are not made. This relieves the lessor of the necessity of complying with the requirements of creating a security interest in property which he sells.

Under Article 2A, the term "lease" was defined specifically to exclude hidden security agreements. Rather, the sales provisions of Article II are extended to the commercial leasing of goods because of the common practice of leasing equipment rather than making an outright purchase (even though the lease may provide for an option to purchase at the end of the lease period). Common law rules and principles still apply to lease agreements except where specifically provided otherwise.

7.4 Article IX

Article IX of the UCC allows for *secured transactions*. A secured transaction is defined as any transaction that is intended to create a security interest in personal property or fixtures, including tangible goods, intangibles, and documents. A tangible good is any good that can be touched and moved such as an automobile or furniture. An intangible good is a right to property rather than a physical object. Examples of intangible goods include stock certificates, patents, or bonds. A document, under this provision of the UCC, is an item such as a bill of lading or dock receipt.

A *secured transaction* is a kind of debtor-creditor relationship in which the debtor puts up collateral, or security, for the credit or loan obtained from the creditor. The creditor may be someone who loans money to the debtor so the debtor can make a purchase, or the creditor may be a seller who sells goods to the debtor on credit.

A *security interest* represents the right of the holder of the interest to attach specific property, the collateral, in case of a default by the debtor. In other words, if the debtor defaults on his contractual obligation to pay for the property and the creditor has a security interest, the creditor can attach the property that is subject to the security interest in order to satisfy the default. Thus, the innocent party is afforded greater protection in the event of a breach of contract because he knows there will be, at least, the value of the secured property to lessen his damages in the event that the debtor fails to pay as required by the contract between the parties. A creditor who holds a security interest in property has greater rights to that specific property of the debtor than do other creditors of the debtor.

Example 7m:

Brett buys a new car and finances the purchase through his local credit union. The credit union loans Brett the money to pay for the car and requires him to give the credit union a security interest in the vehicle. The new car is collateral for the loan. Should Brett default on the loan, the credit union can repossess his car and sell it to satisfy Brett's debt. The security interest exists until the loan is paid in full.

Nearly all security interests in personal property and fixtures are covered under Article IX of the UCC. A few types of transactions such as those involving real estate, wage assignments, and claims arising out of judicial proceedings are not covered.

To create a valid security interest, three requirements must be met:

- There must be a *security agreement* executed in writing between the parties. A security agreement is a writing signed by both parties which describes the collateral, the property that is subject to the security interest, and states that a security interest is being created in that property.

- There must be *attachment* or an indication of the moment when the creditor gives consideration for the security interest. Attachment is the timing element of the security interest. Typically, this occurs when the agreement is signed or when the debtor takes possession of the collateral.

- There must be *perfection*. Perfection is the process of protecting a creditor's rights to the collateral from all other claimants.

    - Perfection by attachment - In some instances, the attachment itself is sufficient to perfect the interest. Perfection by attachment usually involves a purchase-money security interest which is a security interest that is held by the seller of the collateral to secure all or part of the sales price or is held by the person lending money that the debtor uses to acquire the collateral. This type of perfection usually involves consumer goods other than fixtures or vehicles.

    - Perfection by filing a financing statement - Most often, perfection occurs by the filing of a financing statement in the appropriate government office. This puts the public, and, most importantly, other potential creditors of the debtor on notice of the existence of the interest.

A financing statement must contain the names of the both the debtor and the creditor as well as a description of the collateral. The financing statement must also be signed by the debtor. Perfection by filing a financing statement is necessary if the creditor is not in possession of the collateral and if the transaction does not involve automatic perfection, usually via a consumer purchase money security interest. The secured party has the duty to file the financing statement and must file in the office where one would record a mortgage on real estate. In Georgia, this is the County Clerk of Court's office. The UCC Financing Statement form used in Georgia is found Appendix III of this text.

Article IX also establishes the order of priorities for creditors in case of the debtor's default so that, in the event of conflicting claims, the claimant with the highest priority will prevail. Generally speaking, secured creditors have greater priority than unsecured creditors. Among secured creditors, priorities date from the time of filing or perfection of the security interest.

Amoco Oil Company v. G. Sims & Associates
162 Ga.App. 307, 291 S.E.2d 128 (1982)
Court of Appeals of Georgia

Facts: Turner operated a service station. Amoco Oil Company extended credit to Turner who failed to pay his account balance of $19,946.02. Amoco filed three separate financing statements purporting to take a security interest in all of Turner's personal property. Thereafter, Turner sold all the equipment, supplies, and merchandise of the service station to McLarty with the proceeds of the sale being deposited with an escrow agent, Sims. Amoco demanded payment from the escrow agent, The agent refused because the Georgia Department of Revenue had also asserted a claim to the funds because Turner had outstanding tax liabilities. The Department of Revenue had filed a series of fi. fas. on the general execution docket. All were filed after the Amoco financing statements were filed.

Issue: Who has the priority claim to the escrow funds, Amoco or the Department of Revenue?

Holding: A lien for State taxes takes priority over a security interest, except where the security interest is perfected by filing a financing statement prior to the time the execution for taxes is entered on the execution docket. There is nothing in the record to show that Amoco had an enforceable security interest. The record merely shows that Amoco filed three financing statements.

A security interest is not enforceable against the debtor or third parties unless the debtor has signed a security agreement which contains a description of the collateral. A financing statement by itself cannot constitute a security agreement. The general rule is that a financing statement does not create or impose any personal obligation. The financing statement is a paper separate and apart from the security agreement itself. A financing statement merely gives notice of the existence of a security interest but in itself does not create a security interest for which a security agreement is required. A financing statement cannot serve as a security agreement because it does not grant the creditor a security interest in the collateral and does not identify the obligation owed to the creditor.

In this case, Amoco does not have a valid security interest which would take priority over the Department of Revenue's tax lien.

If a debtor fails to pay the debt owed to the creditor, the creditor has several options. The creditor may:

- retain the collateral in satisfaction of the debt;
- sell the collateral to satisfy the debt provided that if the collateral sells for more than the amount of the debt owed, the overage belongs to the debtor; or
- sue the debtor.

Review Questions and Exercises

1. Give two examples of a warranty which you have encountered with a product you have purchased.

2. Why was the UCC enacted?

3. Jamie has a garage sale in preparation for a move from Atlanta to Charlotte. Would Jamie be characterized as a "merchant" under the UCC? Why or why not?

4. Assume Jamie regularly has garage sales, conducting at least one such sale each month and sometimes more. Would that change your opinion?

5. How does the perfect tender rule change the common law rule of performance?

6. How does Article II of the UCC define "goods?"

7. Claire contracts with Suzy Seamstress to make Claire's wedding dress. As Claire enters the church for her wedding, the side seams of the dress begin to unravel and come apart. Is Suzy Seamstress strictly liable? Why or why not?

8. Mike, a building contractor, has been purchasing plumbing supplies from George for several years. It is Mike's practice to use 2.5 inch pipe and this is what George has always supplied. When Mike orders 500 feet of "standard" pipe, George delivers 2 inch pipe which is the industry standard, but not what Mike uses. Does Mike have a breach of contract claim against George? Why or why not?

9. The instructions for the Georgia UCC-1 financing statement state: *"use exact, full name; do not omit, modify, or abbreviate any part of the Debtor's name."* Why is this important?

10. What is a secured transaction? Why would a debtor agree to enter into a secured transaction? What are the advantages of a secured transaction to a creditor?

Practical Applications

1. Snyder and his partners planned the construction of 228 apartments, and entered into a contract with Greenbaum to supply and install carpeting and carpet pad for all 228 units. Greenbaum estimated that the project would require 19,000 to 20,000 yards of carpeting. The written contract which was signed by the parties made no mention of the amount of carpeting to be installed, but simply provided that Greenbaum would supply and install carpeting for 228 apartments for a total consideration of $87,600

Over the next four months, Greenbaum purchased large amounts of carpet and carpet pad from various wholesalers to be used on the Snyder job. However, no carpet was ever installed because Snyder canceled the contract. It had become apparent at some point that the estimation of 19,000 to 20,000 yards of carpet was too high and that the actual figure needed was between 17,000 and 17,500 yards. Greenbaum sued for breach of contract and was awarded a judgment of $19,407.20. Snyder appeals from this judgment.

Consider:
(a) Is this contract one for the sale of services which is not covered by the UCC? Explain.

See – *Snyder v. Herbert Greenbaum and Associations, Inc.*, 38 Md.App. 144, 380 A.2d 618 (1977), Court of Appeals of Maryland.

Chapter 8 Third Party Contracts

OUTLINE

When discussing contracts, we generally speak only of two parties, the offeror and the offeree, and the traditional view was that only the parties to the contract could assert rights under the contract, and only the parties to the contract had duties because of it. Sometimes, however, at the time they make their agreement, the offeror and the offeree may intend for the performance of the contractual obligations to benefit another person who is not a party to the contract. Additionally, one or both parties may later wish to change who is responsible for the contractual obligations.

In this chapter, we will explore *who*, outside of the contracting parties, may have an interest in the agreement, *how* their interests are created and perfected, and *what* effect they have on the performance obligations in the agreement.

8.1 *Third Party Beneficiary Contracts*

Two parties who enter into a contractual agreement with one another are said to have *privity of contract* with each other. Privity is the common law requirement that for a person to have a legal interest or right in a contract, that person must be a party to the contract. For many years, under the common law, an outsider, or third party, had considerable difficulty in enforcing someone else's contract because the outsider lacked privity of contract. A ruling by the Court of Appeals of New York in the mid-nineteenth century gave rise to the doctrine of third-party beneficiary rights.

Lawrence v. Fox
20 N.Y. 268 (1859)
Court of Appeals of New York

Facts: Mr. Holly owed a $300 debt to Mr. Lawrence. After that debt had been incurred, Mr. Fox approached Holly seeking a loan, and Holly loaned Fox the sum of $300. The money was loaned by Holly to Fox with the express provision that, in consideration of the loan, Fox would repay Holly's original debt to Lawrence. Fox agreed to this term.

Fox failed to pay Lawrence the $300 which he had agreed to pay in satisfaction of Holly's debt to Lawrence and of Fox's debt to Holly. When Fox failed to pay Lawrence, Lawrence sued.

Fox defended himself on the theory that he had no contractual agreement with Lawrence and, thus, owed Lawrence no money.

Issue: Was Fox contractually obligated to pay $300 to Lawrence with whom he had no privity of contract as satisfaction of his debt to Holly?

Holding: The Court relies heavily on the case of *Farley v. Cleaveland*, decided more than a quarter of a century earlier by the Supreme Court of New York. In the *Farley* case, "one Moon owed Farley and sold to Cleaveland a quantity of hay, in consideration of which Cleaveland promised to pay Moon's debt to Farley." The defendant in the Farley case raised as a defense a failure of consideration, and the Supreme Court found "the decision in favor of Farley's right to recover was placed upon the ground that the hay received by Cleaveland from Moon was a valid consideration for Cleaveland's promise to pay Farley, and that the subsisting liability of Moon to pay Farley was no objection to the recovery." The promise in the Farley case was a promise, in all material respects, like the one under consideration in the instant case.

Holly's loan to Fox was made for the benefit of Lawrence in that under the contract between Holly and Fox, Holly intended to repay Lawrence the monies owed by Holly to Lawrence. Since this was the intent of the parties at the time they entered into their contract, the lack of privity of contract between Lawrence and Fox is not a bar to recovery, and Lawrence is entitled to recover Holly's $300 from Fox.

Following the decision in *Lawrence v. Fox*, the courts have adopted a modern doctrine of third party contracts which does not require privity of contract between the third party and the other original contracting party who is to perform for the benefit of the third party.

Third party beneficiary contracts are agreements in which the original intent of one of the contracting parties, at the time of entering into the contractual agreement, is to have the promised-for consideration pass not to the contracting party, but to some outside, or third, party. A classic example of a third party contract is an insurance policy. For instance, if Roger takes out a life insurance policy with MetLife Insurance Company, naming his wife, Sally, as the beneficiary, the two contracting parties are Roger and MetLife, but the purpose of the contract is to confer a benefit on Sally in the event of Roger's death. The promised-for consideration, the death benefit, is intended by Roger to be paid to Sally.

In order to be considered a valid third party beneficiary, the contract must usually specifically name the third party in the formative stage of the contract. The parties must have, at the time of the contract, intended to benefit the third party. This element is critical as it defines the third-party beneficiary contract. Was the purpose of the contract to benefit a third party? If so, that third party, although not a party to the contract, may have certain rights with respect to the contract.

Biddle, et al v. BAA Indianapolis, LLS

830 N.E.2d 76 (2005)

Court of Appeals of Indiana

Facts: This suit stemmed from airport traffic over the homeowners' property. The Indianapolis airport authority paid a group of homeowners compensation for noise disturbances caused by overhead air traffic. Thereafter, some of these homeowners sold their homes. Biddle, a purchaser of one such home, and others then sought compensation for themselves from the airport authority.

When a homeowner in this group purchased his home, he made an offer to purchase by submitting a written "Purchase Agreement" to the seller. The seller then submitted an addendum to the agreement which included language to the effect that the parties were availing themselves of the Airport Authority's Noise Compatibility Program. The Airport Authority would make a payment to the seller of a percentage of the contract price in exchange for the placement of a Noise Disclosure Statement in the deed conveying title to the property.

Issue: Is the Airport Authority a third party beneficiary to the real estate sales contract with enforceable rights?

Holding: One who is not a party to an agreement may nevertheless enforce it by demonstrating that the parties intended to protect the non-party by the imposition of a duty in the non-party's favor. For an obligation to be enforceable, it must clearly appear that it was the purpose, or a purpose of the contract, to impose an obligation on one of the contracting parties in favor of the third party. It is not enough that performance would benefit the third party. It must appear that one of the parties intended to require performance of some part of the agreement in favor of the third party, and that the other party to the agreement intended to assume some duty imposed. The intent of the parties should be gathered from the terms of the contract itself, considered in its entirety against the background of the circumstances known at the time of execution.

While the buyers are correct in asserting that the agreement here does not specifically state that it was written for the protection of the Airport Authority from claims arising out of complaints about noise, it is clear that the above provision was included to place the buyers on notice about the noise. More importantly, one need not perform any mental gymnastics to deduce that the provision was included to protect the Authority from noise claims. The provision specifically stated that the Authority has compensated the sellers in exchange for them providing the notice to the buyers. If the provision were not intended to induce the buyer's agreement to refrain from filing claims against the Authority because of noise from the operation of the airport, there would be no reason for the seller to notify the buyer that the Authority had provided compensation in exchange for the notice. Thus, we conclude that the intent of the agreement was that the buyers would not seek compensation from the Authority because of noise disturbances from the operation of the airport.

Situations can arise in which a party does derive some benefit from the contract but was not intended to do so. If it is just serendipitous that the third party happened to gain something from the transaction, he is considered an *incidental* beneficiary and does not have enforceable rights under the contract. Compare and contrast the case above with the following case for examples of intended third party beneficiaries and incidental third party beneficiaries.

Bain v. Gillispie
357 N.W.2d 47 (1984)
Court of Appeals of Iowa

Facts: James Bain, a college basketball referee, had a contract with the Big 10 Basketball Conference to referee varsity basketball games. During a game which took place on March 6, 1982, Bain called a foul on a University of Iowa player that permitted free throws by a Purdue University player.

That player scored the point that gave Purdue a last-minute victory and eliminated Iowa from the Big 10 championship. Some Iowa fans, including John and Karen Gillispie, asserted that the foul call was clearly in error.

The Gillispies operated a novelty store in Iowa City which sold University of Iowa sports memorabilia. They filed a complaint against Bain, alleging that his negligent refereeing constituted a breach of his contract with the Big 10 Conference and destroyed a potential market for their products. The Gillispies sought $175,000 in compensatory damages plus exemplary damages.

Issue: Do the Gillispies have a valid breach of contract action?

Holding: The Gillispies were merely incidental beneficiaries of the contract between Bain and the Big 10 Conference. While the Gillispies contended that they were direct donee beneficiaries, the real test was whether the contracting parties intended, at the time they entered into their contract, that a third person should receive a benefit that might be enforced in the courts. Here, the contracting parties, Bain and the Big 10, clearly did not intend any benefit to the Gillispies.

If the intent of one of the contracting parties comes about *after* the contract has been formed then the contract is not a third party beneficiary contract but, instead, is an assignment. Assignments are discussed later in this chapter.

An important element of a third party contract is the fact that the third party has legally enforceable rights under the contract and, although not a party to the transaction, can sue for its enforcement. The third party has the ability to bring suit against the contracting parties to have the contract enforced in his favor. This is true even though the beneficiary is neither a party to the agreement nor has any enforceable obligation with respect to the agreement. In the event of such a lawsuit, the focus becomes whether or not the promisor has some legitimate reason for not performing his obligations under the contract. In other words, the court will consider the defenses the promisor may raise when the third party sues him on the contract. In such a case, the general rule is that the promisor can raise against the beneficiary any defense that the promisor could have raised against the promisee.

Recall that, generally, the parties to a contract may agree to cancel or modify their contract at any time. However, this rule does not apply in third party beneficiary contracts. The third party beneficiary rights in the contract become vested at the time the third party learns of the agreement. Thus, if the third party beneficiary knows of and consents to the contract, the parties cannot cancel or modify the agreement without the beneficiary's consent.

Consider the interesting problems which can arise with regard to life insurance policies. A life insurance policy is often a third party beneficiary contract – the beneficiary of the policy is not one of the contracting parties. The beneficiary under the policy may sue to enforce the performance (payment) of the policy if the insurance company fails to pay a valid claim. Ordinarily, the original promisee retains the right to sue for enforcement for the benefit of the third party, but, of course, that's not possible in the life insurance contract situation where the promisee, as a condition precedent of the promisor's performance, has died. Thus, the third party beneficiary must be entitled to enforce the policy.

Example 8a:

Kristen's parents enter into a contract with Calvin Construction to build a new home for her. Kristen is directly referenced in the construction contract as the party with whom Calvin should consult regarding all design features. Kristen's parents are merely paying for the house. After Kristen moves in, she discovers several construction defects that affect the habitability of the house. Kristen, as the intended third party beneficiary of the contract, may sue Calvin for breach of contract. Additionally, Kristen's parents retain the right to sue Calvin for breach of contract.

Now assume Calvin fully performs under the contract and that the final payment due to Calvin pursuant to the contract is not made, Calvin may sue Kristen's parents because it is their duty as the promisee under the contract. However, Calvin may not sue Kristen, the third party beneficiary, for payment because she is under no legal duty under the contract to make payment.

The modern view of third party contracts is set out in the *Restatement (Second) of Contracts*, which characterizes someone as a third party beneficiary if "recognition of a right to performance in the beneficiary is appropriate to effectuate the intention of the parties." One of two things must be true. Either the performance of the promise must be for the purpose of paying a debt on behalf of one of the two contracting parties, or it must be for the purpose of making a gift from one of the contracting parties to a third party. This preserves the idea that both creditor and donee beneficiaries have legitimate, enforceable third party rights. The Restatement further states that "an incidental beneficiary is a beneficiary who is not an intended beneficiary," thus, reiterating the traditional and modern view that only "intended" beneficiaries have enforceable rights.

Recall from Chapter 7 that both the UCC and common law recognize a variety of warranties associated with contract law. Since no privity of contract is required with regard to warranties, they may cause the manufacturer/seller of goods to be liable, not only to the buyer, but also to the ultimate consumer of the product – a third party.

O.C.G.A. § 11-2-318

A seller's warranty whether express or implied extends to any natural person who is in the family or household of his buyer or who is a guest in his home if it is reasonable to expect that such person may use, consume, or be affected by the goods and who is injured in person by breach of warranty. A seller may not exclude or limit the operation of this Code section.

Third Party Creditor Beneficiary Contracts

One subset of third party beneficiary conracts is the *third party creditor beneficiary* contract. In this type of contract, the purpose of the promisee's agreement is to extinguish a debt or obligation owed to the third person, the creditor beneficiary. In other words, the promisor agrees to pay a debt owed by the promisee. The party receiving the payment is the third-party creditor.

The debt must be in existence prior to the third party contract being formed. The creditor is considered a real party in interest whose detrimental reliance is assumed to be his willingness to accept payment from the promisor.

Example 8b:

John owns a warehouse worth $250,000 on which he has a mortgage of $100,000. ABC Mortgage Company holds the mortgage. John sells his warehouse to Stan who assumes the mortgage. Under the assumption contract, Stan agrees with John that he, Stan, will take over and pay John's mortgage owing to ABC Mortgage Company. ABC is the creditor beneficiary of the assumption agreement and may bring suit against Stan even though ABC's mortgage contract was not with Stan. ABC may also sue John, the original mortgagor, if Stan does not pay.

The third party creditor is considered to be a real party in interest with regard to the contract between the promisor and promisee because the contract was formed to benefit the creditor. Generally, rights vest, or become enforceable in a court, as soon as a party detrimentally relies on the contract's existence. With a creditor beneficiary, detrimental reliance is assumed to be the creditor's willingness to accept payment from the promisor. Recall that the debt must exist as a prerequisite to the formation of the third party creditor beneficiary contract. Thus, the creditor can always sue the debtor, the promisee in the third party contract, to enforce the contract. But, because the creditor is choosing not to do so and to, instead, rely on the contract between the debtor and the promisor, his rights in the third party contract are deemed to have vested.

Third Party Donee Beneficiary Contracts

In a *third party donee beneficiary contract*, the purpose of the contract is to confer a gift on a third person. Thus, the major difference between a third party creditor beneficiary and a third party donee beneficiary contract is that there is no underlying debt in a third party donee beneficiary contract.

To have a third party donee beneficiary contract, it must be shown that the promisee intended to confer a gift on the donee. The promisor confers the benefit at the request of the promisee. The donee beneficiary is considered a real party in interest and, once he learns of the contract, has enforceable rights against the promisor. However, the donee beneficiary has no enforceable rights against the promisee because the promisee has only promised a gift. Since a promise to make a gift cannot serve as the consideration for a contract, there is no contract between the donee and the promisee.

Example 8c:

When Dylan graduates from college, his parents agree to give him a new car. Dylan and his father visit a car dealership where Dylan selects a car. A sales contract is entered into between Dylan's father and the dealer. Dylan is the donee, Dylan's father is the promisee, and the car dealer is the promisor.

8.2 Assignments

In most cases, neither party, at the time of the making the contract, contemplates that the consideration will flow to an outside party. This does not mean, however, that such a transfer in the future is necessarily precluded by law. If the parties did not originally intend to benefit a third party but, rather, decided to change the arrangement after the formation of the contract to include a third-party benefit, it is considered an *assignment*. Thus, an assignment is merely the transfer of a promisee's rights under an existing contract. The contract must already be in existence before the transfer of rights takes place in order for the transfer to be considered an assignment.

Special vocabulary terms are used to describe the parties involved in an assignment. The *assignor* is the contracting party who makes the transfer of his contractual rights. The *assignee* is the third party who receives the transfer of rights. Finally, the *obligor* is the other original contracting party who remains obligated to render performance to the assignee.

In Georgia, the term "*chose in action*" is sometimes used in contract assignment cases. Very simply, a "chose" is a thing, or an article, of personalty. This definition includes rent, bank deposits, financial payments, and judgments. A "chose in action" is a personal right recoverable by a lawsuit. It is the money, thing, or damages owing. As the Georgia Court of Appeals explained, "The terms 'choses in action' and 'debts' are used by courts to represent the same things when viewed form opposite sides;

the chose in action is the right of the creditor to be paid, while the debt is the obligation of the debtor to pay."[8]

> O.C.G.A. § 44-12-20
>
> A chose in action is personalty to which the owner has a right of possession in the future or a right of immediate possession which is being wrongfully withheld.

> O.C.G.A. § 44-12-22
>
> Except as may be otherwise provided in Title 11, all choses in action arising upon contract may be assigned so as to vest the title in the assignee, but he takes it, except for negotiable instruments, subject to the equities existing between the assignor and debtor at the time of the assignment, and until notice of the assignment is given to the person liable.

Chancellor et al. V. Gateway Lincoln-Mercury, Inc. et al.
233 Ga.App. 38, 502 S.E.2d 799 (1998)
Court of Appeals of Georgia

Facts: Peggy Chancellor and her mother, Betty Mitchell, entered into a retail installment sales contract with Gateway Lincoln-Mercury, Inc., to purchase a used Honda Prelude. The retail installment sales contract provided in its very terms an immediate and automatic assignment from Gateway to Mercury Finance Company of Georgia as soon as Chancellor and Mitchell executed the contract.

Mercury took the assignment and paid Gateway the face amount of the retail installment sales contract less a discount of $450.00. Chancellor and Mitchell objected because the discount was not disclosed to them at the time they entered into the sales contract.

Issue: Was the assignment to Mercury Finance proper?

Holding: When the plaintiffs executed the contract, Gateway acquired an inchoate right or chose in action to the sales price as well as finance charges and interest. This was an assignable property right which Gateway immediately assigned to Mercury Finance at a prearranged, discounted price. The non-UCC law is clear that all choses in action arising upon contract, including accounts receivable, may be assigned so as to vest title and the right to sue on them in the assignee. Gateway had the absolute right to sell this uncollected chose in action for payment of installments by Chancellor and Mitchell for whatever price that such chose in action could bring in the fair market.

An assignment is a transfer of the rights of the assignor. An assignor, like every party to a contract, has both rights and obligations under his contract. Even after an assignment of rights, the assignor is still liable for his or her performance ,as promised under the contract. An assignment does not relieve the assignor of his or her contractual obligations and duties. He must perform his duties or be in breach of the contract.

To be an assignment, the transfer must be made *after* the original contract is created. Whenever rights are assigned, the assignee, that is, the party to whom they are assigned, is simply substituted for the maker of the assignment, the assignor. This substitution of parties gives the assignee exactly the

[8] This explanation is found in Water Processing Co. v. Toporek, 158 Ga.App. 502, 280 S.E.2d 901 (1981).

same rights as the assignor. Once the assignor (the person transferring rights under the contract) makes the assignment, which can be either partial or full, the assignee (the person to whom rights are transferred) becomes the real party in interest and has enforceable rights against the promisor. The assignee is said "to stand in the shoes of the assignor." Once the assignment is effective, the assignor can no longer obtain the benefit of the rights transferred. Only the assignee is entitled to the benefit of those assigned rights.

Example 8d:

Returning to the 8a example of the construction of Kristen's home, if Calvin owes money to his sister, Claudia, who lent him the money to start up his business, Calvin, as the assignor, may assign his right to receive payment from Kristen's parents to his sister, Claudia, to whom he is indebted. Kristen's parents, the obligors, will then make payments directly to Claudia, the assignee.

Generally, no formalities are required for a valid assignment of rights. While the assignor often uses the word "assign," other words such as "sell," "transfer", or "convey" are sufficient to indicate an intent to transfer a contractual right. An assignment may be oral or written with one exception. If the original contract was one which had to be in writing under the Statute of Frauds, then any assignment of rights under that contract must also be in writing.

An assignment does not substantially change the obligations of the obligor. While there is, of course, some change (the obligor is now paying a different party), the law does not consider this to be a material change.

Under general contract law principles, most contract rights are generally assignable. There are, however, exceptions. There are three types of contracts which cannot be assigned.

- The right to personal services cannot be freely assigned. If Ashley agrees to perform bookkeeping services for Mary's store, and Mary sells the store to Debra, Debra cannot claim the services of Ashley even though Mary may have wanted to assign the employment agreement to Debra.

- A contract which is dependent on the personal confidence or circumstances of the recipient cannot be assigned. This includes the right to purchase goods on credit. Because the decision to extend credit is based on the credit worthiness of the original party, the right to purchase goods on credit cannot be assigned.

Example 8e:

If Meg, a healthy thirty year old, purchases a life insurance policy from Best Western Insurance, she cannot assign her contract rights to seventy-eight year-old Ralph. The insurance company sold Meg the policy based on her age and health. The company would be unlikely to sell a policy with the same terms and premiums to Ralph.

- A contract which expressly forbids assignment by one or both parties cannot be assigned. If the contract contains a provision prohibiting assignment, any attempt to assign the rights of either party under the contract is a breach of the original contract.

Additionally, Georgia law provides that rights of action are generally assignable – that is, the right to bring a lawsuit for damages is generally an assignable right. There are exceptions to this rule however. Specifically, lawsuits that arise from contracts that are covered by the UCC and lawsuits for personal injuries are not assignable. Additionally, while legal malpractice claims are not generally assignable, a claim that involves solely a financial loss involves a right of property, and has been held to be assignable.

O.C.G.A. § 44-12-24

Except for those situations governed by Code Sections 11-2-210 and 11-9-406, a right of action is assignable if it involves, directly or indirectly, a right of property. A right of action for personal torts, for legal malpractice, or for injuries arising from fraud to the assignor may not be assigned.

Government Employees Insurance Company v. Hirsh
211 Ga.App. 374, 439 S.E.2d, 59 (1993)
Court of Appeals of Georgia

Facts: David Matthews and Kathleen Hirsh were involved in a motor vehicle collision. Pursuant to an automobile insurance policy it issued covering Matthews' vehicle, the Government Employees Insurance Company (GEICO) paid Matthews $2,392 for medical expenses incurred as a result of the injuries he sustained in the collision. GEICO, as subrogee of its insured, subsequently commenced an action against Hirsh to recover those medical expense benefits.

Issue: Did the subrogation provision in GEICO's insurance policy constitute a prohibited assignment of a personal injury claim under Georgia law?

Holding: Georgia law provides that a right of action for personal torts may not be assigned, codifying the common law prohibition against assignment of personal injury claims.

The medical payment subrogation clause in GEICO's policy provided: "If we make a payment under this coverage, we have the right to sue or otherwise recover the loss from anyone else who may be responsible. The person to whom we make payment must execute and deliver to us all necessary papers, help us to enforce our recovery right and do nothing to prejudice such rights." This subrogation clause amounts to no more than an agreement to assign a personal injury claim to the insurer.

Allowing GEICO to proceed in its own name against an alleged tortfeasor in a personal injury claim to recover the amount of medical benefits paid to its insured would violate the common law and statutory prohibition against assignments of personal injury causes of action.

Sheppard v. State Farm Fire & Casualty Company
222 Ga.App. 619, 475 S.E.2d 675 (1996)
Court of Appeals of Georgia

Facts: Connie Sheppard was injured in an automobile collision while operating a vehicle insured by State Farm, and she elected to receive medical expense benefits under that policy. Sheppard and her husband then brought a claim against the tortfeasor and obtained a recovery under an agreement settling those claims. Pursuant to the terms of its policy, State Farm sought reimbursement from Sheppard of the amounts paid to her as medical expenses. Sheppard refused to reimburse State Farm. State Farm then instituted this action against her.

Issue: Does the language in the medical payments provision of the State Farm policy create an invalid assignment of a personal injury cause of action?

Holding: O.C.G.A. § 44-12-24 provides, in pertinent part, that "[a] right of action for personal torts . . . may not be assigned." This Court has held in several cases that policy language authorizing an insurer to recover benefits paid to an insured by bringing an action against the third party tortfeasor amounts to such an invalid assignment of a cause of action for personal injury.

Other policies, however, contain language that does not authorize the insurer to bring an action directly against the tortfeasor, but merely requires an insured receiving medical payment benefits to reimburse the insurer for such payments out of any recovery the *insured* may obtain from the tortfeasor. In such cases, this Court has held the policy provision valid and enforceable.

The insurance contract provision in this case contemplates that the insured has a right to bring an action against the tortfeasor to recover damages for personal injury, and that recovery of medical expenses will be a portion of that recovery. State Farm requires only that the insured reimburse it from such a recovery for those medical expenses for which it paid benefits. This provision does not violate the Georgia statute.

As the two cases above illustrate, there is a difference under Georgia law in assigning the right to bring the lawsuit and assigning a portion of the proceeds derived from the lawsuit.

If a dispute arises after an assignment, any defense is good against the assignee to the same extent as that defense is good against the assignor.

If the assignor makes the assignment for consideration, the assignment is irrevocable, but if the assignment is gratuitous, the assignor may revoke the assignment, thereby cancelling the assignee's rights except in certain limited situations.

Assignments are common in mortgages and other types of credit. For instance, it is not unusual for a home buyer to obtain a mortgage through one company only to receive a letter some time later informing him that the mortgage company has assigned its right to collect the monthly mortgage payments to another company. The buyer now writes his monthly mortgage check to a company with whom he had no previous obligation and with whom he had no contract or intention to contract. Along with the assignment of the right to receive the payments goes the right to sue the homeowner if he fails to pay his mortgage.

Another very common assignment situation involves commercial lines of credit. Assume that a furniture manufacture sells its products to retail furniture stores around the country. The stores may not be able to pay cash for their inventory, and, in order to boost sales, the manufacturer extends credit, giving the stores some period of time to pay for their purchases. The sales are contracts between the manufacturer and the stores who are its customers. The manufacturer may need funds in order to purchase raw materials to keep its production line operating – it may have thousands of dollars of accounts receivables (the money due to it on the sales accounts) but little cash on hand. If the manufacturer goes to a bank for a loan, the bank will likely consider the accounts receivables as a valuable asset of the manufacturer. The bank may agree to give the manufacturer a line of credit in exchange for an assignment of the accounts receivable. The furniture manufacturer would then transfer its right to receive payment from its customers to the bank in order to obtain the line of credit. The transfer of this right to receive payment is an assignment of rights under the sales contracts between the manufacturer and the retail stores which are the manufacturer's customers.

William Iselin & Company, Inc. v. Davis
157 Ga.App. 739, 278 S.E.2d 442 (1997)
Court of Appeals of Georgia

Facts: William Iselin & Company is a commercial factor[9] located in New York. Davis is a resident of Georgia who bought fabric from Kramer & Brothers, Inc. Kramer entered into a standard factoring contract with Iselin. Iselin collected Kramer's accounts and was entitled to commissions for doing so. Kramer sold fabric to Davis on open account and was required, by the contract with Iselin, to factor the sale with Iselin.

Some months after Kramer entered into the factoring contract with Iselin, Kramer, Iselin, and Irving Trust Company Bank entered into an assignment agreement. Under the assignment agreement, the Bank agreed to make loans to Kramer. Iselin would provide monthly statements to the Bank showing the accounts receivable purchased by Iselin from Kramer under the factoring agreement. Kramer assigned to the Bank all moneys and claims for moneys due under the factoring agreement. Kramer specifically assigned to the Bank the right to file any claims or take any action to collect monies due under the factoring agreement.

When Davis became indebted to Kramer in the amount of $48,137.25, Iselin filed suit against Davis to collect the account. Davis defended, asserting that it owed nothing to Iselin.

Issue: Was Iselin the proper party to collect the debt owed by Davis?

Holding: Under the assignment agreement, Kramer assigned to the Bank all of its interest in all claims due it under the factoring contract; and the gross amount of Kramer's accounts receivable factored by Iselin for a month less the specified deductions and commissions due to Iselin, was to be remitted to the Bank. Only the Bank was authorized to take any legal action necessary to protect its interest in these net proceeds. This suit was brought by Iselin and yet it is clear that Iselin did not initiate this action at the instigation of or with the consent of the Bank or on behalf of the Bank. Under the assignment agreement, the Bank was the proper party to take whatever action was necessary to protect its interest in the net proceeds, and not Iselin.

8.3 *Delegations*

Unlike the first two forms of third party contracts - third party beneficiary contracts and assignments - the third type, *delegations*, does not involve a transfer of rights. Rather, in a delegation, the promisor of a contract authorizes another person to perform some duty owed by the promisor under the contract. The *duty to perform* obligations owed under the contract is what is transferred in a delegation.

---

[9] A factor is one who buys discounted accounts receivable

There is a special vocabulary for delegations. The *delegant* (obligor), or *delegator*, is the contracting party who is delegating or transferring his contractual duties to a third party. The third party who receives the transfer of contractual duties to perform, or assumes the duties to be performed, is referred to as the *delegate*, or *delegatee*. Finally, the other original contracting party to whom the delegated duty is still owed is called the *obligee*.

Generally, all non-personal duties owed under a contract may be delegated. The delegation of duties does not relieve the party making the delegation (the delegant or the delegator) of the obligation to perform in the event that the party to whom the duty has been delegated, the delegate, fails to perform. The delegator, who was the promisor under the contract, always remains liable under the contract if the delegate fails to perform. The obligee must look first to the delegate for performance of the transferred contractual duties, but if the delegate fails to perform, the obligee can then look to the delegator to perform those duties.

Example 8f:

Returning a final time to the construction of Kristen's new house, if Calvin suffers a serious injury and becomes unable to finish work on the house, he may contract with Ben's Best Builders to take over the job. Calvin, the delegator, has delegated his duties to perform and complete construction of the house to Ben, the delegate. Kristen's parents remain obligors (obligated to pay under the original contract) and they now have the right to sue both Ben and Calvin if the job is not completed to the contract specifications.

As a general rule, any duty can be delegated, although there are certain circumstances in which delegation is prohibited. These include:

- when special trust has been placed in the obligor (the person who is contractually obligated to perform);
- when performance depends on the personal skill or talents of the obligor;
- when performance by a third party will vary materially from that expected by the obligee under the contract;
- when the contract expressly prohibits delegation.

Example 8g:

Lily, a famous actress, has a contract with Universal Pictures to play the lead in a new movie. After the contract is signed, Lily decides to take some time off and delegates her responsibilities to her personal assistant, Laura. This delegation is prohibited because Lily's contract with Universal involves personal services.

The delegation scenario is commonly seen in subleases. The original tenant, the delegant, re-rents his apartment to another person, the assignee. The delegate, or sub-lessee, steps into the shoes of the original tenant and owes the rent and any other obligations to the landlord. The landlord can sue both the original tenant (the delegant) and the sublessee (the delegate) if the sublessee fails to pay the rent.

8.4 Novation

Another way in which a third party can be brought into a contract is through a *novation*. A novation is a full substitution of a new party for one of the original contracting parties. The new third party not only receives the all of the benefits of the transferor under the contract but also assumes all of the transferor's obligations. After a novation, the contract reads as though the original contracting party never existed.

A novation requires the consent of everyone involved - both parties to the original contract and the consent of the new, third, party. An individual may be willing to contract with one party, but may not have the same confidence in someone else's willingness or ability to perform the obligations required by the contract. For this reason, novations are rare.

Review Questions and Exercises

1. How does an assignment differ from a delegation?

2. How does an assignment differ from a third party beneficiary contract?

3. What factors might influence a third party beneficiary to sue the promisee rather than the promisor? Give examples.

4. How can one distinguish between a third party beneficiary and an incidental beneficiary?

5. If the assignee sues the obligor after a valid assignment is made, what defenses may the obligor raise against the assignee?

6. Assume the following facts: Larry is a talented minor league baseball player. Though he is a professional athlete, he has not yet made it to a Major League roster. When Larry and his coach have a falling out, Larry sends the coach an e-mail stating that he is delegating his responsibilities to his first cousin Barry who is talented but not under contract with any team. Can Larry do this? Why or why not?

7. What is the meaning of the following: "The assignee stands in the shoes of the assignor"?

8. Will enters into an agreement to work as a paralegal at a prestigious law firm for a period of one year for a salary of $50,000 per year. Discuss:
   (a) Will's right to delegate his duties as a paralegal to his friend, Elaine, who is a highly qualified and respected paralegal;
   (b) The law firm's right to assign Will's contract to another law firm in town;
   (c) Will's right to assign his salary to a bank in order to secure a loan.

9. Assume Jackie hires an attorney to draft a will, directing the attorney to leave all of her property to her best friend, Mara. Assume further that, after Jackie dies, it is determined that the attorney was negligent in drafting the will with the result that the will is invalid. Rather than Mara inheriting, Jackie's assets go to her distant relatives. Discuss:
   (a) Whether there was a contract between Jackie and the attorney;
   (b) Whether Mara was an intended beneficiary of any such contract;
   (c) Whether Mara has any claim against the attorney.

10. Under what circumstances does an assignment become irrevocable?

Practical Applications

(1) Robert Scott constructed a dam on a real estate development but was not fully paid for the

job. While the work was in progress, two interim invoices were paid. Scott finished the project and submitted his last invoice. The developer, by this time, had run into financial difficulties and Scott's final invoice went unpaid.

The last agreement that was entered into by the developer concerning financing of the development was supported by final invoices from Scott and other contractors and stated that the contractors had all been paid for their work. Although the bank disbursed a check in the amount of the agreed upon financing, Scott was not paid.

When he was unable to recover from the developer with whom he had contracted, Scott filed claims against the developer's creditors claiming that he was a third-party beneficiary to financing agreements related to the development.

Consider:
(a) Was Scott an intended beneficiary of the developer's agreement concerning financing? Explain.
(b) Does the intent to pay a third party with loaned money create a beneficiary interest in the contract?

See - *Scott v. Mamari Corporation*, 242 Ga.App. 455, 530 S.E.2d 208 (2000), Court of Appeals of Georgia.

(2) Several vehicles which were insured by Allstate Insurance Company were taken to Fran and John's Doylestown Auto Center for repairs after being damaged in automobile accidents. Allstate's adjustor prepared an estimate for each vehicle and issued checks to Doylestown Auto Center in the amount of the estimates. In the process of repairing the autos, Doylestown requested supplemental sums which it claimed were necessary in order to complete the repairs.

Disputes arose between Allstate and Doylestown Auto Repair over the amounts of the supplemental payments. Doylestown requested each of the customers who owned the cars insured by Allstate to execute a document which Doylestown labeled "Assignment." The language of each "Assignment" was identical except for the name of the insured and the date and is as follows: "I, (name of insured), for good and valuable consideration and intending to be legally bound to hereby assign and convey to Fran and John's Doylestown Auto Center, Inc., any and all claims, rights, actions, and causes of action which I may have against Allstate Insurance Company in connection with the repair of my vehicle which was damaged in an automobile accident on (date). (signature)"

The "General Provisions" page of each Allstate policy contains a "Transfer" clause which reads, in part, "This policy can't be transferred to another person without our written consent..." Allstate contends that the language of the insurance policy prohibits the "Assignment" to Doylestown Auto Center.

Consider:
(a) Whether the document labeled "Assignment" by Doylestown is sufficient to create an assignment;
(b) Whether the language of the Allstate policy prohibits the Doylestown "Assignment;"
(c) Whether Doylestown Auto Center is a third party beneficiary of the contract of insurance between Allstate and the vehicle owners.

See – *Fran and John's Doylestown Auto Center, Inc., v. Allstate Insurance Company*, 432 Pa.Super. 449, 638 A.2d 1023, (1994), Superior Court of Pennsylvania.

Chapter 9 Discharge, Damages and Remedies

OUTLINE

Even if a contract is complete and meets all of the legal requirements to be enforceable, situations may still arise in which a contracting party's obligation to perform is discharged without his actually having fulfilled his obligations under the contract. These cases most often involve situations in which either the other party or some external circumstance or condition relieves the party of the obligation to perform.

If, however, no such circumstance exists, and one party fails to perform as he is required by the contract, the innocent party will incur damages. That injured party will then want to examine the possible remedies which are available to him or her. In this chapter, the circumstances under which one may be excused from performance are discussed as well as the damages which may be incurred as a result of a breach of contract and the other remedies the non-breaching party may seek.

9.1 Methods of Discharge

Discharge is a legal term meaning the completion of a contract or its termination due to other causes or means. While the simplest method of discharging one's obligations under a contract is to perform these obligations, performance is just one of several ways in which a contract can be brought to an end.

Performance

Simply *performing the obligations* required of one under the contract excuses further performance. Once performed, the duties are executed, and there is nothing more for the promisor to do. Full performance is, of course, the goal of the contracting parties at the time they enter into their contract, and most contractual obligations are fulfilled in this fashion. If, however, difficulties arise between the parties after the formation of the contract, one of the parties may be reluctant to go forward. A party, to discharge his obligations, must tender performance.

A *tender of complete performance* is legally sufficient to discharge a party from his contractual obligations. A tender of complete performance occurs when one party tenders, or presents, an unconditional offer to perform his obligations under a contract and is ready, willing and able to perform. If one party tenders complete performance and the other side refuses the performance, the first party is excused of all further obligations of performance.

OCGA § 13-4-20

Performance, to be effectual, must be accomplished by the party bound to perform, or by his agent where personal skill is not required, or by someone substituted, by consent, in his place, and must be substantially in compliance with the spirit and the letter of the contract and completed within a reasonable time.

OCGA § 13-4-22

Where the conditions as to performance of a contract are concurrent, if one party offers to perform and the other refuses to perform, the first shall be discharged from the performance of his part of the contract and may maintain an action against the other.

In most cases, the parties perform their contractual obligations acceptably to one another. To be an effective, full performance of the contract, the parties must substantially comply with the terms of the agreement. Performance means good faith and substantial compliance with spirit, and not just the letter, of the agreement.

Brown, et al. v. Pounds, et al.
289 Ga. 338, 711 S.E.2d 646 (2011)
Supreme Court of Georgia

Facts: Cobb Electric Membership Corporation ("Cobb EMC") members filed a derivative action against Cobb EMC, its president, and the board of directors. The parties subsequently entered into a settlement agreement which was approved by the trial court. The agreement stipulated that the members "will seek an amendment to the by-laws at the next meeting of Cobb EMC members ... Such amendment will seek to allow members the right to vote for directors by mail-in ballots..."

Nine days after the Court approved the agreement, the Board of Directors met and voted unanimously to amend the by-laws to allow proxy voting at member meetings when election of directors is *not* on the agenda.

Issue: Did the Board of Director's amendment of the by-laws violate the trial court's order by violating the provisions of the Settlement Agreement requiring a proposed resolution submitted by members regarding the method to be used in future director elections be presented for consideration and vote?

<u>Holding:</u> The Board's amendment violates the order approving the agreement because it significantly changes the conditions under which the parties' agreed-upon plan for proposing proxy voting to the members is implemented. It would allow the Board to unilaterally change the method of voting on the issue of the method of voting for directors. The Board's proxy voting by-law amendment violates the spirit, if not the letter, of the agreement. Georgia law provides that performance of contractual obligations must be substantially in compliance with both the spirit and the letter of the contract.

Further analysis is required with regard to the question of what happens when a party, instead of completely performing under the contract or tendering complete performance, only partially performs his obligations under the contract. A *breach of contract* may be either minor or material, and there is no specific formula available for determining whether a specific breach should be classified as minor or material. The difference is one of degree.

If the breach is a *minor breach,* the contract itself is still in force and effect. In a minor breach, the performance is substantially what was expected by the terms of the contract, and the performing party will be discharged. Note that, although discharged, the breaching party may have to compensate the innocent party for the difference between the value of full performance and the value of the substantial performance given.

Example 9a:

Connie agrees to sell her used car, in running condition, to Gary for $3,500. When Gary takes possession of the car, he discovers that the spark plugs are worn out. Although the contract specified that the car was to be in working order, this is only a minor breach because replacing the spark plugs is not significant. Gary has a cause of action against Connie for the cost of replacing the plugs, but the contract is still valid and enforceable.

However, if the performance delivered by one of the parties fails to substantially comply with the performance expected under the terms of the contract, the promisor is not relieved of his contractual obligation. A *material breach* occurs where there has been so little performance that a significant part of what the non-breaching party had achieved by obtaining the contract is seriously threatened, interfered with, or destroyed. A material breach gives rise to an immediate cause of action for breach of the entire contract because it goes to the heart of the contract itself. Insubstantial performance never discharges a promisor's contractual obligation unless the promisee accepts that performance.

Example 9b:

Connie agrees to sell her used car, in running condition, to Gary for $3,500. When Gary takes possession of the vehicle, he discovers that the car's transmission is frozen in gear and will not work. This does not meet the contract specifications. This is a breach of the entire contract, giving Gary an immediate cause of action for the full purchase price.

Some courts and some experts, including the drafters of the *Restatement (Second) of Contracts,* use the terms partial breach and total breach. While these terms have some advantages, they, alone, are unrealistic in describing a not uncommon situation. A breach may have such a serious impact on the expectations of the innocent party under the contract that it is "material" even though it is not really "total." Such situations arise when the breaching party's performance is seriously deficient but the breaching party has not failed to do absolutely everything that he is required to do. The Restatement recognizes this and has created three categories of breach – minor, material, and total. Note that not all jurisdictions use this vocabulary.

Remember, regardless of how breaches are defined, they all entitle the innocent, or non-breaching, party to sue for breach of contract. Whether a contracting party actually does sue immediately, or at all, for a minor breach depends more on practicality than on legal rights or theory. Often, a contracting party will decide that is not desirable, cost-effective, or even affordable to engage in litigation. Having a legal right to pursue litigation does not make doing so practical. The right to sue can still be of some benefit, however. If the breaching party acknowledges that there has been a breach, knows that the right to sue exists, and is operating in good faith, he or she may be more inclined to remedy the defect in his performance and avoid the risk of litigation.

Agreement of the Parties

The parties to a contract are always free to rearrange their contractual agreements by mutual assent. Since the contract came about by mutual agreement, it can be ended at any time by mutual agreement. So long as *both* parties agree, they may be discharged from the original obligation without any negative consequences. A *mutual rescission* occurs when both parties to the contract agree that they do not want to proceed any further under the agreement.

Example 9c:

Don and Joe agreed last year to enter into a partnership for the purpose of building new homes with their project to begin this coming summer. Given a down-turn in the housing market, they now decide the business venture is no longer feasible and both want to rescind the contract. They are free to do so.

Another type of discharge of a contract by agreement is a *release*. A release is a contract in which one side relieves the other of any obligation existing under a previous contract in situations where one party has already given some performance. A release is usually obtained by the payment of consideration, usually money, and is valuable protection when a person has, or may have, breached a contract and wishes to avoid any possibility of litigation.

Example 9d:

Elizabeth contracts with Peter to paint both the inside and outside of Elizabeth's house. After painting the inside, Peter gets an extremely profitable contract to paint a large, commercial building which must be undertaken immediately. Peter cannot perform both jobs at once. Peter informs Elizabeth that he will not finish her job (painting the outside of the house). Peter is, of course, in breach of his contract. Elizabeth has the right to sue. Peter may ask Elizabeth to release him from any further obligation to paint her house.

An *accord and satisfaction* is a special contractual situation in which the parties to a disputed contract agree to settle their dispute by changing the obligations of the contract itself with a new agreement. In other words, the parties agree to substitute a new performance in place of, and in satisfaction of, an existing obligation or right of action (right to sue). An essential element is acceptance of the new performance. The *accord* is the agreement to accept the substitution, and the performance of the accord is the *satisfaction*.

OCGA § 13-4-101

Accord and satisfaction occurs where the parties to an agreement, by a subsequent agreement, have satisfied the former agreement, and the latter agreement has been executed …

Example 9e:

Farmer Green has a contract to sell 1000 bushels of Grade A apples to Ace Food Stores for $10 per bushel. Upon delivery of the apples, the parties get into a dispute as to whether the apples are Grade A or Grade B. Rather than sue one another, the parties may agree to an accord and satisfaction, and agree to a price of $9 per bushel, with no comments about grade.

Example 9f:

Continuing with the facts of the example 9d above, Peter want to induce Elizabeth to enter into a new agreement. He may offer to paint the outside of the house at a later date for a discounted price in order to ensure Elizabeth does not sue him for breach of contract. If Elizabeth agrees, she and Peter have entered into an accord and satisfaction.

The parties may also agree to a novation. Recall from Chapter 8 that a novation is a substitution of parties in a contract. In a novation, a third person is substituted for one of the original parties to the contract, and the third person not only receives the benefits of the transferor but also assumes all of the transferor's obligations. The contract, after the novation, reads as though the original contracting party never existed. Recall that all parties, the original parties and the new party, must agree to the novation, and that novations are rare.

A *substituted agreement* is a new contract which incorporates the original contract between the parties in the provisions of a new contract that is entered into between the same parties. The original obligations are now absorbed by the new agreement, and, thus, the original contract duties are deemed discharged.

Example 9g:

Katherine is shopping for a pearl necklace and sees one she likes at Frank's Fine Jewelry. She and Frank agree on a price for the necklace. However, before paying for the necklace, Katherine spies the matching pearl bracelet and decides she would also like to have it. After some haggling, Frank agrees on a price for both items. The original contract for the sale of the necklace is now absorbed into this substituted agreement.

Excuse of Conditions

Recall that a *condition* is a timing element of a contractual agreement which either creates or extinguishes a party's duty to perform. Thus, performance may not be required if a given condition fails to occur. Likewise, a condition subsequent can terminate the obligation to perform after performance has begun. Ordinarily, there is a breach of contract, with the ensuing liability, for a broken promise or covenant. However, if the occurrence or non-occurrence of a condition terminates a contractual obligation, there is no breach.

Impossibility of Performance

Circumstances may arise which make it impossible to perform under the contract through no fault of one of the parties. In such cases, it would be unjust and unfair to hold a person responsible for a contractual obligation that could not possibly be met. Such circumstances can arise from the death or incapacity of a party or from the destruction of the subject matter.

OCGA § 13-4-21

If performance of the terms of a contract becomes impossible as a result of an act of God, such impossibility shall excuse nonperformance, except where, by proper prudence, such impossibility might have been avoided by the promisor.

While the *death or incapacity of a party* may seem self-evident, the language of the contract or the type of contract may dictate otherwise. The contract may provide for contingent performers to fulfill the obligations of the original, but now deceased, party. Similarly, if the contract is not "personal" in nature, meaning only that specific party is capable of performing, then the contract can be carried out by the deceased's estate or personal representative.

Example 9h:

Watson contracted to sell his house to Brian. Before closing, Watson dies. It does not matter that the seller, Watson, is no longer alive. His estate is capable of transferring the real estate interest and fulfilling the contractual obligations owed to Brian.

If the contract is one that is personal in nature, and one of the parties becomes incapacitated to the extent that he or she cannot perform, then that parties' performance under the contract may be excused.

The *destruction of the subject matter* excuse may also seem obvious. One cannot perform the obligations of the contract if the very subject matter of the agreement has been lost or destroyed. This is true provided that the object in question is unique and is not destroyed by an act of one of the parties. If the object is capable of near exact replacement, the promisor is expected to find substitute product and fulfill his obligation. The fact that it might be more expensive for him is of no concern to the law. However, if the subject of the contract is unique or irreplaceable, then the doctrine of impossibility of performance relieves the obligor of performance.

Example 9i:

Tommy has agreed to let his prize show-dog stud with Terri's dog for a fee. Before consummation of the contract, Tommy's dog dies. Both parties are relieved of their contractual obligations.

Note Georgia's definition of "impossibility" is quite restrictive, being limited to "acts of God." An act of God, as noted by the Court in the *Elavon* case at the end of this chapter, is "an overwhelming, unprevenable event caused exclusively by forces of nature, such as an earthquake, flood, or tornado." Does the Illinois court use the same definition in the case below?

Parker v. Arthur Murray, Inc.
295 N.E.2d 487 (1973)
Appellate Court of Illinois

Facts: In November, 1959, Ryland Parker, a 37-year-old college-educated bachelor, went to the Arthur Murray Studios in Oak Park, Illinois, to redeem a certificate entitling him to three free dancing lessons. During the free lessons the instructor told Parker that he had "exceptional potential to be a fine and accomplished dancer." Parker thereupon signed a contract for more lessons. Parker attended lessons regularly and was praised and encouraged by his instructors despite his lack of progress. Contract extensions and new contracts for additional instructional hours were executed, all prepaid. Each written contract contained, in bold-type, the words "NON-CANCELABLE CONTRACT."

In 1961, Parker was severely injured in an automobile accident, rendering him incapable of continuing his dancing lessons. At that time he had contracted for a total of 2,734 hours of dance lessons for which he had prepaid $24,812. When Arthur Murray Studios refused to refund any of the money, Parker sued to rescind the outstanding contracts.

Issue: Does the doctrine of impossibility excuse Parker's performance of the personal services contracts?

Holding: The Court noted that in Illinois, impossibility of performance is recognized as a ground for rescission of a contract. While the studio contended that the bold-type words "NON-CANCELABLE" manifested the parties' mutual intent to waive their respective rights to invoke the doctrine of impossibility, the Court held that the plaintiff never contemplated that by signing the contracts he was waiving a remedy expressly recognized by Illinois courts. Thus, Parker was excused from performing under the contracts.

Supervening Illegality

A *supervening illegality* excuses performance of a contract because illegal contracts are unenforceable. In this circumstance, the subject matter of the contract was not illegal at the time of the making of the agreement, but in the time between acceptance and performance, the law changed. The change in the law made what was previously acceptable under the contract illegal. Since the law will not permit persons to engage in illegal activities, the parties are, therefore, deemed discharged from their contractual duties.

Example 9j:

Robert contracts with Ben Builder for the construction of a new home on his lot. The home will cover 30% of the lot, which, at the time the parties entered into the agreement, was permissible under local zoning laws. However, prior to the commencement of construction, the local zoning board passes a new ordinance which set the maximum lot coverage at 20%. The home cannot be constructed per the contract due to a supervening illegality, and, thus, performance is excused.

Frustration of Purpose

Occasionally, both parties are able to perform on their contractual obligations, but due to changed circumstances, it has become useless for them to do so. In other words, although the contract may appear valid and capable of being performed, the purpose, or underlying reason for the existence of the contract, may no longer exist. In such cases, which are quite rare, performance is excused under the doctrine of *frustration of purpose*.

Example 9k:

The most famous cases regarding frustration of purpose are the Coronation Cases. When Queen Victoria of England died in 1901 after more than sixty years on the throne, the coronation of her son, Edward VII, was highly anticipated. The procession route was announced months in advance, resulting in great demand for spaces overlooking the route. One-day leases were entered into by people with homes and offices overlooking the route so that the "tenants" could have a view of the parade. Two days before the ceremony, Edward developed appendicitis, and the coronation was postponed. The one-day landlords brought suit against the tenants for rent when the tenants refused to pay. The court held that, while the contracts, on their faces, were valid and enforceable, the purpose of the contracts – to view the coronation procession – no longer existed. The tenants were discharged from their rental obligations because of frustration of purpose.

Performance Prevented

If one party engages in some act that makes it impossible for the other party to fulfill his obligation, the innocent party's performance is excused. The party who prevents performance may take some action which affirmatively blocks the other party's attempt to perform his contractual obligations or he may prevent a condition precedent to performance from occurring. If he does so, then the wrongdoer's actions excuse the counter-performance of the innocent party; the wrongdoer, however, is still contractually bound.

OCGA § 13-4-23

If the nonperformance of a party to a contract is caused by the conduct of the opposite party, such conduct shall excuse the other party from performance.

Example 9l:

Walter agrees to paint Michael's house next Saturday. When Walter arrives at Michael's property, he finds that Michael has bolted and locked the gate, blocking access to the house. Michael's conduct excuses Walter's performance, but Michael will still be liable for Walter's costs and expenses.

A *voluntary disablement* occurs when a party prevents his own performance by putting himself in a position where he will be unable to perform according to the contract terms. In other words, his inability to perform his obligations under the contract are not an occurrence outside of the control of that party, but are, instead, the result of his own actions.

Example 9m:

Dan, a real estate developer, is building a subdivision. Dan contracts with Larry, a professional landscaper, to landscape the subdivision entrances, right-of-ways, and recreation areas. In exchange, Dan has agreed to deed to Larry a specific lot selected by Larry. If Dan sells the lot selected by Larry to a third party, Dan has voluntarily disabled himself from being able to perform on his contract with Larry.

In cases where one party has prevented the performance of the other party or in which there has been a voluntary disablement, the wrongdoer always remains contractually bound. A person cannot benefit from his own wrongdoing.

Insolvency

If one party to the contract becomes *judicially insolvent*, the other side is excused, at least temporarily, from performing. The declaration of bankruptcy by a party results in the freezing of all transactions in which the bankrupt party is involved. This is done in order to maintain the status quo until the resolution of the bankruptcy case.

The law does not require that a person become a judicial creditor of a bankrupt party, nor will it permit someone to attempt to fulfill a contract with a bankrupt party which results in increased debts for the insolvent party. Whether or not the performance of contract obligations by the innocent party are permanently excused or merely suspended for a time depends on the nature of the bankruptcy proceeding and the orders of the bankruptcy court.

Anticipatory Breach

If one party, during the time of the contract, states that he has decided not to fulfill his contractual obligation, the innocent party does not have to perform. For the contracting party's conduct to be considered an *anticipatory breach*, the words indicating his or her intentions must be positive, unconditional and unequivocal. An anticipatory breach requires that the breaching party state in no uncertain terms that he will not perform his obligations – merely suggesting that his performance will not be forthcoming is not enough.

In addition to being relieved of his contractual obligations, the innocent party in an anticipatory breach situation may actually sue on the contract before the performance by the other party is due. By permitting the aggrieved party to file suit in anticipation of the breach, the potential damages can be more effectively mitigated since the innocent party may accrue additional damages if he were to be forced to wait for the future breach and then file suit.

As should be apparent, in order for there to be an anticipatory breach, both parties to the contract must still have executory duties to perform. If the innocent party has already performed his obligations under the contract, with no other duty to fulfill, there is nothing "anticipatory" about the breach. The other side is in total breach.

Madison Square Garden v. Ali
430 F.Supp. 679 (1977)
United States District Court for the Northern District of Illinois

<u>Facts</u>: In September, 1976, Muhammed Ali successfully defended his heavyweight boxing championship of the world by defeating Ken Norton. Shortly after the fight, Ali held a press conference where he, as he had done on several occasions before, announced his retirement from boxing. At that time, Ali had beaten every challenger except Duane Bobick whom he had not yet fought.

In November, 1976, Madison Square Garden Boxing, Inc., (MSGB), a fight promoter, offered Ali $2.5 million if he would fight Bobick. Ali agreed, stating, "We are back in business again." MSGA and Ali signed a Fighter's Agreement and MSGA paid Ali $125,000 advance payment. The fight was to take place in Madison Square Garden on a date in February, 1977. On November 30, 1976, Ali told MSGB that he was retiring from boxing and would not fight Bobick in February.

<u>Issue</u>: Does Ali's announcement constitute an anticipatory repudiation, allowing MSGB to sue before the scheduled fight date?

<u>Holding</u>: MSGB does not have to wait until the date performance is due in order to sue Ali for breach of contract. Ali's announcement of his intention to retire was an anticipatory breach of the contract to fight the heavyweight challenger. This announcement was a statement of an intention to refuse to perform under the terms of the contract. At that time, when the announcement was made, the sports arena had a right to sue Ali for breach of contract.

In all of the above described situations in which one party has breached his obligations under a contract, the innocent party is excused from performance. However, the innocent party still has obligations – he has an obligation to attempt to minimize, or mitigate, his injury. The duty to mitigate damages is discussed below.

9.2 Legal Remedies

A breach of contract is really nothing more than a broken promise. If a party to a contract breaches the contract, or breaks his promises and fails to perform his obligations under the contract, then the innocent party has an immediate cause of action provided that the breach is material or serious. Recall that a material breach makes the whole purpose of the contract null since the innocent party is not getting what he or she bargained for. A breach is material if it concerns a term or element that is significant or important to the basis for the agreement. A minor breach, however, is one which has little effect on the expectations of the parties, and gives rise only to a cause of action for that minor or insignificant flaw in performance.

If a valid, enforceable contract is breached, the innocent party has remedies. These include both legal remedies, or money damages, and equitable remedies which include other forms of relief.

Legal remedies or damages are monetary awards granted to the innocent party whenever money would be an appropriate method of rectifying the injury.

Duty to Mitigate

The injured party to the contract cannot simply sit back, do nothing, and later sue the other party for breach of contract. The law imposes a duty on the injured party to a failed contract to attempt to minimize her losses when it is reasonably possible to do so.

This duty on the part of the non-breaching party in the contract to try to lessen the amount of harm she suffers is called *mitigation of damages* and is required. The injured party must make a reasonable attempt to find a replacement for the failed party's contractual performance, thus reducing the amount of her damages. However, only reasonable, not extraordinary or potentially very expensive, efforts to mitigate or minimize damages must be undertaken.

OCGA § 13-6-5

Where by a breach of contract a party is injured, he is bound to lessen the damages as far as is practicable by the use of ordinary care and diligence.

Example 9n:

John has ordered 10,000 units from Acme at a price of $11.00 per unit. When Acme fails to deliver, John must attempt to find replacement units rather than just sue Acme for $110,000. John finds suitable replacements, but will have to pay $12.50 per unit. His damages are $15,000 – the difference between what he expected to pay and what he actually paid.

Compensatory Damages

Compensatory damages, sometimes known as actual damages, are the most common remedy for breach of contract. They are monetary awards designed to put the injured party in the same position he would have been in had the contract been completed as originally contemplated. They are the damages which satisfy a party's expectations under the contract. To determine compensatory damages, take the value of what the injured party started with, add to it the value of what he was promised, and then subtract or add what he was left with.

OCGA 123-6-2

Damages recoverable for a breach of contract are such as arise naturally and according to the usual course of things from such breach and such as the parties contemplated, when the contract was made, as the probable result of its breach.

Example 9o:

Samantha purchases a gold ring from Jennifer for $150. After the sale is complete, Samantha discovers that the ring is phony and is worth only $4. The amount of Samantha's compensatory damages would be $146, the difference between what she was promised (a genuine gold ring) and what she actually received (a phony gold ring worth $4).

Compensatory damages are intended to insure that the injured party is left in as good of a position as he would have been had the contract not been breached, but had, instead, been completed as intended. If, however, the injured party ends up with more than he was promised under the contract, then there are no damages. Furthermore, in mitigating his damages, the injured party cannot put himself in a better position than he would have enjoyed had the contract been completed as intended.

Gainesville Glass Co. v. Don Hammond, Inc.
157 Ga.App. 640, 278 S.E.2d 182 (1981)
Court of Appeals of Georgia

Facts: Don Hammond, Inc., a general contractor, had a contract for the construction of a recreational center at Lake Lanier Islands. Gainesville Glass orally agreed to supply and install the windows for the project for the sum of $2,003. The contract called for "plexiglass panels." "Plexiglass" is a trade name of a specific product made only by one manufacturer but is a term also used frequently to apply to acrylic products made by different companies.

When Hammond called upon the Gainesville Glass to perform the window work, Gainesville Glass refused to do so for the agreed contract price. Hammond then hired another glass company at a cost of $7,253.95. That supplier installed different, more expensive, materials. Plexiglass would have cost less than half the amount charged for the materials actually installed.

Hammond then sued Gainesville Glass for $5,250.95, the difference between the contract price and what the Hammond actually paid.

Issue: What is the proper measure of damages?

Holding: The measure of damages here would be the reasonable cost of completing the window work for the center. This is the difference between the contract price ($2,003.00) and the reasonable and necessary cost to Hammond to have the windows supplied and installed in accordance with the terms of the original contract.

The materials ultimately supplied were significantly more expensive than those called for in the original agreement to supply "plexiglass panels." The fact that the more expensive material "complied" with the architectural specifications is of no moment. The plaintiff must prove that each of the items of expense incurred by him was necessary in obtaining what he was entitled to have under his contract. He cannot use materials which were more expensive than those called for in the contract. If the injured party could fulfill the terms of the contract by using more expensive materials than specified in the original agreement and have the breaching party assume the burden, the result would be an unwarranted windfall to the injured party.

Where a party seeks damages for violation of a contract, the measure of damages is not what he has suffered by performing his part, but what he has suffered by the failure of the other party to perform his part. Damages are given as compensation for the injury sustained and an injured party cannot be placed in a better position than he would have been in if the contract had not been breached.

Punitive Damages

Punitive damages, also known as exemplary damages, are monetary awards designed to punish the breaching party. Punitive damages are not intended to make the innocent party whole, but are designed solely to punish the wrongdoer and deter future wrongful conduct. Punishment is not a usual aspect of contract law; thus, punitive damages are seldom awarded in contract actions. Generally, punitive damages are only awarded when authorized by statute and in cases where the breach of contract is accompanied by some other wrong. If the case is one in which there are, in addition to allegations of breach of contract, allegations of the commission of a tort such as fraud which would authorize punitive damages and such damages are awarded, the injured party receives compensatory damages as well as the award of punitive damages.

Consequential Damages

Consequential damages are monetary damages beyond the standard measure of compensatory damages. They are awarded due to the special circumstances and expenses incurred because of the injury. In other words, consequential damages are economic losses caused *indirectly* by a breach of contract. Lost profits are often claimed as consequential damages. For the innocent party to be entitled to lost profits as consequential damages, the lost profits must be capable of definite ascertainment and traceable directly to the acts of the breaching party.

It is important not to confuse consequential damages with *speculative* damages. Speculative damages are those damages which an injured party might allege she is due but which are not ascertainable or provable.

Example 9p:

Devon, an aspiring novelist, tries for months to get an appointment with a literary agent in New York. After finally securing the appointment, Devon books a flight on TransCoast Airlines. When his flight is delayed four hours, Devon misses his appointment. While Devon may have hoped to secure the agent's services to sell his unpublished novel, his allegation that his damages caused by the airline's delay are millions of dollars, is purely speculative.

Liquidated Damages

Liquidated damages are reasonable damages the parties themselves have agreed to in the contract itself. Normally, parties to a contract would specify liquidated damages if it would be difficult or impossible to compute compensatory damages because of the uncertain nature of the contract or the subject matter. Because liquidated damages are determined at the outset of the contract in order to avoid lengthy litigation later on, the court will simply abide by the parties' agreement under the concept of freedom of contract.

OCGA 13-6-7

If the parties agree in their contract what the damages for a breach shall be, they are said to be liquidated and, unless the agreement violates some principle of law, the parties are bound thereby.

However, a liquidated damages provision may be unenforceable if it is, in fact, meant to punish the breaching party rather than to ease recovery of hard-to-determine losses. Liquidated damages are not meant to be punitive in nature.

H.S. Perlin Company, Inc. v. Morse Signal Devices of San Diego
California Court of Appeals
209 Cal.App.3d 1289 (1989)

<u>Facts:</u> In December, 1974, H.S. Perlin Company, Inc., a retail store, and Morse Signal Devices of San Diego, a security company, entered into a contract under which Morse agreed to provide burglar and fire alarm services to Perlin's coin and stamp store. Pursuant to the contract, Perlin agreed to pay $50 per month for this service. The contract also contained a liquidated damages clause which provided that Perlin's total damages in the event of a loss based on a failure of service by Morse would be limited to $250.00.

On August 25, 1980, Perlin's store was burglarized. Before entering the store, the burglars cut the telephone line which ran from the burglar alarm system in Perlin's store to Morse's central location. When the line was cut, a signal indicated the interruption of service at Morse's central location. However, Morse took no steps to investigate the interruption of service at Perlin's store. The burglars stole stamps and coins with a wholesale value of $958,000. Perlin did not have insurance against this loss. Perlin sued Morse to recover damages.

Issue: Is the liquidated damages clause enforceable?

Holding: The defendants' negligence caused Perlin's losses. However, there was no inequality in bargaining strength between the parties which would make the provision unreasonable. Further, the plaintiff was not unfairly surprised by the provision, particularly in view of the testimony of plaintiff that he had a custom and practice of not reading any contracts of any kind at all, while the burglar alarm salesman testified to his usual practice of informing subscribers of the liquidated damages clause. Moreover, plaintiff was aware that the subscription price to the burglary alarm service was far less than the insurance premium required to protect the value of the inventory in the event of theft. The trial court's ruling awarding the plaintiff $250 in liquidated damages is upheld.

A liquidated damages clause should not be confused with a *limitation of damages* provision. If a contract contains a limitation of damages, the parties have agreed, at the outset, that there is a ceiling or maximum amount of damages for which a breaching party will be liable under the contract. If the actual loss is less than the ceiling, the injured party is awarded the smaller sum; if, however, the actual amount of damages is greater, the liability of the breaching party is capped at the amount provided by the limitation of damages clause.

9.3 *Equitable Remedies*

Equitable remedies are available when monetary damages are insufficient to compensate a party injured by a breach of contract. Historically, courts of equity, called chancery courts, were more concerned with the merits of a case rather than the legal procedure and sought to provide remedies which were fair and just given the circumstances of the particular case before the court. Today, these largely non-monetary remedies are designed to prevent unfairness and unjust enrichment.

Injunction

An *injunction* is a court order to stop someone from engaging in a specific action or to stop a particular activity. The legal term is "to enjoin" a party from engaging in a specific activity. The order can be temporary or permanent. Courts do not usually order injunctions easily - a litigant may be entitled to a *temporary restraining order (TRO)* if he can show irreparable harm would result from a refusal to order the injunction. As indicated by its name, a TRO is only a temporary measure by the court until a hearing for full injunctive relief can take place.

Example 9q:

Paul owns a tract of land in the country on which he plans to build his retirement home. The land has several hundred-year-old oak trees on it. Paul contracts with Sam for the removal of scrub brush, and is horrified to find Sam cutting the old oaks. Sam insists he is entitled by the terms of the parties' contract to cut all timber on the land. Monetary damages will not fully compensate Paul since he will not live long enough to see the oaks replaced. An order enjoining Sam from further cutting until the issue can be heard will protect Paul and the trees from further harm.

Specific Performance

Specific performance is a court order requiring the breaching party to perform exactly what he promised to do under the contract. This remedy is granted only when the subject matter of the contract is considered unique and therefore not replaceable – real estate or an antique, for instance. Other appropriate subjects for this remedy include rare collectibles or original works of art.

Example 9r:

Sarah has a contract with Rachel to purchase Rachel's farm. On closing day, Rachel refuses to perform. Because real estate is generally considered unique, Sarah could go to court to seek specific performance. The court would then order Rachel to convey the farm to Sarah pursuant to the contract.

O.C.G.A. § 23-2-130

Specific performance of a contract, if within the power of the party, will be decreed, generally, whenever the damages recoverable at law would not be an adequate compensation for nonperformance.

Note that with an injunction, the court is ordering a party to stop doing some specific thing, whereas with specific performance, the court is ordering a party to take action or to do some specific thing.

Recall from the discussion, in Chapter 5 the requirements of a writing sufficient to satisfy the Statute of Frauds. The subject matter of the contract must be identified in such a manner that no question can arise between the parties who have entered into the agreement regarding the subject matter. In Georgia, real property must be described in detail – a legal description or reference to a plat of survey is required.

Kirkley v. Jones

250 Ga.App. 113, 550 S.E.2d 686 (2001)

Court of Appeals of Georgia

Facts: Richard Jones borrowed a sum of money from William Kirkley. Kirkley and Jones entered into a handwritten loan agreement which provided that if Jones failed to repay the money he had borrowed from Kirkley, he, Jones, would release all his interest in certain property in Williamson, Georgia, to Kirkley. The property was described as "Lot 13 on Blanton Mill Road," with no further description being given. After Jones defaulted on the note, Kirkley filed suit seeking Jones' interest in the property. The trial court declined to grant specific performance, and, instead, awarded a monetary judgment.

Issue: Was specific performance appropriate in this case?

Holding: The handwritten contract between Kirkley and Jones did not sufficiently describe or identify the land to be conveyed in the event of a default. Specific performance of a contract for the sale of land will not be granted unless the land is clearly identified. The contract must identify the land to be conveyed with reasonable definiteness by describing the particular tract or furnishing a key by which it may be located with the aid of extrinsic evidence.

Here, there is no physical description of the land. It is described only as "Lot 13 on Blanton Mill Road." There is no indication of where Blanton Mill Road is located, where Lot 13 is located or the size, shape and boundaries of the lot. In fact, there may be another Lot 13 somewhere on Blanton Mill Road. This court has previously found that an adequate description of property cannot be found within the four corners of a contract that provides nothing more than an address. The contract in the present case does not even provide a specific address. Because of the lack of a sufficient description of the land, specific performance is not appropriate in this case.

Gilleland v. Welch
199 Ga. 341, 34 S.E.2d 517 (1945)
Supreme Court of Georgia

Facts: Gilleland and Welch entered into a contract whereby Gilleland agreed to buy certain land from Welch for the sum of $3,500, to be paid as follows: $750 cash, $1,650 to be paid December 1st, and assumption of a loan in the amount of $1,100, payment due to the Land Bank Commissioner. The agreement was later modified to provide for a payment of $1,000 cash, rather than $750, in order to cover attorney's fees in connection with the sale.

The parties signed the final agreement on August 14th and agreed to meet at the Bank of Norcross on August 15th to execute the deed. Gilleland was to take possession of the property on January 1st. Welch did not appear, having advised Gilleland that he had changed his mind. Gilleland tendered to Welch the amount of the payment due, $1,000, and advised Welch that he was "ready and willing to comply with all terms of the contract, including the future payment of the sum of $1,650." Welch still refused. Gilleland then immediately sued for specific performance of the contract.

Issue: Was specific performance an appropriate remedy in this case?

Holding: The contract between the parties constituted a valid, complete and unambiguous agreement requiring payment by Gilleland, in the manner agreed, of the full purchase price and his assumption of the specified loan before title should be transferred. Upon the anticipatory breach, Gilleland had two options: he could accept the anticipatory breach and sue at once for damages, or he could treat the contract as remaining in force until the time set for performance (January 1st) and then sue for specific performance.

Before equity will decree specific performance of a contract for the sale of land, at the instance of the purchaser, there must be an unconditional tender of the purchase price. In this case, the prerequisite as to a tender of complete performance has not been met. The time set for performance of the contract had not arrived at the time Gilleland filed his suit, and he had not paid (or tendered) the entire purchase price. Simply stating that he is "ready and willing" to pay in the future is not enough. Gilleland failed to wait for the time for performance to come due; thus, his suit for specific performance was premature.

As seen from the above cases, in Georgia, the courts appear reluctant to grant specific performance in cases where real property is at issue.

Rescission and Restitution

Rescission and restitution is a court order in which the court rescinds, or revokes, the contract in the interest of fairness. Here, it is the party who wants to breach the contract who is seeking relief from the court. To obtain that relief, he must be able to demonstrate to the court that fulfillment of the contract would be so burdensome as to be unjust. Mere economic loss, unless it is very substantial, is insufficient since economic loss is, quite naturally, a risk of contract.

Reformation

Reformation is a remedy much like an accord and satisfaction, but it is ordered by the court when the parties cannot resolve a conflict themselves. Recall that under the rules of construction, contracts are to be upheld if at all possible. Therefore, if the dispute merely involves a question of quality or quantity of the subject matter, the court can reform the contract to correspond to what was actually delivered. In this manner, the contractual relationship can go forward and neither of the parties will be in breach.

Example 9s:

Recall the facts from the earlier Example 9e: Farmer Green and Ace Food Stores are in dispute as to whether Farmer Green's apples are Grade A or Grade B. If the parties cannot resolve the dispute themselves and the disputed delivery was the first on a multi-year contract, the court might choose to reform the contract to remove the mention of grade and substitute a compromised price.

Quasi-Contractual Remedies

Quasi-contractual remedies are the only equitable remedies which involve money damages. Recall that implied-in-law, or quasi, contracts were discussed in Chapter 3. Quasi-contractual remedies are available in situations in which no contract actually exists but where there has been an unjust enrichment to one of the parties to the dispute. There can be no breach of contract because there is no contract; however, one party has rendered a benefit to the other and fairness and equity require compensation.

Quantum merit is the *value of services* rendered and may be awarded when the defendant has been unjustly enriched by receiving uncompensated for services. The defendant will be required to pay for the value of the services.

Quantum valebant is the *value of property* received and may be awarded when the defendant has been unjustly enriched by receiving a conveyance of property. The defendant will be required to pay for the value of the property he received.

9.4 *Other Remedial Provisions*

A *waiver* is the forgiveness by a party to a contract of the other side's failure to meet a contractual obligation. A party cannot be sued for breaching his obligation under a contract if the innocent party waives that breach. A waiver may be either express or implied by the actions of the innocent party. For instance, if a tenant's lease prohibits subletting the apartment, but the tenant asks for and is given permission by the landlord to sublet, the tenant is not in breach of the contract. The landlord has waived any claim of breach by granting permission to the tenant to act in a fashion contrary to the provisions of the lease agreement.

Litigation is time-consuming and expensive. Therefore, parties to a contract may specify that disputes will be decided, not by going to court, but by having the matter resolved by *arbitration.* Arbitration is a non-judicial method of settling legal disputes in which both sides agree to submit the claim to an agreed-upon arbitrator for relief. Because arbitration is now so popular, it must be considered when determining appropriate remedies for a contractual dispute.

9.5 *The Perils of the Lack of Foresight*

As we have seen in this text, inexpertly drafted contracts can create large-scale problems for the parties involved. Such issues are not limited to lay persons acting without professional advice. Because it is so difficult to anticipate every contingency, from time to time, even very large organizations with acess to the very finest in legal representation can find themselves in deep water.

The financial crisis of 2008 wrought much conflict, confusion, and despair for virtually everyone. Some of this, predictably, resulted in litigation. In January, 2009, a lawsuit was filed against Wahovia and Wells Fargo seeking roughly $1 billion in damages. Below is an excerpt from the federal district judge's ruling with regard to various issues arising out that case. The order is well-written, easy to understand, and addresses several of the issues discussed in this text.

Elavon v. Wachovia Bank and Wells Fargo
United States District Court for the Northern District of Georgia
841 F. Supp. 2d 1298; 2011 U.S. Dist. LEXIS 152004 (2011)

ORDER OF THE COURT:

This case is before the Court on the cross-motions for summary judgment.

Plaintiff Elavon, Inc., (formerly known as NOVA) is a Georgia corporation with its principal place of business in Atlanta, Georgia. Elavon is in the business of providing merchant processing services, specifically processing credit-debit card and certain other electronic transactions. At relevant times Defendant Wachovia Bank was a national banking association with its designated main office in North Carolina. Defendant Wells Fargo is a Delaware corporation with its principal place of business in California.

The parties agree that Georgia law applies. The agreement at issue states that Georgia law applies.

Plaintiff brought this suit against Defendants alleging breach of contract. Plaintiff claims that Defendants did not have a right to unilaterally cancel a written agreement between Plaintiff and Wachovia.

Defendants respond that cancellation was allowable under the express terms of the agreement. Defendants argue in the alternative that Wachovia Bank's performance under the agreement was excused on grounds of: (1) impossibility and/or impracticability in light of the economic conditions in 2008, and (2) force majeure.

Undisputed Facts

Between 2002 and December 31, 2008, Elavon and Wachovia had a written agreement through which Elavon provided credit/debit card charge processing services for merchants who banked with Wachovia. The agreement called for Wachovia Bank to refer its merchant customers to Elavon for "merchant processing services." The written agreement was called an "Alliance Agreement" and was amended and extended several times with the last extended termination date being December 31, 2012.

The Alliance Agreement called for Wachovia and its "successors and assigns" to refer its merchant customers exclusively to Elavon for merchant processing services. Elavon made certain payments to Wachovia, and Elavon and Wachovia agreed to share the "merchant account royalties" generated by the merchant processing services, with Wachovia Bank getting 25% of the royalties and 75% going to Elavon.

In 2008 the U.S. banking system experienced serious liquidity and solvency problems. During September and October, 2008, the United States was, according to Dr. Alan Greenspan, the former Chairman of the Federal Reserve, "in the midst of a once in a century credit tsunami." Bank of America purchased Merrill Lynch; Lehman Brothers filed for bankruptcy; Goldman Sachs and Morgan Stanley were approved for conversion to bank holding companies; Fannie Mae and Freddie Mac were placed into receivership by the United States government; and Washington Mutual failed and was purchased by JP Morgan Chase.

Wachovia reported a $664 million loss in the first quarter of 2008 and an $8.9 billion quarterly loss in the second quarter of 2008. Wachovia's stock price fell and investors considered a Wachovia default increasingly likely. On October 3, 2008 Wells Fargo announced that it had reached an agreement with Wachovia whereby it would be merged into Wells Fargo.

Both sides agree that at the time the Wachovia-Wells Fargo Agreement and Plan of Merger was signed on October 3, 2008, Wells Fargo had no specific awareness of the Wachovia-Elavon Alliance Agreement that was to be in effect until December 31, 2012. Wells Fargo had not inquired about Wachovia's merchant processing business by that date. Debra Rossi, the head of Wells Fargo's merchant services business, became aware of the Wachovia-Elavon Alliance Agreement no later than October 21, 2008, but at that point the Agreement and Plan of Merger had already been executed and changes in the merger agreement would not be allowed. Ms. Rossi reviewed the Alliance Agreement in November 2008. The Court infers that particular scrutiny was caused by the fact that, at that time, Wells Fargo already had their own contract for merchant processing services with First Data Merchant Process Services, a joint venture between Wells Fargo and others. Ms. Rossi was the principle negotiator of that agreement. The First Data contract which existed in October 2008 was set to last until December 31, 2009, but on December 31, 2008, (after the merger) it was extended to December 31, 2014. There is substantial evidence in the record that Ms. Rossi and other Wells Fargo representatives were concerned about liability to Elavon under the Alliance Agreement.

On December 29, 2008, Wachovia notified Elavon that they were cancelling the Alliance Agreement effective upon Wells Fargo's merger with Wachovia. The letter stated:

Pursuant to § 17.2 of the Amended ... Alliance ... Agreement between ... Elavon ... and Wachovia ..., Wachovia hereby states its intent to cancel the contract and therefore terminate the Alliance Agreement effective December 31, 2008, subject to consummation on the date of Wachovia's anticipated merger with Wells Fargo ....

On January 5, 2009, Elavon responded, "*Wachovia has [no] right to cancel or terminate the Alliance Agreement effective December 31, 2008*" and "*notwithstanding the Wachovia Letter, the Alliance Agreement remains in full force and effect in accordance with its terms.*" Elavon also wrote Wachovia on January 28, 2009 informing Defendants that it was "*ready, willing, and able to make the Elavon Payments if Wachovia and Wells Fargo promptly rescind or revoke their repudiation of the Agreement and give Elavon reasonable assurances that they will honor their continuing obligations thereunder.*

On December 31, 2008, Wachovia was merged into Wells Fargo. Presumably Wells Fargo assumed all obligations of Wachovia. Wells Fargo began referring merchants to First Data, including former Wachovia customers.

Elavon brought suit seeking unspecified damages for Defendants' alleged failure to honor Wachovia's obligations under the Alliance Agreement.

Motions for Summary Judgment

The Court will grant summary judgment when "there is no genuine dispute as to any material fact and the movant is entitled to judgment as a matter of law." *FED. R. CIV. P. 56 (a).*

Plaintiff's Motion for Summary Judgment

In its Motion for Partial Summary Judgment, Elavon contends that under the undisputed evidence, no reasonable jury could find for Defendants on their affirmative defenses claiming that performance under the Alliance Agreement was legally excused because of (1) impossibility and/or impracticability and (2) force majeure. Elavon also argues that it should be granted summary judgment on Wachovia's counterclaim for conditional breach of contract because Wachovia's anticipatory repudiation of the contract released Elavon from any future duty to perform under the contract. Summary judgment in Elavon's favor is warranted on these claims.

Defendants' Impossibility and/or Impracticability Defenses

Elavon contends that Defendants' impossibility and/or impracticability defenses fail as a matter of law because (1) Defendants themselves created the "impossibility scenario," (2) Defendants cannot show that their breach was caused by "the occurrence of an event the non-occurrence of which was a basic assumption on which the contract was made," (3) the financial downturn cannot excuse Defendants' performance, and (4) performance of the contract was objectively possible. Defendants counter that in a period of one month, a series of unprecedented, unpredictable, and unthinkable events occurred which caused the banking landscape to deteriorate, and Defendants could not have foreseen the market destruction that resulted. Defendants assert that the question of whether the economic downturn was foreseeable is a question of fact that should be left to the jury, and such economic crisis made it impracticable and/or impossible for Defendants to honor the Alliance Agreement obligations.

Georgia law states: "If performance of the terms of a contract becomes impossible as a result of an act of God, such impossibility shall excuse nonperformance, except where, by proper prudence, such impossibility might have been avoided by the promisor." *O.C.G.A. § 13-4-21.* An act of God is defined as " [a]n overwhelming, unpreventable event caused exclusively by forces of nature, such as an earthquake, flood, or tornado." BLACK'S LAW DICTIONARY (9th ed. 2009). The economic downturn of 2008 was not an "act of God." Further, financial inability does not excuse contract performance as impossible. See *Hampton Island, LLC v. HAOP, LLC, 306 Ga. App. 542, 547-48, 702 S.E.2d 770 (Ga. Ct. App. 2010)*("[T]he fact that one is unable to perform a contract because of his inability to obtain money, whether due to his poverty, a financial panic, or failure of a third party . . . will not ordinarily excuse nonperformance . . .").

Defendants' impossibility defense fails as a matter of law. The fundamental question is whether it was impossible for Wachovia/Wells Fargo to continue to honor the merchant referral requirements of the Alliance Agreement after December 31, 2008. Obviously, this was not impossible. Wells Fargo had its own merchant processing agreement with a joint venture which, as of December 31, 2008, Wells Fargo controlled. Wells Fargo could have modified that agreement if it wished to do so. It also could have made a cash payment in satisfaction of its obligation to Elavon. Whether the parties could have foreseen the financial debacle of 2008 is irrelevant; Wells Fargo decided to acquire Wachovia with full knowledge of the crisis in the banking industry. No one forced Wells Fargo to merge with Wachovia. The possibility of Wachovia being acquired by another company was foreseen in the Alliance Agreement (which gave Elavon but not Wachovia the right to cancel the Agreement in the event Wachovia was acquired by another company). Wells Fargo knew about the Alliance Agreement before the merger was concluded and had actual notice of its provisions.

An impossibility defense is difficult to establish.[10] Defendants have failed to identify evidence which shows that performance of their obligations under the Alliance Agreement was "impossible" as defined by the doctrine of impossibility.

As to Defendants' impracticability defense, Georgia law states that a party has not breached a contract by non-performance "if performance as agreed has been made impracticable by the occurrence of a contingency the nonoccurrence of which was a basic assumption on which the contract was made." *O.C.G.A. § 11-2-615*. The Georgia Court of Appeals has determined that the defense of impracticability contemplates the impracticability of performance by a seller of commercial goods. *Calabro v. State Med. Educ. Bd., 283 Ga. App. 113, 115, 640 S.E.2d 581 (Ga. Ct. App. 2006)*. Thus, the impracticability defense is inapplicable here because Defendants were not in the business of selling commercial goods to Elavon. Even if the impracticability defense were applicable here, it would fail because the economic downfall of 2008 was not a contingency "the non-occurrence of which was a basic assumption on which the contract was made." As discussed above, changes in the economic banking environment and the potential acquisition of Wachovia by another entity were foreseen and accounted for in the Alliance Agreement. Defendants' impracticability defense fails.

The Court GRANTS summary judgment in favor of Plaintiff on Defendants' impossibility and/or impracticability defense.

Defendants' Force Majeure Defense

Elavon argues that summary judgment as to Defendants' force majeure defense is proper because Defendants themselves, not any force majeure or third party, created the conflict with the Alliance Agreement. Defendants did this when Wells Fargo chose to sign a six-year contract with First Data when Wells Fargo knew that a merger with Wachovia was pending and knew of Wachovia Bank's contract with Elavon. Plaintiff also contends that even if the drastic changes in the financial market were considered a force majeure, the Alliance Agreement's force majeure clause did not include financial crises in the list of what force majeure instances would constitute a reason to terminate the contract. Defendants counter that the enumerated list of events that constituted force majeure under the Alliance Agreement contract is not exhaustive but instead "without limitation as to other events beyond the control of the parties." Defendants argue that the unprecedented economic crisis in 2008 was an event "reasonably beyond the control" of Wachovia and because the Alliance Agreement defines force majeure as "factors attributable to events reasonably beyond the control of the party obligated to perform," the force majeure provision of the contract applies in this case. Defendants also assert that the question of whether an event qualifies as force majeure is a question reserved for the jury.

The Alliance Agreement defines force majeure as follows:

[10] In Felder v. Oldham, the Georgia Supreme Court determined that even World War II was not an unforseen event that would support an impossibility defense to contract termination. *Felder v. Oldham, 199 Ga. 820, 824-25, 35 S.E.2d 497 (Ga. 1945)*. The Georgia Supreme Court reasoned that the war could "in no sense be said to be an act of God" and instead may be anticipated. Id. If the Georgia Supreme Court determined that World War II was a foreseeable event that could be anticipated and protected against in a contract, certainly a financial downturn--such as that upon which Defendants rely in their impossibility and/or impracticability defense--can be anticipated and protected against when formulating a contract.

"Force Majeure" means factors attributable to events reasonably beyond the control of the party obligated to perform, including, without limitation, war, armed conflict, acts of terrorism or other similar events, conditions or events of nature, civil disturbances, failures of telephone lines and equipment, computer hardware or software failures or fires.

The Alliance Agreement also contains a force majeure clause:

Article XVII – Miscellaneous ***17.13 Force Majeure.*** *Notwithstanding any provision to the contrary contained herein, no party hereto shall have any liability to any other party hereto for any failure or deficiency in performance of obligations hereunder occurring by reason of Force Majeure.*

The economic downturn in 2008 and the subsequent events that followed do not constitute a force majeure which excused Defendants' performance of their obligations under the Alliance Agreement. While the economic perils that faced the banking industry during 2008 may have been "reasonably beyond the control" of Wachovia, the decision to extend the Wells Fargo-First Data contract was well within Defendants' control. Thus, there was no external force majeure that prevented Wachovia from continuing to perform under the Alliance Agreement.

The financial crises in 2008 did not objectively prevent Wachovia from continuing to refer customers for merchant processing services to Elavon; Defendants themselves decided to stop making the referrals. Additionally, as discussed above, the possibility of the acquisition of Wachovia was contemplated in the Alliance Agreement. More fundamentally, the issue here is whether Wells Fargo's/Wachovia's performance of their obligation under the Alliance Agreement was excused. This is different from the question whether the banking crisis constitutes a force majeure. There remains no question of fact as to whether a force majeure excused Defendants' performance under the Alliance Agreement as amended.

The Court GRANTS summary judgment in favor of Plaintiff on Defendants' force majeure defense.

Defendant Wachovia's Conditional Breach of Contract Counterclaim

Elavon asserts that summary judgment should be granted in favor of Elavon as to Wachovia Bank's conditional breach of contract counterclaim because Wachovia's December 29, 2008, termination letter and subsequent actions constituted anticipatory repudiation, releasing Elavon from any future duty to perform under the Alliance Agreement contract. The Court agrees.

Anticipatory repudiation occurs "when one party thereto repudiates his contractual obligation to perform prior to the time such performance is required under the terms of the contract." *Textile Rubber & Chem. Co. v. Thermo-Flex Techs., Inc., 301 Ga. App. 491, 494, 687 S.E.2d 919 (Ga. Ct. App. 2009).* Here, Defendants repudiated the contract when they sent a letter to Elavon on December 29, 2008, stating, "Wachovia hereby states its intent to cancel the contract and terminate the Alliance Agreement effective December 31, 2008 . . ." On January 5, 2009, Elavon replied to Defendants' December 29, 2008, letter, insisting that the Alliance Agreement remained in full force and effect. In a January 28, 2009, follow up letter, Elavon wrote Defendants stating:

Elavon stands ready, willing, and able to make the Elavon Payments if Wachovia and Wells Fargo promptly rescind or revoke their repudiation of the Agreement and give Elavon reasonable assurances that they will honor their continuing obligations thereunder.

Defendants never rescinded their termination nor provided the requested assurances, effectively repudiating the Alliance Agreement contract. Defendants cannot now claim that Elavon breached the exact same contract that Defendants first repudiated.

The Court GRANTS summary judgment in favor of Plaintiff as to Defendant Wachovia Bank's conditional breach of contract counterclaim.

Defendants' Motion for Summary Judgment

Defendants argue that summary judgment should be granted in their favor because as a matter of law, Wachovia and Wells Fargo properly terminated the Alliance Agreement when they invoked the Contract Cancellation Fee provision in ¶ 2.10 of the contract. Defendants alternatively argue that as a matter of law, Elavon cannot collect damages based on Wells Fargo's failure to refer merchant customers to Elavon and also because Elavon's claim for future lost profits is too speculative. The Court disagrees with these arguments.

Whether Wachovia/Wells Fargo breached the Alliance Agreement

Defendants contend that they did not breach the Alliance Agreement by cancelling it because Wachovia properly invoked the Contract Cancellation Fee provision in Section 2.10 of the Alliance Agreement "providing that Wachovia could terminate the Agreement for any reason, as long as it paid the fee required under that provision". Elavon counters that Article IV - Term and Termination - of the Alliance Agreement provides the grounds for termination; Article IV states that the contract is for a definite five-year term which is not terminable at will and further specifies events of default, none of which apply in this case.

Article II--Financial Terms--Section 2.10 of the Fourth Amendment of the Alliance Agreement states:

Contract Cancellation Fee. *In the event this Agreement is terminated for any reason and by any party prior to December 31, 2012 (except as limited by the following provision), then NOVA shall be entitled to receive a "Contract Cancellation Fee," calculated as set forth below; provided, however, that in the event Wachovia terminates this Agreement pursuant to Section 4.3(a) 4.3(b), or 4.3(d) hereof, then NOVA shall not be entitled to any such Contract Cancellation Fee. The Contract Cancellation Fee payable to NOVA shall be calculated as follows, and based upon the Calendar Year during which the effective date of such termination may occur:*

(a) If the effective date of termination occurs in the Calendar Year ending December 31, 2008, the Contract Cancellation Fee shall be calculated by multiplying $11,000,000 (representing the advance amounts paid by NOVA to Wachovia toward the Alliance Extension Payment and Program Support Payment, respectively, for the Agreement Year ending December 31, 2008) by a fraction, the numerator of which is the number of days from the effective date of termination until December 31, 2008, and the denominator of which is 365.

Article IV--Term and Termination—provides:

Article IV – Term and Termination **4.3** ***Termination by Wachovia.*** *In the event that:*

(a) NOVA materially defaults in the performance of any of its material obligations under this Agreement and fails to cure such default within 30 days after written notice (which notice indicates

that Wachovia may terminate this Agreement pursuant to this Section 4.3(a) if such default is not cured as provided herein) and demand for cure by Wachovia . . .;

(b) any material amount due and payable to Wachovia by NOVA under this Agreement is not paid within fifteen Business Days after NOVA receives written notice (which notice indicates that Wachovia may terminate this Agreement pursuant to this Section 4.3(b) if such non-payment is not cured as provided herein) of such non-payment, and demand for cure (provided that Wachovia has attempted to debit, or cause to be debited, the Settlement Account for such amount in accordance with Section 8.2(e) hereof) . . .;

(c) USB or NOVA experiences a consummated Change in Control; or

(d) there occurs a Voluntary Bankruptcy Proceeding with respect to NOVA;

then, in any such case, Wachovia, at its option, may immediately terminate this Agreement upon written notice to NOVA ...

Elavon is correct on this issue. The provisions of Article IV govern grounds for termination, not Article II which pertains to financial terms. There is no ambiguity in the Alliance Agreement, as amended on this point. Also, Defendants' argument that Section 2.10 is a liquidated damages clause is misguided. Section 2.10 is designed to rebate unearned portions of the Alliance Extension Payment and the Program Support Payment if the Alliance Agreement were to end before December 31, 2012. Section 2.10 does not purport to estimate Elavon's total damages for breach.

"Georgia law does not interpret contracts as providing for liquidated damages unless it is clear that the parties intended it." *ADP-Fin. Computer Servs., Inc. v. First Nat'l Bank of Cobb Cnty., 703 F.2d 1261, 1264 (11th Cir. 1983).* "While the words 'liquidated damages' are not specifically required, some manifestation of the parties intent to agree to liquidated damages is." Id. Nowhere in Section 2.10 of the Alliance Agreement do the parties indicate an intent to agree to liquidated damages nor does Section 2.10 specify that the designated "Contract Cancellation Fee" extinguishes, satisfies, or liquidates the damages in the event of a breach of the Alliance Agreement. Therefore, Wachovia cannot terminate the Agreement "for any reason" as long as it has paid the fee (which Defendants call a liquidated damages fee) required under Section 2.10.

The Court need not address the parol evidence presented by Elavon in its memorandum in opposition to Defendants' Motion for Summary Judgment because the Alliance Agreement contract itself shows without ambiguity that Article IV controls. Under Article IV no event of default occurred which entitled Wachovia/Wells Fargo to cancel the Alliance Agreement.

Lost Profits from the Wells Fargo Business

Defendants assert that Elavon cannot seek to recover lost future profits for nonreferral of merchants because such future profits would be speculative and therefore unenforceable under Georgia law. Elavon counters that the lost future profits can be shown by the evidence of past earnings, expenses, and profits with reasonable certainty and the collection of such profits as damages is therefore not precluded by Georgia law.

In Georgia, lost profits of a commercial venture are not recoverable unless the profits are capable of "reasonably accurate computation" because they are based on "an established business with clearly defined business experience as to profit and loss." *Molly Pitcher Canning* [*1313] *Co. v. Cent, of Ga. Ry. Co., 149 Ga. App. 5, 10-12, 253 S.E.2d 392 (Ga. Ct. App. 1979).* " [L]ost profits can be shown by the evidence of past earnings, expenses, and profits with reasonable certainty to enable the jury to calculate the damages." *Witty v. McNeal Agency, Inc., 239 Ga. App. 554, 562, 521 S.E.2d 619 (Ga. Ct. App. 1999).*

The Court cannot say as a matter of law that Elavon's claim for lost profits is too speculative for the trier of fact to consider.

While it is true that Elavon did not provide services to Wells Fargo prior to the Wachovia-Wells Fargo merger, industry experts may be able to calculate what Elavon's profits would have been from Wells Fargo referrals because both Elavon and Wells Fargo have extensive track records with merchant referral contracts. There is a question as to whether the merchant processing services provided by Elavon are the same as, or similar to, the services provided by the Wells Fargo/First Data Joint Venture. The Court cannot resolve this issue because it lacks sufficient information on which to base this determination. At this time, the record does not permit a ruling as a matter of law. Accordingly, summary judgment is DENIED on this claim.

The Court DENIES Defendants' Motion for Summary Judgment.

Conclusion

For the reasons stated above, Plaintiff's Motion for Partial Summary Judgment is GRANTED and Defendants' Motion for Summary Judgment is DENIED. The parties are DIRECTED to file a proposed consolidated pre-trial order no later than June 22, 2011.

SO ORDERED, this 23 day of May, 2011
/s/ Orinda D. Evans
ORINDA D. EVANS
UNITED STATES DISTRICT JUDGE

Review Questions and Exercises

1. Give an example of impossibility of performance.

2. Explain the difference between a minor breach of a contract and a material breach. What are the effects of each type of breach on the parties.

3. Give an example of a situation in which punitive damages might be awarded.

4. Assume the following facts: The Walkers bought a home in a subdivision developed by Sloan. Due to an error by the closing attorney, the deed conveying the home to the Walkers included not only their lot but also the adjoining vacant lot. When Sloan discovered the error some months later, he approached the Walkers regarding the execution of a corrective deed. The Walkers refused even though they knew they had not contracted for the vacant lot. What possible remedies does Sloan have?

5. Calculate the damages in the following situation: Sally contracts with Marvin for the construction of a house at a contract price of $265,000. Marvin completes the foundation and framing but then abandons the job. The house had to be "dried in" immediately and Sally had to pay a roofer $12,500 for this work. She then found another contractor to complete the construction of the house. The new contractor is charging Sally $248,000 to finish the job. Marvin's work is valued at $18,000.

6. What duty does an innocent party have to mitigate damages?

7. What are speculative damages? Why are they not permitted?

8. How is the reformation of a contract like an accord and satisfaction? In what ways is it different?

9. What is specific performance? Under what circumstances is this remedy appropriate? Give an example of a case in which specific performance would be an appropriate remedy.

10. Assume Roger enters into a contract with Village Apartments to repaint apartments in its 60 unit complex as they become vacant. Roger is to be paid $400 for each apartment he paints and is required to complete the painting within four business days of his notice by Village that the apartment is vacant. The contract provides that Roger will lose 10% of the contract price for each day that he is late completing the painting. When he completes the painting of the first apartment three days late, Roger is paid $280.00. Can he sue for breach of contract? Discuss. What effect would the following facts have on your answer?
    (a) Apartments at Village Apartments rent for $500 per month.
    (b) Village Apartments has a vacancy rate of 16%.
    (c) The painting was completed on the 27th day of the month. Alternatively, assume:
    (d) The painting was completed on the 3rd day of the month

Practical Applications

1. The California and Hawaiian Sugar Company owns sugar plantations in Hawaii and transports raw sugar to its refinery in California. Sugar is a seasonal crop with about 70% of the harvest occurring between April and October. C&H requires reliable seasonal shipping of the raw sugar since sugar stored on the ground or left unharvested goes to waste.

C&H commissioned the design of a large vessel to be built by Sun Ship at a contract price of $25,405,000. The contract provided for a delivery date of June 30th and contained a liquidated damages clause calling for a payment of $17,000 per day for each day the vessel was not delivered. Sun Ship did not complete the vessel until the following March. C&H had been unable to find other means of shipping all of the crop during the season, and suffered actual damages of $368,000. C&H filed suit to recover the $4,413,000 in liquidated damages under the contract.

Consider:
(a) Does the liquidated damages clause in the C&H contract impose such a penalty for a breach of the contract and is so oppressive as to be more accurately be a provision for punitive damages?
(b) Are the liquidated damages provided for in the C&H contract speculative?
(c) Is the liquidated damages clause enforceable?

See - *California and Hawaiian Sugar Co. v. Sun Ship, Inc.*, 749 F.2d 1433 (1986), United States Court of Appeals for the Ninth Circuit.

2. In May, 2001, Alexandra Bush booked an African safari as a honeymoon trip through ProTravel International, a travel agency located in Manhattan. At the time of booking, Alexandra paid a deposit of $1,516.00. She and her fiancé were to travel on November 14, 2001. The terms of the contract provided that Alexandra could cancel the trip and receive a refund of her deposit provided that

she did so not later than September 14, 2001. A cancellation after September 14th would result in the forfeiture of the deposit.

As a result of the September 11th attacks, other terrorism alerts and airline scares, Alexandra and her fiancé decided almost immediately after the World Trade Center attacks to cancel their trip. Alexandra endeavored to contact ProTravel of her decision on September 12th and continued her attempts for several days afterwards, but due to difficulties with telephone lines, access to Manhattan, and closures of its office, she was unable to speak to anyone from ProTravel until September 27, 2001.

Consider:

(a) Whether the attack on the World Trade Center and the civil upset of its aftermath in the days which immediately followed excuses Alexandra's admittedly late notice of cancellation based on the doctrine of impossibility?

(b) Did the governmental actions of the mayor of New York City in declaring a state of emergency and of the governor of the State of New York in declaring a state disaster emergency make Alexandra's performance objectively impossible?

See – *Bush v. ProTravel International, Inc.*, 192 Misc. 2d 743, 746 N.Y.S.2d 790 (2002), Civil Court of the City of New York.

PART III – Business Organizations

Chapter 10 Franchises, Sole Proprietorships and General Partnerships

OUTLINE

Anyone who wants to start his own business faces the basic question of what form of business organization to employ. There are a number of forms from which the entrepreneur may choose. Some forms are more appropriate for small businesses while other forms lend themselves to larger businesses. Other considerations include the tax consequences of each form, issues pertaining to the potential liability of the owners of the business, and the availability of ready financing. In this chapter, we will examine sole proprietorships and partnerships, two of the most basic, and oldest, forms of business organization.

We will begin, however, with a brief consideration of franchises. Although a franchise is not really a form of business organization, franchises are widely used by today's entrepreneurs and, thus, an understanding of this common business relationship is fundamental to a discussion of business organizations.

10.1 Introduction to Franchises

A *franchise* is an arrangement in which one party (the franchisor) licenses another party (the franchisee) to use the franchisor's trade name, trademarks, patents, copyrights, and other property in the distribution and selling of goods and services. We all do business with franchises even though we seldom give thought to the legal significance of that fact. Who has not patronized, at least on occasion, a McDonald's, a Holiday Inn, or a 7-Eleven? Many of these individual business outlets are franchises, owned by a franchisee.

A franchise is obviously a business arrangement, but it is important to remember also that this is a contractual relationship between two parties. Generally, the *franchisor* and *franchisee* are separate legal entities. These separate business entities may be sole proprietorships, partnerships or corporations. The franchisee operates an independent business while, at the same time, being economically dependent on the franchisor's integrated business system. In the discussion of franchises, it is important to note that the term "franchise" refers to the contract between the parties as well as to the franchise outlet itself.

There are several advantages to franchising. There are advantages to all parties, the franchisor, the franchisee, and the consumer. These include:

- The franchisor can reach lucrative new markets with greater efficiency while having access to capital provided by the franchisees who also absorb much of the risk of losses;

- The franchisee has access to the franchisor's business expertise, knowledge, marketing and other resources while operating an independent business which the franchisee is able to start with limited capital and experience; and

- Consumers are assured of uniform product quality.

Types of Franchises

There are three basic types of franchises:

- *Distributorship Franchises* – The franchisor manufactures a product and licenses retail dealers to distribute the product to the public. For example, Ford Motor Company franchises dealers to sell Ford automobiles.

- *Processing Plant Franchises* – The franchisor provides a secret formula or essential ingredients to the franchisee. The franchisee then manufactures the product at its own location and distributes it to either wholesale or retail dealers. Coca-Cola, which franchises bottling plants, is an example of a processing plant franchisor.

- *Chain Style Franchises* – The franchisor licenses the franchisee to make and sell its products or services to the public from a retail outlet often serving an exclusive geographical territory. Usually, the franchisee must follow standardized methods of operation and maintain certain performance standards prescribed by the franchisor. Pizza Hut, for example, franchises its restaurants.

The Franchise Agreement

The relationship between a franchisor and a franchisee is, in its simplest terms, a contractual one. A prospective franchisee must apply to the franchisor for a franchise. Many entrepreneurs view a franchise as a means of starting up and operating an independent business with a relatively modest capital investment and, perhaps, limited experience. The franchisor sees a potential franchisee as a means of expanding the business (sales) in an efficient and cost effective method. If the applicant is approved, the parties enter into a *franchise agreement*, a contract, which sets forth the terms and conditions of the franchise.

Both federal and state laws govern certain aspects of franchise relationships. A potential investor is able to weigh the potential risks and benefits of an investment only if he or she has adequate information about the investment. Thus, the Franchise Rule of the Federal Trade Commission requires franchisors to disclose to prospective franchisees material facts which are necessary to enable potential franchisees to make informed decisions regarding the purchase of the franchise.

These protections are particularly important because, generally, franchise agreements do not allow much room for negotiation. Usually, the agreement is a standard form contract which is prepared by the franchisor and is then entered into between the franchisor and franchisee. Franchise agreements are generally very lengthy documents which cover many aspects of the franchisor-franchisee relationship. These agreements specify the terms and conditions of the franchise. The agreement also sets out the rights and duties of both the franchisor and franchisee, and these rights and duties can be enforced in the same manner as any other contract obligation.

Franchise agreements differ from franchise to franchise and different types of franchises will obviously cover different topics. However, the following topics are typical of those usually covered by such agreements:

- Business Premises – The franchisor may require that the franchisee construct a building which meets the specifications of the franchise agreement. In other cases, the building which serves as the business premise for the franchise may be constructed by the franchisor and then leased to the franchisee. The premises may also be leased from a third party.

- Location of the Franchise – The franchisor will generally determine the geographic area to be served by the franchisee. In some cases, the franchisor will give the franchisee exclusive rights to a certain area.

- Quality Control Standards – The franchisor's most important assets are its name and reputation. Quality control standards and the right to make inspections are intended to protect these assets. The franchisor can exercise considerable control in this area since it has a legitimate interest in maintaining the quality of its products or services, and, thus, its reputation.

- Training Requirements – Franchisees and their personnel usually are required to attend training programs dictated by the franchisor.

- Covenant Not To Compete – Covenants prohibiting franchisees from competing with the franchisor during a specific time period and in a specified area after termination of the franchise are common.

- Arbitration Clause – Most franchise agreements contain an arbitration clause which provides controversies arising from the franchise agreement are subject to arbitration.

- Other Terms and Conditions – The agreement may include capital requirements; restrictions on the use of the franchisor's name and trademarks; standards of operation; hours of operation; duration of the franchise; record-keeping requirements; sign requirements; and conditions for termination of the franchise.

Kerl v. Dennis Rasmussen, Inc.
273 Wis.2d 106, 682 N.W.2d 328 (2004)
Wisconsin Supreme Court

Facts: Robin Kerl and David Jones were shot in their workplace parking lot. Kerl was seriously injured and Jones was killed by Kerl's former boyfriend, Harvey Pierce. Pierce was a work-release inmate at the Dane County jail who was employed at a nearby Arby's, Inc., restaurant. Pierce had left work without permission at the time of the shooting. The Arby's franchise was operated by Dennis Rasmussen, Inc., the franshisee. Kerl and the estate of Jones sued Dennis Rasmussen, Inc., and Arby's, Inc. The franchise agreement contained a large number of general controls on the operation of the franchisee's restaurant.

Issue: Is Arby's, Inc., as the franchisor, vicariously liable for the negligent supervision of an employee, Pierce, by the franchisee?

Holding: A franchise is a business format typically characterized by the franchisee's operation of an independent business pursuant to a license to use the franchisor's trademark or trade name. A franchise is ordinarily operated in accordance with a detailed franchise or license agreement designed to protect the integrity of the trademark by setting uniform quality, marketing, and operational standards applicable to the franchise.

The provisions of the franchise agreement in this case are consistent with the quality and operational standards commonly contained in franchise agreements to achieve product and marketing uniformity and to protect the franchisor's trademark. They do not establish that Arby's controlled or had the right to control Rasmussen's hiring and supervision of employees. This is the aspect of Rasmussen's business that is alleged to have caused the plaintiff's harm. The franchise agreement's provisions regarding the specific issue of personnel are broad and general, and further provide that Rasmussen has sole control over the hiring and supervision of its employees. Arby's could not, pursuant to the agreement, step in and take control over the management of Rasmussen's employees. In the absence of close supervisory control or right of control over a franchisee, there can be no imposition of vicarious liability on the franchisor.

Franchise fees payable by the franchisee are usually stipulated in the franchise agreement. These may include some or all of the following fees:

(1) Initial License Fee – A lump-sum payment for the privilege of being granted a franchise.

(2) Royalty Fee – A fee for the continued use of the franchisor's trade name, property, and assistance that is often computed as a percentage of gross sales.

(3) Assessment Fee – A fee for such things as advertising and promotional campaigns.

(4) Lease Fees – Payment for any land or equipment leased from the franchisor.

(5) Cost of Supplies – Payment for supplies purchased from the franchisor. For example, the fanchisee may purchase cups or napkins printed with the franchisor's logo.

The franchise agreement is a lawful, enforceable contract. Each party owes a duty to the other to adhere to and perform under the terms of the agreement. If the agreement is breached, the aggrieved party can sue the breaching party for rescission of the agreement, restitution and damages. Many franchise agreements provide, however, that arbitration shall be the method used to resolve any disputes which may arise between the franchisee and franchisor.

Franchisors and franchisees are liable for their own *contracts* with third parties. The franchisor has no liability with regard to the contract obligations of the franchisee, and, likewise, the franchisee has no liability with regard to the contract obligations of the franchisor.

Example 10a:

Big Boy Burgers, Inc., franchises its restaurants. Bob owns a Big Boy Burgers franchise. Bob enters into a contract with Crystal Cleaners for janitorial services at his restaurant. When Bob fails to pay Crystal Cleaners the contract price, Crystal Cleaners may bring an action against Bob to enforce the contract, but would have no claim against Big Boy Burgers, the franchisor.

YI v. LI

313 Ga.App. 273, 721 S.E.2d 144 (2011)

Court of Appeals of Georgia

Facts: *Recall the facts in the case of the sale of the ice cream shop:* Yi operated a Bruster's ice cream. Li was interested in acquiring the Bruster's franchise owned and operated by Yi. Li submitted an application for the right to operate a franchise store to Bruster's and met multiple times with Bruster's vice president of sales. At a meeting on May 26, 2007, Li signed a franchise agreement (although it was not signed by Bruster's). Li also paid Bruster's a franchise transfer and training fee.

Yi and Li entered into a purchase agreement for the sale of the ice cream store, conditioned upon Bruster's consent. Although Bruster had not yet consented, Li took possession of the store and operated it. During this time, Li acted in the role of franchisee despite not having Bruster's consent. Several months later, Bruster's notified Li that it was withholding its consent of the transfer based on financial concerns regarding the volume of the store versus the proposed purchase price.

Li then sought to rescind the contract.

Issue: Could Li rescind the contract based on the failure of the condition precedent, the Franchisor's consent?

Holding: A condition precedent must be performed before the contract becomes absolute and obligatory upon the other party. The obtaining of Bruster's consent was a condition precedent and the failure to satisfy the condition precedent would have excused the parties' obligations and performance under the Purchase Agreement. However, Bruster's was not a party to the contract between Yi and Li, and Li's failure to obtain Bruster's consent to the transfer *prior* to closing the sale doesn't justify rescission.

The same is true of *tort liability* – franchisors and franchisees are liable for their own tortious conduct. Sometimes, however, both the franchisor and the franchisee may be liable for injuries arising out of the same incident. This is especially true where an apparent agency has been created – that is, where the actions of the franchisor have led third parties to believe that the franchisee is an agent of the franchisor. For example, a franchisor and franchisee who use the same trade name and trademarks and make no effort to inform the public of their separate legal status may find that an apparent agency has been created. For this reason, franchisees are often required to post, in a place visible to the customer, a notice indicating that the business is operated independently from the franchisor.

Example 10b:

Bob, a franchisee, operating a Big Boy Burgers restaurant, is obligated by his franchise agreement, to make his customers aware that his in an independent business. To comply, Bob hangs a notice at the order counter, which reads, "This restaurant locally owned and operated by Bob Bentley."

The franchise agreement usually contains provisions pertaining to the duration of the franchise and that permit the franchisor to terminate the franchise if certain events occur. Usually, a franchise agreement will provide that a franchisor must give a franchisee notice of termination of a franchise. If no set notice requirement is specified, then a reasonable notice is implied, since the franchisee must be given a reasonable amount of time to wind up the business.

Most franchise agreements permit franchisors to terminate the franchise "for cause," such as the death of the franchisee or the insolvency of the franchisee. Another example of cause would be the franchisee's failure to meet legitimate quality control standards. However, unreasonably strict application of a just cause termination clause, a single failure to meet a quality control standard, for example, constitutes wrongful termination.

Generally, the law emphasizes the importance of good faith and fair dealing in terminating a franchise relationship. If the court determines that a franchisor has arbitrarily or unfairly terminated a franchise, the franchisee can sue the franchisor for wrongful termination. If, however, on the other hand, the court determines that the franchisor's decision to terminate a franchise was made in the ordinary course of business and a reasonable notice of termination was given to the franchisee, the court will most likely not consider the termination to be wrongful.

10.2 *Sole Proprietorships*

For many entrepreneurs, the sole proprietorship is an ideal way of realizing their dream of owning their own business. Almost any type of business may be conducted as a sole proprietorship, which is simply a business managed and owned by one person. Indeed, some sole proprietors do not even think of themselves as the owners of a business – the neighborhood teen who cuts lawns during the summer is a sole proprietor although he may not consider himself a businessman. Likewise, the nurse who is skilled at hanging wallpaper and does so for extra money is the sole proprietor of a wallpaper hanging business even though she self-identifies herself as an employee of the local hospital.

The *sole proprietorship* is the oldest and most common form of business entity and is defined as an unincorporated business that that is owned and operated by one person. The owner may hire managers and employees to assist him or her in the operation of the business, but the owner is the sole decision maker. For instance, a physician may operate his medical practice as a sole proprietor and may employ a nurse, medical assistants, clerical help, and others, but the doctor remains the sole owner of the business.

Sole proprietorships are governed exclusively by state and local laws, excepting only that they are subject to various federal tax and employment laws. No permission is required from the state to form a sole proprietorship, although certain licensing requirements, as discussed hereinbelow, may be required.

Advantages of Sole Proprietorships

There are several key advantages to operating a business as a sole proprietorship including:

- Ease of Formation – A sole proprietorship is easily and inexpensively created and operated, and does not require much, if anything, in the way of legal formalities. Those that are required can often be satisfied very easily by the sole proprietor without the necessity of hiring anyone to act for him.

- Managerial Discretion – The sole proprietor, as owner of the business, is free to make all decisions regarding the business. For example, she may select the name under which the business will operate or be known, establish its location, hire all (or no) employees, and decide what products and services will be offered. Additionally, the owner may make changes in the business or even sell the business to someone else at any time without securing the approval of anyone else.

- Retention of Profits – The sole proprietor keeps all profits generated by the business. This, of course, assumes that there are profits. Unfortunately, many small businesses fail.

- Pass-Through Tax Status – The income generated by the business is passed through to the owner, the sole proprietor, who pays taxes at her appropriate individual tax rate. The business itself oes not file a tax return and pays no tax.

Disadvantages of Sole Proprietorships

The sole proprietorship form of business organization is not without significant disadvantages which include:

- Unlimited Personal Liability – The chief disadvantage of operating a business as a sole proprietorship is that the owner, the sole proprietor, is personally liable for the debts and obligations of the business. This liability extends beyond what the sole proprietor has invested in the business and may include the personal assets of the owner. Additionally, the sole proprietor is liable not only for business debts but also for the torts (civil wrongs) committed by both the sole proprietor and any employees acting in the course of their employment.

Example 10c:

Martha operates her high-end clothing boutique as a sole proprietor. Due to a downturn in the economy, sales have fallen off dramatically, leaving Martha unable to pay her suppliers. The suppliers may sue Martha on their accounts. They may collect the judgments owed to them out of Martha's business account as well as seeking payment by attaching her personal bank account, personal stock portfolio account, her home, and any other personal assets belonging to Martha.

- Difficulty in Raising Capital – A sole proprietor is limited in the methods available to him for obtaining funds for his business. He may invest his personal funds in his business. If the sole proprietor doesn't have enough cash to see the business through the start-up phase or through an expansion, he may need to obtain a loan to secure additional funds for the business. However, if the sole proprietor cannot find a lender willing to let him borrow money, the sole proprietorship may collapse.

- Lack of Continuity – A sole proprietorship is generally terminated by the death of the owner. If an heir inherits the business assets and continues to operate the business, a new sole proprietorship has been created.

Vernon v. Schuster, d/b/a Diversity Heating and Plumbing
688 N.E.2d 1172 (1997)
Illinois Supreme Court

Facts: James Schuster was a sole proprietor doing business as Diversity Heating and Plumbing. George Vernon needed a new boiler and hired Diversity to install it. James Schuster, doing business as Diversity, gave Vernon a warranty that the boiler would not crack for ten years.

Four years later, James Schuster died. His son, Jerry Schuster, inherited the assets of his father's business, and thereafter ran the business as a sole proprietorship under the same d/b/a his father had used prior to his death, Diversity Heating and Plumbing. The next year, Vernon's boiler broke. Vernon notified Diversity of the boiler's failure and demanded that Jerry Schuster honor the warranty his father had made and replace the boiler. When Jerry refused, Vernon sued.

Issue: Is Jerry Schuster liable for the warranty made by his father?

Holding: Common identity of ownership is lacking when one sole proprietorship succeeds another. The individual who does business as a sole proprietor under a trade name remains one person, personally liable for all his obligations. But, in these circumstances, there is no continuity of existence because on the death of the sole proprietor, the sole proprietorship ends. Here, it must be remembered that Diversity Heating has no legal existence. Diversity Heating was only a pseudonym for James Schuster. Once James died, Diversity Heating ceased to exist. Now, Diversity Heating is only a pseudonym for Jerry Schuster. James and Jerry, one succeeding the other, cannot be the same entity, and Jerry Schuster is not responsible for the obligations of James.

Note: Vernon should have made a claim against the estate of James Schuster, the sole proprietor who made the warranty, and not against the son, Jerry Schuster.

- Management Vulnerabilities – The sole proprietor, as the sole decision-maker, may lack the expertise needed for the business to succeed. It may be necessary for him to expend funds to hire outside consultants or advisors

Figure 10-1

SOLE PROPRIETORSHIPS

ADVANTAGES	DISADVANTAGES
Easy to form and maintain Inexpensive to form Owner is sole decision maker Management is informal and flexible All profits retained by owner Pass-through taxation status	Unlimited personal liability Limited ways to raise capital Lack of continuity Possible lack of expertise in management

10.3 Formation of Sole Proprietorships

One of the most significant advantages of a sole proprietorship is the lack of formalities required in forming and organizing the business. Thus, is it often easier and less costly to start a sole proprietorship than to start up any other kind of business. Most of the requirements that are involved in creating a sole proprietorship are common to almost any business.

Many types of businesses require the operator obtain a license specific to that profession. For example, in this state, an attorney must be licensed by the State Bar of Georgia in order to practice law; a restaurant that serves alcohol must obtain a liquor license from the local government; and a cosmetologist must obtain a license issued by the State Board of Cosmetology. A sole proprietor who wants to operate such a business must obtain the proper license to do so.

Many sole proprietors choose to operate their business under a name other than their own. Such a name is called a *trade name* or a *fictitious name*. Generally, if a sole proprietor intends to operate under a fictitious name, the name must be registered with the local or state authority. This filing allows consumers to determine the actual owner of a business in the event that litigation is brought against the owner. Sometimes this statement is called a "DBA," meaning "doing business as," because it identifies that the true owner is doing business as or under another name. Finally, the sole proprietor may not operate under a name which is likely to cause confusion with another enterprise. The agency that accepts the fictitious name statement may check to see if the name is available in that locality.

In Georgia, trade names are registered in the office of the Clerk of Superior Court of the county in which the business is located. The form used by the Clerks' offices is found in Appendix IV.

OCGA § 10-1-490

(a) Every person, firm or partnership carrying on in this state any trade or business under any trade name or partnership name or other name which does not disclose the individual ownership of the trade, business or profession carried on under such name shall, within 30 days from March 29, 1937, or thereafter before commencing to do business, file in the office of the clerk of the superior court of the county in which the business is chiefly carried on or, in the case of a domestic corporation using any name other than its corporate name, in the county of its legal domicile, a registration statement, verified by affidavit, setting forth the name or names and addresses of the person, persons, firm or partnership owing and carrying on said trade or business and stating the nature of the business being carried on and the trade, partnership, or other name used and shall, upon any change or ownership, likewise file a new and amended statement of registration. Notice of such filing giving the names and address of each person, firm, or partnership to engage in business under such trade name or partnership name shall be published in the paper in which the sheriff's advertisements are printed once a week for two weeks. No person, firm or partnership already registered shall be required to reregister except in the event of a change of ownership.

(b) The clerk shall register the same by filing the verified statement in his office and shall keep an alphabetical index of all such registrations in a permanent record book to be kept in his office, the index to show trade, partnership, or other name registered and in connection therewith the names of the owners. The applicant for registration shall accompany each registration statement with the fee prescribed by Code Section 15-6-77, relating to fees of clerks of the superior courts, as amended.

Many jurisdictions, including municipalities, require that the sole proprietor obtain a basic license to do business (Recall the *Miles v. City Council of Augusta* case from Chapter 1). Additionally, if the sole proprietor will be selling goods, he or she must make arrangements to pay appropriate sales taxes to the state and/or municipality. A sole proprietor who has employees working for him must apply with the Internal Revenue Service for an employer identification number in order to withhold federal income and Social Security taxes on his employees plus any applicable state income tax.

10.4 *Taxation of Sole Proprietorships*

As mentioned above, one of the advantages of doing business as a sole proprietor is that the sole proprietorship itself does not pay income tax. Income derived from the operation of the business is simply added to any other income the sole proprietor makes from any other source, and the sole proprietor pays tax on this entire amount according to the IRS tax brackets or schedules.

The income earned from the business is reported by the sole proprietor on a form called Schedule C which is attached to the sole proprietor's individual income tax return Form 1040. The sole proprietor may declare and deduct various business expenses such as rent, advertising costs, business insurance, employees' salaries and the like, and use these to offset income. The sole proprietor must pay tax on all net income, that is, gross receipts less business expenses, even if he retains the money in the business for anticipated business needs rather than taking the money out of the business for his personal use.

Example 10d:

Ben owns a muffler shop which he operates as a sole proprietor. Last year, Ben's Muffler Shop had a net income of $50,000. In addition, Ben earned $2,000 in interest income on his savings, and won $4,000 gambling in Las Vegas. Ben must pay tax on his total income of $56,000.

10.5 *General Partnerships – Characteristics and Formation*

A general partnership is defined as a voluntary association of two or more persons who agree to carry on a business together for profit. Partners are co-owners of a business and have joint control over the operation of the business and the right to share in its profits, not just receive wages or compensation. Note that partners may be individuals (natural persons) or artificial persons such corporations.

> OCGA § 14-8-6
>
> A partnership is an association of two or more persons to carry on as co-owners a business for profit...

Unlike corporations, partnerships usually require no special formalities in order to be created. All that is needed is a partnership agreement. Since a partnership agreement is a contract, it, like most other contracts, can be express or implied, and no writing is necessary except for contractual matters generally covered by the statute of frauds. Thus, for example, a partnership agreement that permits partners to transfer real estate, or that has a set term exceeding one year, must be written to be enforceable, at least with respect to these matters. However, from a practical standpoint, a written partnership agreement is usually the best way to assure that the partners, from the outset, understand the nature of their agreement. The absence of such a writing probably increases the chances of disputes between partners and may make it harder to settle any dispute which does arise.

Formation by Express Agreement

Once the parties have agreed to form a partnership, few formalities remain. Partnerships can be legally formed orally. However, while not required, the parties often decide to incorporate the terms of their agreement into a written document, and this is certainly the better practice. This insures that all the partners, from the outset, understand the nature and terms of their agreement. Additionally, a written agreement can provide important evidence of the terms of the parties' agreement in the event that a dispute later arises between them. The partnership agreement can include virtually any term that the parties wish, provided that those terms are not illegal or contrary to public policy or statute.

Commonly included terms are listed in Figure 10.2 below.

Figure 10-2 *TERMS COMMONLY INCLUDED IN PARTNERSHIP AGREEMENTS*

Basic Structure	• Name of the partnership • Names of the partners • Location of the business and state law under which the partnership is organized • Purpose of the partnership • Duration of the partnership
Capital Contributions	• Amount of capital contributed by each partner • Agreed-upon value of contributions other than cash
Sharing of Profits And Losses	• Percentage of profits and losses each partner will receive • When distributions of profit will be made
Management and Control	• How management responsibilities are divided among partners • Name of managing partner or partners • Whether there are any silent partners
Accounting and Partnership Records	• Name of bank the partnership will use • Statement that accounting of partnership records will be maintained and right of partners to review • Date of partnership's fiscal year
Dissolution	• Events that will dissolve partnership • How partnership property will be valued and apportioned on dissolution
Miscellaneous	• Whether arbitration will be required for any disputes

Initially, partnerships derive the capital necessary to function through the contributions to the partnership made by the partners. It is important to note that partners can contribute capital to the partnership either in the form of cash or assets or in the form of services, depending on the specific terms of their agreement. If the partners are contributing services or assets other than cash, they usually need to agree upon the value of those assets or services.

Example 10e:

Don and Brent agree to form a partnership to operate a business to manufacture and sell surf boards. They have decided to call their business Surfs Up. Don contributes the start-up and operating capital and Brent, who has extensive experience in the field, contributes his management services. Even though Brent has not contributed capital in the form of cash, he is an equal partner with Don in Surfs Up (unless the two agree otherwise).

Formation by Implied Agreement

Since a written partnership agreement is not required, a partnership may be implied from the conduct of the parties. If the parties are voluntarily carrying on a business as co-owners with the intent to make a profit, they have formed a partnership, even if they have not thought of themselves as partners. Thus, a partnership may be formed inadvertently.

OCGA § 14-8-7

In determining whether a partnership exists, the following rules shall apply:

(1) Except as provided by Code Section 14-8-16 persons who are not partners as to each other are not partners to third persons;
(2) Joint tenancy, tenancy in common, tenancy by the entireties, joint property, common property, or part ownership does not itself establish a partnership, whether such co-owners do or do not share any profits made by the use of the property;
(3) The sharing of gross returns does not itself establish a partnership, whether or not the persons sharing them have a joint or common right or interest in any property from which the returns are derived;
(4) The receipt by a person of a share of the profits of a business in prima-facie evidence that he is a partner in the business; provided, however, that no such inference shall be drawn if profits were received in payment of the following, even though the amount of payment varies with the profits of the business:

(A) A debt, whether by installments or otherwise;
(B) Wages, salary, or other compensation to an employee or independent contractor;
(C) Rent to a landlord;
(D) An annuity or other payment to a surviving spouse or representative of a deceased partner;
(E) Interest or other payment or charge on a loan;
(F) Consideration for the sale of goodwill of a business or other property, whether by installments or otherwise.

Since partnerships may be formed by implied agreement, the courts must occasionally determine whether the parties intended to actually form a partnership. Co-ownership of a business is essential to create a partnership. The most important factor in determining co-ownership is whether the parties share the business's profits and management responsibilities. Receipt of a share of business profits is prima facie evidence of a partnership because non-partners usually are not given the right to share in the business's profits.

Vohland v. Sweet
435 N.E.2d 860 (1982)
Court of Appeals of Indiana

Facts: Norman Sweet began working for Charles Vohland as an hourly employee at a garden nursery owned by Vohland when Sweet was a teen and worked there for many years.

When Charles retired, his son, Paul, took over the business. At that time, Sweet's status changed: it was agreed between Paul and Norman that Norman was to receive 20% of the net profit of the business rather than an hourly salary. Sweet contributed no capital to the business. Every few weeks, Vohland and Sweet would compute the income received and the expenses paid, and Sweet would be issued a check for 20% of the net income. No Social Security or income taxes were withheld from Sweet's checks. No written partnership agreement was entered into and no partnership returns were filed. Sweet's tax returns declared him to be self-employed, and he paid self-employment Social Security tax. Vohland made most of the sales for the nursery and Sweet managed the physical aspects of the nursery.

When Sweet and Vohland had a falling out, Sweet brought an action for dissolution of the alleged partnership and for an accounting.

Issue: Did Vohland and Sweet enter into a partnership?

Holding: The receipt of a share of the profits is prima facie evidence of a partnership. Absence of contribution of capital is not controlling, and contribution of labor and skill will suffice. Where, as here, the profits of the business are divided, it can be inferred that the parties intended to do the things that amount to the formation of a partnership, regardless of how they characterized the relationship.

The Uniform Partnership Act

The Uniform Partnership Act (UPA), first approved in 1914, governs the operation of partnerships in the absence of an express agreement and has done much to reduce controversies in the law relating to partnerships. Except for Louisiana, all of the states, as well as the District of Columbia, have adopted the UPA. Georgia adopted its version of the Uniform Partnership Act in 1984. The National Conference of Commissioners on Uniform State Laws adopted a Revised Uniform Partnership Act of 1997 which updates many of the provisions of the original UPA.

For some purposes, partnerships are treated as entities with a legal identity separate from that of the partners or owners of the partnership. For instance, in most states, the partnership can sue or be sued in the partnership name. In addition, judgments against a partnership must usually be collected from the partnership before collection actions are instigated against individual partners. In other instances, a partnership is considered an aggregate of the individual partners. Under federal tax law, the partnership is not taxed separately; rather, the individual partners are taxed on their share of the profits. Additionally, partners cannot disclaim personal liability for the partnership's acts or omissions, and, since the partnership is not an employer of the partners, departing partners are not entitled to unemployment benefits.

If the parties' written partnership agreement fails to provide for an essential term or contingency, the provisions of the UPA control. Thus, the UPA acts as a gap-filling device to the partners' agreement. Recall that the partners may agree to virtually any term they see fit. However, if the agreement of the partners is silent as to the following issues, the provisions of the UPA provide:

- all partners have equal management rights;

- each partner has an equal vote, regardless of the relative size of his or her capital contribution; and

- partnership decisions require a majority vote of the partnership, unless otherwise agreed, except in the following cases, which require unanimous consent:
  (1) altering the essential nature of the partnership's business or entering a wholly new business;
  (2) admitting new partners or altering the capital structure of the partnership;
  (3) assigning partnership property into a trust for the benefit of creditors, disposing of goodwill, or undertaking any act which would make conduct of the partnership's business impossible;
  (4) confessing judgment against the partnership; or
  (5) amending the partnership agreement.

10.6 *Advantages and Disadvantages of Partnerships*

The partnership form of business offers a variety of advantages to the partners, but also has three key disadvantages.

Among the advantages to this form of business are:

- Ease of Formation – A general partnership can be easily formed with little or no formality. Often no filings need be made with any state or local agency and no written agreement is required, making general partnerships simple and inexpensive to form. The partnership may be required, however, to obtain a business license or to file a fictitious name statement if it is going to do business under a name other than its own.

- Flexible Management – General partnerships offer their partners the ability to share management. Partnerships can appoint certain partners to manage the business or partners may co-manage the business.

- Ease of Raising Capital – Partnerships may raise capital by requiring additional contributions from their members or by admitting new partners.

- Pass-through Taxation – Partnerships do not pay federal income tax. Income earned is passed through to the individual partners, who declare and pay tax on their respective share of partnership profits.

There are three primary disadvantages in doing business in the general partnership form. The first of these concerns the liability of partners. A partnership creates unlimited personal liability for each partner with regard to the debts and obligations of the partnership. This liability is joint and several – thus, any creditor of the partnership or any claimant can sue the partners individually or together, and any partner can be held liable for the entire amount of the damages or obligation. This includes both contract and tort liability, provided that the tort was committed in the course of partnership business.

Mansour et al. v. Mobley
96 Ga App. 812, 101 S.E.2d 786 (1957)
Court of Appeals of Georgia

Facts: Alfred Mansour, George Mansour and Nasor Mansour operated a department store in Columbus, Georgia, as partners. Mattie Ruth Mobley was shopping in the Mansours' department store when she was accused, in a loud and angry tone, of shoplifting. The accusation, which ultimately proved to be false, was made by George Mansour. Neither Alfred Mansour nor Nasor Mansour was present at the time. Mrs. Mobley sued the three Mansours for false imprisonment in connection with the incident.

Issue: Whether Alfred Mansour and Nasor Mansour are personally liable for the actions of George Mansour.

Holding: The department store is undoubtedly a partnership, with the three Mansours inviting the general public to come in for the purpose of buying and doing business to the profit of the three brothers. The Mansours co-own the business. A partnership, in the conduct of its business, is a legal entity, both as to its rights and in the performance of its duties to the public and to its employees. It is

> also a legal entity as to its obligations. Partners are, in respect to the business in which they are engaged, agents of each other, and therefore one partner might be liable for the tortious acts of another done in the usual course of the business of the firm. Partners are not responsible for the torts of each other merely by reason of their relationship as partners. In order for such liability to exist, the wrong must have been committed within the legitimate scope of the partnership business. Such is clearly the case here.

Another disadvantage of the general partnership form of business organization is the difficulty in transferring a partnership interest. The only transferable property a partner has is his share of the partnership's profits. Because a partnership is a voluntary arrangement, one partner may not simply transfer all of his partnership rights to another individual - the other partners have not agreed to do business with a newcomer. Admission of a new partner requires consent from the other partners. Because this consent may not be forthcoming, transferring an interest in a partnership may not be easy or even possible.

Finally, the lack of continuity can pose a significant drawback to the general partnership form. Traditionally, a partnership could not survive the death or withdrawal of a partner, and this lack of continuity was an unattractive feature of a general partnership. The Revised Uniform Partnership Act attempts to reduce this harsh effect by providing that partnerships no longer dissolve every time a partner dies.

> OCGA § 14-8-42
>
> When any partner withdraws or dies, and the business is continued under any of the conditions set forth in subsection (a) of Code Section 14-8-41 or paragraph (2) of subsection (b) of Code Section 14-8-38, without any settlement of accounts as between the withdrawn partner or legal representative of the estate of a deceased partner and the persons or partnership continuing the business, unless otherwise agreed:
>
> (1) Such persons or partnership shall obtain the discharge of the withdrawn partner or the legal representative of the estate of the deceased partner, or appropriately hold him harmless from all present or future partnership liabilities, and shall ascertain the value of his interest at the date of dissolution; and
>
> (2) The withdrawn partner or legal representative of the estate of the deceased partner shall receive as an ordinary creditor an amount equal to the value of his interest in the dissolved partnership with interest, or, at his option, in lieu of interest, the profits attributable to the use of his right in the property of the dissolved partnership, provided that the creditors of the dissolved partnership as against the separate creditors, or the representative of the withdrawn or deceased partner, shall have priority on any claim arising under this Code section, as provided by subsection (d) of Code Section 14-8-41.

10.7 Rights and Duties of Partners

A partnership is a fiduciary relationship, meaning that each partner owes his co-partners the duty of the highest loyalty and must deal with the co-partners in good faith. Partners should do everything for the benefit of the partnership and nothing to its detriment. The partners must not engage in outside activities that compete with or are detrimental to the partnership. Partners must not behave in a manner that is considered negligent or reckless and must not engage in intentional misconduct or knowingly commit a violation of the law when conducting partnership business. Each partner has a right of access to the books and records of the partnership.

Agency

Each partner is an agent of the partnership for business purposes. This means that each partner can legally bind the partnership and has the authority to sign contracts, execute documents, enter into contracts, make purchases, enter into leases and do other things in the name of the partnership which bind the partnership or make the partnership legally responsible. As a result of this general agency, the partnership, together with all of its partners, becomes legally liable for obligations entered into by any one partner on behalf of the partnerhip. This is true even though the other partners may have had no knowledge of the acts of the partner who is acting alone.

> OCGA § 14-8-9
>
> Subject to the provisions of Code Section 14-8-10.1:
>
> (1)Every partner is an agent of the partnership for the purpose of its business, and the act of every partner, including the execution in the partnership name of any instrument, for apparently carrying on in the usual way the business of the partnership of which he is a member binds the partnership …

The third party who sues to recover on a partnership debt or contract may bring his suit against the partnership and all of the partners. If the suit is successful and a judgment is entered in favor of the third party, that plaintiff can collect the entire amount of his judgment from partnership assets or from any one of or all of the partners. If the partnership lacks sufficient assets to satisfy the judgment, the third party can go after the "deepest pocket" even though that partner may not have been the partner who entered into the contract. A partner who is made to pay more than his proportionate share of the liability may seek indemnification from the partnership and from those partners who have not paid their share of the obligation.

Example 10f:

> James, Matt and Peter enter into a partnership agreement for the operation of a new restaurant. Matt, unknown to James and Peter and without authority or consent of his partners, orders very expensive furnishings for the new restaurant. The partnership is obligated to pay for the furnishings. The law will protect the innocent third party, the supplier of the furnishings, and will require that the partnership pay the debt. The partners must later sort out among themselves the allocation of liability due to Matt's breach of fiduciary duty.

Alternatively, the third party may sue the partnership and the specific partner or partners seen to be at fault. The third party may still enforce the judgment against any or all of the partners, but he will be required to bring a separate action against those partners not named in the original suit. This is, obviously, a less efficient method of collecting the debt.

J.T. Turner Construction Company, Inc. v. Summerour, et al.

301 Ga.App. 323, 687 S.E.2d 612 (2009)

Court of Appeals of Georgia

<u>Facts:</u> J.T. Turner Construction Company, Inc., obtained a judgment against SWI Partners, a general partnership, and Ernest Burns, one of SWI's partners. Turner was unable to collect the judgment from the partnership or from Burns.

Turner then filed a lawsuit against Summerour and Hatcher, two other SWI partners, alleging they were jointly and severally liable for the judgment against SWI.

Issue: Are Summerour and Hatcher liable with regard to the judgment against the partnership? Can their personal assets be attached to pay it?

Holding: As a general rule, all partners in a general partnership are jointly and severally liable for all debts, obligations, and liabilities of the partnership. A judgment rendered in a suit against a general partnership binds the partnership assets and the individual assets of any general partners who were properly served in the suit. A general partner's individual assets may not be bound unless the partner himself was personally served with process and has "had his day in court." However, partners not personally served in the original suit or who do not appear in the original trial against the partnership are nonetheless subject to be sued individually.

Three elements that must be proven before a partner served in a subsequent lawsuit can be held individually liable for a prior judgment rendered on a general partnership debt: the plaintiff must prove that (1) the individual sued was a general partner of the partnership; (2) the indebtedness of the partnership was proved; and (3) the account sued upon was the identical account upon which the former suit against the partnership was based. Summerour and Hatcher admit they are general partners of SWI, and there is no dispute that Turner obtained a valid judgment against SWI on the same indebtedness upon which he now sues Summerour and Hatcher as general partners of SWI.

Permitting general partners in a subsequent suit to attack the merits of a judgment rendered against the partnership is in direct opposition to *OCGA § 14-8-15 (a)* and could lead to inconsistent judgments.

Summerour and Hatcher had the opportunity to show a question of fact as to one or all of the three elements, but they have presented no evidence that contradicts Turner's proof. Had Summerour and Hatcher denied they were partners of SWI, argued that the judgment against the partnership was void for some reason, or denied that the present action involved the same indebtedness as the previous action, they would have been entitled to a trial on those issues. Since these matters were not at issue in this case, however, Turner was entitled to judgment as a matter of law.

Management

Unless the partners agree otherwise, all partners have equal rights in the management and conduct of the partnership business. Each partner will have one vote. This is true regardless of the initial and later capital contributions of the various partners to the partnership. This rule recognizes that some partners may bring valuable assets such as experience to the partnership while others contribute the capital necessary to the start-up of the business. Furthermore, unless the partners agree otherwise, decision-making in the partnership is by majority vote.

Example 10g:

Using the scenario from Example 10f of above, if the partners agreed that James would make an initial contribution to the partnership of $70,000, while Matt contributed $25,000, and Peter contributed his expertise in the restaurant business, and, assuming the three had not agreed otherwise, Matt and Peter could, by voting together, control decisions made about the restaurant, despite the much larger financial stake James has in the business.

In many partnerships, the partners agree to a voting formula which is often tied to the contributions of each partner in the partnership. Additionally, new partners cannot be admitted to the partnership without the consent of all of the existing partners. Recall that a partnership is a voluntary association; therefore, one cannot be forced into a partnership with another against one's will.

Profits and Accounting

Partners do not normally receive a regular and fixed salary from the partnership (unless they are employed by the partnership). Rather, each partner has an interest in the profits of the partnership which will, quite naturally, vary from time to time. A partner's share of the profits of the partnership is the personal property of the partner, and each partner may transfer or assign his or her share of profits in the partnership to another party. This right to transfer profits does not carry with it the right to transfer one's other rights and obligations with regard to the partnership. The transferor partner retains all of his or her partnership rights and duties, and the transferee of profits receives nothing except the right to receive the distributions of the transferor.

Unless the partners agree otherwise, all partners are entitled to an equal share of the profits of the partnership and are responsible for an equal share of partnership losses. It is quite common for the partnership agreement to provide that profits and losses are to be shared by the partners in proportion to the amount of each partner's contribution to the partnership, but the partners are free to devise any formula they see fit regarding the distribution of profits and losses.

In addition to his or her share of profits, each partner is entitled to reimbursement for expenses incurred on behalf of the partnership. Partners are also entitled to inspect the partnership books and records so that each might determine whether distributions are correct.

10.8 Termination of Partnerships

The dissolution of a partnership triggers a winding up of the business affairs of the partnership. Dissolution may be caused by:

- The ending of the term of the partnership;
- Unanimous agreement of all partners;
- The withdrawal at will of any partner;
- The death, expulsion or bankruptcy of a partner (unless there is a written agreement between the partners expressly providing otherwise);
- Any event which makes it unlawful for the business of the partnership to be carried on or for the members to carry it on in a partnership; or
- By court decree.

A partner, thus, has the *power* to withdraw and dissolve a partnership at any time, but he may not have the *right* to do so. For example, a partner who withdraws from a partnership before the expiration of the term stated in the partnership agreement has the power to withdraw but does not have right to do so. His action, in withdrawing prematurely, cause, a wrongful dissolution, and the withdrawing partner is liable for damages caused by the wrongful dissolution of the partnership.

Arford v. Blalock

199 Ga.App. 434, 405 S.E.2d 698 (1991)

Court of Appeals of Georgia

Facts: In 1982 Eulas Blalock and Anthony Arford commenced a mortgage banking business operating under the name of Gulf States Mortgage Company. The partnership between Blalock and Arford was oral and for an indefinite duration. The partnership was an independent contractor of Gulf

States Mortgage Company, Inc. Blalock and Arford were financially successful and the enterprise continued to grow until early 1987 when the two had some disagreements.

On February 11, 1987, the president of Gulf States informed Blalock his relationship with Gulf States was terminated but Gulf States continued conducting business with Arford. The locks on the building were changed so that Blalock no longer had unsupervised access to it.

Issue: Does Blalock have a cause of action for wrongful termination?

Holding: Because the partnership was for an indefinite duration and was, therefore, terminable at will, Arford argues he had a right to terminate the partnership.

Blalock's cause of action is for wrongful dissolution of the otherwise terminable-at-will partnership. A wrongful dissolution is one made either in contravention of the partnership agreement or as a result of other wrongful conduct of a partner. Any partnership agreement includes, as a matter of law, an agreement for each partner to act in "the utmost good faith" toward the other partner. The power of a partner to dissolve the partnership at will, like any other power held by a fiduciary, must be exercised in good faith. A partner may not 'freeze out' a co-partner and appropriate the business to his own use. Even though a partner has a right to dissolve the partnership, if it is proved that the partner acted in bad faith and violated his fiduciary duties by attempting to appropriate to his own use the new prosperity of the partnership without adequate compensation to his co-partner, the dissolution would be wrongful, and the partner would be liable for violation of the implied agreement not to exclude the other partner wrongfully from the partnership business opportunity.

Arford argues the only remedy available to Blalock for the dissolution of the partnership is an accounting and payment of net assets owed to him as a one-half partner in the now-dissolved partnership. A partner who has been wrongfully excluded from the partnership business has a right to a formal accounting. In the case of wrongful dissolution of a partnership, however, a partner who did not wrongfully cause the dissolution is entitled not only to payment for his net interest in the partnership (which would be calculated pursuant to an accounting) but also damages for wrongful dissolution. We find instructive the holding by the California Supreme Court that damages for wrongfully excluding a partner from a partnership business opportunity should include compensation to the ousted partner for his share of the prospective business opportunity.

Unless the partners have agreed otherwise in their partnership agreement, any time a partner leaves the partnership, the partnership is dissolved and must wind up its affairs. To wind up the business of the partnership, the business must complete all contracts, collect its assets, pay its creditors, and then distribute any remaining assets to the partners in accordance with the terms of their partnership agreement.

Notice of the dissolution must be given to certain third parties. Those who have actually dealt with the partnership must be given actual notice. Those who have not dealt with the partnership but have knowledge of it must be given constructive notice by the publication of a notice of dissolution in the newspaper.

10.9 Taxation of Partnerships

A partnership is not a tax paying entity. Rather, all profits (and losses) are passed through to the partners who report their respective share on a Schedule K-1 which is attached to their individual

Form 1040 tax returns. Each partner's share of profits must be reported in this manner regardless of whether the profits have been distributed or not. In this regard, the taxation of partnerships is much like the taxation of sole proprietorships. To ensure the individual partners accurately report their share of partnership income and losses, the partnership is required to file an informational return, Form 1065, to report income, gains and losses.

Finally, because there may be certain advantages to paying tax at corporate rates, the IRS will allow partnerships to elect to be taxed as a corporation. A partnership which has substantial profits that have not yet been distributed may elect this form of taxation because income not distributed by corporations is not taxed to the owners. If no election is affirmatively made, the default provision is that the partners' income will automatically be taxed under the pass-through taxation provisions.

Review Questions and Exercises

1. Give four customary provisions in a franchise agreement.

2. How would you characterize the relationship between the franchisee and the franchisor?

3. Why might one want to purchase a franchise? What are the advantages to the franchisee? To the franchisor? To the customers?

4. Larry, a sole proprietor, operates a fitness center. The center is located in a building which Larry rents. The landlord is owed $5,000 in back rent. The business has $3,000 in its accounts. From what sources may the landlord seek to recover the debt? Is there any action which Larry could have taken to protect himself? Discuss.

5. Larry, the sole proprietor of the fitness center, employs Diana as an instructor. During a class, Diana accidentally drops a weight on a customer, injuring the customer. Discuss the liability of both Larry and Diana for this act.

6. Maria is employed as a software designer. Her hobby is painting. One of Maria's friends suggests Maria attempt to sell some of her work at a local outdoor festival. To her surprise and pleasure, Maria sells four canvases. Are there any business implications in Maria's participation in the festival? Discuss.

7. When is it necessary to file a fictitious name (trade name) statement? Why is this done?

8. What are the major disadvantages one must consider when entering into a general partnership?

9. Mary and Martha have entered into a partnership agreement with a term of two years. After one year, Mary decides to terminate the partnership. Does she have the power to end the partnership? Does she have the right to do so? Dicuss.

10. James, Matt, and Peter formed a partnership for the purpose of operating a new restaurant.

    a. They made no provision in their partnership agreement regarding the division of profits and losses. Last year the partnership made a profit of $45,000. How will this be divided among the partners?

b. The restauarant partnership owes $15,000 to its landlord and has $7,500 in its bank account. Who is liable for payment of the money owed to the landlord. Discuss.

c. Two years ago, when the partnership was initially formed, James contributed $70,000, Matt contributed $25,000 and Peter contributed his expertise in the restaurant business. Now, the partnership has decided that it should raise an additional $15,000. What share of this sum must each partner contribute?

d. Matt ran into financial difficulties and was forced to borrow $25,000 from his brother, Mark. Matt has decided to transfer his partnership interest to Mark. What rights, if any, does Mark have in the partnership? Discuss

e. After four years, the partners have all agreed that the partnership should be dissolved. The partnership owes $5,000 to vendors and owes $4,000 to its bank. The partnership has $20,000 in its accounts. Discuss how the debts will be paid and how the remaining cash and any assets will be distributed.

Practical Applications

1. Clifford Clark is a sole proprietor who owns Clark Enterprises in Salina, Kansas. Through representatives, trade shows and his web-site, Clark sells "The Exercise Machine," an aerobic exercise device. Clark's machine is in direct competition with "The Chi Machine" manufactured and sold by a Hsin Ten Enterprise USA, Inc., a corporation with its principle place of business in Farmingdale, New York. This corporation owns the "Chi" trademark and manufactures other products under this name. Clark began using the name "Chi Exerciser 2000" to promote its machine.

Hsin Ten filed a suit in federal district court in New York against Clark, asserting trademark infringement and other claims. Clark filed a motion to dismiss on the ground the court did not have venue under 28 U.S.C. Section 1391(c) which provides that, "For purposes of venue ..., a defendant that is a corporation shall be deemed to reside in any judicial district in which it is subject to personal jurisdiction." Hsin Ten argued that although Clark is an unincorporated sole proprietorship with its offices in Kansas, it should be deemed a "corporation" for venue purposes.

Consider:
(a) Should Clark be subject to suit in federal district court in New York?
(b) Why or why not?

See - *Hsin Ten Enterprises USA, Inc., v. Clark Enterprises,* 138 F.Supp.2d 449 (2000), United States District Court, Southern District of New York.

2. Clifford W. Davis and Dr. William D. Mitchell formed a general partnership for the purpose of purchasing and operating rental properties. The partnership purchased a parcel of real property from the Edward A. Kemmler Memorial Foundation. To pay for the purchase, Davis signed a promissory note in the amount of $150,000 as "Cliff Davis, Partner."

Prior to the purchase of the Kemmler Memorial Foundation property, Davis and Mitchell had agreed between themselves that only Davis, and not Mitchell, would be personally liable on the note to the Foundation. However, they did not inform the Foundation of this agreement.

The partnership defaulted on the note and the Foundation sued both partners. Mitchell asserted that his side agreement with Davis relieved him of personal liability.

Consider:
(a) Are both partners, Davis and Mitchell, jointly liable on the note?
(b) What is the impact of the failure to disclose their agreement to the Kemmler Foundation?

See - *Edward A Kemmler Memorial Foundation v. Mitchell*, 584 N.E.2d 695 (1992), Supreme Court of Ohio.

3. McDonald's Corporation is a franchisor. One of its franchises was located in Oak Forest, Illinois, and was owned and operated by a corporate franchisee, McDonald's Restaurants of Illinois, Inc. McDonald's Corporation recognized the threat of armed robbery at its franchises, especially in the period immediately prior to closing. McDonald's established an entire corporate division to deal with security problems at franchises.

Jim Carlson was McDonald's regional security manager for the area in which the Oak Forest franchise was located. Carlson visited the Oak Forest franchise to inform the manager of security procedures. He specifically mentioned two rules: (1) No one should throw garbage out the backdoor after dark; (2) trash and grease were to be taken out of the side glass door at least one hour prior to closing. During his inspection, Carlson noted that the lock on the backdoor needed to be replaced and that the restaurant had no alarm. Carlson never followed up to determine whether these security measures had been taken. The employees were not instructed about the security measures.

About a month later, a crew of six teenage girls was working to clean up and close the restaurant. A robber appeared at the back door, used by the crew, with a gun. He ordered the crew to open the safe and then ordered them into the refrigerator. During the robbery, one crew member was shot and killed and two others assaulted.

The family of the murdered girl, together with the injured girls, sued both the franchisee and the franchisor, McDonald's Corporation.

Consider:
(a) Is there a benefit to the franchisor in establishing security rules for franchisees?
(b) Are there any potential problems for the franchisor in establishing security rules?
(c) Is McDonald's Corporation liable for the girls' injuries?

See - *Martin v. McDonald's Corporation*, 572 N.E.2d 1073 (1991), Appellate Court of Illinois.

Chapter 11 Limited Partnerships, Limited Liability Companies, and Professional Corporations

OUTLINE

In this chapter, we will explore limited partnerships. We will also look at limited liability partnerships, limited liability companies and professional corporations. All of these forms of business have a very significant common characteristic – they are all creatures of statute. While sole proprietorships and general partnerships may be formed with little, if any, government involvement, these types of business organizations may be formed only by strict compliance with state law.

11.1 Limited Partnerships – Characteristics and Formation

At the outset, it is important to note when the term "partnership" is used, the use of the single word denotes a general partnership as opposed to a limited partnership, discussed here.

Limited partnerships are partnerships formed by two or more persons or entities which consist of one or more general partners and one or more limited partners. As indicated by the use of the word "entities," the partners in a limited partnership may be natural persons or other entities such as corporations or other partnerships or any combination thereof.

All states have enacted statutes that provide for the creation of limited partnerships. Limited partnerships provide a means for limited partners, sometimes called "silent partners," to make investments knowing that the amount of the investment represents their maximum possible loss. In other words, a limited partnership enables the limited partners to put a cap on their exposure while the general partner(s) retain(s) unlimited personal liability. Limited partnerships developed as a tool to enable wealthy individuals a means of investing in business opportunities and, at the same time, protect all of their other assets from the unlimited personal liability inherent in general partnerships.

A limited partnership can be created only by strict adherence to the requirements of the appropriate statute. The Uniform Limited Partnership Act, drafted and approved in 1916, was updated by the Revised Uniform Limited Partnership Act (RULPA) in the mid-1970's, and every state, excepting only Louisiana, has adopted some version of it. Georgia adopted its version of the RULPA in 1988.

The name of a limited partnership must contain the words "limited partnership" or the abbreviation "L.P." and must be distinguishable from the name of any other limited partnership organized in the state or doing business in the state. One may apply to reserve a name for the purpose of forming a limited partnership by making a request to the Secretary of State's office and paying the specified fee. The Secretary of State will then determine whether the requested name is distinguishable and, if it is, will reserve the name for thirty (30) days.

Under the RULPA, two or more persons must execute a certificate of limited partnership, containing specified information. That certificate is then filed with the Secretary of State and the limited partnership is formed when the certificate is filed.

OCGA § 14-9-201

(a) In order to form a limited partnership, a certificate of limited partnership must be executed and filed in the Office of the Secretary of State. The certificate must set forth:

(1) The name of the limited partnership;

(2) The address of the registered office and the name and address of the initial agent for service of process required to be maintained by Code Section 14-9-104;

(3) The name and the business address of each general partner; and

(4) Any other matters the general partners determine to include therein.

(b) A limited partnership exists from the time of the filing of the certificate of limited partnership in the office of the Secretary of State or form a later time or later time and date, not to exceed 90 days from the date of filing, specified in the certificate of limited partnership, to the time of cancellation pursuant to subsection (c) of Code Section 14-9-206.

Defective formation of a limited partnership may occur if the certificate of limited partnership is not properly filed or if there is some defect in the certificate. If there is a substantial defect in the creation of a limited partnership, persons who thought they were limited partners may find themselves liable as general partners.

- The Limited Partner's Role in a Limited Partnership

Limited partners in a limited partnership are merely investors who are liable only for the debts and obligations of the limited partnership up to the amount of their capital investment. Thus, in the worst-case scenario, the complete failure of the business, a wealthy individual who is a limited partner may lose all of his investment in the business but his personal assets are protected from the creditors of the limited partnership.

In exchange for this protection, limited partners, at least in theory, forgo any management in the enterprise. The general partner is the manager of a limited partnership and makes all decisions as to the running of the business. A limited partner is not an agent of the limited partnership and has no right to bind the partnership with regard to contracts. A limited partner does, however, have a right to review the books and financial records of the partnership and the right to be informed about the affairs of the business.

Traditionally, a limited partner who acted as a general partner would lose his limited liability status. Thus, he could not "control" the business and still enjoy his limited liability status. The RULPA still takes this position. While the RULPA does not specify exactly what acts constitute an exercise of control, it does provide that a limited partner may engage in certain activities without jeopardizing his limited liability status. These include:

- Being a contractor, agent or employee of the limited partnership;
- Consulting with and advising a general partner with respect to the business;
- Requesting or attending a partners' meeting; or
- Proposing any of the following matters:
    - the dissolution and winding up of the business
    - the sale or transfer of all or substantially all of the partnership's assets
    - the admission or removal of a partner, general or limited
    - an amendment to the partnership certificate or agreement

Georgia, however, has taken a somewhat different view. In adopting its version of the RULPA in 1988, Georgia eliminated the rule that a limited partner is liable as a general partner if he takes part control of the partnership. Several reasons for doing so were given.[11] Specifically, it was noted that the control rule has, over the years, been greatly watered down, as evidenced by the RUPLA's broad safe harbor as to what constitutes control. Thus, the resulting uncertainty of the control rule was believed to operate as a disincentive to limited partnership investments. It was also noted that the control rule is not effective in fulfilling the objective of ensuring that only those with personal liability, and thus, a strong incentive to be careful, will manage the business. General partners can always incorporate or delegate control to individuals other than limited partners. The control rule may actually serve to weaken the quality of management since the risk of liability for participation in control deters limited partners from monitoring the general partners. Finally, third parties are protected if they are misled by a limited partner's participation in control since the limited partner may be liable on estoppel or fraud grounds, or on general equitable grounds under "veil-piercing" theory. "Veil piercing" is discussed in Chapter 12 in conjunction with liability of corporate owners

> OCGA § 14-9-303
>
> A limited partner is not liable for the obligations of a limited partnership by reason of being a limited partner and does not become so by participating in the management or control of the business.

- The General Partner's Role in a Limited Partnership

Every limited partnership must have at least one general partner, but may have more than one. The general partner (or partners) controls the partnership and is fully responsible for managing the business. Thus, the general partner in a limited partnership has essentially the same rights and duties as do partners in a general partnership. This means the general partner owes fiduciary duties to both the limited partners as well as the limited partnership, and the general partner is an agent of the limited partnership who can bind the partnership in contracts.

---

[11] These reasons are set out in the comment which follows the Georgia code section. The comments were prepared under the supervision of the Joint Committee on Partnership Law of the Real Property and Corporate and Banking Sections of the State Bar of Georgia and were included in the Official Code of Georgia Annotated at the request of those committees.

OCGA § 14-9-402

(a) ...a general partner of a limited partnership has the rights and powers and is subject to the restrictions of and liability to the partnership and to the other partners of a partner in a partnership without limited partners.

(b) ...a general partner of a limited partnership has the liabilities of a partner in a partnership without limited partners to persons other than the partnership and the other partners.

General partners have personal and joint and several liability for the debts and obligations of the limited partnership. Thus, the personal assets of the general partner can be reached by creditors if the assets of the limited partnership are insufficient to satisfy those debts.

Advantages and Disadvantages of a Limited Partnership

Forming a business as a limited partnership has several advantages. A limited partnership is often an ideal vehicle for attracting capital. As mentioned above, wealthy persons can invest money in a business enterprise knowing that their maximum exposure is the amount of their contribution. The limited partner knows exactly how much he is risking, if the worst happens, making limited partnerships an attractive investment vehicle for some investors. Additionally, if more capital is needed, it is quite easy to admit new limited partners assuming persons who are interested in becoming new limited partners can be found. If those new limited partners are not readily available, obtaining financing can pose problems.

General Electric Credit Corporation v. Stover
708 S.W.2d 355 (1986)
Missouri Court of Appeals

Facts: Linnane and Stover formed a limited partnership for the purpose of operating a home entertainment store. Linnane was the sole general partner and Stover was the sole limited partner. Stover was the silent partner who provided the capital for the partnership and took no part in the day-to-day managment of the business. When additional financing for the business was needed, the limited partnership applied to GE Credit, but GE Credit refused to provide financing to the undercapitalized partnership unless Stover signed as the guarantor of the credit. When the partnership defaulted on the note and the general partner, Linnane, was adjudicated bankrupt, GE Credit sued Stover.

Issue: Was the limited partner, Stover, personally liable for the limited partnership's debt?

Holding: GE Credit would not extend credit to the limited partnership unless Stover signed the credit agreement after providing GE Credit with his personal financial statement. Stover's signature on the credit application induced GE Credit to extend credit to the business. GE relied upon Stover's personal guarantee. Stover cannot now hide behind his status as a limited partner.

The ease of transferability of a limited partner's interest is another significant advantage to this form of business organization. A partner has no interest in specific property that is owned by the limited partnership, but his partnership interest itself is personal property. Limited partners can easily transfer their interests in a limited partnership to others. So long as either the limited partnership agreement permits it or the other partners agree, the assignee of a limited partner's interest will be a new limited partner. Georgia's RULPA provides that a limited partnership interest is assignable in whole or in part unless the partnership agreement provides otherwise. Thus, assignability is the default position, and if the partners want to provide otherwise, they must explicitly so provide in their partnership agreement. Furthermore, the partners can agree that an assignee automatically assumes the status of a limited partner so that, like corporate shares, a partner's entire status and not merely his financial rights would be transferable.

Because limited partners do not control or manage the business enterprise, the withdrawal of a limited partner does not cause a dissolution of the limited partnership. This is a significant advantage over the general partnership form in which one partner's withdrawal dissolves the business.

The limited partnership form of business does, however, pose major disadvantages for both the limited partner(s) and the general partner(s). Since, in most states, limited partners have no control over the business, they must have complete confidence in the general partner. The disadvantage for the general partner is, of course, the unlimited personal liability the general partner has for the debts and obligation of the limited partnership. Finally, as mentioned above, a limited partnership can only be created by strict adherence to the requirements of the appropriate statute. Since the creation of a limited partnership is more complex than the creation of general partnership, significant filing fees and legal fees are often incurred.

Taxation of Limited Partnerships

The taxation of a limited partnership is nearly identical to that of a general partnership. The limited partnership does not pay federal income tax but does file an informational tax return with the IRS. All of the income earned by the limited partnership is passed through to the partners, regardless of whether that income has been distributed to the partners or not. The partners then declare their share of the income on their own individual tax returns.

A limited partnership, just like a general partnership, may elect to "check the box" and be taxed as a corporation.

11.2 Limited Liability Partnerships

Limited Liability Partnerships (LLPs) were created as a way to shield partners from liability for the wrongful acts of their co-partners. LLPs are ideal for professionals such as doctors, attorneys, or accountants and were created with these professionals in mind.

When large numbers of saving and loan institutions failed in the 1980s, creating a financial crisis, investors lost millions of dollars. Since the institutions were insolvent, investors sought to recoup some of their money by suing the attorneys and accountants who had provided professional advice to the savings and loans. Because these professionals operated as general partnerships, many innocent professionals, partners of the wrongdoers, were subjected to unlimited joint and several liability even though they had not personally performed work for the institutions. To remedy this harsh situation, a new form of business organization was created to shield partners from liability for the malpractice of their co-partners.

An LLP is very similar to a general partnership, with the critical difference being that there is no unlimited personal liability. Instead, all partners are limited partners who stand to lose only their capital contribution in the event the partnership should fail. None of the partners is personally liable for the debts and obligations of the partnership beyond his or her own capital contribution, except, of course, that every partner is personally liable for his or her own torts and misconduct. Thus, the LLP allows professionals to avoid the unlimited personal liability for the malpractice of other partners which accompanies the general partnership form of organization.

Example 11a:

Kevin is one of three attorneys who form an LLP. When Kevin fails to file his client's complaint in a timely fashion and misses a statute of limitation, Kevin is liable for his malpractice. The firm is also liable, but Kevin's co-partners are not personally liable for Kevin's malpractice.

Note, however, that there are a couple of exceptions to the protection from liability for acts of co-partners. There are discussed in more detail later. Basically, a partner who had a supervisory role over the wrongdoer does not escape liability, nor does a partner who had knowledge of the wrongful act and failed to take measures to stop it. Of course, the LLP itself is always fully liable for the negligent acts and omissions of any of its partners.

In 1995, Georgia's legislature enacted laws which made it possible for a general partnership to elect to become a limited liability partnership by filing a statement electing that status with the appropriate government office. Additionally, limited partnerships were also permitted to continue their operations as limited liability partnerships.

O.C.G.A. § 14-8-62

(a) To become and to continue as a limited liability partnership, a partnership shall record in the office of the clerk of the superior court of any county in which the partnership has an office a limited liability partnership election. Such election shall be recorded by such clerk in a book to be kept for that purpose, which may be the book in which are recorded statements of partnership recorded pursuant to code Section 4-7-10.1, and open to public inspection…

(g) A limited partnership organizing under or subject to chapter 9 of this title may become and continue as a limited liability partnership…

Full Shield States vs. Partial Shield States

Most states, including Georgia, are Full Shield states, meaning that a partner is not personally liable for either the wrongful acts or omissions of other partners, and additionally, the partners are not liable for the commercial, contractual, or other obligations of the partnership. Thus, a partner's personal assets are not at risk with regard to the past due lease payments on the firm's office building or his co-partner's malpractice.

In the three Partial Shield states, a partner in an LLP is not personally liable for the wrongful acts or omissions of his co-partners, but does retain liability for other partnership obligations such as contract obligations. Thus, a partner will incur no liability for his co-partner's malpractice, but will be personally liable for other debts and obligations incurred by either the partnership or by a partner since any partner, as an agent of the partnership, can bind the partnership.

Example 11b:

Assuming the same facts in example 11a, because of Kevin's malpractice, the partnership has lost many clients and is unable to pay for its expensive new computer network. When the partnership is sued by the computer supplier, all of the partners are personally liable for payment of the debt in a partial shield state, but not in a full shield state.

Formation and Operation of Limited Liability Partnerships

The formation of a limited liability partnership is similar to the formation of a limited partnership. In Georgia, LLPs are formed as either general partnerships or limited partnerships and then elect to be treated as LLPs. This election is made by the filing of a "limited liability partnership election" in the office of the clerk of the superior court in any county in which the partnership has an office.[12]

The name of a Limited Liability Partnership must contain some indication of its status as such. Appropriate indications include "LLP," or "limited."

> O.C.G.A. §14-6-63
>
> (a) Except as provided in subsection (b) of this Code section, the name of a limited liability partnership shall contain the words "limited liability partnership," it being permitted to abbreviate the word "limited" as "ltd.," or the abbreviation "L.L.P." or the designation "LLP" as the last words or letters of its name.
>
> (b) The name of a limited partnership that is a limited liability partnership shall contain the words "limited liability limited partnership," it being permitted to abbreviate the word "limited" as "ltd.," or the abbreviation "L.L.L.P." or the designation "LLLP" as the last words or letters of its name.

As evidenced from the above code section, a limited partnership may also elected limited liability status thus becoming a limited liability limited partnership (LLLP).

Advantages and Disadvantages of Limited Liability Partnerships

As the name indicates, limited liability partnerships are a form of partnership and thus, are governed almost exclusively by partnership laws and principles. Additionally, the Revised Uniform Partnership Act (RUPA) has been amended to recognize this form of business organization. However, because of their unique nature, limited liability partnerships have specific advantages and certain disadvantages which are not found in general partnerships.

The advantages of doing business as an LLP include:

- Partners in an LLP are protected against unlimited personal liability for the negligent acts and misconduct of their co-partners unless:
    - A partner supervised or directed the partner who engaged in wrongful acts, or
    - A partner was directly involved in the act giving rise to liability, or
    - A partner had knowledge or notice of the act giving rise to liability and failed to take reasonable steps to prevent or cure it;
- Partners share management duties and responsibilities; and
- Partners have the ability to raise capital by admitting new partners.

The disadvantages of LLPs include:

- LLPs can be formed only with strict compliance with state statutes making them somewhat more complicated and expensive to form;
- Many states require LLPs to have liability insurance in place;

---

[12] See. O.C.G.A. § 14-8-62.

- Operating an LLP on a nationwide basis may be difficult because of the differences in state law in full shield states and partial shield states; and
- LLPs may encourage senior partners to avoid supervising junior partners in order to avoid the liability imposed on supervising partners.

Taxation of Limited Liability Partnerships

Like other forms of partnerships, an LLP itself does not pay federal income taxes but does file an informational tax return. The income earned by the LLP is passed through to the individual partners, regardless of whether the income has been distributed to the partners or not. The partners then declare their share of the income on their individual returns and pay the appropriate tax on it based on their individual personal rates. Additionally, just as with general and limited partnerships, LLPs may choose to "check the box" and elect to be taxed as a corporation.

11.3 Limited Liability Companies

Another non-corporate entity which entrepreneurs may opt to use is the *limited liability company* which, like the corporate form, offers the advantage of limited personal liability to its owners. In terms of structure and management, some have described an LLC as being much like a limited partnership with no general partner, but this analogy is not entirely accurate.

LLCs are a relatively new form of business organization in this country, having first been introduced in the 1970s. When the Internal Revenue Service ruled, in 1988, that a limited liability company would be classified as a partnership for federal tax purposes, eliminating the potential for double taxation, the LLC explosion began. Since then, all fifty states and the District of Columbia have adopted legislation providing for the formation of this type of business organization, although the legislation varies considerably from state to state. The first Georgia LLC was formed in 1994. Since that time, the LLC has become the dominant form of organization for newly-created small businesses.[13]

A limited liability company is a legal entity separate and distinct from its owners. The owners, in Georgia and as well as in most other states, are referred to as *members*. In many states, including Georgia, a single individual may form an LLC. A sole proprietor is, thus, afforded a means of maintaining sole ownership and complete control of his business while, at the same time, insulating himself from personal liability for the debts and obligations associated with that business. This has made the LLC form of business organization extremely attractive for many small business owners.

Formation and Operation of Limited Liability Companies

In most states, a limited liability company may be formed for virtually any purpose, although a few states limited this form of business to the practice of specified professions. Georgia places no limitations on the purpose for which a limited liability company may be formed.

O.C.G.A. §14-11-201

(a) A limited liability company may be formed under this chapter for any lawful purpose...

[13] The Georgia Secretary of State's office reports that for the calendar year 2013, 64,943 LLCs were formed in Georgia while only 13,582 for-profit corporations were formed.

Statutory compliance is required to form an LLC, although, in Georgia, the formalities are few. An organizer who desires to form an LLC must decide upon a name for his business enterprise. There are few requirements with regard to the name. The name must not be confusingly similar to that of another corporation, limited liability company, or limited partnership organized or doing business in the state. Additionally, the name must include the words "limited liability company," "limited company," or the abbreviation "L.L.C.," "LLC," "L.C." or "LC." The organizer may reserve his preferred name with the Secretary of State's office, provided, of course, that the chosen name meets the statutory requirements. Additionally, the LLC may, like other business forms, operate under a fictitious or trade name subject to the same provisions required of a sole proprietorship using a fictitious name.[14]

The formation of an LLC closely parallels the formation of a corporation. The document which creates the LLC is called the *articles of organization*. After the articles have been prepared and signed by one organizer or member, that person will then submit this document to the Secretary of State for filing, enclosing payment of the required filing fee. The articles of organization must contain the information prescribed by the statutes of the state in which the LLC is formed.

Typically, the articles will include:

- The name of the limited liability company;
- The address of the company's initial designated office;
- The name and street address of the initial agent for service of process;
- The name and address of each organizer;
- Whether the LLC will be member managed or manager managed; and
- Whether the company is to exist perpetually.

In Georgia, remarkably little information is required to be included in the articles of organization. Below is the example form from the Georgia Secretary of State's website for the Articles of Organization for a Georgia Limited Liability Company:

Exhibit 11-1:

Articles of Organization
Of
ABC and Associates, LLC

Article 1.
The name of the limited liability company is ABC and Associates, LLC.

(Note: Article 2. below is optional. It, and other provisions not inconsistent with law, may be set forth in the Articles of Organization.)

Article 2.
Management of the limited liability company is vested in one or more managers whose names and addresses are as follows:

IN WITNESS WHEREOF, the undersigned has executed these Articles of Organization.

This _________ day of ________, 2012.

(*signature*)
John Doe (*Capacity of signer*)

---

[14] See. O.C.G.A. § 14-11-207

O.C.G.A. §14-11-204

(a) The articles of organization shall set forth the name of the limited liability company, which name must satisfy the requirements of Code Section 14-11-207.

(b) The articles of organization may set forth:

(1) That management of the limited liability company is vested in one or more managers; and

(2) Any other provisions not inconsistent with law.

In Georgia, the other information typically required to be included in the articles of organization, such as the names of the members, the address of the limited liability company, and name and street address of the initial agent for service of process, is provided in a separate document, called a Transmittal Form, which must accompany the filing of the articles of organization. The Secretary of State's website has a Transmittal Form which can be filled out electronically

O.C.G.A. § 14-11-203

(a) One or more persons may act as the organizer or organizers of a limited liability company by delivering articles of organization to the Secretary of State for filing and supplying to the Secretary of State, in such form as the Secretary of State may require, the following information:

(1) The name and address of each organizer;

(2) The street address and county of the limited liability company's initial registered office and the name of its initial registered agent at that office; and

(3) The mailing address of the limited liability company's principal place of business.

(b) An organizer need not be a member of the limited liability company at the time of formation or thereafter.

(c) A limited liability company is formed when the articles of organization become effective pursuant to Code Section 14-11-206.

The limited liability company is formed upon the filing of the articles of organization with the Secretary of State unless a later effective date is specified. The Secretary of State will issue a Certificate of Organization. An example of a Certificate of Organization and accompanying Articles of Organization are found in Appendix V.

O.C.G.A. § 14-11-206

(a) A signed original and one exact or conformed copy of any document required or permitted to be filed pursuant to this chapter shall be delivered to the Secretary of State; provided, however, that if the document is electronically transmitted, the electronic version of such person's name may be used in lieu of a signature. Unless the Secretary of State finds that the document does not conform to the filing provisions of this chapter, upon receipt of all filing fees and additional information required by law, he or she shall:

(1) Stamp or otherwise endorse his or her official title and the date and time of receipt on both the original and copy;

(2) File the original in his or her office; and

(3) Return the copy to the person who delivered the document to the Secretary of State or the person's representative.

(b) If the Secretary of State refuses to file a document, he or she shall return it to the limited liability company or its representative within ten days after the document was delivered, together with a brief written explanation of the reason for his or her refusal. ...

> (e) … a document accepted for filing is effective:
>
> (1) At the time of filing on the date it is filed, as evidenced by the Secretary of State's date and time endorsement on the original document; or
>
> (2) At the time specified in the document as its effective time on the date it is filed.
>
> (f) A document may specify a delayed effective time and date, and, if it does so, the document shall become effective at the time and date specified. …

The *operating agreement* contains provisions for the operation and governance of the LLC and is very similar to a partnership agreement. The operating agreement represents the contract of the members with regard to the operation of their business. The operating agreement is a private document which is not filed with any state agency.

Generally speaking, members in an LLC are entitled to information or records of the LLC such as financial statements, and they owe one another duties of good faith, fair dealing, and loyalty. Otherwise, members are free to regulate the affairs of the LLC as they see fit.

Typically, an operating agreement will contain provisions pertaining to the following:

- Names of all members – The names of members as well as the members' addresses will be included so notices and other information may be communicated to them.

- Recitals - A recitation confirms the intent of the members to form an LLC.

- Purpose – The purpose of the LLC is stated, but it may be stated in very general terms, such as "the purpose of the LLC is to engage in any lawful business."

- Address – The principal place of business of the LLC is provided.

- Financial Provisions – A description of the initial contributions by members to the LCC which may be in the form of cash, property or services is included.

- Operation of the LLC – The type of management the LLC will have must be described. Member-managed LLCs operate similarly to general partnerships with each member having an equal right to manage the business. An LLC may also be manager-managed, particularly if there are a large number of members such that member management is difficult or cumbersome.

- Meetings and Voting – Provisions should be included setting out how often regular meetings will be held, where they will be conducted, and the procedure for sending notices of meetings and how meetings will be conducted.

- Admission of New Members – Unless the operating agreement provides otherwise, the admission of a new member to an LLC requires unanimous agreement (under the ULLCA).

- Dissociation of Members – Unless provided otherwise in the operating agreement, a member may withdraw or dissociate from the LLC upon notice to the LLC.

- Transferability of Interest – A member's financial interest in an LLC is that member's personal property and is transferable. A member may always transfer, or assign, his right to distributions from the LLC, but the transferee will become a member of the LLC only if the operating agreement so provides.

- Dissolution – Often an operating agreement will provide that certain events will trigger the dissolution of the LLC. These events often include the expiration of the fixed period of duration, the unanimous agreement of all members, or the death or bankruptcy of any member.

If an LLC desires to operate in state other than the one in which it is organized, it must qualify to do business in that state. Specific state statutes must be consulted because the requirements for qualifying to do business vary from state to state. Under Georgia law, if a foreign LLC wants to qualify to do business here, the LLC must procure a certificate of authority to transact business in Georgia from the Secretary of State's office.[15] This is done by submitting to the Secretary of State an application which includes certain basic information about the foreign LLC including its name, the name of the jurisdiction under whose laws it was organized, the address of the principle place of business, and the name of a person who has substantial responsibility for managing the business activities of the foreign LLC. Most importantly, the application must give the name and street address of the LLC's registered office in Georgia and the name of its registered agent for service of process at that office.[16] If the foreign LLC failes to appoint or maintain a registered agent for service, then the Secretary of State is, by law, appointed as the agent for service.[17]

Many activities are *not* considered to be transacting business, and thus, no certificate of authority is required. In Georgia these include maintaining or defending a lawsuit, maintaining bank accounts, owing real property, making loans, holding meetings, effecting sales through independent contractors, and soliciting or procuring orders where such orders require acceptance outside the state before becoming a binding contract. Additionally, conducting an isolated transaction not part of a number of repeated similar transactions is *not* considered to be transacting business.

Advantages and Disadvantages of Limited Liability Companies

The rise in popularity of LLCs is due to the significant advantages of this form of business organization. The greatest of these is the complete protection the LLC provides to its members from personal liability. The liability of any member is limited to the amount of the investment he contributed to the LLC. An investor in an LLC may be active in the management of the LLC and yet protect his other assets from exposure to liability.

Bonner v. Brunson

262 Ga.App. 521, 585 S.E.2d 917 (2003)

Court of Appeals of Georgia

<u>Facts</u>: T.I. Brunson, LLC, is organized under the laws of the State of Georgia with a sole member, Thomas Brunson. T.I. Brunson, LLC, acting through its agent, Thomas Brunson, subcontracted with Fred Bonner to perform roofing work on a condominium construction project. Bonner completed the work and submitted a bill for $288,000. When payment was not received, Bonner sued both the LLC and Brunson in his individual capacity.

<u>Issue</u>: Is the individual who is the sole member of an LLC personally liable for the debt of the LLC?

---

[15] See the requirements of O.C.G.A. § 14-11-702.

[16] See O.C.G.A. § 14-11-702.

[17] See O.C.G.A. § 14-11-703.

Holding: Just as the corporate veil protects an individual shareholder of a corporation from personal liability for the debts of the separate corporate entity (so long as the corporate forms are maintained) so is a member of a limited liability company "veiled" from personal liability for the debts of the separately maintained LLC entity. In order to pierce this veil and hold Brunson personally liable for the alleged debt of the LLC, there must be evidence that he abused the forms by which the LLC was maintained as a separate legal entity apart from his personal business. A court may disregard the separate LLC entity and the protective veil it provides to an individual member of the LLC when that member, in order to defeat justice or perpetrate fraud, conducts his personal and LLC business as if they were one by commingling the two on an interchangeable or joint basis or confusing otherwise separate properties, records, or control. In the instant case, there is no basis for concluding that Brunson abused the form of the LLC.

As a practical matter, it is often necessary for an entrepreneur to give a personal guarantee in order to obtain a loan or other financing for his small LLC. In such case, while the member is not liable for the debts of the LLC, he may find himself called upon to pay the obligation based on his personal guarantee.

In the following case, two medical doctors were required to personally guarantee payment on a lease agreement. The *Winzer* case is included in these materials, however, for the holding of the court on another important issue.

Winzer et al. v. EHCA Dunwoody, LLC
277 Ga.App. 710, 627 S.E.2d 426 (2006)
Court of Appeals of Georgia

Facts: Doctors Winzer and Serwitz formed Northside Medical Care Center, LLC, which leased medical office property from EHCA Dunwoody, LLC. Winzer and Serwitz guaranteed the obligations of their LLC to EHCA Dunwoody. When Northside failed to pay rent under the lease agreement, EHCA Dunwoody sued the LLC. Northside appeared at the bench trial without an attorney and was, instead, represented by Dr. Serwitz. EHCA was awarded a judgment in the amount of $104,609. Dr. Serwitz filed a notice of appeal. The appeal, however, was not accepted by the Court of Appeals since it was filed by Dr. Serwitz representing the LLC, rather than by an attorney.

Unable to collect on the judgment, EHCA then sued Winzer and Serwitz individually, alleging that they had each personally guaranteed the lease obligations of Northside and were thus liable for the unpaid rent. Neither timely filed an answer, and default judgments were entered against both of them. Winzer and Serwitz filed a notice of appeal from that judgment.

Issues: Did the Court of Appeals improperly fail to accept the appeal of the LLC, Northside Medical Care Center? Were Winzer and Serwitz liable to EHCA Dunwoody?

Holding: With regard to the issue of the liability of Winzer and Serwitz for the unpaid rent, a default judgment was properly entered as a result of the failure of the doctors to file an answer to the suit filed against them in their individual capacities by EHCA Dunwoody.

As to the issue of the representation of Northside by Dr. Serwitz, it has been established that only a licensed attorney is authorized to represent a corporation in a proceeding in a court of record.

> Like a corporation, a limited liability company is a business entity which protects its members from personal liability for business debts. Like a corporation, a limited liability company can act only through its agents. Like a corporation, allowing a limited liability company to be represented in court by a non-attorney agent would permit the practice of law by an unlicensed layman who is not subject to the discipline of the court. And, like those who accept the benefits of incorporation, those who accept the benefits of a limited liability company must also accept its burdens, including the need to hire counsel.

The LLC itself is liable for the wrongful acts of its members, and each LLC member is, of course, liable for his or her own wrongful acts. Thus, if one member of a professional LLC commits an act of malpractice, both that member and the LLC have liability for that act of malpractice, but the other LLC members are not personally liable.

Limited liability is a particularly attractive feature of the limited liability company form since one member LLCs are permitted in almost all jurisdictions including Georgia. Thus, the LLC form allows a sole proprietor to protect his assets from liability while still affording him sole decision-making, management and control of his business. This makes the LLC an ideal form of organization for a small business owner who wants to shield his personal assets from the unlimited personal liability he risks if he does business as a sole proprietorship.

Another advantage to the LLC form of business organization is the flexibility of management it offers. Most LLCs are managed by their members. However, the members may elect to appoint a manager or managers to operate and manage the LLC. An appointed manager need not be a member of the LLC. Thus, the members have the option of employing a professional to run their business.

The most significant disadvantages to the LLC form of business organization arise from the newness of the form. Because LLCs did not exist until a few years ago, there is little case law interpreting the various statutes pertaining to them. Furthermore, while each state now recognizes the LLC form, there are considerable variations among the state statutes and those variations may make it somewhat complicated to operate an LLC in more than one state.

Taxation of Limited Liability Companies

The income of an LLC is passed through the LLC to the members just as with a partnership. All income, regardless of whether it has been distributed to the members or not, flows through the LLC to the individual members who declare their share of the LLC income on their individual income tax returns and pay tax on this amount. Likewise, losses sustained by the LLC are passed through and may be used to offset members' other income, thereby decreasing their tax liability.

The LLC does not pay taxes itself, but must file the same informational tax return required of general partnerships. Also, like other entities, an LLC may elect to be taxed as a corporation at corporate rates by "checking the box."

11.4 Professional Corporations

At common law, professionals, such as doctors and lawyers, were allowed to practice only as individuals or as partners in general partnerships. Of course, by practicing their professions in a general partnership, professionals exposed themselves to unlimited personal liability for the wrongful acts of their partners. Several decades ago, states began to enact statutes designed to provide some protection for professionals against unlimited personal liability. Most began with statutes permitting the formation of professional corporations. Now, all states have passed such statutes with most of them being based on the Model Professional Corporation Act (MPCA).

As the name implies, professional corporations are designed for use only by those practicing the professions. Some state statutes, including Georgia's, enumerate the types of professions covered by the statute. Usually, the statutes also provide that only one profession may be practiced by a given P.C. Thus, a dentist, a lawyer and a veterinarian may not form a single professional corporation.

O.C.G.A. § 14-7-2

"Profession" means the profession of certified public accountancy, architecture, chiropractic, dentistry, professional engineering, land surveying, law, pharmacy, psychology, medicine and surgery, optometry, osteopathy, podiatry, veterinary medicine, registered professional nursing, or harbor piloting.

Most states require that all shareholders in a professional corporation be members of the designated profession – persons who are licensed to practice the profession for which the corporation is organized.

In the event of the death or retirement of a shareholder, the shares must be redeemed or canceled by the corporation or transferred to a person who is authorized to hold the shares, that is, a member of the profession. The shares cannot be held by a non-professional.

O.C.G.A. § 14-7-4

(a) A professional corporation may practice only one profession, but for the purpose of this chapter, the practice of architecture, professional engineering, and land surveying shall be considered the practice of only one professional to the extent that existing laws permit overlapping practices by members of those specific professions not inconsistent with the ethics of the professions involved.

(b) A professional corporation shall engage in the practice of a profession only through its officers, employees, and agents who are duly licensed or otherwise legally authorized to practice the profession in this state. This restriction shall not, however, prevent the corporation from employing unlicensed persons in capacities in which they are not rendering professional services to the public in the course of their employment.

(c) At least one member of the board of directors and the president of a professional corporation shall be licensed to practice the profession for which the corporation is organized. If the governing board of a professional corporation includes persons not so licensed, the corporation shall, by creation of a standing committee of the board of directors or otherwise, vest the responsibility for decisions relating wholly to professional considerations in persons who are so licensed.

Licensed professionals are always personally liable for their own acts of wrongdoing such as professional malpractice. However, professionals practicing in a group may incorporate in order to provide protection against personal liability for the acts and omissions (torts) of their associates, the other professionals practicing with them.

11.5 Professional Associations

Prior to 1970, Georgia law prohibited the practice of some professions by corporations. However, the General Assembly had recognized the desire of professionals to limit their personal liability while still practicing their profession with others. In 1961, the Georgia legislature passed legislation authorizing the formation of *professional associations*. Professional associations are defined as unincorporated associations and are limited to those rendering professional services "which may be legally performed only pursuant to a license from a board ..."

The members of any professional association are not individually liable for the obligations or debts of the professional association. Specifically, a member is not liable for any acts of malpractice committed by another member, unless that member has personally participated in the transaction for which the debt of claim is made or out of which it arises. Of course, the formation of a professional association does not alter the liability a professional may have for malpractice.

The legislature, in enacting the Professional Associations statute, intended it for the benefit of doctors, lawyers and the like. However, the courts have interpreted the definition of "profession" in a broader fashion and have expanded the "professions" covered by the statute to include any profession which requires licensing by the state.[18]

> O.C.G.A. § 14-10-3
>
> Any two or more persons duly licensed to practice a profession under the laws of this state may form a professional association, as distinguished from a partnership, by associating themselves for the purpose of carrying on a profession and dividing the gains therefrom ...

Professional associations are prohibited from rendering services in more than one type of profession. However, an opinion by Georgia's Attorney General provides that doctors in different specialty areas may form a professional association. Additionally, professional associations are also prohibited by statute from engaging in any business other than that for which the association was formed.[19]

Professional associations are governed generally by laws applying to corporations and are specifically not deemed to be partnerships.

Review Questions and Exercises

1. What is the limited partner's role in a limited partnership? What is the role of the general partner?

2. How does Georgia law differ from the RULPA with regard to the participation in management by a limited partner? Is Georgia's modification an improvement over the RUPLA? Why or why not? Given the Georgia law in this regard, what is the significant difference between a general partnership and a limited partnership under Georgia law?

3. Why might an investor prefer to become a member of an LLC rather than a limited partner in a limited partnership?

---

[18] While intended for attorneys, physicians, dentists, etc., the courts expanded the definition. In *Colston v. Fred's Pest Control, Inc.*, 210 Ga.App. 362, 436 S.E.2d 23 (1993), the Georgia Court of Appeals determined that a pest control company's control and treatment of wood-destroying organisms is a profession for purposes of filing a professional malpractice action since the pest control company must secure a license from the State Structural Pest Control Commission in order to legally render services.

[19] See O.C.G.A. § 14-10-5.

4. What are the advantages to doing business in the Limited Liability Partnership form? What are the disadvantages? Explain the difference between partial shield and full shield states.

5. Under what circumstances may one partner in an LLP be liable for the malpractice of another partner?

6. Who may be a shareholder in a Professional Corporation? What is the liability of shareholders in a PC?

7. Assume Mike and his two nephews, Dan and Don, decide to form a limited liability company to operate a landscaping and lawn service business. Dan and Don will each contribute $10,000 to the LLC and Mike's initial contribution will be $30,000. Can the operating agreement provide that Mike's distributions will be three times the amount of distributions to Dan and Don? If the operating agreement is silent with regard to distributions, how would a $10,000 distribution be divided among the three members?

8. Assume Alisha is forming a limited liability company which will own and operate several art galleries. Alisha will begin with one gallery in Atlanta but wants to expand to Birmingham, Tallahassee and Memphis. What steps might she take during the organization process to plan for her future expansion?

9. Are members of an LLC always protected from personal liability for the debts and obligations of the company? What are some circumstances in which members may be personally liable for the company's debts?

10. John forms a Limited Liability Company for the purpose of buying, renovating, and renting houses. He is the only member of the LLC. The LLC rents a house to a tenant who causes some damage to the home. John wants to sue the tenant in magistrate (small claims) court to recover the repair costs. Can John do this himself or must he hire an attorney? Does it matter that John is the only member of the LLC? Does it matter if John is the only person who has dealt with the tenant and seen the damage which the tenant caused?

Practical Applications

1. Jerry Thomas, Larry Conner and Diana McDonald formed a professional corporation, and the next day, entered into a sublease with Swiss Bank Corporation to sublease office space. The terms of the sublease were prepared by Swiss Bank Corp., and both the lease and the signature lines referred to "Thomas, Conner, & McDonald, P.A.," as the tenant. The defendants' signatures did not indicate they were signing the sublease in their capacities as agents for the professional corporation.

When the professional corporation failed to make lease payments, Swiss Bank Corp., sued, seeking to hold the members personally liable.

Consider:

(a) How does an entity such as a professional association enter into an agreement such as a lease?

(b) Does it matter whether the signers of the lease indicated they were signing for the association as opposed to signing in their individual capacities?

(c) What importance, if any, is attached to the fact that Swiss Bank, Corp., prepared the sublease agreement?

See – *Swiss Bank Corporation v. Thomas, Conner & McDonald, P.A. at al.*, 236 Ga.App. 890, 514 S.E.2d 68 (1999), Court of Appeals of Georgia.

2. Dan Gardner, acting through his manager, approached Rob Marcum regarding investing up to $150,000 in an album by Gardner. Marcum agreed to make the investment and gave the manager a check for $50,000 to be used for producing, releasing and promoting the album. For "tax reasons," and at the request of the manager, the check was made payable to "DG Productions, LLC," a limited liability company owned solely by Gardner. On the check was the written notation "for 1/3 investment in Dan Gardner."

At the time of the initial payment, the parties agreed that they would negotiate the terms of an acceptable written contract as to the terms of the investment. The parties were unable to agree upon the terms of a formal agreement regarding further investment by Marcum, and Marcum demanded that Gardner return the $50,000 "partial payment."

Consider:
(a) What is the effect of the lack of a written contract between the parties?
(b) Was there an enforceable verbal contract between the parties?
(c) Is DG Productions, LLC liable for repayment of Marcum's $50,000?
(d) Is Gardner personally liable for repayment of Marcum's $50,000?

See - *Gardner v. Marcum,* 292 Ga.App. 369, 665 S.E.2d 336 (2008), Georgia Court of Appeals.

Chapter 12 Corporations – Organization and Formation

OUTLINE

Corporations, which have existed for hundreds of years, are the most dominant form of business organization in the United States, generating about 85% of the country's gross business receipts. Corporations are creatures of statute, artificial beings which exist only in the law. The corporation is an entity separate and distinct from the individuals who own it and operate it. While there are a very few public corporations which are created pursuant to federal law, corporations are considered the product of state law with the overwhelming majority of corporations being created pursuant to the laws of the various states.

Each state has its own body of laws which govern the formation, operation, regulation and dissolution of corporations, and these laws, while similar, are not entirely uniform from state to state. The Model Business Corporation Act (MBCA) was quite influential in the codification of state corporation laws, and today the majority of state statutes are guided by the most recent revision of the MBCA, often referred to as the Revised Model Business Corporation Act (RMBCA).

12.1 The Nature of Corporations

A corporation is an artificial entity created by operation of law. In 1819, Chief Justice of the United States Supreme Court John Marshall described the corporate form by saying, "A corporation is an artificial being, invisible, intangible and existing only in the contemplation of law." The corporation is, in legal theory, an artificial person that exists independently of the people who own it, independently of the people who run it, and independently of the people who work for it.

This separation gives a corporation a life of its own. Thus, as an artificial person, a corporation normally exists in perpetuity, and the death or bankruptcy of any or all of the shareholders, directors, officers, or employees of a corporation, while perhaps having dire practical consequences to the continued operation of the corporation's business, would not mean the end of the corporation itself.

It is important to note, however, that not all corporations exist in perpetuity. The corporation's articles of incorporation may provide for a specific duration for a corporation or the shareholders may vote to voluntarily terminate a corporation. Additionally, a corporation's creditors may, in appropriate circumstances, petition the bankruptcy court for involuntary termination of the corporation.

A corporation, being an artificial person, can act only through its agents, specifically, its officers and directors, but it does have the power to engage in virtually all business activities that a natural person may pursue. Thus, a corporation can enter into contracts in its own name, can buy, sell, lease, and mortgage property in its own name, can sue and be sued in its own name, and can make donations in its own name. A corporation is also responsible for its acts in much the same manner as a natural person. A corporation can incur civil liability and can also be charged with criminal acts. Obviously, a corporation cannot be sentenced to prison time, but other criminal penalties, such as fines or the revocation of licenses, can be imposed on a corporation.

Most corporations are profit-motivated business entities, and most large businesses are organized as corporations. While only about one-quarter of all businesses in the U.S. are organized as tax-paying corporations (C corporations under the IRS code), they account for the vast majority of business receipts. Over time and particularly in recent years, however, the number of tax-paying corporations has begun a steady decline as more forms of business organizations that offer tax advantages to the owners, such as LLCs, have come into being.

As with any business entity, there is a tension between the interests of the shareholders, who may be preoccupied with making the highest possible profits, and the interests of others including society as a whole. This is particularly true with regard to large, multi-national corporations. For example, the shareholders of a manufacturing company which sells its products overseas may want the company to use a cheaper but more dangerous component part in order to maximize profits. At the same time, others, such as consumer advocates, may believe the company has a responsibility to consumers, including those in poor, third-world countries who are unlikely to file civil lawsuits for damages, to produce a safer product although the profit margin on the safer product will be less.

This notion of "corporate social responsibility" came to the forefront in the early 1970s with the dramatic increase in the number of multi-national corporations. The term "stakeholder" is used to describe persons other than shareholders on whom an organization's activities have an impact. Stakeholders may include consumers, employees, persons who live near a company's facilities and many others. Proponents of corporate social responsibility argue that, while short-term profits may suffer, corporations make more long-term profit by operating in a manner that promotes the overall good of all stakeholders while critics argue that such a perspective merely distracts from the economic role of business. Still others contend that talk of corporate social responsibility is merely window-dressing designed to preempt governments who serve as watchdogs over powerful corporations.

Advantages and Disadvantages of the Corporate Form of Business

The fact that there are significant advantages to the corporate form of business organization is apparent when one considers that corporations have existed in various forms since medieval times. The principle advantage is the limited liability that the shareholders of the corporation enjoy. The owners of the corporation, the shareholders, are not personally liable for the debts and obligations of the corporation. When one buys stock in a corporation, one knows that his maximum exposure is the price paid for the stock. In other words, the investor knows he may, in an extreme case, lose his entire investment, but he is not liable for the contract or tort obligations of the corporation.

Example 12a:

Melissa and John incorporate their business as ABC, Inc. Each owns 50% of the stock of ABC for which each contributes $50,000. After incorporation, ABC, Inc., borrows $200,000 from Business Financial Corp. After months of struggling, ABC, Inc., defaults on the loan and declares bankruptcy. ABC has assets worth only $20,000 and this sum is paid to Business Financial Corp. Melissa and John have each lost their investment of $50,000 but neither is personally liable for the $180,000 balance still owed to Business Financial.

Note: As a practical matter, Business Financial, when making the loan, would most likely seek a personal guarantee from one or both of the shareholders of ABC, Inc., since it is a new corporation without a proven history of credit worthiness.

In certain, very limited situations, the courts may ignore the corporate entity and *pierce the corporate veil.* That is, a creditor may seek to hold individual shareholders liable for corporate obligations. If the corporate form is used as a false front behind which the owners perpetrate fraud upon creditors or others with whom they deal, the courts may disregard the corporate form. Commonly in these cases, the shareholders have not acted as if the corporation is a separate entity, but have viewed the corporation as their alter ego.

The usual "piercing the veil" case is brought against a small corporation whose shareholders are all active in managing the business. One or more of the following types of conduct are usually involved in piercing of the corporate veil cases:

- Commingling of Assets – Shareholders dip into corporate accounts to pay personal expenses or the corporation informally borrows money from the shareholders to meet its obligations.

- Lack of Formalities – The corporation never issues stock, never elects directors, never appoints officers, and/or never holds meetings.

- Inadequate Capitalization – The corporation is so inadequately capitalized that is could not expect to meet its responsibilities.

Kinney Shoe Corp. v. Polan

939 F.2d 209 (1991)

United States Court of Appeals, Fourth Circuit

Facts: Lincoln Polan formed Industrial Realty Company, a West Virginia corporation. Polan was the sole shareholder. The state of West Virginia issued a certificate of incorporation, but no organizational meeting was ever held and no directors elected or officers appointed. Industrial Realty Company issued no stock certificates and nothing was ever paid into the corporation.

Polan, on behalf of Industrial Realty, signed a lease for commercial space owned by Kinney Shoe Corp. The first rental payment was made out of Polan's personal funds. No further payments were made. Eventually, Kinney filed suit against Industrial Realty Company and obtained a judgment in the amount of $66,400 for unpaid rent. When Industrial failed to pay the judgment, Kinney sued Polan individually and sought to pierce the corporate veil and collect the monies owed.

<u>Issue:</u> Is Polan personally liable for the debt owed by Industrial Realty Company?

<u>Holding:</u> Polan's failure to carry out the corporate formalities, together with the gross under-capitalization of Industrial Realty Company, resulted in damage to Kinney. Industrial had absolutely no assets and no paid-in capital because Polan had put nothing into the corporation as he had failed to purchase any stock in Industrial Realty. Polan was, in this court's opinion, obviously trying to limit his liability by setting up a paper curtain constructed of nothing more than Industrial's certificate of incorporation. Given these facts, it is proper to pierce the corporate veil to produce an equitable result.

The Georgia courts have shown reluctance to pierce the corporate veil on the basis of undercapitalization without additional evidence of wrongdoing. The Court of Appeals of Georgia has noted that undercapitalization "is in itself a perfectly legal business device."[20] The Georgia appellate courts have been more receptive to the notion of holding shareholders liable for corporate debts in cases in which undercapitalization has been coupled with preferences granted to majority stockholders. These cases typically involve personal loans from the shareholder to the corporation. When the corporation becomes insolvent, and the assets of the corporation are used first to satisfy the outstanding debts owed to the shareholder leaving the corporation without sufficient resources to pay other creditors, the courts may hold the shareholder liable. In such cases involving insolvency, the finances of the corporation will be closely examined to determine whether the corporate form has been used as a "cloak for a preference granted to an officer, majority stockholder, etc."[21]

Another significant advantage of doing business in the corporate form is the free transferability of shares of stocks. The stocks of many major corporations are traded over exchanges and are freely bought and sold by investors. Stocks are also generally transferable by gift or assignment. It is, however, quite common for the articles of incorporation of close corporations, discussed later in this chapter, to restrict the transferability of shares to outside persons by requiring that shareholders offer their shares to the corporation itself or other shareholders before selling them to an outside purchaser.

As mentioned above, most corporations exist in perpetuity. Although the articles of incorporation may provide that a corporation exist only for a stated period of time, such provisions are extremely unusual. Perpetual existence gives the business a life of its own separate and apart from that of its owners, officers, or directors. Thus, the death of one person, even a founder or majority shareholder, will not result in the demise of the corporation itself although, of course, any business may be significantly impacted by the loss of one of its leaders. Likewise, the business is not terminated by the withdrawal or bankruptcy of one or more of its owners.

While the significant advantages of the corporate form of business have made it an extremely popular option, there are disadvantages which must be considered when deciding upon a form of organization for a new business. The most significant disadvantage of the corporate form is double taxation. Corporate profits are subject to taxation at both the state and federal levels. After paying these taxes, the corporation may distribute some of its profits to its shareholders in the form of cash dividends. When these profits are distributed to the shareholders, they are taxed again by the federal and state governments since they must be included as income on the personal income tax returns of the shareholders who receive the dividends.

---

[20] See *Fountain v. Burke*, 160 Ga.App. 262, 287 S.E.2d 39 (1981); *Hyzer v. Hickman*, 195 Ga.App 213, 393 S.E.2d 79 (1990).
[21] *Fountain*, at page 40.

In practice, however, it must be noted that the disadvantage of double taxation is largely theoretical for many large, international corporations. According to a 2008 study by the Government Accountability Office, two out of three U.S. corporations pay no corporate income tax.[22] Large corporations are able to do this; however, most small corporations, without the benefit of powerful Congressional lobbyists and sophisticated corporate accountants to create and take advantage of tax loopholes, are subject to double taxation. Taxation is discussed at greater length in Chapter 13.

The formation and operation of a corporation requires strict compliance with state law. Thus, electing to do business in this form may result in more expense since one may incur, in addition to the fees required by the state, attorney's fees, accountant's fees or other expenses in setting up a corporation. After the corporation is formed, it must comply with various statutorily mandated formalities. Additionally, each state imposes annual filing and reporting requirements. Finally, the corporation must also file an annual tax return.

The owners of a corporation are, of course, the shareholders. They do not, however, manage the corporation. Rather, the shareholders vote for and elect directors who make policy decisions and govern the corporation as a board. The directors then appoint officers who manage the day-to-day operations of the corporation. Thus, the owners of a large corporation, the shareholders, are simply investors. In a small corporation, however, management is usually not centralized because the shareholders most often elect themselves as directors and appoint themselves as officers, thereby managing the corporation and its business themselves.

Figure 12.1

Advantages of the Corporate Form	Disadvantages of the Corporate Form
• Limited liability for owners • Exists in perpetuity • Free transferability of shares	• Double taxation • Corporate formalities • Centralized management

Corporate Powers

Corporations are granted very broad powers, and, in most states, can perform any act which is not inconsistent with law. A corporation's powers are separate from those of its shareholders, directors, or officers. However, since corporations are formed pursuant to state law, a corporation has only those powers which are granted to it by statute, and it may not exceed the authority given it by the state.

O.C.G.A. § 14-2-302

Every corporation has perpetual duration and succession in its corporate name, unless its articles of incorporation … provides otherwise. Unless its articles of incorporation provide otherwise, every corporation has the same powers as an individual to do all things necessary or convenient to carry out its business and affairs, including without limitation power:

(1) To sue, be sued, complain, and defend in its corporate name;

(2) To have a corporate seal which may be altered at will, and to use it, or a facsimile of it, by impressing or affixing it or in any other manner reproducing it;

---

[22] As reported by the New York Times on March 24, 2011, General Electric reported worldwide profits of $14.2 billion in 2010, but paid no federal income taxes to the United States government. In fact, GE claimed a tax benefit of $3.2 billion. According to the New York Times, GE used an "aggressive strategy that mixes fierce lobbying for tax breaks with innovative accounting …" to obtain these results.

(3) To make and amend bylaws, not inconsistent with its articles of incorporation or with the laws of this state, for managing the business and regulating the affairs of the corporation;
(4) To purchase, receive, lease, or otherwise acquire, own, hold, improve, use, and otherwise deal with real or personal property or any legal or equitable interest in property, wherever located;
(5) To sell, convey, mortgage, pledge, lease, exchange, and otherwise dispose of all or any part of its property;
(6) To purchase, receive, subscribe for, or otherwise acquire, own, hold, vote, use, sell, mortgage, lend, pledge, or otherwise dispose of, and deal in and with shares or other interests in, or obligations of, any other entity;
(7) To make contracts and guarantees, incur liabilities, borrow money, issue its notes, bonds, and other obligations … and secure any of its obligations by mortgage or pledge of any of its property, franchises, or income;
(8) To lend money, invest and reinvest its funds, and receive and hold real and personal property as security for repayment;
(9) To be a promoter, partner, member, associate, or manager of any partnership, joint venture, trust or other equity;
(10) To conduct its business, locate offices, and exercise the powers granted by this chapter within or without this state;
(11) To elect directors and appoint officers, employees, and agents of the corporation, define their duties, fix their compensation; and lend them money and credit;
(12) To pay pensions and establish pension plans, pension trusts, profit sharing plans, share bonus plans, share option plans, and benefit or incentive plans for all or all of its current or former directors, officers, employees, and agents;
(13) To make donations for the public welfare or for charitable, scientific, or educational purposes;
(14) To transact any lawful business that will aid governmental policy;
(15) To provide insurance for its benefit on the life or physical or mental ability of any of its directors, officers, or employees or any other person whose death or physical or mental disability might cause financial loss to the corporation; …
(16) To make payments or donations or do any other act not inconsistent with law that furthers the business and affairs of the corporation.

While corporate rights and powers are quite broad, they are not synonymous with those enjoyed by an individual or natural citizen, particularly with regard to constitutionally protected rights. While we speak of corporations as "artificial persons," they have not traditionally been considered to be "citizens" as that word is used in the federal Constitution.[23] For instance, the Fifth Amendment, which protects citizens from self-incrimination, applies only to natural citizens and not to corporations. Thus, corporate records may be seized even if they incriminate the corporation itself or persons who work for the corporation.

In addition to the limitations placed upon it by state law, a corporation's power may also be limited by its articles of incorporation. The articles of incorporation, as we will see later, are usually broadly drawn, but they may provide some limits on the ability of the corporation to do certain things. For instance, the articles of incorporation may place restrictions on the corporation with regard to the salaries paid to officers or directors or on the purchase of certain kinds of assets.

If a corporation takes action that is beyond its powers, it is said to be acting *ultra vires*, or "beyond the power." Given today's modern statutes which give corporations very broad powers and given that most articles of incorporation give the corporation the power to do all things permitted by law, the ultra vires doctrine is not so important today as it once was. Under the MBCA approach, a corporation is not permitted to escape its duties when dealing with third parties on the theory that the

---

[23] Although as seen in Chapter 1, the Supreme Court has, in recent decisions, extended to corporations First Amendment rights which previously were generally associated with natural persons.

corporation lacked authority to act. However, the shareholders of a corporation can file suit to enjoin ultra vires acts by a corporation. Additionally, shareholders can file a derivative suit, discussed in the next chapter, against an officer or against the board of directors because of an unauthorized action.

12.2 *Classifications of Corporations*

Corporations can be classified in several different ways. Classification normally indicates either the location, purpose, or ownership characteristics of the corporation.

Domestic, Foreign and Alien Corporations

The classification of a corporation as a domestic, foreign, or alien corporation indicates the location of the corporation, or, more specifically, the jurisdiction in which the corporation was created. A corporation is known as a *domestic corporation* in the state in which it incorporates. If a corporation is formed in one state but is doing business in another state, that corporation is referred to as a *foreign corporation* in the other state.

A corporation does not have an automatic right to do business in a state other than its state of incorporation. However, as we saw in Chapter 1, the U.S. Constitution does not permit any state to restrict or regulate interstate commerce. The phrase "doing business" does not mean transacting any business whatsoever, but has a rather more specific meaning. Generally, a foreign corporation is "doing business" in another state if it maintains sufficient contacts or ties within a state on a continuous or regular basis such that it is fair to hold that corporation accountable in the foreign state. If a corporation wishes to do business in a state other than its state of incorporation, it must qualify to do so. In most cases, this means that the foreign corporation must register to do business with the secretary of state's office in the state in which it desires to do business, pay a fee, and designate a registered agent in that state to receive service of process and other legal papers. This is discussed in more detail in Chapter 14.

Example 12b:

ABC Corp., in incorporated pursuant to the laws of the State of Georgia. ABC Corp., is a domestic corporation in Georgia. If ABC Corp., qualifies to do business in Alabama, then ABC is referred to as a foreign corporation in Alabama.

An *alien corporation* is one formed in one country and doing business in another country. For instance, Volvo Car Corporation is a Swedish corporation which transacts business in many countries, including the United States and is, therefore, an alien corporation in the U.S.

Public and Private Corporations

A *public corporation,* sometimes referred to as a government-owned corporation, is one formed for the direct function of government. Many cities and towns are organized as municipal corporations. Additionally, the federal government operates a number of organizations which are public corporations. These are generally created for narrow and specific purposes and include such entities as the U.S. Postal Service and the Federal Deposit Insurance Corporation.

Public utilities are sometimes known as quasi-public corporations. They are privately owned businesses which have been created for public purposes. They often have monopolies, or partial monopolies, for the provision of utility services and are strictly controlled both as to their services and prices charged for their services. These corporations are permitted, through regulatory agencies, to make a reasonable return on investment. Southern Company, the owner of Georgia Power Company which provides electric power to much of Georgia, is an example of a public utility company.

Private corporations, on the other hand, are created for private purposes, specifically to conduct business, and most corporations are private corporations. The phrase "private corporation" means that the stock of the corporation is owned by individuals or other entities, not the government. Take care not to confuse "public corporations" with "publicly traded companies." Public corporations are government-owned, while publicly traded corporations are private, business corporations whose stocks are traded on stock exchanges and may be purchased by the public.

Nonprofit Corporations

Corporations which are formed for purposes other than making a profit are called *nonprofit* or *not-for-profit corporations*. These include many educational institutions, charities, and religious organizations. By organizing as nonprofit corporations, these organizations are able to own property, enter into contracts, and engage in other activities necessary to the accomplishment of their purposes without exposing the individual members to personal liability.

Commercial law is primarily concerned with corporations organized for profit, and the focus of this text is on these for-profit business corporations.

Close Corporations

A *close corporation* is one whose shares are held by a relatively few persons, frequently members of a family. Close corporations may also be referred to as closely held or privately held corporations. In virtually all cases, the stockholders of a close corporation are known to each other.

Because the number of stockholders is so small, there is no trading market for the shares. In most cases, the transferability of shares is restricted, either through a provision in the articles of incorporation or by means of a shareholder agreement. Such provisions usually require that any shareholder of a close corporation who wants to sell his shares offer them first to the corporation itself or to the other shareholders before selling them to an outside purchaser. In this way, the shareholders are able to ensure that the corporation remains in the hands of a small group of family members or others with an existing relationship. Georgia's Close Corporations code follows this model.[24] It is specifically because of the small number of shareholders that close corporations hold special potential perils for minority shareholders who have little control over the corporation.

Comolli, et al. v. Comolli et al.
241 Ga. 471, 246 S.E.2d 278 (1978)
Supreme Court of Georgia

Facts: The three Comolli brothers owned all of the stock of Comolli Granite Company, with Felix owning 375 shares, Louis owning 375 shares, and Mario owning 250 shares. When Mario died, a contest developed between Louis and Felix over control of the company. Both Felix and Louis aggressively sought to purchase Mario's shares from his widow who had inherited them. Mario's widow, Maria, agreed to sell 10 shares to Louis for $800 per share which gave Louis control of the company.

[24] See O.C.G.A. § 14-2-9 et seq.

Thereafter, Louis caused the board of directors to approve the corporation's purchase of Maria's remaining 240 shares for $800 per share, partially out of earned surplus. The corporation also borrowed money from the Granite City Bank in order to fund the purchase. Felix sued, seeking to set aside the stock purchase by the corporation.

Issue: Was the directors' approval of the purchase of Maria's shares a breach of the directors' fiduciary duty and not done for a legitimate business purpose?

Holding: Directors are required to act in "good faith" and with ordinary diligence in all transactions. Good faith is not just a question of what is proper for the corporation. It also requires that the stockholders be treated fairly and that their investments be protected. In close corporations, minority stockholders may easily be reduced to relative insignificance and their investment rendered captive, because ordinarily there is no market for minority stock in a close corporation and a minority stockholder cannot easily liquidate his investment for its true value.

The control and management of corporations is always dictated by the majority. Directors may decide in good faith what is best for the corporation, but this interest must be consistent with good faith to the minority stockholder. The minority stockholder has an interest in the liquidity of the corporation. He looks to the earned surplus for payment of dividends. If directors use corporate funds to purchase corporate stock, the interest of the minority stockholder is depreciated and his investment is frozen.

In this case, the action of the directors demonstrates a lack of good faith. Good faith requires that the directors authorize a corporate purchase of Felix's stock at the same price and terms given to Mario's widow. In the event the corporation elects not to do so, the corporate purchase of Maria's stock is invalid. This will eliminate any question of a preferential distribution of assets and provide an opportunity for Felix to liquidate his investment.

Because a close corporation has a small, closely knit group of shareholders, these same persons usually hold positions as directors and officers of the corporation. Thus, in practice, the management and operation of a close corporation resembles that of a partnership.

S Corporations

Subchapter S of the Internal Revenue Code provides that a close corporation which meets certain requirements can operate as an *S corporation,* also called a "subchapter S corporation." An S corporation is taxed like a partnership. Thus, by choosing this form of organization, a close corporation can avoid the imposition of income tax on corporate earnings and thereby do away with the disadvantage of corporate "double taxation."

An S corporation must meet a number of requirements in order to qualify for this special taxation treatment. Among the most important:

- The corporation must be a domestic corporation.
- The corporation must have no more than one hundred shareholders.
- The corporation must have only one class of stock.
- No shareholder of the corporation may be a non-resident alien.
- Individuals, estates, charitable organizations, and certain trusts can be S corporation shareholders. Ordinarily, corporations, partnerships, or other non-natural persons

cannot be S corporation shareholders, although an S corporation can wholly own another S corporation.

An S corporation must file an informational tax return with the IRS, but it does not pay income tax on corporate earnings. Instead, the entire income is taxed to the shareholders who declare the income on their individual tax return, regardless of whether or not the income is distributed to the shareholders.

12.3 The Creation of Corporations

The formation of corporations consists of two basic steps: first, the promoters engage in the preliminary organization or planning of the corporation, and secondly, the legal process of incorporation must be completed by the preparation and filing of the articles of incorporation.

The Promoters

The incorporator, the person who takes the preliminary steps to organize the proposed corporation, is referred to as the *promoter*. Of course, there may be more than one promoter, in which case the promoters are joint venturers who owe fiduciary duties to one another.

An initial task for the promoter is to decide in which state to incorporate. A business may incorporate in any state, but most small corporations incorporate in the state of the principle place of business, particularly if the corporation will operate in only one state. For large corporations which will operate in several states or nationwide, several factors must be considered. Incorporating in one state and doing business in another will subject the corporation to filing and reporting requirements in both states. Additionally, the costs of incorporation as well as annual reporting requirements and state taxes vary from state to state and must be considered when making the decision as to where to incorporate. Furthermore, some states favor their own domestic corporations by awarding public contracts to them, a fact which also must be considered depending on the nature of the business to be conducted by the corporation.

One of the primary tasks of the promoter is to ensure that the proposed corporation will have sufficient capital to begin operation. Usually, the promoters are persons who will also own stock in the corporation once it is formed, but they may also look to other sources of capital investment.

In order to obtain sufficient capital for the proposed corporation, the promoters of the corporation may take steps to attract subscribers in addition to themselves who agree to purchase shares of stock in the proposed corporation. They may do this by issuing a prospectus that describes the financial operations of the proposed corporation, thus allowing potential investors to make informed investment decisions. In preparing a prospectus, the promoters must take care to abide by all provisions of federal and state securities law. Specifically, the Securities Act of 1933 governs the initial sale of stock and requires disclosure of all essential information concerning the issuance of stocks and other securities to the investing public. As is evident from the stringent disclosure requirements, one of the primary purposes of the Securities Act is to prohibit fraud.

In addition to securing capital for the proposed corporation, the promoter may also enter into contracts on behalf of the proposed corporation. The services of various professionals including attorneys and accountants are usually required in the planning stages of the proposed corporation, and the promoter may enter into contractual agreements with these professionals. The promoter may deem it appropriate to enter into other types of contracts for the benefit of the proposed corporation. For example, the promoter may purchase or lease property for use by the proposed corporation once it is formed. These third parties with whom the promoter contracts prior to the actual creation of the corporation may be understandably anxious about the possibility of suffering a loss if problems arise leading the promoter to abandon of the creation of the corporation.

> O.C.G.A. § 14-2-204
>
> All persons purporting to act as or on behalf of a corporation, knowing there was no incorporation under this chapter, are jointly and severally liable for all liabilities created while so acting.

The promoter is not an agent of the proposed corporation because the corporation has not yet come into existence. Thus, the promoter is personally liable on any pre-incorporation agreements into which he enters. To avoid this liability, the promoter may secure the agreement of the contracting party that only the corporation, and not the promoter, will be liable in the event of any breach of the pre-incorporation agreement. Once the corporation is formed, it may assume the pre-incorporation contract by novation. This will release the promoter from personal liability and make the corporation liable for performing the contractual obligations. If novation of the pre-incorporation contract does not occur, the promoter remains personally liable on the contract.

Zuberi v. Gimbert
230 Ga.App. 236, 398 S.E.2d 741 (1990)
Court of Appeals of Georgia

Facts: Steven and Janis Gimbert leased a warehouse to a toilet cleaner manufacturing business owned by Manzar Zuberi. Zuberi signed the lease as the purported representative of a nonexistent corporation, "ATM Manufacturing, Inc." Zuberi later manufactured toilet bowl cleaner on the premises under the name of an existing corporation, "Ameri-Pak International, Inc." Zuberi was the president of Ameri-Pak. Zuberi never formed ATM Manufacturing, Inc. The Gimberts claimed the business's use of hydrochloric acid in its operations severely damaged the premises. They sued both Ameri-Pak and Zuberi for damages.

Issue: Was Zuberi personally liable for damage to the Gimberts' warehouse?

Holding: Zuberi knowingly signed the lease agreement with the Gimberts on behalf of a corporation (ATM Manufacturing, Inc.) that simply did not exist, either before or after the signing of the lease. Zuberi suggests that because the Gimberts believed they were dealing with a corporation, they should be estopped from holding him personally liable. However, Zuberi entered into the lease agreement on behalf of a company that did not exist, and thus, is personally liable. The mere fact that Zuberi later occupied the premises under the corporate form, "Ameri-Pak International," does not relieve Zuberi of personal liability with regard to the obligations he incurred on behalf of the never formed corporation, ATM Manufacturing, Inc.

Share Subscriptions

As mentioned above, one of the primary duties of the promoters is to secure capital for the proposed corporation. This may be done by contacting potential investors who may agree to purchase shares of stock in the future corporation. An agreement to purchase shares in a yet to be formed corporation is called a *subscription agreement*. The potential investor is referred to as a *subscriber*.

The promoters must be assured that sufficient capital will be raised to support the corporate venture. Thus, subscribers are bound by their promises, or contracts, to purchase stock in the future corporation. If a subscriber fails to pay under a subscription agreement, the corporation may collect the amount owed as it would any other debt; however, the stock subscription agreement must be in writing in order to be enforced. Section 6.20 of the RMBCA and the Georgia statute both provide that if the corporation has not yet been organized, a subscription is irrevocable for a period of six months unless the subscription agreement provides otherwise or unless all subscribers consent to revocation.

Reservation of the Corporate Name

Before the corporation can come into existence, the promoters must decide upon a name for the new corporation. The selection of a name may be critical to the marketing and business strategy of the corporation.

The promoters may choose any name they wish for the new corporation provided that:

- The name includes the word corporation, incorporated, company, or limited, or some abbreviation of one of those words, to insure that persons doing business with the corporation understand that the entity is a corporation; and

- The name is not the same as, or deceptively similar to, the name of any other domestic corporation in the state or any foreign corporation doing business in the state.

O.C.G.A. § 14-2-401

(a) A corporate name:

(1) Must contain the word "corporation," "incorporated," "company," or "limited," or the abbreviation "corp.," "inc.," "co.," or "ltd.," or words or abbreviations of like import in another language; ...

(b) Except as authorized by subsections (c) and (d) of this Code section, a corporate name must be distinguishable upon the records of the Secretary of State from:

(1) The corporate name of a corporation incorporated or authorized to transact business in this state;

(2) A corporate name reserved under Code Section 14-2-402;

(3) The fictitious name adopted by a foreign corporation authorized to transact business in this state because its real name is unavailable;

(4) The corporate name of a nonprofit corporation incorporated or authorized to transact business in this state;

(5) The name of a limited partnership or professional association filed with the Secretary of State; and

(6) The name of a limited liability company formed or authorized to transact business in this state.

The Secretary of State will determine whether the name sought by the promoters is available and, if so, will reserve the name for a short time, pending completion and fling of the articles of incorporation with the Secretary of State. If the promoter fails to file the articles of incorporation within the specified time, the name may be again reserved for another period by the same or another applicant. Thus, the promoter is not guaranteed his preferred name if he doesn't act with the specified time period.

O.C.G.A. § 14-2-402(a)

A person may apply to reserve a name for the purpose of incorporation by paying the fee specified in Code Section 14-2-122. If the Secretary of State finds that the corporate name applied for is available, he or she shall reserve the name for the applicant's use for 30 days or until articles of incorporation are filed, whichever is sooner. ...

12.4 *The Articles of Incorporation*

The document which creates a corporation is most commonly called the *articles of incorporation*, although some states use the term "certificate of incorporation" or the word "charter." The articles of incorporation are, in essence, the constitution of the corporation.

Incorporation matters are handled in almost all states, including Georgia, by the Secretary of State. The *articles of incorporation* provide the basic framework for the corporation.

The articles must comply with all statutory requirements, which vary somewhat from state to state. Generally, the articles of incorporation will include the following:

- Name – the corporation's name as reserved with the Secretary of State;
- Registered Address – the street address of the corporation's initial registered office must be provided to facilitate communication with the corporation;
- Agent for Service of Process – the designated individual to receive service of legal process;
- Purposes – the purposes of the corporation may be stated in broad terms such as "any lawful activity." A full purpose clause eliminates the possibility that the corporation may engage in *ultra vires* acts or acts beyond the powers of the corporation;
- Description of Stock – the corporation's shares should be fully described. If more than one class of stock is authorized, all of the provisions, privileges, and restrictions relating to each class must be set out. The number of shares authorized – that is, the maximum number of shares the corporation may issue – must be stated for each class. The par value, or minimum issue price, may also be stated; and
- Incorporators – the names and addresses of the incorporators. At least one of the incorporators must also sign the articles of incorporation.

The articles of incorporation may include much more information, including the names and addresses of the individuals who are to serve as the initial directors. In many states, the articles of incorporation must specify the intended business activities of the corporation. However, in Georgia, it is not mandatory that this information be included in the articles of incorporation.

When completed, the articles of incorporation are filed with the appropriate state agency, usually the Secretary of State's office, and the required filing fee is paid to that agency. In Georgia, the articles of incorporation may be submitted on paper or in electronic fashion.

Once filed, it may be costly and somewhat burdensome to amend the articles of incorporation because amendment generally requires shareholder approval. Because of this, many experts recommend tht the articles include only what is required by statute and that optional provisions be included in the corporation's bylaws. As we will see later, bylaws are relatively easy to amend and are not a public document open for public review.

O.C.G.A. § 14-2-202

(a) The articles of incorporation must set forth:

(1) A corporate name for the corporation that satisfies the requirements of Code Section 14-2-401;

(2) The number of shares the corporation is authorized to issue;

(3) The street address and county of the corporation's initial registered office and the name of its initial registered agent at that office;

(4) The name and address of each incorporator; and

(5) The mailing address of the initial principal office of the corporation, if different from the initial registered office.

(b) The articles of incorporation may set forth:

(1) The names and addresses of the individuals who are to serve as the initial directors;

(2) Provisions not inconsistent with law regarding:

(A) The purpose or purposes for which the corporation is organized;

(B) Managing the business and regulating the affairs of the corporation;

(C) Defining, limiting, and regulating the power of the corporation, its board of directors, and shareholders;

(D) A par value for authorized shares or classes of shares; and

(E) The imposition of personal liability on shareholders for the debts of the corporation to a specified extent and upon specified conditions

(3) Any provision that under this chapter is required or permitted to be set forth in the bylaws;

(4) A provision eliminating or limiting the liability of a director to the corporation or its shareholders for monetary damages for any action taken, or any failure to take any action, as a director, except liability:

(A) For any appropriation, in violation of his or her duties, of any business opportunity of the corporation;

(B) For acts or omissions which involve intentional misconduct or a knowing violation of law;

(C) For the types of liability set forth in Code Section 14-2-832; or

(D) For any transaction from which the director received an improper personal benefit, provided that no such provision shall eliminate or limit the liability of a director for any act or omission occurring prior to the date when such provision becomes effective; and

(5) A provision that, in discharging the duties of their respective positions and in determining what is believed to be in the best interests of the corporation, the board of directors, committees of the board of directors, and individual directors, in addition to considering the effects of any action on the corporation or its shareholders, may consider the subsidiaries, the communities in which offices or other establishments of the corporation and its subsidiaries are located, and all other factors such directors consider pertinent; provided, however, that any such provision shall be deemed solely to grant discretionary authority to the directors and shall not be deemed to provide to any constituency any right to be considered.

(c) The articles of incorporation need not set forth any of the corporate powers enumerated in this chapter.

The articles must include the name and physical address of the corporation's initial registered agent. The requirement that a corporation maintain a registered office and a registered agent at that office is based on the premise that at all times a corporation should have an office where it may be found and a person at that office upon whom any notice or process may be served. In other words, the agent for service of process is the individual upon whom the summons and complaint will be served in the event the corporation is sued and that person's identify and location must be set out in the documents filed with the Secretary of State's office. It is an easy matter to check the Georgia Secretary of State's website and ascertain the name and address of the registered agent for any Georgia corporation.

The address of the agent for service may be different from that of the corporation's principal office. The agent's address must be given as a street address, as opposed to a post office box address, since process must usually be personally served.

It is not unusual for a corporation's registered agent for service or registered office to change, sometimes many times over the years. Additionally, the registered agent for service may change addresses. These are considered routine changes and may require only the filing of an amendment to the corporation's annual registration to accomplish.[25]

While all states provide forms or templates for the articles of incorporation, it is not mandatory that the incorporators use the state form. The Georgia Secretary of State's website includes a template for the preparation of articles of incorporation shown as Exhibit 12.1 below.

Exhibit 12.1:

Articles of Incorporation
Of
ABC and Associates, Inc.

Article 1.
The name of the corporation is ABC and Associates, Inc.

Article 2.
The corporation is authorized to issue (fill in the number) shares. (*Number may not be "0".*)

Article 3.
The street address of the registered office is 123 Magnolia Lane, Atlanta, Georgia 12345. The registered agent at such address is John Doe. (*The registered office address must be a street address at which the agent may be personally located.*) The county of the registered office is ____________.

Article 4.
The name and address of each incorporator is:

John Doe	Jane Doe	Jack Doe
123 Magnolia Lane	123 Magnolia Lane	123 Magnolia Lane
Atlanta, Georgia 12345	Atlanta, Georgia 12345	Atlanta, Georgia 12345

Article 5.
The principal mailing address of the corporation is 123 Magnolia Lane, Atlanta, Georgia 12345.

IN WITNESS WHEREOF, the undersigned has executed these Articles of Incorporation.

This _________ day of ________, 2012.

(*signature*)
John Doe (*Capacity of signer*) (i.e. incorporator or attorney in fact))

Holmes & Company of Orlando v. Carlisle
289 Ga.App. 619, 658 S.E.2d 185 (2008)
Court of Appeals of Georgia

Facts: Holmes & Company of Orlando is a Florida corporation doing business in Georgia pursuant to a certificate of authority issued by the Secretary of State. Carlisle was injured in an automobile accident involving one of Holmes's employees and filed suit seeking to recover damages for his injuries. Holmes's registered agent for service was Donna West, whose address was listed as 6340 Lake Oconee Parkway, Greensboro, Georgia. This address was the location of the BankSouth branch where West was employed. The return of service as filed in this case shows that the sheriff served "Melinda Walker, in charge of the office and place of doing business of said corporation in this county."

---

[25] See O.C.G.A. § 14-2-502.

Holmes alleged that service of the complaint in this case was insufficient because Walker had no authority to accept service on the company's behalf. Walker was the BankSouth branch manager, but was not an employee of Holmes and was not Holmes's registered agent for service of process. Walker testified that she was in charge of the BankSouth branch and that West was an employee at the bank but was not authorized to do business there as an agent of anyone except the bank. She further stated that as West's supervisor, she had authority to accept documents on West's behalf.

Issue: Was service of process on the manager where an out-of-state corporation's registered agent worked sufficient to accomplish service on the corporation?

Holding: A corporation is served through service upon its registered agent. Holmes's principal address was a post office box in Florida. Its registered agent for service of process in Georgia was Donna West whose address was given as the address of the BankSouth branch. In other similar cases, service has been found to be proper where the recipient of papers said the agent was unavailable but she would accept service. While Walker was not authorized to accept service on behalf of Holmes, there is nothing establishing that Walker was not authorized to accept service on behalf of West, the registered agent. It is undisputed that Walker, as the manager, was authorized to accept service on behalf of the employee whom she supervised. Since West was the person upon whom service was required and as Walker was authorized to accept service on behalf West, Holmes was properly served.

To file the articles of incorporation, the incorporator simply mails or electronically submits the articles to the office of the Secretary of State or other official designated by state statute and pays the required filing fee. In most states, including Georgia, corporate existence begins upon the filing of the articles of incorporation. A certification of incorporation is mailed to the applicant after the articles are reviewed and approved.

The First Organizational Meeting

While the corporation is formed upon the filing of the articles of incorporation, an *organizational meeting* generally must be held to complete the incorporation activities and commence the business of the corporation. Georgia law permits the incorporators to take the actions normally taken at the organizational meeting without a formal meeting provided that all of the incorporaters consent in writing to each action taken.[26]

At the organizational meeting:

- directors are elected if they were not named in the articles of incorporation;
- officers are appointed by the directors;
- the bylaws are adopted;
- any preincorporation contracts are ratified;
- preincorporation share subscriptions are accepted;
- the form of the corporate seal and stock certificates are approved;
- the directors authorize the officers to begin issuing stock and fix the price for each share.

The organizational meeting is usually attended by the incorporters and the initial directors and and officers of the corporation and any anticipated shareholders.

---

[26] See O.C.G.A. § 14-2-205

The Bylaws

Bylaws are the rules that govern the operation and management of the corporation and are always much more detailed than the articles of incorporation. Bylaws are not maintained with any public agency but are maintained by the corporation. For this reason, the promoters may choose to draft articles of incorporation, which are filed with the state, that contain only the information required by law and then include a much greater level of detail in the bylaws.

The bylaws are presented to the shareholders for adoption at the first organizational meeting. Bylaws are easily amended by the shareholders and may also be amended by the board of directors unless the articles of incorporation reserve that right for the shareholders.

The bylaws should contain various provisions relating to the managers of the corporation – that is, the board of directors – including:

- Requirements for Position – these may include whether directors must be shareholders of the corporation or residents of the state of incorporation;
- Number, Tenure and Compensation – bylaws state the number of directors as well as when and how they will be selected and their compensation;
- Authority to Manage – directors are given express authority by the bylaws to manage the business affairs of the corporation;
- Meetings – when and where regular meetings of the directors are to be held as well as when and how special meetings may be called;
- Liability – whether the corporation will indemnify directors for acts taken in good faith.

O.C.G.A. § 14-2-206

(a) The incorporators or board of directors of a corporation shall adopt initial bylaws for the corporation. Bylaws adopted by the incorporators or board of directors prior to or contemporaneously with the issuance of any of the corporation's shares shall constitute bylaws adopted by the shareholders for all purposes of this chapter.

(b) The bylaws of a corporation may contain any provision for managing the business and regulating the affairs of the corporation that is not inconsistent with law or the articles of incorporation.

The bylaws should also identify the corporate officers and should specify the duties of each officer. The bylaws include information about regular shareholders' meetings and special meetings, including notice requirements, quorum requirements and method for voting.

12.5 Defective Incorporation

On rare occasions, the process of forming a corporation is improperly or imperfectly handled.

In the past, a defect in the incorporation process might leave the shareholders personally liable for the debts of the corporation. In cases of an alleged imperfect incorporation process, the courts were called upon to examine the nature of the defect. Based upon that examination, a court might classify the corporation as a *de jure corporation,* meaning that it had complied substantially with state law and could not be attacked by anyone. Alternatively, a court might determine a corporation to be a *de facto corporation* or one that had failed to substantially comply with state law and could be attacked by its creator or by the state, but not by a third party such as a creditor. Finally, the court could determine that the defect was so significant that the corporation was neither a de jure corporation nor a de facto corporation, and, in such a case, the corporation and its shareholders could be attacked by anyone including a third party creditor.

The MBCA and most states now provide that the Secretary of State's filing of the articles of incorporation is conclusive proof that the corporation is validly formed and the formation of the corporation cannot be attacked by third parties although it can still be challenged by the state.

> O.C.G.A. § 14-2-203
>
> (b) The Secretary of State's filing of the articles of incorporation is conclusive proof that the incorporators satisfied all conditions precedent to incorporation except in a proceeding by the state to cancel or revoke the incorporation or involuntarily dissolve the corporation.

This means that there are very few cases filed in which third party creditors allege that a corporation's shareholders should be liable for the corporation's debts due to defects in the incorporation process. The filing of the articles with the Secretary of State's offices acts as a bright line - before the filing of the articles of incorporation, the promoters have personal liability but after the filing of the articles, the corporation is viewed as a validly formed entity and, thus, is not subject to attack excepting only by the state.

Review Questions and Exercises

1. Southern Peach Farms, Inc., is incorporated in the state of Georgia. Southern Peach does business in Georgia, South Carolina and Florida. Southern Peach Farms, Inc., is a domestic corporation in what state(s)? A foreign corporation in what state(s)?

2. What are the significant advantages to doing business in the corporate form? What are the disadvantages?

3. Marcus is the sole promoter of a future corporation being formed to manufacture and sell street legal golf carts. While the corporation has not yet been formed, Marcus has located a facility ideally suited to his needs. Can Marcus legally sign a contract for the purchase of the property for his future corporation? What is his liability on the contract if the corporation is never formed? What is his liability on the contract once the corporation is formed? What can Marcus do to limit his liability?

4. Prior to the incorporation of Marcus' golf cart business, his sister, Renee, agreed to buy 50 shares of stock in the corporation. May Renee revoke her share subscription?

5. Marcus desires to incorporate his street legal golf cart business. Marcus believes that naming his business "Ford Motor Products, Inc." will give him an advantage over his competitors. Should he be able to use this name? Why or why not?

6. If Marcus is the sole promoter of the corporation, must he hold an organizational meeting after the articles of incorporation are filed? Why or why not? What would be accomplished at such a meeting if one were held?

7. Assume the following facts: Brad, Brandon, Brian, and Brooke are the only shareholders in BR Timber Products, Corp. The net income of BR Timber Products, Corp., is taxed at the corporate level, after which each of the shareholders pays income tax on distributions received from the corporation. How can BR Timber Products, Corp., retain its corporate status and, at the same time, avoid this double taxation? Discuss the requirements which must be met.

8. What is a close corporation? Why are the shares of a close corporation not typically as freely transferable as thos of many other types of corporations? What is the disadvantage of being a minority shareholder in a close corporation? Is this disadvantage any different from that of a minority shareholder in any corporation?

9. Why would a promoter not include as many details as possible in the articles in incorporation?

10. Why must the street address of the registered agent for service be included in the articles of incorporation? Why is a post office box number not sufficient?

Practical Applications

1. In May, 1985, Harold Korey opened an account for telephone service with BellSouth for Atlanta Temps, Inc. Atlanta Temps, Inc., was not incorporated at the time the account was opened, but was subsequently incorporated in August, 1986. BellSouth provided telephone service and submitted bills to Atlanta Temps, Inc., for several years after the account was established. When telephone service was disconnected on July 20, 1992, BellSouth sued Korey for amounts due on the account.

In his answer to the lawsuit, Korey stated that the entity that ordered and received the telephone service was Atlanta Personnel Services, Inc. Atlanta Personnel Services, Inc., was incorporated in April, 1989. BellSouth contends that Korey established service for Atlanta Temps, Inc., and that it was never knew of the existence of Atlanta Personnel Services, Inc.

Consider:

(a) What is the effect of Korey's contention that the true recipient of telephone services was Atlanta Personnel Services, Inc.

(b) If Korey had agreed that Atlanta Temps, Inc., was the entity for whom telephone service was established, would he be liable for the unpaid bill?

(c) Who would be liable if, at the time Atlanta Personnel Services, Inc., was incorporated Korey had advised BellSouth that Atlanta Personnel Services, Inc., was assuming the account?

See – *Korey v. BellSouth Communications, Inc.*, 225 Ga.App. 857, 485 S.E.2d 498 (1998), Court of Appeals of Georgia.

2. In the fall of 1985, Mike Shean and Earl Hickman met and decided to enter the home construction business. Hickman, an attorney, was to secure financing of the project while Shean would provide technical knowledge and supervise the actual construction. A corporation was formed to conduct the business. Shean was not a shareholder but was merely an employee of the corporation. No more than $500 was ever designated as capital of the corporation. Hickman and two other investors held all of the stock. The initial funding for construction came from loans to the corporation. Later, additional loans were obtained to continue construction. The loans eventually totaled about $700,000.

Six houses were started, but only one was ever completed. It was sold to Peter and Bette Hyzer. The Hyzers discovered various defects in the construction of their home and attempted to have the problems remedied under the corporation's warranty of the house. They were unsuccessful. When Walk

Softly, Inc., filed an action asserting a labor and materialman's lien arising from the construction of the Hyzers' home, the Hyzers sued Hickman individually, seeking to pierce the corporate veil.

Consider:
(a) What is the effect of the corporation's financing coming from loans as opposed from capital?
(b) Was the corporation grossly undercapitalized?
(c) If so, is the undercapitalization alone enough to justify piercing the corporate veil? Why or why not?

See – *Hyzer v. Hickman*, 195 Ga.App. 213, 393 S.E.2d 79 (1990), Court of Appeals of Georgia

Chapter 13 Shareholders and Corporate Stock

OUTLINE

Recall from the last chapter that immediately after the filing of the articles of incorporation, the first organizational meeting is conducted. At that meeting, pre-incorporation share subscriptions are accepted. The shareholders, the owners of corporation's stock, are the actual owners of the corporation. The issuance of stock is the corporation's source of initial financing.

13.1 The Shareholders

The owners of a corporation are its *stockholders* or *shareholders*. The two terms are synonymous and may be used interchangeably. Shareholders own the corporation through their ownership of the corporation's equity securities or stock. A shareholder has three ownership interests in the corporation:

- Right to Vote – The owners of shares of stock typically vote, usually one vote per share, to elect the persons who will serve as the directors of the corporation and be responsible for governance of the corporation.

- Distribution Rights – While the directors are not obligated to declare dividends, the shareholders are entitled to participate in the distribution of the corporation's profits if dividends are declared by the board.

- Liquidation Rights – In the event the corporation is liquidated, the shareholders are entitled to a proportionate share of the corporation's net assets after the payment of all other obligations.

Rights and Responsibilities of Shareholders

With most forms of business organization, the owners are active in the management of the business. This is not the case with corporations. Stockholders are not involved in the day-to-day operation of the corporation but simply vote on the election, and removal, of directors and the approval of fundamental changes in the corporation such as amending the articles of incorporation. Of course, in small corporations, the stockholders are often more actively involved in the running of the business, often serving as directors and/or officers of the corporation.

Shareholders have only one responsibility to the corporation – to pay for the stock issued to them. After the shareholder pays for his stock, he has no liability to the corporation. Furthermore, the shareholder has no liability to the corporation's creditors for the corporation's debts and obligations.

O.C.G.A. § 14-2-622

(a) A purchaser from a corporation of its own shares in not liable to the corporation or its creditors with respect to the shares except to pay the consideration for which the shares were authorized to be issued.

(b) Unless otherwise provided in the articles of incorporation, a shareholder of a corporation is not personally liable for the acts or debt of the corporation except that he may become personally liable by reason of his own acts or conduct.

Shareholders, as the owners of the corporation, have the right to be informed about the affairs of the corporation. This includes the right to inspect corporate records such as the articles of incorporation, the bylaws, and the minutes of shareholders' meetings.

When someone buys shares of stock in a business corporation, that purchaser is desirous of making money and hopes that the corporation will make a profit. In fact, his purchase of stock is his bet that the business will be successful and make money. A stockholder can share in the corporation's profitability in two ways. First, the owner hopes that his capital investment appreciates in value. That is, he hopes that the value of his stock increases over time and that he can ultimately sell the stock for more than he paid for it. Additionally, the stockholder may receive *dividends* from the corporation. Dividends are simply the distribution of the corporation's profits to the shareholders as the owners of the corporation.

There is no requirement that a corporation ever pay dividends. The determination to declare and distribute dividends is a discretionary decision for the board of directors. The corporation may not make a profit or the profit may be small. Even if the corporation's profits are substantial, the directors may elect to retain the profits, rather than pay dividends to the shareholders, so that the profits can be used for some corporate purpose such as expanding the business's operations or paying off corporate debt.

A shareholder may bring a lawsuit on behalf of the corporation if the corporation has some right which the corporation is not enforcing on its own. In a *derivative action*, the shareholder is not suing because of a direct injury to himself but, rather, he is pursuing an action that derives from the shareholder's ownership interest in the corporation. Derivative actions usually involve allegations of wrongdoing by individual directors or officers of the corporation. For instance, if a corporate officer is accused of wasting corporate assets and the board of directors refuses, perhaps because of the close relationship between them, to sue the officer for reimbursement, a shareholder may bring the suit in his name as plaintiff. Both the corporation and the alleged wrongdoer are the defendants.[27]

---

[27] As with any civil suit, the party bringing the suit must have standing. In derivative actions, this means the plaintiff must have been a shareholder of the corporation at the time of the act or omission complained of. Additionally, the plaintiff must fairly and adequately represent the interest of the corporation in enforcing the right of the corporation. See O.C.G.A. § 14-2-741.

In order to bring a derivative suit, the shareholder must first demand that the directors bring the lawsuit. If the directors refuse, the shareholder may proceed. If the shareholder wins the lawsuit, the recovery belongs to the corporation since the suit was brought for the benefit of the corporation. However, the corporation is required to reimburse the shareholder for his attorney's fees expended in pursuing the case.

Shareholders' Meetings

Shareholders meet at two types of meetings – *annual* and *special*. Most state statutes, including Georgia's, provide that the shareholders of a corporation meet annually.[28] Usually, the bylaws of the corporation specify the date of the annual shareholders' meeting. For example, the bylaws may provide that the annual shareholders' meeting will be held on the second Friday in March of each year. Annual meetings may be conducted at a place specified in the bylaws. This is usually the corporation's principal office. Alternatively, the bylaws may provide that the directors will select the place of the annual meeting.

In addition to the regular annual shareholders' meetings, special shareholders' meetings may be called by the board of directors or by a group of shareholders. Special meetings may be held to consider important or emergency issues. Such issues might include a merger or consolidation of the corporation with another corporation, the removal of a director or directors, an amendment of the articles of incorporation, or the dissolution of the corporation. Only the business which resulted in the special meeting being called may be conducted at the special meeting.

O.C.G.A. § 14-3-702

(a) A corporation shall hold a special meeting of the shareholders:

(1) On call of its board of directors or the person or persons authorized to do so by the articles of incorporation or bylaws:

(2) ...(I)f the holders of at least 25 percent, or such greater or lesser percentage as may be provided n the articles of incorporation or bylaws of all the votes entitled to be cast on any issued proposed to be considered at the proposed special meeting, sign, date and deliver to the corporation one or more demands in writing or by electronic transmission for the meeting describing the purpose or purposes for which it is to be held; ...

(d) Only business within the purpose or purposes described in the meeting notice required ... may be conducted at a special shareholders' meeting.

All shareholders are entitled to notice of shareholders' meetings. State statutes are usually very detailed in specifying the information which must be provided to the shareholders in the meeting notice. Thus, the statute must be consulted when preparing a notice of a shareholders' meeting. The notice must contain the specifics regarding the date, time, and place of the meeting. A notice of a special meeting must also contain a description of the purpose of the special meeting.

Voting Rights

The shareholders do not actively manage the affairs of the corporation. Instead, shareholders have a very limited role in the operation of the corporation. They participate only through voting for the members of the board of directors. The articles of incorporation must grant at least one class of stock of a corporation voting rights.

---

[28] See O.C.G.A. § 14-2-701.

All shareholders who own stock as of the *record date* are entitled to notice of the shareholders' meeting and are entitled to vote. The record date is a date selected in advance of the meeting and may be specified in the corporation's bylaws. Any shareholder who owns shares of stock as of the record date will receive the notice. Unless that shareholder has waived the notice requirement, she will be entitled to attend the annual shareholders' meeting and vote her shares. A shareholder who owns stock as of the record date but subsequently sells his stock before the date of the annual meeting is still entitled to attend the meeting and vote his shares even though he no longer owns the shares. Likewise, an individual who buys shares of stock after the record date, but before the meeting date, has no right to vote at the annual shareholders' meeting even though he owns stock at the time of the meeting.

Example 13a:

The annual shareholders' meeting of NuTech, Inc., will be held on June 1. The record date is May 1. Oscar own 500 shares of NuTech stock and receives the notice of the annual meeting. On May 15, Oscar sells his 500 shares to Felix. Oscar is entitled to attend the meeting on June 1 and vote his shares even though he no longer owns the shares. Felix, however, is ineligible to vote the shares he now owns since he purchased them after the record date.

Shareholders do not have to physically attend the shareholders' meeting. Instead, they may vote by *proxy*. Voting by proxy requires the appointment of another person (the proxy) as the agent for the shareholder.[29] The proxy then attends the meeting and votes the shares for the shareholder. The shareholder may decide to give the proxy exact directions as to how to vote the shareholder's shares or the proxy may be given authority to vote the shares at his or her discretion. Proxies must be given in writing or posted online. Note that the word "proxy" means both the individual given the authority to vote another's shares as well as the written document making the appointment of this individual.

In order for directors to be elected or other action to be taken at a shareholders' meeting, a *quorum* must be present.[30] A quorum is defined as a majority of shares entitled to cast votes on a given matter unless the articles of incorporation provide otherwise. If no quorum is present, the meeting must be adjourned. Provided that a quorum is present, action on a matter is approved if the votes cast in favor of the action exceed the votes cast opposing the action.

Example 13b:

ABC Corp., has 10,000 shares outstanding. If 5001 shares are represented at the shareholders' meeting, a quorum is present. Assume that the shareholders are considering an amendment to the articles of incorporation. If 2501 of the shares represented vote in favor of the amendment, it passes.

Unless the articles of incorporation provide otherwise, voting for the election of directors is by the *straight voting*, or noncumulative voting, method. Straight voting is the most common form of voting. Each outstanding share is entitled to one vote for each director's position. Thus, each shareholder votes the number of shares he owns for each position on the board which is up for election. If the articles of incorporation provide for this method of voting, a majority shareholder can control the election of the entire board of directors.

To give minority shareholders a greater voice in management, the articles of incorporation may provide for *cumulative voting* with regard to the election of directors. Under this method, each share is multiplied by the total number of vacancies to be filled on the board of directors. The total number of votes may then be cast in any manner desired by the shareholder.

---

[29] See O.C.G.A. § 14-2-722.

[30] See O.C.G.A. § 14-2-725.

Example 13c:

ABC Corp. has 10,000 shares outstanding. Albert owns 2,000 shares. If, at the shareholders' meeting, three directors are to be elected, Albert, by multiplying his number of shares by the number of positions to be filled, will have 6,000 votes to cast. If Albert casts all 6,000 votes for one director, he will be able to elect one director of his choosing to the board. He will have no votes to cast in the election of the directors to fill the remaining two vacancies, but he is now assured of some representation on the board.

13.2 Equity Securities – Stock

Every corporation needs funds with which to finance the start-up of business operations. While every for-profit corporation hopes to eventually generate revenues through its business operations, the corporation must first get the business up and running. Doing so requires money. Additionally, a corporation which desires to expand its operations must often secure additional financing, either through the issuance of additional shares of stock or through borrowing.

The most common way of obtaining financing, particularly initial financing, is through the sale of *equity securities*. Equity securities, or stocks, represent ownership rights in the corporation. Stockholders invest in the corporation and, of course, hope to make a return on that investment. The types of stock and number of shares of stock are identified in the articles of incorporation.

It is quite common for the promoters of a corporation to try to raise capital for the new corporation before the corporation comes into legal existence. *Pre-incorporation share subscriptions* are agreements in which investors commit to purchase a specified number of shares of stock at a specified price when the corporation is later formed. Such agreements are irrevocable for a certain period of time. In Georgia, this is six months unless other agreed.[31] At the organizational meeting, held after the articles of incorporation are filed, the subscriber will pay the agreed upon price for his shares and the stock will be issued to him. If a subscriber fails to pay for his stock, the subscriber becomes a debtor of the corporation and the corporation may collect the amount owed as it would any other debt.

The total number of shares that a corporation is authorized to issue, as set forth in the articles of incorporation, is referred to as *authorized shares*. Simply because the articles of incorporation authorize a corporation to issue a given number of shares does not mean that the corporation has issued, or will ever issue, all of that number. Shares that have actually been issued and are owned by third parties are called *outstanding shares*. Only these shares are entitled to vote at corporate meetings. Equally important, only issued and outstanding shares are entitled to receive dividends.

The articles of incorporation may authorize more than one class or type of stock. Historically, these classes of stock have been referred to as *common stock* and *preferred stock*. Preferred stock is simply a type of stock that enjoys some rights or preferences over other types of shares. Most typically, these preferences pertain to distribution rights, conversion rights, and/or redemption rights. These terms are discussed in detail later in this chapter.

The terms "common stock" and "preferred stock" are not always used in describing classes or types of stock since "old statutory distinctions between common and preferred shares have been abandoned, in favor of complete contractual flexibility" by many states, including Georgia.[32] Articles of

---

[31] See O.C.G.A. § 14-2-620.

[32] See Comment to O.C.G.A. §14-6-601.

incorporation may create one or more "series" within a specific class of stock. This is permitted so long as the articles include some distinguishing designation for each series.

O.C.G.A. § 14-2-601

(a) The articles of incorporation must prescribe the classes of shares and the number of shares of each class that the corporation is authorized to issue. If more than one class of shares is authorized, the articles of incorporation must prescribe a distinguishing designation for each class, and, prior to the issuance of shares of a class, the preferences, limitations and relative rights of that class must be described in the articles of incorporation. …
(c) The articles of incorporation must authorize:
(1) One or more classes of shares that together have unlimited voting rights; and
(2) One or more classes of shares (which may be the same class or classes as those with voting rights) that together are entitled to receive the net assets of the corporation upon dissolution.

(d) The articles of incorporation may authorize one or more classes or series of shares that:
(1) Have special, conditional, or limited voting rights, or no right to vote …
(2) Are redeemable, exchangeable, or convertible as specified in the articles of incorporation;
(A) At the option of the corporation, the shareholder, or another person or upon the occurrence of a designated event;
(B) For cash, indebtedness, securities, or other property; or
(C) In a designated amount or in an amount determined in accordance with a designated formula or by reference to extrinsic data or events;
(3) Entitle the holders or distributions calculated in any manner, including dividends that may be cumulative, noncumulative, or partially cumulative; and
(4) Have preference over any other class or series within a class of shares with respect to distributions, including dividends and distributions upon the dissolution of the corporation.

The decision to issue stock and the price at which it is to be issued are both made by the board of directors. The directors may not issue a greater number of shares than is authorized by the articles of incorporation since that number is the maximum number of shares that can be issued. With that caveat, the board can decide exactly how many shares to issue and at what price. The board may issue stock in exchange for any virtually any consideration. This may include any tangible or intangible benefit such as cash, property, services performed, or contracts for services to be performed in the future.

When determining the price at which to issue stock, the directors are, theoretically, limited by the *par value* of the stock as established in the articles of incorporation. The par value is the nominal value set for each share and represents the minimum amount for which stock may be issued or sold although stock is usually issued for a much higher price. The modern trend in this regard is reflected by the MBCA which does require that a par value be stated in the articles of incorporation. In any event, the directors must determine that the price for which shares are issued is adequate and appropriate.

When a corporation issues stock, the corporation may, but is not required to, issue paper certificates evidencing ownership of the stock. For many years, the use of paper certificates was common; however, given the speed at which trading transactions are completed today, the use of paper certificates is uncommon. The ownership of shares issued without stock certificates is recorded in the corporate books and the owners of such shares enjoy the same rights as all stock holders.

Finally, note that a corporation may own its own stock. Assuming that the corporation has sufficient funds to do so, the corporation may buy back outstanding shares from its own shareholders. There are several reasons that a corporation may wish to acquire its own stock. The corporation may wish to decrease the supply of shares in the market, thereby increasing the price per share. In some cases, usually involving close corporations, the corporation may agree to purchase shares in order to prevent a shareholder from selling them to others.

When a corporation buys its own stock, the corporation may hold those shares as *treasury shares*. Treasury shares are issued but not outstanding shares. Treasury shares cannot be voted by the corporation at the stockholders' meeting and dividends are not paid on treasury shares. Alternatively, the corporation may cancel the shares with the result that the shares are returned to the status of authorized but unissued.

Common Stock

If a corporation issues only one class of stock, as most corporations do, that stock is referred to as *common stock*. The articles of incorporation may, of course, provide for additional classes of stock or even for different series within the same class of stock. Different classes of stock, or series within the same class, may be entitled to different voting rights so long as at least one class has unlimited voting rights.

Example 13d:

The articles of incorporation of ABC, Corp., provide for two types of common stock. Common X shareholders are entitled to one vote per share of stock while Common Y shareholders are entitled to two votes per share of stock.

Assuming only one class of stock, the common stockholders have the right to vote for and elect the directors of the corporation. Additionally, they have the right to vote on fundamental changes to the corporation. Included in this category are the amendment of the articles of incorporation, the removal of directors, the consolidation or merger of the corporation with another corporation, and the dissolution of the corporation.

Common stockholders may also have *pre-emptive rights* if these rights are granted to them in the articles of incorporation.[33] Pre-emptive rights give an existing shareholder the ability to maintain his or her proportionate ownership interest in the corporation. This is done by giving the shareholder the option of subscribing to new shares, in the same proportion as his ownership interest, anytime new shares are issued by the corporation. Of course, if the shareholder fails to exercise his option, the shares are sold to others. Exercising this option can prevent the shareholder's interest in the corporation from being diluted.

Example 13e:

ABC Corp. has 200,000 shares authorized and 100,000 shares outstanding. Philip owns 10,000 shares or 10% of the outstanding stock. ABC wants to raise capital for a new expansion of its product line by issuing an additional 50,000 shares. If Philip has pre-emptive rights, he must be offered the option to purchase 5,000 of the new 50,000 shares. If Philip exercises this option, he will continue to own 10% of the corporation (15,000 shares of 150,000 shares outstanding). If he does not exercise his option, his ownership interest in the corporation will be reduced to 7.5%.

Preferred Stock

Preferred stock is an equity security that, as its name implies, enjoys certain preferences and rights over common stock. The owners of these securities are called preferred stockholders. A

[33] See O.C.G.A. § 14-2-30.

corporation has the option of issuing only one class of stock, but if the corporation issues preferred stock, the creation of this class of stock must be authorized by the articles of incorporation. Owners of a corporation's preferred stock enjoy the same limited personal liability that common stockholders enjoy, and, additionally, enjoy certain preferences. Often these preferences are tied to the distribution of corporate profits. Thus, preferred stock may be attractive to conservative investors who desire regular and predictable returns on their investments.

The preferences that preferred stock has over common stock must be set out in the articles of incorporation. The common preferences include:

- *Dividend Preference* – A dividend preference is the right to receive a fixed dividend at regular intervals during the year provided that the corporation has sufficient profit to pay the dividend. Such a preference is usually set as a percentage of the initial offering price.

Example 13f:

Julia purchases a $1,000 preferred stock in XYZ, Inc. The stock pays a 1% quarterly dividend. Julia has a right to receive $10 every three months as a dividend on the preferred stock.

- *Liquidation Preference* – A liquidation preference is the right to be paid before common stockholders if the corporation is dissolved and liquidated. A liquidation preference is normally stated as a specific dollar amount.

Example 13g:

Julia's preferred stock in XYZ, Inc., has a liquidation preference of $500. If the corporation is dissolved and liquidated, Julia will receive at least $500 before the common stockholders receive anything. However, the corporation's creditors will be paid before Julia; thus, even though she has a preference over the common shareholders, she is not guaranteed of receiving anything upon liquidation.

- *Cumulative Dividend Preference* –If the stock is a cumulative preferred stock, the corporation must pay any missed dividend payments to the preferred stockholders before the common shareholders are entitled to receive any dividends. If the stock is noncumulative preferred stock, the corporation does not have to pay any missed dividends since there is no right of accumulation.

Example 13h:

Julia's preferred stock has a cumulative dividend preference. XYZ, Inc., does not make a profit during the first three quarters of the year. During the fourth quarter, the corporation makes a profit of $50 per share. Julia is entitled to receive the dividend arrearages of $30 plus this quarter's dividend of $10 before the common stockholders receive anything.

- *Conversion Right* – *Convertible preferred stock* give the preferred stockholders the right to convert their shares into common stock under terms that are established when the preferred stock is issued.

- *Redemption Rights* - If a preferred stock is issued with redemption rights, the corporation has the power to reacquire them from the shareholders at a future date.

Preferred shareholders may be given one or more of the above preferences in any combination. However, preferred shareholders generally are not given the right to vote for the election of directors.

13.3 Dividends

If a corporation has been profitable over a given period of time, the board of directors may pass a resolution directing the profits be distributed to the owners of the corporation. As we have seen, this is done by the payment of dividends to the shareholders. Dividends are paid to the shareholders in direct proportion to the respective ownership interest which the shareholders have in the corporation. Thus, the greater an individual shareholder's stake in the corporation, the greater his share of the dividends or profits earned by the corporation.

Example 13i:

ABC Corp., has only one class of stock and Bill owns 5% of it. If the board of directors of ABC declares a total dividend of $10,000 for the quarter, Bill is entitled to receive $500 or 5% of the total.

If the corporation has more than one class of stock, all shareholders within a given class must be treated uniformly. For instance, all common shareholders must be treated the same. One group of shareholders cannot be given cash dividends while other shareholders holding the same class of stock receive share dividends. However, different classes of shareholders or holders of different series of stock within the same class may be treated differently.

Example 13j:

XYZ, Inc. has two classes of stock, preferred stock and common stock. XYZ cannot declare a cash dividend of $3 per share to all common shareholders who own more than 5% of the total outstanding common stock and $2 to all common shareholders who own less than 5% of the outstanding common stock. XYZ may, however, declare a cash dividend of $2 per share to all common stockholders and a cash dividend of $3 per share to all preferred shareholders.

Types of Dividends

There are three types of dividends which may be declared by the board of directors. These are:

- Cash Dividends – Cash dividends are the most common type of dividend and are sent to the shareholders in the form of a check.

- Property Dividends – The least common form of dividend, property dividends may consist of a product that the company manufactures or coupons entitling the bearer to discounts at the corporation's stores or restaurants. Property dividends can present significant difficulties, especially for large corporations. General Mills, one of the world's largest cereal manufacturers, has more than 303 million shares of common stock outstanding. If General Mills declared a property dividend of one box of cereal per share of common stock, a shareholder who owned just 1/100 of 1% of the stock would receive more than 30,000 boxes of cereal. Thus, property dividends are quite rare.

  A more common variation of a property dividend occurs when a corporation issues shares of stock in its subsidiary corporation as a property dividend.

- Share Dividends – Sometimes a corporation may give its shareholders a dividend in the form of additional shares of stock, assuming that the corporation has a sufficient number of authorized but unissued shares to distribute. After a share dividend has been declared, the actual number of shares owned by any given shareholder is increased; however, that shareholder's proportionate ownership interest in the corporation remains the same since all other shareholders in the class will be treated the same.

A share dividend requires that the corporation possess sufficient shares available for the dividend. If the number of shares is insufficient, the articles of incorporation must first be amended to increase the number of shares the corporation is authorized to issue.

Example 13k:

ABC Corp., has 50,000 shares of common stock authorized and 20,000 shares issued and outstanding. If ABC's board declares a share dividend of one share for every five shares outstanding, the total number of outstanding will increase to 24,000. If Bob owns 1,000 shares before the share dividend, his total number of shares after the dividend will increase to 1,200. Before the share dividend, Bob owned 5% of the corporation. After the share dividend, he continues to own 5%.

If a corporation declares a share dividend, a shareholder may end up owning a fraction of a share. For example, if a corporation declares a share dividend of one share for every 100 owned, the owner of 150 shares would receive 1 ½ shares. The owner of a fractional share is entitled to the factional voting rights, dividends, and other shareholder rights.

If the corporation is one that issues paper stock certificates, the corporation will issue *scrip*. Scrip is the written document that evidences ownership of a partial share. When the shareholder has accumulated enough scrip to total one share, the scrip may be surrendered to the corporation for a certificate evidencing one full share.

Procedures for Declaring and Paying Dividends

Only the board of directors can decide to declare a dividend. This decision is made by a majority vote of the directors and is left to the discretion of the directors. The board determines when, how, and how much will be paid in dividends. Shareholders have no right to receive a dividend and cannot force the directors to declare one.

The decision to declare and distribute a dividend is one for the directors to make subject only to the *business judgment rule*. In making their decision, the directors may rely on the corporation's financial statements as well as reports of the corporation's officers, accountants, attorneys, or other experts. So long as the directors have a reasonable basis for making their decision and are acting in good faith, the law provides them with immunity.

Despite the great discretion the directors have, there are some limits placed on their ability to declare a dividend. Recall that dividends are designed to be a distribution of profits to the owners of the business, the shareholders. When a dividend is paid, the corporation is transferring assets, usually cash, from the corporation itself to the shareholders. If the corporation is not financially healthy, this action could have an impact on the ability of the corporation to pay its debts and obligations.

In order to protect the creditors of the corporation, restrictions exist in the law to ensure that a corporation has adequate resources before the corporation is allowed to pay a dividend. If this were not the case, one can readily imagine the temptation of a majority shareholder who is also a director of a financially unhealthy corporation to take the corporation's few profits or assets and distribute them as a dividend. The majority shareholder would thus benefit himself but leave the corporation's creditors holding bad debt when the corporation became insolvent.

The MBCA provides two approaches to ensuring corporations can legally pay a dividend:

- Under the *equity solvency test*, a corporation may pay a dividend only if the corporation is solvent or able to pay its debts as they come due in the usual or ordinary course of business.

- Under the *excess assets test*, a dividend may be paid if, after giving the dividend effect, the corporation's assets will exceed the total of its liabilities plus the amount required to be paid to satisfy the rights of preferred shareholders in the event of the liquidation of the corporation.

Georgia follows the model act in this regard and, only if a corporation is able to satisfy both of these tests, may it pay a dividend.

O.C.G.A. § 14-2-640

(a) A board of directors may authorize and the corporation may make distributions to its shareholders subject to restriction by the articles of incorporation and the limitation in subsection (c) of this Code section. ...

(c) No distribution may be made if, after giving it effect:

(1) The corporation would not be able to pay its debts as they become due in the usual course of business; or

(2) The corporation's total assets would be less than the sum of its total liabilities plus (unless the articles of incorporation permit otherwise) the amount that would be needed, if the corporation were to be dissolved at the time of the distribution, to satisfy the preferential rights upon dissolution of shareholders whose preferential rights are superior to those receiving the distribution.

Dougherty, McKinnon & Luby, P.C. v. Greenwald, et al.
225 Ga.App. 762, 484 S.E.2d 722 (1997)
Court of Appeals of Georgia

Facts: Dougherty, McKinnon & Luby, P.C., (DML) is a professional corporation of certified public accountants. Richard Greenwald and Richard Denzik are former shareholders/employees of the firm. When Greenwald and Denzik became shareholders, they signed a Termination Agreement with the corporation. This agreement provided that upon the termination of their employment with the corporation, the corporation would buy back the capital stock Greenwald and Denzik purchased in the corporation, paying the original purchase price of the stock plus interest. When Greenwald and Denzik left the firm and sought to enforce the Termination Agreement, DML argued that the purchase of Greenwald's and Denzik's stock would be an illegal distribution in that, after such a purchase, DML would be unable to pay its debts as they became due in the usual course of business.

Issue: Would re-acquisition of former shareholders' stock be a distribution subject to the provisions of O.C.G.A. § 14-2-640?

Holding: On its face, O.C.G.A. § 14-2-640 applies only to "distributions to shareholders." Greenwald and Denzik are no longer shareholders of DML. Under the terms of the Termination Agreement, their relationship with DML, including their status as shareholders, ended upon the termination of their employment. At that time, pursuant to the Termination Agreement, DML incurred the obligation to repurchase all of Greenwald's and Denzik's capital stock, and Greenwald and Denzik became creditors of DML rather than shareholder/employees.

Even if a corporation has sufficient profits to pay a dividend, the board of directors may elect not to declare one. The board may take this action for any of a variety of reasons. The board may opt to retain the profits to be used for another corporate purpose such as an expansion of the corporation's business, investment in another business entity, or any other legitimate corporate purpose the board sees fit. The business judgment rule provides that the decision of the board of directors may not be second guessed by shareholders in the absence of director abuse or bad motives such as the deliberate withholding of accumulated cash without good cause. However, once a dividend has been declared by a properly adopted resolution of the board of directors, the obligation to pay the dividend is a legal debt of the corporation. This debt is enforceable in a court of law. Shareholders can sue to recover declared, but unpaid, dividends.

Dividends are not paid on the same date that the board declares them. Thus, when declaring a dividend, the board of directors will establish a *record date*, usually a few weeks prior to the actual payment. The record date determines the shareholders who are eligible to receive dividends. Shareholders who own stock on the record date will receive the dividend even in the event that the shareholder sells his stock after the record date but before the time the dividend is actually paid. A shareholder who purchases stock after the record date purchases it *ex-dividend*.

Example 13l:

ABC Corp., has 10,000 shares of common stock outstanding. On March 1, the board of directors declares a dividend of $2.00 per share and sets the record date as March 15. The dividends are actually paid on April 15. Cory owns 1,000 shares of ABC common stock as of March 1, but sells 200 shares to Amanda on March 20. Cory will receive dividends in the amount of $2,000 since he owned 1,000 shares on the record date. Even though Amanda owns 200 shares of ABC common stock at the time the dividends are paid, she receives nothing as she purchased her stock ex-dividend.

Some states require that dividends be paid only from certain corporate accounts, such as a retained earnings account or surplus account. If the board of directors declares a dividend while the corporation is insolvent or pays dividends from unauthorized accounts, the distribution is an unlawful or illegal dividend. Shareholders who receive dividends while the corporation is insolvent must usually return them. Directors who vote for an illegal dividend are personally liable for the amount of the illegal dividend – the portion which exceeds the amount that could have been lawfully distributed.

13.4 Stock Splits

Recall that when one buys stock in a corporation, the purchaser hopes to make money. This can happen in two ways, the first of which is through the payment of dividends by the corporation. Additionally, if a corporation is profitable, its stock price increases and the purchaser is able to sell the stock for more than he paid for it. He has then, of course, made money.

Sometimes, a corporation's stock price will increase to such a level that the board of directors deems it appropriate to declare a stock split in order to increase the number of shares, thereby decreasng the price per share. A stock split is most often declared in order to increase the attractiveness of the corporation's shares. If the stock has appreciated significantly, the price per share may appear prohibitively high to small investors. Additionally, some investors may be reluctant to buy the stock at the higher price, fearing that the price will, over time, settle back to something closer to the stock's historical trading point.

A stock split increases the number of outstanding shares of corporation, but it does not alter the total value of an individual shareholder's investment in the corporation. Rather, it merely spreads that investment over a greater number of shares. It is analogous to breaking a twenty dollar bill into small denominations – the owner still has $20, but instead of one bill, he now has multiple bills with a total value of $20. While there is no direct increase in the value of an individual shareholder's stock, the corporation hopes that by reducing the per share market price, it will induce more trading in the stock which will lead, ultimately, to a higher per share price.

Example 13m:

ABC Corp., has 10,000 shares of common stock outstanding, which, over several years, has traded at about $40 per share, but has recently increased to $70 per share. The corporation declares a two-for-one split with the result that there are now 20,000 shares of common stock outstanding and the stock is now trading at $35 per share. If Sally owns 200 shares of stock before the split, worth $14,000, after the split, Sally will own 400 shares worth $14,000.

A stock split must not be confused with a stock dividend. A stock split does not alter the amount of capital or surplus of the corporation whereas a stock dividend represents the transfer of earnings or profits to the capital of the corporation.

A reverse stock split is the opposite of a stock split – the corporation reduces, rather than increases, the number of outstanding shares. A corporation may use a reverse stock split to eliminate smaller shareholders, thus avoiding the time, effort, and paperwork of communicating with those minority shareholders who own only a few shares of stock each.

Example 13n:

If ABC Corp., has 100,000 shares of common stock outstanding and declares a four for one reverse stock split, each group of four shares will be exchanged or surrendered for one new share, and the total number of shares will be reduced to 25,000 shares.

13.5 *Taxation of Corporations*

Recall that with all of the other forms of business organizations discussed in this text, sole proprietorships, general and limited partnerships, limited liability partnerships, and limited liability companies, the income earned by the business is passed through to the individuals who own the business. The business entity may be required to file an informational tax return, but the business itself pays no income tax on its profits. Instead, the individual owners pay income tax on the business profits at their individual income tax rates.

However, since corporations are artificial persons created by law, they must pay taxes just as natural persons are required to do. In this regard, corporations are different from other forms of business organizations. In addition to being subject to federal income taxes, corporations may also be required to pay a variety of state and local taxes including income, property, and other taxes.

The profits earned by corporations are subject to *double taxation*. The corporation files a corporate income tax return and pays income tax on its net income at its specified corporate rate. Then when the profits, on which tax has already been paid, are distributed to the shareholders in the form of dividends, the shareholders must declare the dividends as income on their personal tax returns and pay income tax on the distributions received by them at their applicable individual income tax rates. This double taxation of profits is one of the biggest disadvantages to doing business in the corporate form.

Corporate tax rates are different from the rates that exist for natural persons. Furthermore, a corporation pays tax only on its net income. Gross income is defined as total sales minus the cost of the goods sold. To determine a corporation's net income, other expenses incurred in operating the business are deducted from gross income. These expenses include salaries paid to employees, rent, interest paid to lenders, contributions to employee benefit plans, and many other expenses.

Exhibit 13.1 Federal Income Tax Rates for Individuals Filing Singly - 2013

If Taxable Income Is:		The Tax Is:	
Not over $8,925		10% of the taxable income	
Over $8,925	but not over $36,250	$ 892.50 plus	15% of the excess over $8,925
Over $36,250	but not over $87,850	$ 4,991.25 plus	25% of the excess over $36,250
Over $87,850	but not over $183,250	$ 17,891.25 plus	28% of the excess over $87,850
Over $183,250	but not over $398,350	$ 44,603.25 plus	33% of the excess over $183,250
Over $398,350	but not over $400,000	$115,586.25 plus	35% of the excess over $398,350
Over $400,000		$116,163.75 plus	39.6% of the excess over $400,000

Exhibit 13.2 Federal Income Tax Rates for Corporations – 2013

If Taxable Income Is		The Tax Is:	
Not over $50,000		15% of the taxable income	
Over $50,000	but not over $75,000	$7,500 plus	25% of the amount over $50,000
Over $75,000	but not over $100,000	$13,750 plus	34% of the amount over $75,000
Over $100,000	but not over $335,000	$22,250 plus	39% of the amount over $100,000
Over $335,000	but not over $10,000,000	$113,900 plus	34% of the amount over $335,000
Over $10,000,000	but not over $15,000,000	$3,400,000 plus	35% of the amount over $10,000,000
Over $15,000,000	but not over $18,333,333	$5,150,000 plus	38% of the amount over $15,000,000
Over 18,333,333		35% of the taxable income	

Currently, the top corporate tax rate in the U.S. is 35%, and the complaint is often made by corporate lobbyists and politicians that this tax rate is too high and puts U.S. companies at at a competitive disadvantage with the rest of the world. However, as noted in Chapter 12, the disadvantage of double taxation is largely theoretical for many large, international corporations whose lobbying efforts have resulted in significant loopholes being created which allow them to minimize their tax burden. In fact, most multi-national corporations are paying lower tax rates in the United States than they pay on their foreign operations.[34] One would expect a struggling corporation with small profits to pay little in the way of federal income taxes, but a five year study by the group Citizens for Tax Justice found that from 2008-2012, many of the most profitable U.S. corporations paid little or no federal income tax.[35]

Additionally, the effect of double taxation is minimized by the special tax treatment afforded to dividend income. Currently, dividend income is not taxed at the recipient's tax rate for earned income. For most dividend income, the maximum tax rate is just 15%.

---

[34] According to Robert McIntyre, director of Citizens for Tax Justice.

[35] The study was published Februay 25, 2014, and found that Boeing, Co., General Electric Co. and Verizon, all of which had profits in the billions, paid no federal income taxes during the five year period 2008-2012. During the five year period analyzed, Verizon had profits in excess of $30 billion.

While many corporations must simply accept double taxation as a cost of doing business, small corporations may take advantage of various methods to minimize their taxes. If the number of shareholders is fewer than 100 and the corporation meets certain other requirements, the corporation may elect S corporation status. In this case, all income earned by the corporation is passed through to the individual shareholders who will pay tax on it at their individual rates.

If the small corporation is one in which the shareholders are actively involved in running the corporation, the corporation may pay these shareholder/employees larger salaries or bonuses. The corporation is thus able to minimize corporate profits since salaries and bonuses are deductible expenses. The salaries or bonuses are taxable income to the employees, but the corporation is paying tax on a smaller amount of profit.

Example 130:

ABC Corp., has only four shareholders, all of whom are employed by the corporation. ABC is on track to make a profit of $200,000 this year. ABC elects to pay each of the four shareholders a bonus of $40,000, thereby reducing the corporation's net income or profit to $40,000. On $200,000 income, ABC would pay $61,250 in taxes (see Exhibit 13.2 above) or 30.625% of its income. On $40,000, ABC's tax obligation is just $6,000 or 15% of its income. Each of the four shareholders would report the $40,000 bonus as income on his or her individual income tax return.

Another method a corporation may use to reduce its tax burden is to obtain funds through debt financing (borrowing money) rather than equity financing (issuing shares). This would reduce the corporation's taxes since interest paid to creditors is a tax-deductible corporate expense while dividends paid to shareholders are not tax deductible.

There are risks in utilizing this method in addition to the obvious risk of the corporation being unable to pay its debts. The Internal Revenue Service theory of *thin incorporation* was designed to discourage corporations from engaging in excessive borrowing. If the IRS determines a corporation's debts to be excessive, the IRS may characterize the interest payments on the debt as dividends. Dividends are non-deductible to the corporation but remain subject to taxation by the recipient.

Shareholders in a corporation are required to pay income tax only on dividends received by them. If a corporation does not distribute its profits to the shareholders in the form of dividends, the shareholders are not obligated to pay tax on the profits. The IRS has devised penalties to discourage corporations from simply holding onto profits rather than distributing them has dividends. If a corporation hoards its profits beyond the reasonable needs of the business in order to avoid having shareholders pay taxes on dividends distributed to them, the corporation may be subject to an *accumulated earnings tax*. Through 2012, the accumulated earnings tax imposed is 15% of accumulated earnings over $250,000.[36]

Corporations are also required to pay a variety of state and local taxes. A corporation that owns property may be required to pay property taxes in the jurisdiction in which the property is located. Corporations engaged in the sale of goods may be required to collect sales taxes from customers and remit these taxes to the appropriate state and local governments. If a corporation transacts business in a state that imposes a state income tax, the corporation is usually subject to that tax in addition to its federal income taxes.

---

[36] According to a study done by Standard & Poor's Corp., U.S. corporations are hoarding $1.15 trillion which was earned overseas and is kept out of the country so as to avoid paying corporate taxes on it.

Finally, a corporation must pay to the secretary of state's office or other appropriate state agency in the state of incorporation a filing fee upon the filing of the articles of incorporation. In Georgia, this fee is $100.00 as of January 1, 2011. Each corporation must also pay an annual filing fee, currently $50.00 in Georgia, which must accompany the corporation's annual registration. Every foreign corporation wishing to qualify to do business in another jurisdiction must pay a fee to the appropriate state agency. In Georgia, a foreign corporation seeking authorization to transact business in Georgia must pay a fee of $225.00 when the corporation applies for a certificate of authority to do business in this state.[37]

Review Questions and Exercises

1. Identify the advantages and disadvantages to a corporation of raising money by the issuance of stock.

2. Describe the three ownership interests a shareholder has in a corporation.

3. Do shareholders have the right to force the board of directors of a corporation to declare a dividend? Are there any constraints on the board's decision regarding as to whether to declare a dividend? Discuss.

4. Sally owns 500 shares of stock in NuTech, Inc. Sally receives a notice of the annual shareholders' meeting to be held on November 15. The notice recites that the record date is October 31. On November 5, Sally sells 100 of her shares to Susan.

   (a) Who is entitled to attend the shareholders' meeting?
   (b) Who is entitled to vote the 500 shares that Sally owned at the time she received the notice of the shareholders' meeting? Explain.

5. What is meant by corporate double taxation? Describe the methods a corporation may use to reduce the burden of double taxation.

6. Stuart Hudson Holding Corp. has 200 shareholders and two classes of stock, Common A (100 shares) and Common B (100 shares). The board of directors has decided to declare a dividend.

   (a) The board would like to distribute a cash dividend to one-half of the Common A shareholders and a share dividend to the other one-half of the Common A shareholders. Is this permissible? Discuss.
   (b) Is it permissible for the Common A shareholders to receive a cash dividend while the Common B shareholders receive a share dividend? Discuss.
   (c) Due to soaring fuel costs and increased insurance premiums, the corporation is having financial difficulties. Bills are often paid late and it has been necessary to secure a line of credit in order to be assured of meeting payroll. What affect do the corporation's finances have on the ability to declare a dividend? Discuss.

7. What is a stock split? Why might a corporation want to split its stock?

8. What is the difference between authorized shares and outstanding shares?

---

[37] See O.C.G.A. §14-2-122. Fees cited are rates applicable as of 2011.

9. What is a proxy? Why might a shareholder give someone else his proxy to use in the context of shareholder meetings?

10. If the shareholders of a corporation feel that their stock has lost its value due to the mismanagement and/or misconduct of the corporation's officers and directors, what, if any, recourse do they have?

Practical Applications

1. Mary Katherine Rosenfeld and William Spencer Rosenfeld were husband and wife. They were also the only to shareholders in a family business corporation, with the wife owing 25% of the stock and the husband owning 75% of the stock. Both served as officers and directors of the corporation, with the husband being the Chief Executive Officer. For many years, the parties used corporate funds to pay their personal and family expenses, routinely transferring corporate funds into a family checking account.

After 30 years of marriage, the husband filed for divorce and terminated the wife's access to the corporation although he continued to use corporate funds for his personal expenses. The wife sued in her capacity as a minority shareholder, alleging that the husband, in so using corporate funds, had breached his fiduciary duties that he, as the presiding officer, owed to the corporation and its shareholders.

Consider:

(a) If the husband and wife are the only two shareholders of the corporation, is a resolution by the directors required before a distribution can be made to the shareholders?

(b) Does it matter that the wife also used corporate funds for personal expenses prior to the separation? In other words, can she complain about the husband doing what she also did in the past?

(c) Is the husband, as a director, required to show that he acted in good faith when he used corporate funds for his personal expenses? Did he do so?

See – Rosenfeld v. Rosenfeld, 186 Ga.App. 61, 648 S.E.2d 399 (2007), Court of Appeals of Georgia.

2. Carolee Davies was the sole shareholder and officer of Carolee's Combine, Inc., a Georgia Corporation organized for the purpose of conducting a single auction of architectural antiques. The corporation planned to acquire merchandise such as columns, chandeliers, and railings, restore them, and then sell the merchandise at a no-minimum, no-reserve auction.

Davies contributed little, if any, capital to the business which needed cash to acquire the merchandise. To raise money, Davies promised persons who advanced money to the corporation for the venture, in writing, that on the first day of the two-day auction they would be repaid with ten percent annual interest and a bonus of a flat ten percent of the principal amount of the advance. Davies also deferred until after the auction payment for labor, materials, rent, utilities and other expenses. At the conclusion of the auction owed these trade creditors, laborers, and others more than $250,000.

The auction grossed only $625,000 against liabilities of $850,000. Despite this, the persons who advanced money to the corporation were all paid back in full with interest and the promised bonuses.

Consider:

(a) Was the repayment of the advances in full on the first day of auction equitable when the trade creditors and laborers were owed $250,000 at the conclusion of the two-day auction?

(b) Did the advances by "investors" represent loans to the corporation?

(c) Alternatively, did the advances by the "investors" represent a proprietary or ownership participation in the corporation?

(d) How would the classification of the advances affect the distribution of the corporation's assets?

See – In re: Carolee's Combine, Inc., 3 B.R. 324 (1980), United States Bankruptcy Court.

Chapter 14 *Corporate Management, Changes, and Termination of Existence*

OUTLINE

The shareholders are, of course, the owners of the corporation, but shareholders are not involved in the management of the corporation simply by virtue of owing stock in the corporation. The shareholders' management activity is limited to electing the members of the board of directors who formulate broad policies for the corporation. The officers of the corporation, who are appointed by the board of directors, run the corporation's day-to-day activities.

A profitable corporation with a flourishing business is not static even though it may exist in perpetuity. The law recognizes that, occasionally, the need will arise to amend the articles of incorporation, and procedures exist to accomplish such action. Additionally, a corporation may also desire to conduct business in jurisdictions other than the one in which it was organized. To do so, the corporation must first qualify as a foreign corporation in the other state.

Corporations may also create or acquire other corporations or may merge or otherwise combine with other corporations. Such combinations are not only permitted but common so long as proper procedures are followed. Finally, some corporations fail or outlive their usefulness, and, thus, the decision may be made to terminate the corporation's existence. When a corporation is dissolved and the assets of the corporation liquidated and distributed to the shareholders, careful attention must be paid to the applicable provisions of law.

14.1 Management of the Corporation

The board of directors of the corporation is responsible for the management of the corporation. The board accomplishes this by formulating policy decisions that affect the operation of the corporation but the directors are not involved in the daily management of the corporation. The directors appoint corporate officers who are responsible for running the corporation and carrying out the policy decisions of the directors.

The Directors

The corporation's policy makers are the members of the *board of directors*. Directors are classified as either inside directors or outside directors. An *inside director* is a person who is also an officer of the corporation and, thus, involved in the day-to-day operation of the corporation. For instance, it is fairly common for the president of a corporation to also sit on the board of directors.

An *outside director* sits on the board but is not an officer of the corporation. Outside directors are often asked to sit on the board in order to lend to the board their business knowledge and expertise. They are usually officers and directors of other corporations, bankers, attorneys, or industry experts.

A board of directors can consist of only one director or several directors. The exact number of directors is specified by the articles of incorporation and can be changed unless otherwise provided in the articles of incorporation. The board of directors is permitted to fix the amount of compensation paid to each director. The members of the initial board of directors may be named in the articles of incorporation, but if they are not, they are elected at the corporation's first organizational meeting. These directors will then serve until the first annual shareholders' meeting at which time directors will be elected by the shareholders.

> O.C.G.A. § 14-2-802
>
> Directors shall be natural persons who are 18 years of age or older but need not be residents of this state nor shareholders of the corporation... The articles of incorporation may prescribe additional qualifications for directors.

Often, the articles of incorporation will provide for *staggered terms*, meaning that the directors do not all face election at the same time. If so, the directors will be divided into two or three groups, and the terms of the first group will expire at the first annual shareholders' meeting, the terms of the second group will expire at the second annual shareholders' meeting, and the terms of the third group, if any, will expire at the third annual shareholders' meeting. At each succeeding shareholders' meeting, directors will be elected for terms of two or three years, as the case may be, to succeed those whose terms are then expiring. The use of staggered terms promotes continuity in the make-up of the board. Otherwise, at each election an entirely new board could be elected.

In the past, a director could be removed from a board by the shareholders only "for cause" which generally meant dishonesty, fraud, or incompetence. However, modern statutes recognize that the shareholders, as the corporation's owners, should be allowed to remove directors with or without cause. Shareholders who are dissatisfied with a director can exercise their right to remove that director from the board at a special shareholders' meeting called for the stated purpose of removing the director.

The board of directors acts by adopting resolutions. Actions taken at a directors' meeting are usually approved by a simple majority vote. Once adopted, corporate resolutions are recorded in the minutes of the board of directors' meetings and detail the decisions made by the board. There are some actions that a board of directors may initiate which require shareholder approval. These actions include mergers, the sale of substantially all of the corporation's assets, the amendment of the corporation's articles of incorporation, and the voluntary dissolution of the corporation.

In order to fulfill their duties to the corporation, directors must have access to the corporation's books and records as well as to any other information that affects the operation of the corporation.

Directors must discharge their duties to the corporation in good faith and in the best interests of the corporation. Generally speaking, directors are required to exercise the care that a person in similar circumstances would reasonably believe to be appropriate. The *business judgment rule* immunizes directors from liability for decisions they make in their capacity as directors so long as the directors had a reasonable basis for making the decision and acted in good faith. Obviously, no one would be willing to serve on the board of directors of a corporation if he believed others would be constantly second guessing his decisions and seeking to hold him liable for errors in judgment.

O.C.G.A. § 14-2-830

(a) A director shall discharge his duties as a director, including his duties as a member of a committee:

(1) In a manner he believes in good faith to be in the best interests of the corporation; and

(2) With the care an ordinarily prudent person in a like position would exercise under similar circumstances.

(b) In discharging his duties a director is entitled to rely on information, opinions, reports, or statements, including financial statements and other financial data, if prepared or presented by:

(1) One or more officers or employees of the corporation whom the director reasonably believes to be reliable and competent in the matters presented;

(2) Legal counsel, public accountants, investment bankers, or other persons as to matters the director reasonably believes are within the person's professional or expert competence; or

(3) A committee of the board of directors of which he is not a member if the director reasonably believes the committee merits confidence. …

(d) A director is not liable to the corporation or to its shareholders for any action taken as a director, or any failure to take any action, if he performed the duties of his office in compliance with this Code section.

Georgia law provides a very high level of protection for corporate directors. In adopting the above code section, the General Assembly of Georgia published the following comment which evidences the legislature's intent to protect directors from liability: "In determining whether to impose liability, the courts recognize that boards of directors and corporation managers continuously make decisions that involve the balancing of risks and benefits for the enterprise. Although some decisions turn out to be unwise or the result of a mistake of judgment, it is unreasonable to reexamine these decisions with the benefit of hindsight. Therefore, a director is not liable for any injury or damage caused by his decision, no matter how unwise or mistaken it may turn out to be if, in performing his duties, he met the requirements of Section 14-2-830."

Gallagher v. McKinnon

273 Ga.App. 727, 615 S.E.2d 746 (2005)

Court of Appeals of Georgia

Facts: Gallagher and McKinnon each owned 48% of the stock of Peliton, Inc., a corporation, and were company's sole directors. Gallagher wanted complete control of the corporation. In July, 2000, Gallagher wrote a letter to Peliton's corporate counsel in which he made his intentions regarding control of the company clear. He wrote: "How can I end up with the majority of [Peliton] because, rest assured, I will, or I'll simply do it on my own."

In 2002, Peliton sponsored a birthday party for Gallagher at which a number of employees were drinking alcoholic beverages. At one point, McKinnon got into the back seat of his truck with Annette Yeomans, a Peliton employee. Yeomans testified that McKinnon made sexual advances toward her, but that they did not have sex. McKinnon testified that he was so inebriated that he had no memory of the encounter. The following Monday morning, Gallagher met with McKinnon and told him that he had had sex with Yeomans at the party and that Yeomans was threatening suit against Peliton for sexual harassment. Gallagher then advised McKinnon to go home while he, Gallagher, attempted to work things out.

The next morning Gallagher telephoned McKinnon, requesting a meeting the following day at Peliton's corporate counsel's office. When McKinnon arrived at the meeting, which was, in reality, an unannounced special meeting of directors, Gallagher told McKinnon that he had slept with Yeomans; that he, Gallagher, had investigated the matter, speaking with both employees and nonemployees; that he believed the allegations to be true; and that Yeomans was planning to file a lawsuit. In fact, however, Gallagher had spoken to no one but Yeomans and McKinnon about the matter. Neither one of them told Gallagher they had sex. Importantly, Yeomans did not threaten to sue.

Gallagher then informed McKinnon that, in order to protect Peliton from liability, McKinnon would have to be "disciplined." This discipline included removing McKinnon from his position as secretary of the corporation, demoting him to maintenance supervisor, reducing his salary by 25% and placing him on two years probation. Next, McKinnon was informed that to further protect the corporation's interests, additional shares of stock would have to be issued to Gallagher to give him a controlling interest in the corporation. During the meeting, it was determined that an additional 750 shares would be issued to Gallagher and it is undisputed that, at the time, there was absolutely no attempt to determine the value for the shares being issued. Value and consideration for the shares were not even discussed. Gallagher subsequently fired McKinnon. McKinnon then sued to cancel the issuance of the additional shares to Gallagher, to reinstate him as an employee, and for lost wages.

Issue: Did Gallagher breach his duties as a director of the corporation? Were the actions taken by Gallagher as a director unfairly prejudicial to McKinnon as a shareholder?

Holding: The board of directors may authorize shares to be issued for consideration consisting of cash, property, or benefit to the corporation. The directors are merely required to determine that the consideration received for shares is adequate. In many instances, the value of the property or benefit is uncertain. In such cases, it is only necessary that the board determine that the issuance of the shares for the property or benefit is an appropriate transaction that protects the shareholders from dilution. In this case, there was no attempt to determine the value of the additional shares issued to Gallagher, and there was no attempt to determine that the consideration for the issued shares was adequate. Gallagher was interested in control of Peliton, not the well being of its shareholders. His actions breached his fiduciary duties to the existing shareholders.

Georgia law, O.C.G.A. § 14-2-940, provides that relief may be granted to a minority shareholder where a corporate director has acted in a manner that is illegal, oppressive, fraudulent, or unfairly prejudicial. Gallagher falsely told McKinnon that McKinnon had had sex with an employee and that the employee was threatening to sue the corporation for sexual harassment. He did this to force McKinnon to agree to, in effect, transfer sole control of the corporation to Gallagher.

The Officers

The day-to-day operations of a corporation are conducted by its officers who are appointed by the board of directors. Officers serve at the pleasure of the board of directors and may be removed by the board at any time. The only thing required is that the board determine that the best interests of the corporation will be served by the removal of the officer. An individual's appointment as an officer of a corporation does not create an employment contract between the individual and the corporation;

however, if the officer who is removed has an employment contract with the corporation, the officer's removal does not nullify the contract and the removed officer may sue the corporation for breach of contract.

> O.C.G.A. § 14-2-844
>
> (a) The appointment of an officer does not itself create contract rights.
>
> (b) An officer's removal does not affect the officer's contract rights, if any, with the corporation. An officer's resignation does not affect the corporation's rights, if any with the officer.

The MBCA does not require any specific officers be appointed nor does it require that the officers who are appointed bear any particular titles. Most corporations have, at a minimum, a president, vice-president, secretary, and treasurer although large corporations may have many more officers. Additionally, the articles of incorporation or bylaws may authorize officers to appoint assistant officers to help them in the performance of their duties.

Officers are agents of the corporation. Their authority to act on behalf of the corporation comes from the bylaws or from the board of directors. Because they are agents of the corporation, officers have the authority to bind the corporation to contracts subject to the principles of agency discussed earlier in this text in Chapter 2.

Officers are subject to the same duties of care and the same fiduciary duties as those imposed on directors. Like directors, officers are protected by the business judgment rule. So long as there is some reasonable basis for their decisions, officers of a corporation will not be held liable for their acts done on behalf of the corporation. When officers are determined to be liable, it is usually because of clear and gross abuse or negligence.

14.2 *Debt Securities*

While corporations initially raise capital by issuing stock, a directors or officers may decide that the corporation needs to borrow money. A debt security is the instrument that evidences the corporation's debt to a bank, other financial institution, or individual and creates a debtor-creditor relationship. Like other borrowers, the corporation promises to repay the principal borrowed at some stated maturity date in the future and to pay interest on the amount borrowed. Unlike a shareholder, a debt security holder is not an owner of the corporation and does not have voting rights or the rights to receive distributions of profit. Rather, the debt security holder is simply entitled to be repaid the principal amount owed plus interest. In the event of the liquidation and dissolution of the corporation, the debt security holder will be entitled to repayment prior to any distribution to the shareholders.

Some corporations may be required to offer incentives to make their debt securities more attractive to investors, thus enabling the corporations to obtain needed financing. Common features that may be offered include:

- Higher Interest – A corporation may pay a higher rate of interest than other investments, yielding a higher rate of return for the investor who loans money to the corporation.

- Redemption Terms – A corporation may agree not to redeem the debt before the stated maturity date in order to guarantee the lender the interest the lender expects to earn over the life of the loan. Alternatively, the corporation may agree to pay a penalty in the event that the debt is paid off early.

- Priority and Subordination Rights – If the lender wants to ensure that it will be paid before other creditors, it may require that the corporation agree not to give another creditor priority over the lender's debt and to keep any debts incurred by the corporation at a later date subordinate to that owed to the lender.

- Conversion Terms – A corporation may allow a creditor to trade the debt for shares of stock, thereby becoming a shareholder in the corporation.

- Voting Rights – In a very few states, the articles of incorporation may allow debt security holders to vote on certain issues including the election of directors. Georgia is not one of these states.

Debt securities are usually classified based on two factors – the length of time of the instrument and whether the instrument is secured or not.

Unsecured Debt

A corporation may borrow money based on the corporation's good credit standing and without the necessity of pledging any property as collateral or security for the debt. In the event that the corporation defaults on the debt, the creditor must sue the corporation to receive a judgment against it and then seek to enforce the judgment. Such a debt is referred to as an *unsecured debt.*

A *promissory note* is often used to meet the short-term financing needs of a corporation, while a *debenture*, the name given to a long-term unsecured debt instrument, may be used for financing over longer periods. With both, the corporation will execute a document which sets out the terms of the loan. In addition to naming the parties and the amount of the loan, the note will also specify the maturity date of the loan, that is, the date upon which repayment is due, and the interest rate.

If the corporation is unable to repay an unsecured debt, the holders of the unsecured debts are treated as general creditors of the corporation. They are only paid after the claims of secured creditors are paid. Generally, only a corporation that is in a sound financial situation and has a proven record of credit worthiness will be able to obtain unsecured loans. New or unproven corporations or those experiencing financial difficulties will have to look to other methods of financing.

Secured Debt

If the corporation's debt is a *secured debt*, some specific corporate property is pledged as collateral to ensure that the corporation will repay the loan. If the corporation defaults on the loan, the creditor may then foreclose on the collateral. The holder of the debt will seize the specifically identified corporate asset and sell it in order to satisfy the debt. A corporation's long-term secured debt is called a *bond.*

With a secured debt, the document evidencing the debt will state the names of the parties and will specifiy the principal amount of the loan, the interest rate, the date of repayment, and the property pledged to secure repayment of the loan. The property pledged can be either real property or personal property.

- Real Property – If the corporation pledges real estate to secure a loan, the document executed by the parties is usually called a *mortgage bond.* In addition to its promise to repay the loan, the mortgage agreement will often require that the corporation keep the property insured, keep it in good condition, and pay the property taxes as they come due. The mortgage document will be recorded with the clerk of court in the county where the land is located.

- Personal Property – If the corporation pledges personal property as the security, the parties will execute a security agreement and the creditor will file a *financing statement* with the clerk of court. The financing statement will describe the property pledged, often cars, computers, or equipment. The filing of the financing statement acts to provide notice to others that the lender has a security interest in the property. Financing statements were discussed in Chapter 7.

14.3 Amending the Articles of Incorporation

Various events may occur which require the amendment of a corporation's articles of incorporation. Generally, whenever any significant information contained in the articles of incorporation changes, the articles must be amended in accordance with the statutory provisions of the state of incorporation. Usually, shareholder approval is required in order to amend the articles of incorporation. However, the incorporators or the board of directors have the authority to amend the articles at any time prior to the issuance of stock in the corporation. Additionally, some states, including Georgia, provide that under certain circumstances the board of directors may make routine amendments to the articles of incorporation without shareholder approval.

> O.C.G.A. § 14-2-1001
>
> (a) A corporation may amend its articles of incorporation at any time to add or change a provision that is required or permitted in the articles of incorporation or to delete a provision that is not required in the articles of incorporation.

For amendments to the articles of incorporation that require shareholder approval, the MBCA provides the following procedure:

1. The board of directors must adopt the proposed amendment.

2. The board of directors will either recommend the amendment to the shareholders for approval or make no recommendation as to approval.

3. Each shareholder, including those not entitled to vote, must be notified of the shareholder meeting at which time the amendment will be considered. Consideration may take place at a regular annual shareholders' meeting or at a special meeting called for the purpose of considering the amendment. The notice must state that the purpose of the meeting is to consider an amendment to the articles of incorporation, and it must either set out in the notice itself or be accompanied by a copy or summary of the proposed amendment.

4. The amendment must be approved by a vote of the shareholders. In most states, the vote necessary to approve the amendment is a simple majority vote, although some states require a two-thirds vote for approval.

After an amendment has been approved by the shareholders, *articles of amendment* must be prepared by the corporation and filed with the Secretary of State's office. A filing fee must also be paid when the articles of amendment are filed and any other statutory requirements must be met. For instance, some states, including Georgia, require that in the event the articles of incorporation are amended to change the name of the corporation, a notice of the name change must be published in the newspaper where the corporation's registered office is located.[38] All requirements relating to the

---

[38] See O.C.G.A. § 14-2-1006.1

submission and filing of the original articles of incorporation must be followed. For instance, if a state's statute required the publication of articles of incorporation when the corporation was formed, then the articles of amendment must also be published.

Many third parties, including creditors, suppliers, vendors and others, may have dealt with the corporation prior to the amendment of the articles of incorporation. The amendment of the articles of incorporation has no effect on the rights of third parties who have previously dealt with the corporation. For example, the amendment of a corporation's articles of incorporation does not affect the corporation's relationship with its creditors or alter the course of any litigation in which the corporation may be engaged.

Over time, a corporation's articles of incorporation may be amended many times. The corporation may consider it advantageous to change the company's name as it grows and expands into new markets. The number of authorized shares may need to be increased to allow for share dividends or to raise additional capital. In other words, there can be many business reasons for making changes to the articles of incorporation. Each time that the articles are amended, articles of amendment are filed with the secretary of state. Thus, reading the original articles of incorporation and the various articles of amendment may become confusing. To remedy this problem, almost all states allow corporations to restate their articles of incorporation at any time.

Restated articles combine the original articles with all later amendments into one "clean" document. The restated articles themselves do not include changes, but rather are simply a composite of the original articles of incorporation and the previously approved articles of amendment. Thus, shareholder approval of restated articles is not required.

14.4 Qualification of Foreign Corporations

Recall that a corporation is a domestic corporation in the state of its incorporation and a foreign corporation in all other states and that corporations may be formed in one state and do business in other states. Since a corporation is formed pursuant to the laws of its state of incorporation, it has no legal existence beyond the borders of that state and, thus, has no automatic right to do business in states other than its home state. Therefore, in order to conduct business in other states, the corporation must request permission of those other states. It must qualify or be authorized to do business in the other state as a foreign corporation. While qualification is, in many regards, a formality, the foreign corporation must take certain steps in order to lawfully do business in another state. Specifically, it must apply to the secretary of state's office or other government agency for permission to do business in the state. It must also pay a fee to the local state, and, most importantly, it must designate a registered agent in the state to receive service of process and other legal papers.

GMAC Mortgage Corporation V. Bongiorno
277 Ga.App. 328, 626 S.E.2d 536 (2006)
Court of Appeals of Georgia

Facts: A deputy sheriff served a complaint on Daniel Carr, the local branch manager for GMAC Mortgage Corporation, a foreign corporation. The deputy who performed the service testified that when meeting Carr, he asked if Carr was authorized to accept civil processes on behalf of the corporation and Carr told the deputy, "yes." GMAC contended that its registered agent was the only proper entity for service of process.

Issue: Did the trial court obtain jurisdiction over GMAC Mortgage Corporation by service of the complaint on the local branch manager rather than serving its registered agent?

Holding: Service on the registered agent was not the only method for proper service on a foreign corporation. GMAC has cited no statutory authority or case law supporting its argument that once a foreign corporation has designated a registered agent for service of process, it may only be served through its registered agent. In fact, the statutory authority and case law clearly indicate just the opposite. Even *OCGA § 14-2-1510*, upon which GMAC relies in support of its argument, specifically notes "This Code section does not prescribe the only means, or necessarily the required means, of serving a foreign corporation."

Pursuant to *OCGA § 9-11-4(e)(1),* an action against a foreign corporation may be served on "the president or other officer of the corporation, secretary, cashier, managing agent, or other agent thereof." GMAC argues that the above-referenced individuals may only be used for service of process if the foreign corporation has failed to designate a registered agent for service of process. However, *OCGA § 9-11-4 (e) (2)* directly contradicts such an argument. That Code section specifically states, "If the action is against a foreign corporation ... doing business and having a managing or other agent, cashier, or secretary within this state, [service may be made] to such agent, cashier, or secretary or to an agent designated for service of process."

Here, there is no dispute that Carr was a local branch manager for GMAC. In order for an employee to be authorized to accept service on behalf of a corporation, it is necessary that he occupy some managerial or supervisory responsibility within the organization. The employee's position must be such as to afford reasonable assurance that he will inform his corporate principal that such process has been served on him. As a branch manager, Carr clearly occupied some managerial or supervisory responsibility within GMAC. The trial court was authorized to find that service on the local branch manager was valid service on GMAC

Holmes & Company of Orlando v. Carlisle

289 Ga.App. 619, 658 S.E.2d 185 (2008)

Court of Appeals of Georgia

Facts: *Recall this case from Chapter 12. The relevant facts are these:* David Carlisle sued Holmes & Company of Orlando (Holmes), a foreign corporation, for injuries sustained when he was involved in a motor vehicle accident with a Holmes' vehicle. Holmes' registered agent for service was Donna West, whose address was listed as 6340 Lake Oconee Parkway, Greensboro, Georgia. That location was a BankSouth branch. West was a bank employee at that branch but was not authorized by the bank to do business as an agent of anyone except the bank.

The return of service shows that the sheriff served "Melinda Walker, in charge of the office..." Walker was the branch manager and the person in charge of the office. Walker, as West's supervisor, acknowledged she had the authority to accept documents on West's behalf.

Issue: Was service properly accomplished on the foreign corporation by service on the bank manager?

Holding: Holmes' annual registration showed that its principal address was a post office box in Florida, that its registered agent was Donna West, and that its registered agent's address was 6340 Lake Oconee Parkway, Greensboro.

> The methods of service set out in the Civil Practice Act, *OCGA § 9-11-1 et seq.*, and the Georgia Business Corporation Code, *OCGA § 14-2-[101] et seq.*, are discrete methods of service upon corporations, and a plaintiff may serve a defendant corporation by following the directions of the Civil Practice Act or by following the directions of the Georgia Business Corporation Code.
>
> A corporation may be served through its registered agent as provided in *OCGA § 14-2-504 (a)*. A foreign corporation doing business and having an agent within this state may also be served by delivering a copy of the summons and complaint to the corporation's agent or to an agent designated for service of process, as provided in *OCGA § 9-11-4 (e) (2)*. The Georgia Business Corporation Code requires corporations to maintain a registered office and a registered agent in the state. *OCGA § 14-2-501.*
>
> The deputy sheriff's return of service showed that he served Walker as the person in charge of the business located at the registered agent's address. While Walker was not the company's registered agent and was not authorized to accept service on behalf of the company, Walker was authorized to accept service on West's behalf. While the evidence in this case clearly establishes that the defendant corporation's agent for service was not served personally, it is undisputed that West's supervisor was authorized to accept service on her behalf, thereby accomplishing service on the corporation.

Generally, a foreign corporation may not legally transact business within a foreign state until it obtains a certificate of authority to do so. Recall from Chapter 1 that the federal constitution prohibits a state from restricting interstate commerce. Thus, a state cannot prohibit a corporation from engaging in commerce across state lines. However, if the corporation desires to transact business in the state, it must qualify to do so or be subject to certain penalties. It is through this mechanism that states seek to protect their citizens. Through the qualification process, a state is able to gather some basic information about the foreign corporation and is able provide a means for local citizens to serve the foreign corporation with service of process in the event it becomes necessary to file a lawsuit.

As seen from the above cases, in Georgia service on a foreign corporation may be accomplished by complying with the requirements of the Georgia Civil Practice Act or, alternatively, by complying with the requirements of the Georgia Business Corporation Code.

The meaning of "transacting business" has been the subject of considerable litigation. Generally, a foreign corporation is transacting business if it maintains sufficient contacts or ties within the state on a continuous or regular basis so as make it fair and equitable that the corporation be accountable for in its actions the foreign state. State long-arm statutes give the courts of each state personal jurisdiction over foreign corporations that go into that state for the purpose of transacting business there.

In an attempt to further define the concept of transacting business, the MBCA has designated a list of activities that do *not* constitute transacting business with the caveat that the list is not exhaustive. As the Comment to the Georgia Business Corporation Code notes, the statute does not attempt to formulate an inclusive definition of what constitutes the transaction of business. Instead, the concept is defined in a negative fashion. Georgia's statute follows the MBCA in this regard,[39] providing that the following activities are *not* to be considered transacting business:

---

[39] See O.C.G.A. § 14-2-1501.

- Transacting business in interstate commerce;
- Holding meetings of the board of directors or shareholders;
- Maintaining bank accounts;
- Selling through independent contractors;
- Soliciting or obtaining orders if the orders require acceptance outside the state before they become contracts;
- Owning, without more, real or personal property;
- Conducting an isolated transaction;
- Creating or acquiring indebtedness, mortgages, and security interests in real or personal property;
- Securing or collecting debts or enforcing mortgages and security interests in property securing the debts; and
- Maintaining, defending, or settling any proceeding.

Since a foreign corporation's qualifying to do business is a formality in most regards, any questions about the necessity of qualifying should be resolved in favor of qualification.

O.C.G.A. § 14-2-1503

(a) A foreign corporation may apply for a certificate of authority to transact business in this state by delivering an application to the Secretary of State for filing. The application must set forth:

(1) The name of the foreign corporation or, if its name is unavailable for use in this state, a corporate name that satisfies the requirements of Code Section 14-2-1506;

(2) The name of the state or country under whose law it is incorporate;

(3) Its date of incorporation;

(4) The mailing address of its principal office;

(5) The address of its registered office in this state and the name of its registered agent at that office; and

(6) The names and respective business addresses of its chief executive officer, chief financial officer, and secretary or individuals holding similar positions.

(b) The foreign corporation shall deliver with the completed application a certificate of existence (or a document of similar import) duly authenticated by the secretary of state or other official having custody of corporate records in the state or country under whose laws it is incorporated.

To qualify to do business, a foreign corporation is required to submit an application for qualification to the appropriate state authority, usually the Secretary of State. Certain information must be provided in the application which generally includes the name of the foreign corporation, the state of incorporation, the principal address and agent, and the identities of directors and officers of the corporation. In many states, the application must also be accompanied by a *certificate of good standing* from the corporation's home state.

The name of the corporation cannot be the same or confusingly similar to that of a domestic corporation in the state. In some states, if the secretary of state determines the name to be too similar, the foreign corporation may be required to add some distinguishing word or words to its name. In other states, including Georgia,[40] a foreign corporation may use a fictitious or trade name to transact business in the state if its real name is unavailable provided that the corporation provides to the Secretary of State a resolution of its board of directors adopting the fictitious or trade name.

---

[40] See O.C.G.A. § 14-2-1506.

Example 14a:

Clarke Products, Inc., is a South Carolina corporation which wishes to do business in Georgia. However, there is already a Clarke Products, Corp., incorporated in Georgia. To do business in the state of Georgia, the South Carolina corporation may use the name "Clarke Products of South Carolina, Inc., for all of its business in Georgia.

Upon review of the application, the Secretary of State will issue a *certificate of authority*, after which the foreign corporation is authorized to transact business within the state. Upon qualifying, the foreign corporation is subject to any restrictions imposed on domestic corporations and is subject to service of process in the new state. Additionally, the corporation must pay any fees and taxes imposed by the new state and must file an annual report with the new state.

The state in which a foreign corporation has qualified to do business may revoke the certificate of authority if the foreign corporation fails to file its annual registration, fails to pay taxes or other fees required by the state, or is without a registered agent for service or registered office.

If a foreign corporation transacts business without first obtaining a certificate of authority to do so, that corporation may not maintain any proceeding in any court in the state until it obtains a certificate of authority. Simply put, failing to qualify to transact business means that the foreign corporation may not bring a lawsuit in any court in the state. Additionally, the foreign corporation is subject to civil financial penalties.

14.5 Corporate Combinations

Corporate combinations come about through a variety of methods. One corporation may take control of another or be merged into another. One corporation may purchase all or most of the stock of another corporation or it may purchase the assets of the other corporation. Additionally, one corporation may create another corporation which did not formally exist.

Mergers and Consolidations

The combination of two or more corporations is called a *merger*. Typically in a merger two corporations will combine with the result that one of them, known as the *extinguished corporation*, will cease to exist while the other, known as the *survivor*, acquires everything previously owned by both corporations including assets, liabilities, contracts, rights, and obligations, and usually, the shareholders.

A *consolidation* is quite similar to a merger except that in a consolidation, two or more corporations combine to form an entirely new corporation. At the end of the consolidation the previously existing, and now combining, corporations both cease to exist. All of the assets, liabilities, contracts, rights, and obligations previously owned by both of the combining corporations are acquired by a newly formed corporation which is an entirely different legal entity from either of the combining corporations. Consolidations are rare since it is usually advantageous for one of the combining corporations to survive.

The procedures for accomplishing consolidations and mergers are the same. Both begin with negotiations between the corporations involved which are called the constituent corporations. When an agreement is eventually reached, the constituent corporations will prepare a plan of merger which will set out the details including the terms and conditions of the merger, the manner of converting the shares of the extinguished corporation into shares of the survivor corporation or cash, and any amendments to the survivor's articles of incorporation necessitated by the merger. A merger has dramatic consequences for both constituent corporations – one will be extinguished while the survivor will likely take on the debts and other obligations of the extinguished corporation. Furthermore, power and control of the survivor corporation may shift if shares are issued to the shareholders of the extinguished corporation. If cash, rather than stock, is paid to the shareholders of the extinguished corporation, the survivor's shareholders are affected by the large outlay of cash. Because of the extreme effects on both corporations, approval by the shareholders of both constituent corporations is required in order to complete a merger.

After the shareholders have voted to approve the merger, *articles of merger* must be prepared and filed with the Secretary of State's office. Upon the effective date of the merger, the extinguished corporation ceases to exist, and the survivor corporation assumes the assets, debts, liabilities and properties of the extinguished corporation. The shareholders of the extinguished corporation are either cashed out or issued shares of stock in the survivor corporation.

Not all shareholders may be in favor of a proposed merger. However, since only a majority vote of the shareholders is required to approve the merger, a minority shareholder may find himself in the position of owning stock in a corporation to which he has some opposition.

All states allow these *dissenting shareholders* to have their shares appraised and for the dissenters to be paid the fair value of their shares in cash. Dissenters' rights are generally a dissenting shareholder's only remedy if he is opposed to a merger.

Magner et al. v. One Securities Corporation et al.
258 Ga.App. 520, 574 S.E.2d 555 (2002)
Court of Appeals of Georgia

<u>Facts</u>: One Securities Corporation (OSC) and Benefit Plan Service, Inc., (BPS) were private, closely held corporations in the employee benefits plans business. Barbara and Ronald Balser owned two-thirds of the stock of both corporations and Richard Magner owned one third. At a directors meeting, a plan was approved to merge both corporations into Giotto, Inc. The purpose of the mergers was to cash out Magner's interest in the corporations. The directors agreed to pay Magner the "fair value" of his stock, an amount that had been determined by an independent appraiser.

The mergers were approved at a stockholders' meeting, and became effective. Magner was notified of his dissenter's rights, offered the established fair value of his stock, and directed to tender his shares and demand payment if he intended to perfect his dissenter's rights. Demanding several times the appraised value of his stock, Magner refused, and, instead, sought to declare the mergers void.

<u>Issue</u>: Does a minority shareholder have the power to revoke a merger?

<u>*Holding*</u>: In the absence of fraud or illegality, Magner's exclusive remedy with respect to the cash-out mergers was to dissent and seek payment for the fair value of his shares in accordance with the statutory provision. As the commentary to the applicable code section explains: when a majority of shareholders has approved a corporate change, the corporation should be permitted to proceed even if a minority considers the change unwise or disadvantageous and persuades a court that this is correct. Since dissenting shareholders can obtain the fair value of their shares, they are protected from pecuniary loss.

O.C.G.A. § 14-2-1302

(a) A record shareholder of the corporation is entitled to dissent from, and obtain payment of the fair market value of his or her shares in the event of, any of the following corporate actions:

(1) Consummation of a plan of merger to which the corporation is a party …

(2) Consummation of a plan of share exchange to which the corporation is a party as the corporation whose shares will be acquired, if the shareholder is entitled to vote on the plan;

(3) Consummation of a sale or exchange of all or substantially all of the property of the corporation if a shareholder vote is required on the sale or exchange …

(4) An amendment of the articles of incorporation with respect to a class or series of shares that reduces the number of shares of a class or series owned by the shareholder to a fraction of a share if the fractional share so created is to be acquired for cash …

(b) A shareholder entitled to dissent and obtain payment for his or her shares under this article may not challenge the corporate action creating his or her entitlement unless the corporate action fails to comply with procedural requirements of this chapter or the articles of incorporation or bylaws of the corporation or the vote required to obtain approval of the corporate action was obtained by fraudulent and deceptive means, regardless of whether the shareholder has exercised dissenter's rights ...

A dissenting shareholder must follow the procedure provided for by statute in order to exercise his right to an appraisal and buy-out of his shares. Generally, he must notify the corporation of his intent to demand payment for his shares within the time specified. In some states, he must vote against the merger. An obvious point of contention may be the valuation placed upon the shares. If the parties are unable to agree upon a dollar figure, the courts may be called upon to resolve the issue as illustrated by the following case.

Blitch v. Peoples Bank

246 Ga.App. 453, 540 S.E.2d 667 (2000)

Court of Appeals of Georgia

Facts: Dan Blitch owned 763.5 shares of stock in the Peoples Bank, amounting to 5.5% of the Bank's outstanding stock. When the Bank merged with another corporation, Blitch dissented from the merger and sought the fair value of his shares. The Bank filed a petition seeking a determination of the fair value of Blitch's shares. The Bank's expert determined the value of the shares based upon the profitability of the bank and then discounted the share value because Blitch was a minority shareholder and because there was no public market for the shares. He concluded the shares were worth $1,214 per share. Blitch's expert did not apply either a minority shareholder discount or lack of marketability discount and determined each share was worth $2,342.

Issue: What is the proper basis for determining the value of minority shares when the minority shareholders dissent?

Holding: The Georgia statute provides that shareholders who dissent from corporate action must be paid the fair value of their shares, but the statute does not provide a method for determining fair value and does not indicate whether courts should apply discounts for minority shares and lack of marketability. There is no Georgia case law interpreting the statutory meaning of "fair value."

The majority of other jurisdictions have held that minority and marketability discounts should not be applied when determining the fair value of dissenting shareholders' stock. These courts have reasoned that using discounts injects speculation into the appraisal process, fails to give minority shareholders the full proportionate value of their stock, encourages corporations to squeeze out minority shareholders, and penalizes the minority for taking advantage of the protection afforded by dissenters' rights statutes. The Model Act definition of fair value was modified in 1999 to reflect this view.

Based on the clear expression by the amended Model Act and the sound reasoning of the majority view, we find that under Georgia's dissenters' rights statute, a court should not apply minority or marketability discounts in determining the fair value of dissenters' shares.

Parent and Subsidiary Corporations

One corporation may act as the promoter and form another corporation. The creator corporation is called the *parent corporation* and the corporation it creates is called the *subsidiary*. If the parent corporation owns all of the stock of the subsidiary, the new corporation is referred to as a *wholly owned subsidiary*. Whether the parent corporation owns all or a majority of the stock in the subsidiary, the parent can elect the directors of the subsidiary, or a majority of them, and thereby control the policies of the subsidiary.

There are various reasons why a corporation may deem it advisable to create a subsidiary. For instance, a corporation wishing to branch out into a new type of business may create a subsidiary for the new venture. Additionally, if a corporation decides to engage in a high-risk business venture, it may consider it prudent to establish a subsidiary for this purpose so as to protect the parent corporation's assets from potential liability. For example, if British Petroleum had created a subsidiary corporation to own and operate the Deepwater Horizon oil rig, BP, as the parent company, would have been protected from the substantial liability it incurred when the Deepwater Horizon rig exploded in April, 2010, dumping millions of gallons of crude oil into the Gulf of Mexico. Only the assets of the subsidiary corporation would have been at risk rather than the assets of the parent corporation, BP. Of course, had BP followed such a course of action, no doubt there would have been a great outcry from many of the various stakeholders following the Gulf disaster.

A subsidiary corporation is formed just like any other corporation. There are no special requirements simply because the incorporator of the new corporation is itself a corporation, and the articles of incorporation need not recite that the corporation is being formed as a subsidiary of the parent corporation. Additionally, a corporation may create multiple subsidiaries. If the parent corporation creates several subsidiaries, the subsidiaries are referred to as *affiliates* of one another or *brother-sister corporations*.

14.6 Termination of Corporate Existence

In the same way that corporations are created by compliance with state statutes, they can only be terminated or dissolved in accordance with state statutes. Dissolution ends the corporation's existence as a legal person and may come about in two ways. Dissolution may be voluntarily initiated by the board of directors or the corporation may be involuntarily dissolved by the state, the shareholders or the creditors of the corporation.

Once a decision has been made to dissolve a corporation, the process of winding up the corporation's affairs must begin. The corporation's outstanding business must be completed, the assets of the corporation liquidated, the corporation's creditors paid, and the remaining assets distributed to the shareholders.

Dissolution

Dissolution, or the termination of the corporation's existence, may occur for any of several reasons. The corporation's articles of incorporation may have provided for a fixed duration for the corporation or the corporation may have been merged into another corporation or, unfortunately, the corporation's business may simply be unprofitable, making termination judicious. Additionally, the state of incorporation may, given certain circumstances, take action to dissolve the corporation.

A dissolution initiated by the corporation itself is referred to as a *voluntary dissolution*. If the corporation is dissolved because of the expiration of the period of existence stated in the articles of incorporation, no shareholder approval is needed. For all other voluntary dissolutions, however, the shareholders, as the owners, must approve of the decision to dissolve the corporation.

In most cases, a voluntary dissolution begins with the directors of the corporation who, as the corporation's managers, are often in the best position to determine that dissolution is appropriate. The directors must approve the dissolution of the corporation by a majority vote. The shareholders will then meet in a special meeting called for the purpose of considering dissolution. The notice of the special meeting must specify that the meeting is being called for the purpose of considering dissolution. The shareholders will vote on the matter. In most states, and under the MBCA, a simple majority vote of shareholders is required to approve dissolution of the corporation.

Articles of dissolution are prepared and filed with the secretary of state after the dissolution has been approved by both the directors and the shareholders. After the articles of dissolution are filed, the corporation is referred to as a *dissolved corporation*. Even so, the corporation will continue to exist for the purpose of winding up its affairs, liquidating assets, and making final distributions to shareholders. Winding up often requires that the corporation continue to operate for a brief period of time in order to satisfy outstanding contractual obligations, pay debts, and the like. Dissolution, thus, precedes liquidation. To provide greater finality, some states, including California, require that the winding up process precede the dissolution of the corporation. This approach has a distinct advantage in that the articles of dissolution include a recitation that all known debts have been paid and assets distributed to shareholders.

Fulton Paper Company, Inc. v Reeves
212 Ga.App.314, 441 S.E.2d 881 (1994)
Court of Appeals of Georgia

Facts: Reeves is the president of May Fresh Services, Inc., a Georgia corporation. May Fresh was administratively dissolved by the Secretary of State in January, 1992. Reeves continued to do business as usual on behalf of May Fresh. From May through July, 1992, May Fresh purchased $26,892.53 worth of wholesale paper goods from Fulton Paper. It is undisputed that these purchases were inconsistent with the winding up of May Fresh's affairs. When the account went unpaid, Fulton Paper brought suit against Reeves "d/b/a May Fresh, Inc." After the suit was filed, May Fresh applied for and received a certificate of reinstatement.

Issue: Is Reeves personally liable for the debts incurred by May Fresh after dissolution?

Holding: Even after dissolution May Fresh, Inc., continued to exist as a corporate entity but was not authorized to carry on any business except that necessary to wind up and liquidate its business and affairs. Thus, personal liability cannot be based on the theory that Reeves was acting for a nonexistent corporation since the corporation was still in existence. After dissolution, May Fresh had the power, though no legally authorized purpose, to purchase supplies from Fulton Paper in furtherance of its normal course of business. At all times, Fulton Paper dealt with May Fresh as a corporate entity and expected that it could look only to May Fresh for payment on the open account. As no fraud by Reeves has been demonstrated or alleged, Fulton Paper may only look to May Fresh for payment.

Dissolution of a corporation can occur even though the board of directors and shareholders do not desire that the corporation be dissolved. An involuntary dissolution can be commenced by any of three parties – the shareholders of the corporation, the creditors of the corporation, or the state.

A shareholder or group of shareholders may petition a court to dissolve the corporation if they believe the directors of the corporation are operating the corporation in an illegal or fraudulent manner or if the directors or shareholders are deadlocked with regard to the management of the business. Dissolution of the corporation is an extreme remedy; thus, the shareholder bringing the suit must prove that irreparable injury is being done to the corporation, that corporate assets are being wasted, or that the corporation's management has acted in an illegal or fraudulent manner.

A creditor of the corporation may implement a court action for judicial dissolution of the corporation if the corporation cannot pay its debts in the usual course of business. Typically, to prevail, the creditor must establish that the corporation is insolvent and that the creditor has either (a) obtained a judgment against the corporation which the corporation cannot satisfy, or (b) the corporation has stated in writing that it cannot pay the creditor's claim. Since, upon dissolution, the assets of the corporation are used to pay the corporation's debts, a creditor of an insolvent corporation may view dissolution as the only means available to it of obtaining payment.

Finally, because the state has the authority to ensure compliance with state law, the state of incorporation may seek dissolution if the corporation fails to file its annual report with the secretary of state, fails to pay its annual fees, fails to maintain a registered agent for service, and the like. Such a dissolution is called an *administrative dissolution* because is it handled by the secretary of state's office rather than through the courts. The Secretary of State will notify the corporation that grounds for dissolution exists, and if the corporation does not correct the deficiencies, the Secretary of State will simply file a certificate of dissolution. After dissolution, the corporation will continue to exist in order to wind up and liquidate its business. A corporation that has been administratively dissolved may apply for reinstatement.

O.C.G.A. § 14-2-1420

The Secretary of State may commence a proceeding under Code Section 14-2-1421 to dissolve a corporation administratively if:

(1) The state revenue commissioner has certified to the Secretary of State that the corporation has failed to file a license or occupation tax return and that a period of one year has expired since the last day permitted for timely filing without the filing and payment of all required license and occupation taxes and penalties by the corporation; provided, however, that dissolution proceedings shall be stayed so long as the corporation is contesting, in good faith, in any appropriate proceeding the alleged grounds for dissolution;

(2) The corporation does not deliver its annual registration to the Secretary of State, together with all required fees and penalties, within 60 days after it is due;

(3) The corporation is without a registered agent or registered office in this state for 60 days or more;

(4) The corporation does not notify the Secretary of State within 60 days that its registered agent or registered office has been changed, that its registered agent has resigned, or that its registered office has been discontinued;

(5) The corporation pays a fee as required to be collected by the Secretary of State pursuant to the Code by a check or some other form of payment which is dishonored and the corporation or its incorporator or its agent does not submit payment for said dishonored payment within 60 days from notice of nonpayment issued by the Secretary of State; or

(6) Any notice which is required to be published by Code Section 14-2-201.1, 14-2-1006.1, 14-2-1105.1, or 14-2-1403.1 has not been published.

Liquidation

After dissolution, the corporation must conduct the process of winding up its affairs, called *liquidation*. Liquidation is basically the process of the corporation paying its debts, distributing its assets and apportioning the profit or loss.

As a part of the liquidation process, creditors of the corporation are given notice of the dissolution of the corporation and an opportunity to submit claims to the corporation for payment. In addition to notifying creditors of known claims, the corporation will give notice to the public, by publication, so that if there are any unknown claims against the corporation, they can be submitted and disposed of. If a creditor receives proper notice and does not file a claim with the corporation, the claim will be barred.

The liquidation process involves the following:

- Collecting the assets of the corporation;
- Disposing of any assets that will not be distributed in kind to shareholders;
- Discharging all liabilities by paying creditors or otherwise making provision for the discharge of obligations; and
- Distributing the remaining property to the shareholders in accordance with their respective interests.

The final aspect of liquidation is the distribution of assets to the shareholders of the corporation. After all debts have been paid, the remaining corporate assets are distributed to the shareholders who will receive a pro rata portion of the assets based on the number of shares of stock they own. Distribution must take into account the rights of each particular class of stock. For instance, preferred shareholders may have a priority right to the distribution of assets upon dissolution if such a priority is provided for in the articles in incorporation. The assets of the corporation may be converted into cash prior to distribution or they may be distributed in kind.

Review Questions and Exercises

1. Identify the advantages and disadvantages to a corporation of raising money by the issuance of debt securities.

2. Define the business judgment rule and its purpose.

3. What remedies exist for a minority shareholder who objects to the merger or consolidation of his corporation with another?

4. What is meant by the phrase "conducting business?" Why must a foreign corporation qualify to do business in a state other than the corporation's state of formation? What is the consequence of failing to qualify before doing business in a foreign state?

5. Identify the three parties who may initiate the dissolution of a corporation and discuss the factors that may lead to a dissolution.

6. What role do the directors of a corporation play in the management of the corportation? What is the role of the officers of the corporation with regard to management?

7. Stuart Hudson Holding Corp. is a Georgia corporation whose primary business is long-haul trucking. The directors of the company have decided that the corporate name should be changed to provide third parties with an indication of the type of business SHHC conducts. What steps are necessary to accomplish this?

8. Why would a corporation desire to restate its articles of incorporation? Discuss the procedure to be followed in order to restate the articles of incorporation.

9. Clarke Products, Inc., has decided to merge with NuTech, Inc. NuTech will be the survivor. Is shareholder approval required? Why? Which shareholders must vote on the merger? What will happen to the debts Clarke Products owes to its creditors and to the assets of Clarke Products?

10. Aaron, Avery and Adam form AAA Windows, Inc., a corporation which will manufacture and sell replacement windows. Each owns 30% of the stock and each serves on the board of directors. Additionally, Aaron serves as the corporation's president, Avery as its vice-president, and Adam serves as its secretary/treasurer. The remaining 10% of the stock is held by two investors who do not work for the corporation. Aaron, Avery and Adam ask their friends, Carl, who is in the home construction business, and David, who is in marketing, to serve as directors.

    (c) Who are the inside directors? Who are the outside directors?
    (d) Disputes arise, with Aaron and Adam taking one position and Avery taking another. If Aaron and Adam want to remove Avery from the board of directors, how may they accomplish this?
    (e) AAA Windows, Inc., was formed as a Georgia corporation and originally operated only in Georgia, but later expanded its operations into several neighboring states. The decision to expand was based upon market surveys and other research. Unfortunately, this expansion came immediately before the collapse of the housing market and has been a failure, putting the entire business at risk. Are the directors liable to the minority shareholders for their losses? Why or why not?

Practical Applications

1. Roger Wahl was the sole shareholder of Roger Wahl, C.P.A., P.C., and worked there from the time it opened until March, 1993, when Wahl was being investigated for tax evasion. Wahl subsequently plead guilty. On August 16, 1993, the Wahl firm sold its client files, client contracts, customer lists, computer software, and computer records to Serotta, Maddocks & Devanny, a competing accounting firm.

That afternoon, Maddocks went the Wahl firm's address to tell the remaining Wahl firm employees about the sale. David Crews, the other CPA in the Wahl firm decided to start his own accounting firm. Using the Wahl firm customer list, he and other Wahl employees drafted a letter announcing the formation of the new business and enclosing a release for customers to sign. When they left, Crews and others took computer back-up tapes, equipment, supplies.

The corporate entity, the Wahl firm, now controlled by Serotta, sued Crews and others, alleging conversion and misappropriation of trade secrets including customer lists. Before the case could be tried, the Wahl firm was administratively dissolved.

Consider:
(a) Did the Wahl firm have the capacity to pursue its lawsuit against Crews after the firm was dissolved?
(b) Was the action of the Wahl firm in filing the lawsuit properly a part of the process of "concluding its business?"

See – *Crew, et al. v. Roger Wahl, C.P.A., P.C.,* 238 Ga.App. 892, 520 S.E.2d 727 (1999), Georgia Court of Appeals.

2. Graham and Black were each 50% shareholders of a building supplies business. When they became wholly unable to agree on the management of the business, Graham filed a petition to dissolve the corporation.

Consider:
(a) Were the shareholders deadlocked so as to justify the dissolution of the business?
(b) Was there any way to break the deadlock?
(c) Did the deadlock threaten irreparable harm to the corporation?
(d) Did the court have the power to dissolve the corporation?

See – *Black v. Graham,* Ga. 154, 464 S.E.2d 814 (1996), Supreme Court of Georgia.

Constitution of the United States

We the People of the United States, in Order to form a more perfect Union, establish Justice, insure domestic Tranquility, provide for the common defense, promote the general Welfare, and secure the Blessings of Liberty to ourselves and our Posterity, do ordain and establish the Constitution for the United States of America.

Article I

Section 1. All legislative Powers herein granted shall be vested in a Congress of the United States, which shall consist of a Senate and House of Representatives.

Section 2. The House of Representatives shall be composed of Members chosen every second Year by the People of the several States, and the Electors in each State shall have the Qualifications requisite for Electors of the most numerous Branch of the State Legislature.

No Person shall be a Representative who shall not have attained the Age of twenty five Years, and been seven Years a Citizen of the United States, and who shall not, when elected, be an Inhabitant of that State in which he shall be chosen.

Representatives and direct Taxes shall be apportioned among the several States which may be included within this Union, according to their respective Numbers, which shall be determined by adding to the whole Number of free Persons, including those bound to Service for a Term of Years, and excluding Indians not taxed, three fifths of all other Persons. The actual Enumeration shall be made within three Years after the first Meeting of the Congress of the United States, and within every subsequent Term of ten Years, in such Manner as they shall be Law direct. The number of Representatives shall not exceed one for every thirty Thousand, but each State shall have at Least one Representative; and until such enumeration shall be made, the State of New Hampshire shall be entitled to chose three, Massachusetts eight, Rhode Island and Providence Plantations one, Connecticut five, New York six, New Jersey four, Pennsylvania eight, Delaware one, Maryland six, Virginia ten, North Carolina five, South Carolina five, and Georgia three.

When vacancies happen in the Representation from any State, the Executive Authority thereof shall issue Writs of Election to fill such vacancies.

The House of Representatives shall chuse their Speaker and other Officers; and shall have the sole Power of Impeachment.

Section 3. The Senate of the United States shall be composed of two Senators from each State, chosen by the Legislature thereof, for six Years; and each Senator shall have one vote.

Immediately after they shall be assembled in Consequence of the first Election, they shall be divided as equally as may be into three Classes. The Seats of the Senators of the first Class shall be vacated at the Expiration of the second Year, of the second Class at the Expiration of the fourth Year, and of the third Class at the Expiration of the sixth Year, so that one third may be chosen every second Year; and if Vacancies happen by Resignation or otherwise, during the Recess of the Legislature of any State, the Executive thereof may make temporary Appointments until the next Meeting of the Legislature, which shall then fill such vacancies.

No person shall be a Senator who shall not have attained the Age of thirty Years, and been nine Years a Citizen of the United States, and who shall not, when elected, be an Inhabitant of that State for which she shall be chosen.

The Vice President of the United States shall be President of the Senate, but shall have no Vote, unless they be equally divided.

The Senate shall chuse their other Officers, and also a President pro tempore, in the absence of the Vice President, or when he shall exercise the Office of the President of the United States.

The Senate shall have the sole power to try all Impeachments. When sitting for that Purpose, they shall be an Oath or Affirmation. When the President of the United States is tried, the Chief Justice shall preside: And no Person shall be convicted without the concurrence of two thirds of the Members present.

Judgment in Cases of Impeachment shall not extend further than to removal from Office, and disqualification to hold and enjoy any Office of honor, Trust or Profit under the United States; but the Party convicted shall nevertheless be liable and subject to Indictment, Trial, and Punishment, according to Law;

Section 4. The Times, Places and Manner of holding Elections for Senators and Representatives, shall be prescribed in each State by the Legislature thereof: but the Congress may at any time by Law make or alter such Regulations, except as to the Places of chusing Senators.

The Congress shall assemble at least once in every Year, and such Meeting shall be on the first Monday in December, unless they shall be Law appoint a different Day.

Section 5. Each House shall be the Judge of Elections, Returns and Qualifications of its own Members, and a Majority of each shall constitute a Quorum to do Business; but a small Number may adjourn from day to day, and may be authorized to compel the Attendance of absent Members, in such Manner, and under such Penalties as each House may provide.

Each House may determine the Rules of its Proceedings, punish its Members for disorderly Behaviour, and, with the Concurrence of two thirds, expel a Member.

Each House shall keep a Journal of its Proceedings, and from time to time publish the same, excepting such Parts as may in their Judgment require Secrecy; and the Yeas and Nays of the Members of either House on any question shall, at the Desire of one fifth of those Present, be entered on the Journal.

Neither House, during the Session of Congress, shall, without the Consent of the other, adjourn for more than three days, nor to any other Place than that in which the two Houses shall be sitting.

Section 6. The Senators and Representatives shall receive a Compensation for their Services, to be ascertained by Law, and paid out of the Treasury of the United States. They shall in all Cases, except Treason, Felony and Breach of the Peace, be privileged from Arrest during their Attendance at the Session of their respective Houses, and in going to and returning from the same; and for any Speech or Debate in either House, they shall not be questioned in any other Place.

No Senator or Representative shall, during the Time for which he was elected, be appointed to any civil Office under the Authority of the United States, which shall have been created, or the Emoluments whereof shall have been increased during such time; and no Person holding any Office under the United States, shall be a Member of either House during his Continuance in Office.

Section 7. All Bills for raising Revenue shall originate in the House of Representatives; but the Senate may propose or concur with Amendments as on other Bills.

Every Bill which shall have passed the House of Representatives and the Senate, shall, before it become a Law, be presented to the President of the United States; If he approve he shall sign it, but if not he shall return it, with his Objections to that House in which it shall have originated, who shall enter the Objections at large on their Journal, and proceed to reconsider it. If after such Reconsideration two thirds of that House shall agree to pass the Bill, it shall be sent, together with the Objections, to the other House, by which it shall likewise be reconsidered, and if the other House, by which it shall likewise be reconsidered, and approved by two thirds of that House, it shall become a Law. But in all such Cases the Votes of both Houses shall be determined by Yeas and Nays, and the Names of the Persons voting for and against the Bill shall be entered on the Journal of each House respectively. If any Bill shall not be returned by the President with ten Days (Sundays excepted) after it shall have been presented to him, the Same shall be a Law, in like Manner as if he had signed it, unless the Congress by their Adjournment prevent its Return, in which Case it shall not be a Law.

Every Order, Resolution, or Vote to which the Concurrence of the Senate and House of Representatives may be necessary (except on a question of Adjournment) shall be presented to the President of the United States; and before the Same shall take Effect, shall be approved by him, or being disapproved by him, shall be repassed by two thirds of the Senate and House of Representatives, according to the Rules and Limitations prescribed in the Case of a Bill.

Section 8. The Congress shall have Power to lay and collect Taxes, Duties, Imposts, and Excises, to pay the Debts and provide for the common Defence and general Welfare of the United States, but all Duties, Imposts, and Excises shall be uniform throughout the United States;

To borrow Money on the credit of the United States;

To regulate Commerce with foreign Nations, and among the several States, and with the Indian Tribes;

To establish an uniform Rule of Naturalization, and uniform Laws on the subject of Bankruptcies throughout the United States;

To coin Money, regulate the Value thereof, and of foreign Coin, and fix the Standard of Weights and Measures;

To provide for the Punishment of counterfeiting the Securities and Current Coin of the United States;

To establish Post Offices and post Roads;

To promote the Progress of Science and useful Arts, by securing for limited Times to Authors and Inventors the exclusive Right to their respective Writings and Discoveries;

To constitute Tribunals inferior to the supreme Court;

To define and punish Piracies and Felonies committed on the high Seas, and Offenses against the Law of Nations;

To declare War, grant Letters of Marque and Reprisal, and make Rules concerning Captures on Land and Water;

To raise and support Armies, but no Appropriation of Money to that Use shall be for a longer Term than two Years;

To provide and maintain a Navy;

To make Rules for the Government and Regulation of the land and naval Forces;

To provide for calling forth the Militia to execute the Laws of the Union, suppress Insurrections and repel Invasions;

To provide for organizing, arming, and disciplining, the Militia, and for governing such Part of them as may be employed in the Service of the United States, reserving to the States respectively, the Appointment of the Officers, and the Authority of training the Militia according to the discipline described by Congress;

To exercise exclusive Legislation in all Cases whatsoever, over such District (not exceeding ten Miles square) as may, by Cession of particular States, and the Acceptance of Congress, become the Seat of the Government of the United States, and to exercise like Authority over all Places purchased by the Consent of the Legislature of the State in which the Same shall be, for the Erection of Forts, Magazines, Arsenals, dock-Yards, and other needful Buildings; - And

To make all Laws which shall be necessary and proper for carrying into Execution the foregoing Powers, and all other Powers vested by this Constitution in the Government of the United States, or in any Department or Officer thereof.

Section 9. The Migration or Importation of such Persons as any of the States now existing shall think proper to admit, shall not be prohibited by the Congress prior to the Year one thousand eight hundred and eight, but a Tax or Duty may be imposed on such Importation, not exceeding ten dollars for each Person.

The Privilege of the Writ of Habeas Corpus shall not be suspended, unless when in Cases of Rebellion or Invasion the public safety may require it.

No Bill of Attainder or ex post facto Law shall be passed.

No Capitation, or other direct, Tax shall be laid, unless in Proportion to the Census or Enumeration herein before directed to be taken.

No Tax or Duty shall be laid on Articles exported from any State.

No Preference shall be given by any Regulation of Commerce or Revenue to the Ports of one State over those of another; nor shall Vessels bound to, or from, one State, be obliged to enter, clear, or pay Duties in another.

No Money shall be drawn from the Treasury, but in Consequence of Appropriations made by Laws; and a regular Statement and Account of the Receipts and Expenditures of all public Money shall be published from time to time.

No Title of Nobility shall be granted by the United States; And no Person holding any Office of Profit or Trust under them, shall, without, the Consent of the Congress, accept of any present, Emolument, Office, or Title, of any kind whatever, from any King, Prince, or foreign State.

Section 10. No State shall enter into any Treaty, Alliance, or Confederation; grant Letters of Marque and Reprisal; coin Money; emit Bills of Credit; make any Thing but gold and silver Coin a Tender in Payment of Debts; pass any Bill of Attainder, ex post facto Law, or Law impairing the Obligation of Contracts, or grant any Title of Nobility.

No State shall, without the Consent of the Congress, lay any Imposts or Duties on Imports or Exports, except what may be absolutely necessary for executing its inspection Laws; and the net Produce of all Duties and Imports, laid by any State on Imports or Exports, shall be for the Use of the Treasury of the United States; and all such Laws shall be subject to the Revision and Controul of the Congress.

No State shall, without the consent of Congress, lay any Duty of Tonnage, keep Troops, or Ships of War in time of Peace, enter into any Agreement or Compact with another State, or with a foreign Power, or engage in War, unless actually invaded, or in such imminent Danger as will not admit of delay.

Article II

Section 1. The executive Power shall be vested in a President of the United States of America. He shall hold his Office during the Term of four Years, and, together with the Vice President, chosen for the same Term, be elected, as follows:

Each State shall appoint, in such Manner as the Legislature thereof may direct, a Number of Electors, equal to the whole Number of Senators and Representatives to which the State may be entitled in the Congress: but no Senator or Representative, or Person holding an Office of Trust or Profit under the United States, shall be appointed as Elector.

The Electors shall meet in their respective States, and vote by Ballot for two Persons, of whom one at least shall not be an Inhabitant of the same State with themselves. And they shall make a list of all the Persons voted for, and of the Number of Votes for each; which List they shall sign and certify, and transmit sealed to the Seat of the Government of the United States, directed to the President of the Senate. The President of the Senate shall, in the presence of the Senate and House of Representatives, open all the Certificates, and the Votes shall be counted. The Person having the greatest Number of Votes shall be the President, if such Number be a Majority of the whole Number of Electors appointed; and if there be more than one who have such Majority, and have an equal Number of Votes, then the House of Representatives shall immediately chuse by Ballot one of them for President; and if no Person have a Majority, then from the five highest on the List the said House shall in like Manner chuse the President. But in chusing the President, the Votes shall be taken by States, the Representation from each State having one Vote; A quorum for this Purpose shall consist of a Member or Members from two thirds of the States, and a Majority of all the States shall be necessary to a Choice. In every Case, after the Choice of the President, the Person having the greatest Number of Votes of the Electors shall be the Vice President. But if there should remain two or more who have equal Votes, the Senate shall chuse from them by Ballot the Vice President.

The Congress may determine the Time of Chusing, the Electors, and the Day on which they shall give their Votes, which Day shall be the same throughout the United States.

No person except a natural born Citizen, or a Citizen of the United States, at the time of the Adoption of this Constitution, shall be eligible to the Office of President, neither shall any Person be eligible to that Office who shall not have attained to the Age of thirty five Years, and been fourteen Years a Resident within the United States.

In Case of the Removal of the President from Office, or of his Death, Resignation, or Inability to discharge the Powers and Duties of the said Office, the Same shall devolve on the Vice President, and the Congress may by Law provide for the Case of Removal, Death, Resignation or Inability, both of the President and Vice President, declaring what Officer shall then act as President, and such Officer shall act accordingly, until the Disability be removed, or a President shall be elected.

The President shall, as stated Times, receive for his Services, a Compensation, which shall neither be increased nor diminished during the Period for which he shall have been elected, and he shall not receive within that Period any other Emolument from the United States, or any of them.

Before he enter on the Execution of his Office, he shall take the following Oath or Affirmation: - "I do solemnly swear (or affirm) that I will faithfully execute the Office of President of the United States, and will to the best of my Ability, preserve, protect, and defend the Constitution of the United States."

Section 2. The President shall be Commander in Chief of the Army and Navy of the United States, and of the Militia of the several States, when called into the actual Service of the United States; he may require the Opinion, in writing, of the principal Officer in each of the Executive Departments, upon any Subject relating to the Duties of their respective Offices, and he shall have Power to grant Reprieves and Pardons for Offences against the United States, except in Cases of Impeachment.

He shall have Power, by and with the Advice and Consent of the Senate, to make Treaties, providing two thirds of the Senators present concur; and he shall nominate, and by and with the Advice and Consent of the Senate, shall appoint Ambassadors, other public Ministers and Consuls, Judges of the supreme Court, and all other Officers of the United States, whose Appointments are not herein otherwise provided for, and which shall be established by Law; but the Congress may by Law vest the Appointment of such inferior Officers, as they think proper, in the President alone, in the Courts of Law, or in the Heads of Departments.

The President shall have Power to fill up all Vacancies that may happen during the Recess of the Senate, by granting Commissions which shall expire at the End of their next Session.

Section 3. He shall from time to time give to the Congress Information of the State of the Union, and recommend to their Consideration such Measures as he shall judge necessary and expedient; he may, on extraordinary Occasions, convene both Houses, or either of them, and in Case of Disagreement between them, with Respect to the time of Adjournment, he may adjourn them to such Time as he shall think proper, he shall receive Ambassadors and other public Ministers; he shall take Care that the Laws be faithfully executed, and shall Commission all the Offices of the United States.

Section 4. The President, Vice President and all civil Officers of the United States, shall be removed from Office on Impeachment for, and Conviction of, Treason, Bribery, or other high Crimes and Misdemeanors.

Article III

Section 1. The judicial Power of the United States, shall be vested in one supreme Court, and in such inferior Courts as the Congress may from time to time ordain and establish. The Judges, both of the supreme and inferior Courts, shall hold their Offices during good Behaviour, and shall, at Times, receive for their Services, a Compensation, which shall not be diminished during their Continuance in Office.

Section 2. The judicial Power shall extend to all Cases, in Law and Equity, arising under this Constitution, the Laws of the United States, and Treaties made, or which shall be made, under their Authority; -to all Cases affecting Ambassadors, other public Ministers and Consuls; -to all Cases of admiralty and maritime Jurisdiction; -to Controversies to which the United States shall be a Party; -to controversies between two or more States; -between a State and Citizens of another State; -between Citizens of different States; -between Citizens of the same State claiming Lands under Grants of different States; and between a State, or the Citizens thereof, and foreign States, Citizens or Subjects.

In all Cases affecting Ambassadors, other public Ministers and Consuls, and those in which a State shall be Party, the supreme Court shall have original jurisdiction. In all the other Cases before mentioned, the supreme Fact, with such Exceptions, and under such Regulations as the Congress shall make.

The Trial of all Crimes, except in Cases of Impeachment, shall be by Jury; and such Trial shall be held in the State where the said Crimes shall have been committed; but when not committed within any State, the Trial shall be at such Place or Places as the Congress may by Law have directed.

Section 3. Treason against the United States, shall consist only in levying War against the, or in adhering to their Enemies, giving them Aid and Comfort. No Person shall be convicted of Treason unless on the Testimony of two Witnesses to the same overt Act, or on Confession in open Court.

The Congress shall have Power to declare the Punishment of Treason, but no Attainder of Treason shall work Corruption of Blood, or Forfeiture except during the Life of the Person attainted.

Article IV

Section 1. Full Faith and Credit shall be given in each State to the public Acts, Records, and judicial Proceedings of every other State. And the Congress may by general Laws prescribe the Manner in which such Arts, Records and Proceedings shall be proved and the Effect thereof.

Section 2. The Citizens of each State shall be entitled to all Privileges and Immunities of Citizens in the several States.

A Person charged in any State with Treason, Felony, or other Crime, who shall flee from Justice, and be found in another State, shall on Demand of the executive Authority of the State form which he fled, be delivered up, to be removed to the State having Jurisdiction of the Crime.

No Person held to Service or Labour in one State, under the Laws thereof, escaping into another, shall, in Consequence of any Law or Regulation therein, be discharged from such Service or Labour, but shall be delivered up on Claim of the Party to whom such Service or Labour may be due.

Section 3. New States may be admitted by the Congress into this Union; but no new State shall be formed or erected within the Jurisdiction of any other State; nor any State be formed by the Junction of two or more States, or Parts of States, without the Consent of the Legislatures of the States concerned as well as the Congress.

The Congress shall have Power to dispose of and make all needful Rules and Regulations respecting the Territory of other Property belonging to the United States; and nothing in this Constitution shall be so construed as to Prejudice any Claims of the United States, or any particular State.

Section 4. The United States shall guarantee to every State in this Union a Republican Form of Government, and shall protect each of them against Invasion; and on Application of the Legislature, or of the Executive (when the Legislature cannot be convened) against domestic Violence.

Article V

The Congress, whenever two thirds of both Houses shall deem it necessary, shall propose Amendments to the Constitution, or, on the Application of the Legislatures of two thirds of the several States, shall call a Convention for proposing Amendments, which, in either Case, shall be valid to all Intents and Purposes, as Part of this Constitution, when ratified by the Legislatures of three fourths of the several States, or by Conventions in three fourths thereof, as the one or the other Mode of Ratification may be proposed by the Congress; Provided that no Amendment which may be made prior to the Year One thousand eight hundred and eight shall in any Manner affect the first and fourth Clauses in the Ninth Section of the first Article; and that no State, without its Consent, shall be deprived of its equal Suffrage in the Senate.

Article VI

All Debts contracted and Engagements entered into, before the Adoption of this Constitution, shall be as valid against the United States under this Constitution, as under the Confederation.

This Constitution, and the Laws of the United States which shall be made in Pursuance thereof; and all Treaties made, or which shall be made, under the Authority of the United States, shall be the supreme Law of the Land; and the Judges in every State shall be bound thereby, any Thing in the Constitution or Laws of any State to the Contrary notwithstanding.

The Senators and Representatives before mentioned, and the Members of the several State Legislatures, and all executive and judicial Officers, both of the United States and of the Several States, shall be bound by Oath or Affirmation, to support this Constitution; but not religious Test shall ever be required as a Qualification to any Office or public Trust under the United States.

Article VII

The Ratification of the Conventions of nine States, shall be sufficient for the Establishment of this Constitution between the States so ratifying the Same.

Amendment I (1791)

Congress shall make no law respecting an establishment of religion, or prohibiting the free exercise thereof; of abridging the freedom of speech, or the press; or the right of the people peaceably to assemble, and to petition the Government for a redress of grievances.

Amendment II (1791)

A well regulated Militia, being necessary to the security for a free State, the right of the people to keep and bear Arms, shall not be infringed.

Amendment III (1791)

No Soldier shall, in time of peace be quartered in any house, without the consent of the Owner, nor in time of war, but in a manner to be prescribed by law.

Amendment IV (1791)

The right of the people to be secure in their persons, houses, papers, and effects, against unreasonable searches and seizures, shall not be violated, and no Warrants shall issue, but upon probable cause, supported by Oath or Affirmation, and particularly describing the place to be searched, and the persons or things to be seized.

Amendment V (1791)

No person shall be held to answer for a capital, or otherwise infamous crime, unless on a presentment or indictment of a Grand Jury, except in cases arising in the land or naval forces, or in the Militia, when in actual service in time of War or public danger; nor shall any person be subject for the same offense to be twice put in jeopardy of life or limb; nor shall be compelled in any criminal case to be a witness against himself, nor be deprived of life, liberty, or property, without due process of law; not shall private property be taken for public use, without just compensation.

Amendment VI (1791)

In all criminal prosecutions, the accused shall enjoy the right to a speedy and public trial, by an impartial jury of the State and district wherein the crime shall have been committed, which district shall have been previously ascertained b law, and to be informed of the nature and cause of the accusation; to be confronted with the Witnesses against him; to have compulsory process for obtaining witnesses in his favor, and to have the Assistance of counsel for his defence.

Amendment VII (1791)

In suits at common law, where the value in controversy shall exceed twenty dollars, the right of trial by jury shall be preserved, and no fact tried by a jury, shall be otherwise re-examined in any Court of the United States, than according to the rules of the common law.

Amendment VIII (1791)

Excessive bail shall not be required, nor excessive fines imposed, nor cruel and unusual punishments inflicted.

Amendment IX (1791)

The enumeration in the Constitution, of certain rights, shall not be construed to deny or disparage others retained by the people.

Amendment X (1791)

The powers not delegated to the United States by the Constitution, nor prohibited by it to the States, are reserved to the States respectively, or to the people.

Amendment XI (1798)

The judicial power of the United States shall not be construed to extend to any suit in law or equity, commenced or prosecuted against one of the United States by Citizens of another State, or by Citizens or Subjects of any Foreign State.

Amendment XII (1804)

The Electors shall meet in their respective states and vote by ballot for President and Vice-President, one of whom, at least, shall not be an inhabitant of the same state with themselves; they shall name in their ballots the person voted for as President, and in distinct ballots the person voted for as Vice-President, and they shall make distinct lists of all persons voted for as President , and of all persons voted for as Vice-President, and of the number of votes for each, which lists they shall sign and certify, and transmit sealed to the seat of the government of the United States, directed to the President of the Senate; -The President of the Senate shall, in the presence of the Senate and House of Representatives, open all the certificates and the votes shall then be counted; -The person having the greatest number of votes for President, shall be the President, if such number be a majority of the whole number of Electors appointed; and if no person have such majority, then from the persons having the highest numbers not exceeding three on the list of those voted for as President, the House of Representatives shall choose immediately, by ballot, the President. But in choosing the President, the votes shall be taken by states, the representation from each state having one vote; a quorum for this purpose shall consist of a member or members from two-thirds of the states, and a majority of all the states shall be necessary to a choice. And if the House of Representatives shall not choose a President whenever the right of choices shall devolve upon the, before the fourth day of March next following, then the Vice-President shall act as President, as in the case of the death or other constitutional disability of the President. The person having the greatest number of votes as Vice-President, shall be the Vice-President, if such number be a majority fo the whole number of Electors appointed, and if no person have a majority, then from the two highest numbers on the list, the Senate shall choose the Vice-President; a quorum for the purpose shall consist of two-thirds of the whole number of Senators, and a majority of the whole number shall be necessary to a choice. But no person constitutionally ineligible to the office of President shall be eligible to that of the Vice-President of the United States.

Amendment XIII (1865)

Section 1. Neither slavery nor involuntary servitude, except as a punishment for crime whereof the party shall have been duly convicted, shall exist within the United States, or any place subject to their jurisdiction.

Section 2. Congress shall have power to enforce this article by appropriate legislation.

Amendment XIV (1868)

Section 1. All persons born or naturalized in the United States, and subject to the jurisdiction thereof, are citizens of the United States and of the State wherein they reside. No State shall make or enforce any law which shall abridge the privileges or immunities of citizens of the United States; nor shall any State deprive any person of life, liberty, or property, without due process of law; nor deny to any person within its jurisdiction the equal protection of the laws.

Section 2. Representatives shall be appointed among the several States according to their respective numbers, counting the whole number of persons in each State, excluding Indians not taxed. But when the right to vote at any election for the choice of electors for President and Vice President of the United States, Representatives in Congress, the Executive and Judicial officers of a State, or the members of the Legislature thereof, is denied to any of the male inhabitants of such State, being twenty-one years of age, and citizens of the United States, or in any way abridged, except for participation in rebellion, or other crime, the basis of representation therein shall be reduced in the proportion which the number of such male citizens shall bear the whole number of male citizens twenty-one years of age in such State.

Section 3. No person shall be a Senator or Representative in Congress, or elector of President and Vice President, or hold any office, civil or military, under the United States, or under any State, who, having previously taken an oath, as a member of congress, or as an officer of the United States, or as a member of any State legislature, or as an executive or judicial officer of any State, to support the Constitution of the United States, shall have engaged in insurrection or rebellion against the same, or given aid or comfort to the enemies thereof. But Congress may by a vote of two-thirds of each House, remove such disability.

Section 4. The validity of the public debt of the United States, authorized by law, including debts incurred for payment of pensions and bounties for services in suppressing insurrection of rebellion, shall not be questions. But neither the United States nor any State shall assume or pay any debt or obligation incurred in aid of insurrection of rebellion against the United States, or any claim for the loss or emancipation of any slave; but all such debts, obligations and claims shall be held illegal and void.

Section 5. The Congress shall have power to enforce, by appropriate legislation, the provision of this article.

Amendment XV (1870)

Section 1. The right of citizens of the United States to vote shall not be denied or abridged by the United States or by any State on account of race, color, or previous condition of servitude.

Section 2. The Congress shall have power to enforce this article by appropriate legislation.

Amendment XVI (1913)

The Congress shall have power to lay and collect taxes on incomes, from whatever source derived, without apportionment among the several States, and without regard to any census or enumeration.

Amendment XVII (1913)

The Senate of the United States shall be composed of two Senators from each State, elected by the people thereof, for six years; and each Senator shall have one vote. The electors in each State shall have the qualifications requisite for electors of the most numerous branch of the State legislatures.

When vacancies happen in the representation of any State in the Senate, the executive authority of each State shall issue writs of election to fill such vacancies; *Provided*, That the legislature of any State may empower the executive thereof to make temporary appointments until the people fill the vacancies by election as the legislature may direct.

This amendment shall not be construed as to affect the election or term of any Senator chosen before it becomes valid as part of the Constitution.

Amendment XVIII (1919)

Section 1. After one year from the ratification of this article the manufacture, sale, or transportation of intoxicating liquors within, the importation thereof into, or the exportation thereof from the United States and all territory subject to the jurisdiction thereof for beverage purposes is hereby prohibited.

Section 2. The Congress and the several States shall have concurrent power to enforce this article by appropriate legislation.

Section 3. This article shall be inoperative unless it shall have been ratified as an amendment to the Constitution by the legislatures of the several States, as provided in the Constitution, within seven years from the date of the submission hereof to the States by the Congress.

Amendment XIX (1920)

The right of citizens of the United States to vote shall not be denied or abridged by the United States or by any State on account of sex.

Congress shall have power to enforce this article by appropriate legislation.

Amendment XX (1933)

Section 1. The terms of the President and Vice President shall end at noon on the 20th day of January, and the terms of Senators and Representatives at noon on the 3rd day of January, of the years in which such terms would have ended if this article had not been ratified; and the terms of their successors shall then begin.

Section 2. The Congress shall assemble at least once in every year, and such meeting shall begin at noon on the 3rd day of January, unless they shall by law appoint a different day.

Section 3. If, at the time fixed for the beginning of the term of the President, the President elect shall have died, the Vice President elect shall become President. If a President shall not have been chosen before the time fixed for the beginning of his term, or if the President elect shall have failed to qualify, then the Vice President elect shall act as President until a President shall have qualified; and the Congress may by law provide for the case, wherein neither a President elect nor a Vice President shall have qualified, declaring who shall then act as President, or the manner in which one who is to act shall be selected and such person shall act accordingly until a President or Vice President shall have qualified.

Section 4. The Congress may by law provide for the case of the death of any of the persons form whom the House of Representatives may choose a President whenever the right of choice shall have devolved upon them, and for the case of the death of any of the persons from whom the Senate may choose a Vice President whenever the right of choice shall have devolved upon them.

Section 5. Sections 1 and 2 shall take effect on the 15th day of October following the ratification of this article.

Section 6. This article shall be inoperative unless it shall have been ratified as an amendment to the Constitution by the legislatures of three-fourths of the several States within seven years from the date of its submission.

Amendment XXI (1933)

Section 1. The eighteenth article of amendment to the Constitution of the United States is hereby repealed.

Section 2. The transportation or importation into any State, Territory, or possession of the United States for delivery or use therein of intoxicating liquors, in violation of the laws thereof, is hereby prohibited.

Section 3. This article shall be inoperative unless it shall have been ratified as an amendment to the Constitution by conventions in the several States, as provided in the Constitution, within seven years from the date of the submission hereof to the States by the Congress.

Amendment XXII (1933)

Section 1. No person shall be elected to the office of the President more than twice, and no person who has held the office or President, acted as President, for more than two years of a term to which some other person was elected President shall be elected to the office of the President more than once. But this Article shall not apply to any person holding the office of President when this Article was proposed by the Congress, and shall not prevent any person who may be holding the office of president, or acting as President, during the term within which this Article becomes operative from holding the office of President, or acting as President during the remainder of such term.

Section 2. This article shall be inoperative unless it shall have been ratified as an amendment to the Constitution by the legislatures of three-fourths of the several States within seven years from the date of its submission to the States by the Congress.

Amendment XXIII (1961)

Section 1. The District constituting the seat of Government of the United States shall appoint in such manner as the Congress may direct:

A number of electors of President and Vice President equal to the whole number of Senators and Representatives in Congress to which the District would be entitled if it were a State, but in no event more than the least populous State; they shall be in addition to those appointed by the States, but they shall be considered, for the purposes of the election of President and Vice President, to be electors appointed by a State; and they shall meet in the District and perform such duties as provided by the twelfth article of amendment.

Section 2. This article shall be inoperative unless it shall have been ratified as an amendment to the Constitution by the legislatures of three-fourths of the several States within seven years from the date of its submission to the States by the Congress.

Amendment XXIV (1964)

Section 1. The right of citizens of the United States to vote in any primary or other election for President or Vice President, for electors for President or Vice President, or for Senator or Representative in Congress, shall not be denied or abridged by the United States or any State by reason of failure to pay any poll tax or other tax.

Section 2. The Congress shall have power to enforce this article by appropriate legislation.

Amendment XXV (1967)

Section 1. In case of the removal of the President from office or of his death or resignation, the Vice President shall become President.

Section 2. Whenever there is a vacancy in the office of the Vice President, the President shall nominate a Vice President who shall take office upon confirmation by a majority vote of both Houses of Congress.

Section 3. Whenever the President transmits to the President pro tempore of the Senate and the Speaker of the House of Representatives his written declaration that he is unable to discharge the power and duties of his office, and until he transmits to them a written declaration to the contrary, such powers and duties shall be discharged by the Vice President as Acting President.

Section 4. Whenever the Vice President and a majority of either the principal officers of the executive departments or of such other body as Congress may by law provide, transmit to the President pro tempore of the Senate and the Speaker of the House of Representatives their written declaration that the President that the President is unable to discharge the powers and duties of his office, the Vice President shall immediately assume the powers and duties of the office of Acting President.

Thereafter, when the President transmits to the President pro tempore of the Senate and the Speaker of the House of Representatives his written declaration that no inability exists, he shall resume the powers and duties of his office unless the Vice President and a majority of either the principal officers of the executive department or of such other body as Congress may be law provide, transmit within four days to the President pro tempore of the Senate and the Speaker of the House of Representatives their written declaration that the President is unable to discharge the powers and duties of his office. Thereupon Congress shall decide the issue, assembling within forty-eight hours for that purpose if not in session. If the Congress, within twenty-one days after receipt of the latter written declaration, or, if Congress is not in session, within twenty-one days after Congress is required to assemble, determines by two-thirds vote of both Houses that the President shall continue to discharge the same as Acting President; otherwise, the President shall resume the powers and duties of his office.

Amendment XXVI (1971)

Section 1. The right of citizens of the United States, who are eighteen years of age or older, to vote shall not be denied or abridged by the United States or by any State on account of age.

Section 2. The Congress shall have power to enforce this article by appropriate legislation.

Amendment XXVII (1992)

No law, varying the compensation for the services of the Senators and Representatives, shall take effect, until an election of Representatives shall have intervened.

State of Georgia Uniform Commercial Code - Title 11
(Selected Articles)

ARTICLE 1. GENERAL PROVISIONS

§ 11-1-101. Short title

This Title 11 shall be known as and may be cited as the "Uniform Commercial Code."

§ 11-1-102. Purposes; rules of construction; variation by agreement

(1) This title shall be liberally construed and applied to promote its underlying purposes and policies.
(2) Underlying purposes and policies of this title are:
(a) To simplify, clarify, and modernize the law governing commercial transactions;
(b) To permit the continued expansion of commercial practices through custom, usage, and agreement of the parties;
(c) To make uniform the law among the various jurisdictions.
(3) The effect of provisions of this title may be varied by agreement, except as otherwise provided in this title and except that the obligations of good faith, diligence, reasonableness, and care prescribed by this title may not be disclaimed by agreement but the parties may by agreement determine the standards by which the performance of such obligations is to be measured if such standards are not manifestly unreasonable.
4) The presence in certain provisions of this title of the words "unless otherwise agreed" or words of similar import does not imply that the effect of other provisions may not be varied by agreement under subsection (3) of this Code section.
(5) In this title unless the context otherwise requires:
(a) Words in the singular number include the plural, and in the plural include the singular;
(b) Words of the masculine gender include the feminine and the neuter, and when the sense so indicates words of the neuter gender may refer to any gender.

§ 11-1-103. Supplementary general principles of law applicable
Unless displaced by the particular provisions of this title, the principles of law and equity, including the law merchant and the law relative to capacity to contract, principal and agent, estoppel, fraud, misrepresentation, duress, coercion, mistake, bankruptcy, or other validating or invalidating cause shall supplement its provisions.

§ 11-1-104. Construction against implicit repeal
This title being a general act intended as a unified coverage of its subject matter, no part of it shall be deemed to be impliedly repealed by subsequent legislation if such construction can reasonably be avoided.

§ 11-1-105. Territorial application of the title; parties' power to choose applicable law
(1) Except as provided hereafter in this Code section, when a transaction bears a reasonable relation to this state and also to another state or nation the parties may agree that the law either of this state or of such other state or nation shall govern their rights and duties. Failing such agreement this title applies to transactions bearing an appropriate relation to this state.
(2) Where one of the following provisions of this title specifies the applicable law, that provision governs and a contrary agreement is effective only to the extent permitted by the law (including the conflict of laws rules) so specified:
Rights of creditors against sold goods. Code Section 11-2-402.
Applicability of the article of this title on leases (Article 2A of this title). Code Sections 11-2A-105 and 11-2A-106.
Applicability of the article of this title on bank deposits and collections (Article 4 of this title). Code Section 11-4-102.
Bulk transfers subject to the article of this title on bulk transfers (Article 6 of this title). Code Section 11-6-102.
Applicability of the article of this title on investment securities (Article 8 of this title). Code Section 11-8-110.
Law governing perfection, the effect of perfection or nonperfection, and the priority of security interests and agricultural liens. Code Sections 11-9-301 through 11-9-307.
Governing law in the article on funds transfers (Article 4A of this title). Code Section 11-4A-507.

§ 11-1-106. Remedies to be liberally administered
(1) The remedies provided by this title shall be liberally administered to the end that the aggrieved party may be put in as good a position as if the other party had fully performed but neither consequential or special nor penal damages may be had except as specifically provided in this title or by other rule of law.
(2) Any right or obligation declared by this title is enforceable by action unless the provision declaring it specifies a different and limited effect.

§ 11-1-107. Waiver or renunciation of claim or right after breach
Any claim or right arising out of an alleged breach can be discharged in whole or in part without consideration by a written waiver or renunciation signed and delivered by the aggrieved party.

§ 11-1-108. Severability
If any provision or clause of this title or application thereof to any person or circumstances is held invalid, such invalidity shall not affect other provisions or applications of the title which can be

given effect without the invalid provision or application, and to this end the provisions of this title are declared to be severable.

§ 11-1-109. Section captions
Section captions are parts of this title.

§ 11-1-201. General definitions
Subject to additional definitions contained in the subsequent articles of this title which are applicable to specific articles or parts thereof, and unless the context otherwise requires, in this title:

(1) "Action" in the sense of a judicial proceeding includes recoupment, counterclaim, setoff, suit in equity, and any other proceedings in which rights are determined.

(2) "Aggrieved party" means a party entitled to resort to a remedy.

(3) "Agreement" means the bargain of the parties in fact as found in their language or by implication from other circumstances including course of dealing or usage of trade or course of performance as provided in this title (Code Sections 11-1-205 and 11-2-208). Whether an agreement has legal consequences is determined by the provisions of this title, if applicable; otherwise by the law of contracts (Code Section 11-1-103).

(4) "Bank" means any person engaged in the business of banking. Wherever the word "branch" is used in this title, with reference to a bank, it shall mean "branch office" as that term is defined in Code Section 7-1-600.

(5) "Bearer" means a person in control of a negotiable electronic document of title or a person in possession of an instrument, a negotiable tangible document of title, or a certificated security payable to bearer or indorsed in blank.

(6) "Bill of lading" means a document of title evidencing the receipt of goods for shipment issued by a person engaged in the business of directly or indirectly transporting or forwarding goods. The term does not include a warehouse receipt.

(7) "Branch" includes a separately incorporated foreign branch of a bank.

(8) "Burden of establishing" a fact means the burden of persuading the triers of fact that the existence of the fact is more probable than its nonexistence.

(9) "Buyer in ordinary course of business" means a person that buys goods in good faith without knowledge that the sale violates the rights of another person in the goods, and in the ordinary course from a person, other than a pawnbroker, in the business of selling goods of that kind. A person buys goods in the ordinary course if the sale to the person comports with the usual or customary practices in the kind of business in which the seller is engaged or with the seller's own usual or customary practices. A person that sells oil, gas, or other minerals at the wellhead or minehead is a person in the business of selling goods of that kind. A buyer in the ordinary course of business may buy for cash, by exchange of other property, or on secured or unsecured credit and may acquire goods or documents of title under a preexisting contract for sale. Only a buyer that takes possession of the goods or has a right to recover the goods from the seller under Article 2 of this title may be a buyer in ordinary course of business. A person that acquires goods in a transfer in bulk or as security for or in total or partial satisfaction of a money debt is not a buyer in ordinary course of business.

(10) "Conspicuous," with reference to a term, means so written, displayed, or presented that a reasonable person against which it is to operate ought to have noticed it. Whether a term is "conspicuous" or not is a decision for the court. Conspicuous terms include the following:

(A) A heading in capitals equal to or greater in size than the surrounding text, or in contrasting type, font, or color to the surrounding text of the same or lesser size; and

(B) Language in the body of a record or display in larger type than the surrounding text, or in contrasting type, font, or color to the surrounding text of the same size, or set off from the surrounding text of the same size by symbols or other marks that call attention to the language.

(11) "Contract" means the total legal obligation which results from the parties' agreement as affected by this title and any other applicable rules of law.

(12) "Creditor" includes a general creditor, a secured creditor, a lien creditor and any representative of creditors, including an assignee for the benefit of creditors, a trustee in bankruptcy, a receiver in equity, and an executor or administrator of an insolvent debtor's or assignor's estate.

(13) "Defendant" includes a person in the position of defendant in a cross-action or counterclaim.

(14) "Delivery" with respect to an electronic document of title means voluntary transfer of control and with respect to instruments, tangible documents of title, chattel paper, or certificated securities means voluntary transfer of possession.

(15) "Document of title" means a record (a) that in the regular course of business or financing is treated as adequately evidencing that the person in possession or control of the record is entitled to receive, control, hold, and dispose of the record and the goods the record covers and (b) that purports to be issued by or addressed to a bailee and to cover goods in the bailee's possession which are either identified or are fungible portions of an identified mass. The term includes a bill of lading, transport document, dock warrant, dock receipt, warehouse receipt, and order for delivery of goods. An electronic document of title means a document of title evidenced by a record consisting of information stored in an electronic medium. A tangible document of title means a document of title evidenced by a record consisting of information that is inscribed on a tangible medium.

(16) "Fault" means wrongful act, omission, or breach.

(17) "Fungible" with respect to goods or securities means goods or securities of which any unit is, by nature or usage of trade, the equivalent of any other like unit. Goods which are not fungible shall be deemed fungible for the purposes of this title to the extent that under a particular agreement or document unlike units are treated as equivalents.

(18) "Genuine" means free of forgery or counterfeiting.

(19) "Good faith" means honesty in fact in the conduct or transaction concerned.

(20) "Holder" means:

(a) The person in possession of a negotiable instrument that is payable either to bearer or to an identified person that is the person in possession;

(b) The person in possession of a negotiable tangible document of title if the goods are deliverable either to bearer or to the order of the person in possession; or

(c) The person in control of a negotiable electronic document of title.

(21) To "honor" is to pay or to accept and pay, or where a credit so engages to purchase or discount a draft complying with the terms of the credit.

(22) "Insolvency proceedings" includes any assignment for the benefit of creditors or other proceedings intended to liquidate or rehabilitate the estate of the person involved.

(23) A person is "insolvent" who either has ceased to pay his debts in the ordinary course of business or cannot pay his debts as they become due or is insolvent within the meaning of the federal bankruptcy law.

(24) "Money" means a medium of exchange authorized or adopted by a domestic or foreign government and includes a monetary unit of account established by an intergovernmental organization or by agreement between two or more nations.

(25) Subject to subsection (27) of this Code section, a person has "notice" of a fact if the person:

(a) Has actual knowledge of it;

(b) Has received a notice or notification of it; or

(c) From all the facts and circumstances known to the person at the time in question, has reason to know that it exists. A person "knows" or has "knowledge" of a fact when the person has actual knowledge of it. "Discover" or "learn" or a word or phrase of similar import refers to knowledge rather than to reason to know. The time and circumstances under which a notice or notification may cease to be effective are not determined by this title.

(26) A person "notifies" or "gives" a notice or notification to another person by taking such steps as may be reasonably required to inform the other person in ordinary course, whether or not the other person actually comes to know of it. Subject to subsection (27) of this Code section, a person "receives" a notice or notification when:

(a) It comes to that person's attention; or

(b) It is duly delivered in a form reasonable under the circumstances at the place of business through which the contract was made or at another location held out by that person as the place for receipt of such communications.

(27) Notice, knowledge, or a notice or notification received by an organization is effective for a particular transaction from the time when it is brought to the attention of the individual conducting that transaction, and in any event, from the time when it would have been brought to the individual's attention if the organization had exercised due diligence. An organization exercises due diligence if it maintains reasonable routines for communicating significant information to the person conducting the transaction and there is reasonable compliance with the routines. Due diligence does not require an individual acting for the organization to communicate information unless such communication is part of the individual's regular duties or the individual has reason to know of the transaction and that the transaction would be materially affected by the information.

(28) "Organization" includes a corporation, government or governmental subdivision or agency, business trust, estate, trust, partnership or association, two or more persons having a joint or common interest, or any other legal or commercial entity.

(29) "Party," as distinct from "third party," means a person who has engaged in a transaction or made an agreement within this title.

(30) "Person" includes an individual or an organization (see Code Section 11-1-102).

(31) "Presumption" or "presumed" means that the trier of fact must find the existence of the fact presumed unless and until evidence is introduced which would support a finding of its nonexistence.

(31.1) "Public sale" means a sale:

(A) Held at a place reasonably available to persons who might desire to attend and submit bids; and

(B) At which those attending shall be given the opportunity to bid on a competitive basis; and

(C) At which the sale, if made, shall be made to the highest and best bidder; and

(D) Except as otherwise provided in this title for advertising or dispensing with the advertising of public sales, of which notice is given by advertisement once a week for two weeks in the newspaper in which the sheriff's advertisements are published in the county where the sale is to be held, and which notice shall state the day and hour, between 10:00 A.M. and 4:00 P.M., and the place of sale and shall briefly identify the goods to be sold. The provisions of this paragraph shall not be in derogation of any additional requirements relating to notice of and conduct of any such public sale as may be contained in other provisions of this title but shall be supplementary thereto.

(32) "Purchase" includes taking by sale, discount, negotiation, mortgage, pledge, lien, security interest, issue or reissue, gift, or any other voluntary transaction creating an interest in property.

(33) "Purchaser" means a person who takes by purchase.

(34) "Remedy" means any remedial right to which an aggrieved party is entitled with or without resort to a tribunal.

(35) "Representative" includes an agent, an officer of a corporation or association, and a trustee, executor or administrator of an estate, or any other person empowered to act for another.

(36) "Rights" includes remedies.

(37) "Security interest" means an interest in personal property or fixtures which secures payment or performance of an obligation. The term also includes any interest of a consignor and a buyer of accounts, chattel paper, a payment intangible, or a promissory note in a transaction that is subject to Article 9 of this title. The special property interest of a buyer of goods on identification of those goods to a

contract for sale under Code Section 11-2-401 is not a "security interest," but a buyer may also acquire a "security interest" by complying with Article 9 of this title. Except as otherwise provided in Code Section 11-2-505, the right of a seller or lessor of goods under Article 2 or 2A of this title to retain or acquire possession of the goods is not a "security interest," but a seller or lessor may also acquire a "security interest" by complying with Article 9 of this title. The retention or reservation of title by a seller of goods notwithstanding shipment or delivery to the buyer (Code Section 11-2-401) is limited in effect to a reservation of a "security interest."

Whether a transaction creates a lease or security interest is determined by the facts of each case; however, a transaction creates a security interest if the consideration the lessee is to pay the lessor for the right to possession and use of the goods is an obligation for the term of the lease not subject to termination by the lessee, and

(a) The original term of the lease is equal to or greater than the remaining economic life of the goods,

(b) The lessee is bound to renew the lease for the remaining economic life of the goods or is bound to become the owner of the goods,

(c) The lessee has an option to renew the lease for the remaining economic life of the goods for no additional consideration or nominal additional consideration upon compliance with the lease agreement, or

(d) The lessee has an option to become the owner of the goods for no additional consideration or nominal additional consideration upon compliance with the lease agreement.

A transaction does not create a security interest merely because it provides that

(a) The present value of the consideration the lessee is obligated to pay the lessor for the right to possession and use of the goods is substantially equal to or is greater than the fair market value of the goods at the time the lease is entered into,

(b) The lessee assumes risk of loss of the goods, or agrees to pay taxes, insurance, filing, recording, or registration fees, or service or maintenance costs with respect to the goods,

(c) The lessee has an option to renew the lease or to become the owner of the goods,

(d) The lessee has an option to renew the lease for a fixed rent that is equal to or greater than the reasonably predictable fair market rent for the use of the goods for the term of the renewal at the time the option is to be performed, or

(e) The lessee has an option to become the owner of the goods for a fixed price that is equal to or greater than the reasonably predictable fair market value of the goods at the time the option is to be performed.

For purposes of this subsection (37):

(x) Additional consideration is not nominal if (i) when the option to renew the lease is granted to the lessee the rent is stated to be the fair market rent for the use of the goods for the term of the renewal determined at the time the option is to be performed, or (ii) when the option to become the owner of the goods is granted to the lessee the price is stated to be the fair market value of the goods determined at the time the option is to be performed. Additional consideration is nominal if it is less than the lessee's reasonably predictable cost of performing under the lease agreement if the option is not exercised;

(y) "Reasonably predictable" and "remaining economic life of the goods" are to be determined with reference to the facts and circumstances at the time the transaction is entered into; and

(z) "Present value" means the amount as of a date certain of one or more sums payable in the future, discounted to the date certain. The discount is determined by the interest rate specified by the parties if the rate is not manifestly unreasonable at the time the transaction is entered into; otherwise, the discount is determined by a commercially reasonable rate that takes into account the facts and circumstances of each case at the time the transaction was entered into.

(38) "Send" in connection with a writing, record, or notice means

(a) To deposit in the mail or deliver for transmission by any other usual means of communication with postage or cost of transmission provided for and properly addressed and, in the case of an instrument, to an address specified thereon or otherwise agreed, or if there be none to any address reasonable under the circumstances; or

(b) In any other way to cause to be received any record or notice within the time it would have arrived if properly sent.

(39) "Signed" includes any symbol executed or adopted by a party with present intention to authenticate a writing.

(40) "Surety" includes guarantor.

(41) "Telegram" includes a message transmitted by radio, teletype, cable, any mechanical method of transmission, or the like.

(42) "Term" means that portion of an agreement which relates to a particular matter.

(43) "Unauthorized" signature means one made without actual, implied, or apparent authority and includes a forgery.

(44) "Value": Except as otherwise provided with respect to negotiable instruments and bank collections (Code Sections 11-3-303, 11-4-208, and 11-4-209) a person gives "value" for rights if he acquires them:

(a) In return for a binding commitment to extend credit or for the extension of immediately available credit whether or not drawn upon and whether or not a charge-back is provided for in the event of difficulties in collection; or

(b) As security for or in total or partial satisfaction of a preexisting claim; or

(c) By accepting delivery pursuant to a preexisting contract for purchase; or

(d) Generally, in return for any consideration sufficient to support a simple contract.

(45) "Warehouse receipt" means a document of title issued by a person engaged in the business of storing goods for hire.

(46) "Written" or "writing" includes printing, typewriting, or any other intentional reduction to tangible form.

§ 11-1-202. Prima-facie evidence by third party documents
A document in due form purporting to be a bill of lading, policy or certificate of insurance, official weigher's or inspector's certificate, consular invoice, or any other document authorized or required by the contract to be issued by a third party shall be prima-facie evidence of its own authenticity and genuineness and of the facts stated in the document by the third party.

§ 11-1-203. Obligation of good faith
Every contract or duty within this title imposes an obligation of good faith in its performance or enforcement.

§ 11-1-204. Time; reasonable time; "seasonably."
(1) Whenever this title requires any action to be taken within a reasonable time, any time which is not manifestly unreasonable may be fixed by agreement.
(2) What is a reasonable time for taking any action depends on the nature, purpose, and circumstances of such action.
(3) An action is taken "seasonably" when it is taken at or within the time agreed or if no time is agreed at or within a reasonable time.

§ 11-1-205. Course of dealing and usage of trade
(1) A course of dealing is a sequence of previous conduct between the parties to a particular transaction which is fairly to be regarded as establishing a common basis of understanding for interpreting their expressions and other conduct.
(2) A usage of trade is any practice or method of dealing having such regularity of observance in a place, vocation, or trade as to justify an expectation that it will be observed with respect to the transaction in question. The existence and scope of such a usage are to be proved as facts. If it is established that such a usage is embodied in a written trade code or similar writing the interpretation of the writing is for the court.
(3) A course of dealing between parties and any usage of trade in the vocation or trade in which they are engaged or of which they are or should be aware give particular meaning to and supplement or qualify terms of an agreement.
(4) The express terms of an agreement and an applicable course of dealing or usage of trade shall be construed wherever reasonable as consistent with each other; but when such construction is unreasonable express terms control both course of dealing and usage of trade and course of dealing controls usage of trade.
(5) An applicable usage of trade in the place where any part of performance is to occur shall be used in interpreting the agreement as to that part of the performance.
(6) Evidence of a relevant usage of trade offered by one party is not admissible unless and until he has given the other party such notice as the court finds sufficient to prevent unfair surprise to the latter.

§ 11-1-206. Statute of frauds for kinds of personal property not otherwise covered
(1) Except in the cases described in subsection (2) of this Code section a contract for the sale of personal property is not enforceable by way of action or defense beyond $5,000.00 in amount or value of remedy unless there is some writing which indicates that a contract for sale has been made between the parties at a defined or stated price, reasonably identifies the subject matter, and is signed by the party against whom enforcement is sought or by his authorized agent.
(2) Subsection (1) of this Code section does not apply to contracts for the sale of goods (Code Section 11-2-201) nor of securities (Code Section 11-8-113) nor to security agreements (Code Section 11-9-203).

§ 11-1-207. Performance or acceptance under reservation of rights
(1) A party who, with explicit reservation of rights, performs or promises performance or assents to performance in a manner demanded or offered by the other party does not thereby prejudice the rights reserved. Such words as "without prejudice," "under protest" or the like are sufficient.
(2) Subsection (1) of this Code section does not apply to an accord and satisfaction.

§ 11-1-208. Option to accelerate at will
A term providing that one party or his successor in interest may accelerate payment or performance or require collateral or additional collateral "at will" or "when he deems himself insecure" or in words of similar import shall be construed to mean that he shall have power to do so only if he in good faith believes that the prospect of payment or performance is impaired. The burden of establishing lack of good faith is on the party against whom the power has been exercised.

§ 11-1-209. Subordinated obligations
An obligation may be issued as subordinated to payment of another obligation of the person obligated, or a creditor may subordinate his right to payment of an obligation by agreement with either the person obligated or another creditor of the person obligated. Such a subordination does not create a security interest as against either the common debtor or a subordinated creditor. This Code section shall be construed as declaring the law as it existed prior to the enactment of this Code section and not as modifying it.

ARTICLE 2 - SALES

§ 11-2-101. Short title
This article shall be known and may be cited as "Uniform Commercial Code -- Sales."

§ 11-2-102. Scope; certain security and other transactions excluded from this article
Unless the context otherwise requires, this article applies to transactions in goods; it does not apply to any transaction which although in the form of an unconditional contract to sell or present sale is intended to operate only as a security transaction nor

does this article impair or repeal any statute regulating sales to consumers, farmers, or other specified classes of buyers.

§ 11-2-103. Definitions and index of definitions

(1) In this article unless the context otherwise requires:

(a) "Buyer" means a person who buys or contracts to buy goods.

(b) "Good faith" in the case of a merchant means honesty in fact and the observance of reasonable commercial standards of fair dealing in the trade.

(c) "Receipt" of goods means taking physical possession of them.

(d) "Seller" means a person who sells or contracts to sell goods.

(2) Other definitions applying to this article or to specified parts thereof, and the Code sections in which they appear are:

"Acceptance." Code Section 11-2-606.
"Banker's credit." Code Section 11-2-325.
"Between merchants." Code Section 11-2-104.
"Cancellation." Code Section 11-2-106(4).
"Commercial unit." Code Section 11-2-105.
"Confirmed credit." Code Section 11-2-325.
"Conforming to contract." Code Section 11-2-106.
"Contract for sale." Code Section 11-2-106.
"Cover." Code Section 11-2-712.
"Entrusting." Code Section 11-2-403.
"Financing agency." Code Section 11-2-104.
"Future goods." Code Section 11-2-105.
"Goods." Code Section 11-2-105.
"Identification." Code Section 11-2-501.
"Installment contract." Code Section 11-2-612.
"Letter of credit." Code Section 11-2-325.
"Lot." Code Section 11-2-105.
"Merchant." Code Section 11-2-104.
"Overseas." Code Section 11-2-323.
"Person in position of seller." Code Section 11-2-707.
"Present sale." Code Section 11-2-106.
"Sale." Code Section 11-2-106.
"Sale on approval." Code Section 11-2-326.
"Sale or return." Code Section 11-2-326.
"Termination." Code Section 11-2-106.

(3) "Control" as provided in Code Section 11-7-106 and the following definitions in other articles of this title apply to this article:

"Check." Code Section 11-3-104.
"Consignee." Code Section 11-7-102.
"Consignor." Code Section 11-7-102.
"Consumer goods." Code Section 11-9-102.
"Dishonor." Code Section 11-3-502.
"Draft." Code Section 11-3-104.

(4) In addition Article 1 of this title contains general definitions and principles of construction and interpretation applicable throughout this article.

§ 11-2-104. Definitions: "merchant"; between merchants"; "financing agency."

(1) "Merchant" means a person who deals in goods of the kind or otherwise by his occupation holds himself out as having knowledge or skill peculiar to the practices or goods involved in the transaction or to whom such knowledge or skill may be attributed by his employment of an agent or broker or other intermediary who by his occupation holds himself out as having such knowledge or skill.

(2) "Financing agency" means a bank, finance company, or other person who in the ordinary course of business makes advances against goods or documents of title or who by arrangement with either the seller or the buyer intervenes in ordinary course to make or collect payment due or claimed under the contract for sale, as by purchasing or paying the seller's draft or making advances against it or by merely taking it for collection whether or not documents of title accompany or are associated with the draft. "Financing agency" includes also a bank or other person who similarly intervenes between persons who are in the position of seller and buyer in respect to the goods (Code Section 11-2-707).

(3) "Between merchants" means in any transaction with respect to which both parties are chargeable with the knowledge or skill of merchants.

§ 11-2-105. Definitions: transferability; goods"; "future" goods; "lot"; "commercial unit."

(1) "Goods" means all things (including specially manufactured goods) which are movable at the time of identification to the contract for sale other than the money in which the price is to be paid, investment securities (Article 8 of this title), and things in action. "Goods" also includes the unborn young of animals and growing crops and other identified things attached to realty as described in the Code section on goods to be severed from realty (Code Section 11-2-107).

(2) Goods must be both existing and identified before any interest in them can pass. Goods which are not both existing and identified are "future" goods. A purported present sale of future goods or of any interest therein operates as a contract to sell.

(3) There may be a sale of a part interest in existing identified goods.

(4) An undivided share in an identified bulk of fungible goods is sufficiently identified to be sold although the quantity of the bulk is not determined. Any agreed proportion of such a bulk or any quantity thereof agreed upon by number, weight, or other measure may to the extent of the seller's interest in the bulk be sold to the buyer who then becomes an owner in common.

(5) "Lot" means a parcel or a single article which is the subject matter of a separate sale or delivery, whether or not it is sufficient to perform the contract.

(6) "Commercial unit" means such a unit of goods as by commercial usage is a single whole for purposes of sale and division of which materially impairs its character or value on the market or in use. A commercial unit may be a single article (as a machine) or a set of articles (as a suite of furniture or an assortment of sizes) or a quantity (as a bale, gross, or carload) or any other unit treated in use or in the relevant market as a single whole.

§ 11-2-106. Definitions: "contract"; "agreement"; "contract for sale"; "sale"; "present sale"; "conforming" to contract; "termination"; "cancellation."

(1) In this article unless the context otherwise requires "contract" and "agreement" are limited to those relating to the present or future sale of goods. "Contract for sale" includes both a present sale of goods and a contract to sell goods at a future time. A "sale" consists in the passing of title from the seller to the buyer for a price (Code Section 11-2-401). A "present sale" means a sale which is accomplished by the making of the contract.
(2) Goods or conduct including any part of a performance are "conforming" or conform to the contract when they are in accordance with the obligations under the contract.
(3) "Termination" occurs when either party pursuant to a power created by agreement or law puts an end to the contract otherwise than for its breach. On "termination" all obligations which are still executory on both sides are discharged but any right based on prior breach or performance survives.
(4) "Cancellation" occurs when either party puts an end to the contract for breach by the other and its effect is the same as that of "termination" except that the canceling party also retains any remedy for breach of the whole contract or any unperformed balance.

§ 11-2-107. Goods to be severed from realty; recording
(1) A contract for the sale of timber, minerals, or the like (including oil and gas) or a structure or its materials to be removed from realty is a contract for the sale of goods within this article if they are to be severed by the seller but until severance a purported present sale thereof which is not effective as a transfer of an interest in land is effective only as a contract to sell.
(2) A contract for the sale apart from the land of growing crops or other things attached to realty and capable of severance without material harm thereto but not described in subsection (1) of this Code section is a contract for the sale of goods within this article whether the subject matter is to be severed by the buyer or by the seller even though it forms part of the realty at the time of contracting, and the parties can by identification effect a present sale before severance.
(3) The provisions of this Code section are subject to any third party rights provided by the law relating to realty records, and the contract for sale may be executed and recorded as a document transferring an interest in land and shall then constitute notice to third parties of the buyer's rights under the contract for sale.

§ 11-2-201. Formal requirements; statute of frauds
(1) Except as otherwise provided in this Code section a contract for the sale of goods for the price of $500.00 or more is not enforceable by way of action or defense unless there is some writing sufficient to indicate that a contract for sale has been made between the parties and signed by the party against whom enforcement is sought or by his authorized agent or broker. A writing is not insufficient because it omits or incorrectly states a term agreed upon but the contract is not enforceable under this paragraph beyond the quantity of goods shown in such writing.
(2) Between merchants if within a reasonable time a writing in confirmation of the contract and sufficient against the sender is received and the party receiving it has reason to know its contents, it satisfies the requirements of subsection (1) of this Code section against such party unless written notice of objection to its contents is given within ten days after it is received.
(3) A contract which does not satisfy the requirements of subsection (1) of this Code section but which is valid in other respects is enforceable:
(a) If the goods are to be specially manufactured for the buyer and are not suitable for sale to others in the ordinary course of the seller's business and the seller, before notice of repudiation is received and under circumstances which reasonably indicate that the goods are for the buyer, has made either a substantial beginning of their manufacture or commitments for their procurement; or
(b) If the party against whom enforcement is sought admits in his pleading, testimony, or otherwise in court that a contract for sale was made, but the contract is not enforceable under this provision beyond the quantity of goods admitted; or
(c) With respect to goods for which payment has been made and accepted or which have been received and accepted (Code Section 11-2-606).

§ 11-2-202. Final written expression; parol or extrinsic evidence
Terms with respect to which the confirmatory memoranda of the parties agree or which are otherwise set forth in a writing intended by the parties as a final expression of their agreement with respect to such terms as are included therein may not be contradicted by evidence of any prior agreement or of a contemporaneous oral agreement but may be explained or supplemented:
(a) By course of dealing or usage of trade (Code Section 11-1-205) or by course of performance (Code Section 11-2-208); and
(b) By evidence of consistent additional terms unless the court finds the writing to have been intended also as a complete and exclusive statement of the terms of the agreement.

§ 11-2-203. Seals inoperative
The affixing of a seal to a writing evidencing a contract for sale or an offer to buy or sell goods does not constitute the writing a sealed instrument and the law with respect to sealed instruments does not apply to such a contract or offer.

§ 11-2-204. Formation in general
(1) A contract for sale of goods may be made in any manner sufficient to show agreement, including conduct by both parties which recognizes the existence of such a contract.
(2) An agreement sufficient to constitute a contract for sale may be found even though the moment of its making is undetermined.
(3) Even though one or more terms are left open a contract for sale does not fail for indefiniteness if the parties have intended to make a contract and there is

a reasonably certain basis for giving an appropriate remedy.

§ 11-2-205. Firm offers
An offer by a merchant to buy or sell goods in a signed writing which by its terms gives assurance that it will be held open is not revocable, for lack of consideration, during the time stated or if no time is stated for a reasonable time, but in no event may such period of irrevocability exceed three months; but any such term of assurance on a form supplied by the offeree must be separately signed by the offeror.

§ 11-2-206. Offer and acceptance in formation of contract
(1) Unless otherwise unambiguously indicated by the language or circumstances:
(a) An offer to make a contract shall be construed as inviting acceptance in any manner and by any medium reasonable in the circumstances;
(b) An order or other offer to buy goods for prompt or current shipment shall be construed as inviting acceptance either by a prompt promise to ship or by the prompt or current shipment of conforming or nonconforming goods, but such a shipment of nonconforming goods does not constitute an acceptance if the seller seasonably notifies the buyer that the shipment is offered only as an accommodation to the buyer.
(2) Where the beginning of a requested performance is a reasonable mode of acceptance an offeror who is not notified of acceptance within a reasonable time may treat the offer as having lapsed before acceptance.

§ 11-2-207. Additional terms in acceptance or confirmation
(1) A definite and seasonable expression of acceptance or a written confirmation which is sent within a reasonable time operates as an acceptance even though it states terms additional to or different from those offered or agreed upon, unless acceptance is expressly made conditional on assent to the additional or different terms.
(2) The additional terms are to be construed as proposals for addition to the contract. Between merchants such terms become part of the contract unless:
(a) The offer expressly limits acceptance to the terms of the offer;
(b) They materially alter it; or
(c) Notification of objection to them has already been given or is given within a reasonable time after notice of them is received.
(3) Conduct by both parties which recognizes the existence of a contract is sufficient to establish a contract for sale although the writings of the parties do not otherwise establish a contract. In such case the terms of the particular contract consist of those terms on which the writings of the parties agree, together with any supplementary terms incorporated under any other provisions of this title.

§ 11-2-208. Course of performance or practical construction
(1) Where the contract for sale involves repeated occasions for performance by either party with knowledge of the nature of the performance and opportunity for objection to it by the other, any course of performance accepted or acquiesced in without objection shall be relevant to determine the meaning of the agreement.
(2) The express terms of the agreement and any such course of performance, as well as any course of dealing and usage of trade, shall be construed whenever reasonable as consistent with each other; but when such construction is unreasonable, express terms shall control course of performance and course of performance shall control both course of dealing and usage of trade (Code Section 11-1-205).
(3) Subject to the provisions of Code Section 11-2-209 on modification and waiver, such course of performance shall be relevant to show a waiver or modification of any term inconsistent with such course of performance.

§ 11-2-209. Modification, rescission, and waiver
(1) An agreement modifying a contract within this article needs no consideration to be binding.
(2) A signed agreement which excludes modification or rescission except by a signed writing cannot be otherwise modified or rescinded, but except as between merchants such a requirement on a form supplied by the merchant must be separately signed by the other party.
(3) The requirements of the statute of frauds section of this article (Code Section 11-2-201) must be satisfied if the contract as modified is within its provisions.
(4) Although an attempt at modification or rescission does not satisfy the requirements of subsection (2) or (3) of this Code section it can operate as a waiver.
(5) A party who has made a waiver affecting an executory portion of the contract may retract the waiver by reasonable notification received by the other party that strict performance will be required of any term waived, unless the retraction would be unjust in view of a material change of position in reliance on the waiver.

§ 11-2-210. Delegation of performance; assignment of rights
(1) A party may perform his duty through a delegate unless otherwise agreed or unless the other party has a substantial interest in having his original promisor perform or control the acts required by the contract. No delegation of performance relieves the party delegating of any duty to perform or any liability for breach.
(2) Except as otherwise provided in Code Section 11-9-406, unless otherwise agreed all rights of either seller or buyer can be assigned except where the assignment would materially change the duty of the other party, or increase materially the burden or risk imposed on the other party by the contract, or impair materially the other party's chance of obtaining return performance. A right to damages for breach of the whole contract or a right arising out of the assignor's due performance of the assignor's entire

obligation can be assigned despite agreement otherwise.
(3) The creation, attachment, perfection, or enforcement of a security interest in the seller's interest under a contract is not a transfer that materially changes the duty of or increases materially the burden or risk imposed on the buyer or impairs materially the buyer's chance of obtaining return performance within the purview of subsection (2) of this Code section unless, and then only to the extent that, enforcement actually results in a delegation of material performance of the seller. Even in that event, the creation, attachment, perfection, and enforcement of the security interest remain effective, but (i) the seller is liable to the buyer for damages caused by the delegation to the extent that the damages could not reasonably be prevented by the buyer, and (ii) a court having jurisdiction may grant other appropriate relief, including cancellation of the contract for sale or an injunction against enforcement of the security interest or consummation of the enforcement.
(4) Unless the circumstances indicate the contrary a prohibition of assignment of "the contract" is to be construed as barring only the delegation to the assignee of the assignor's performance.
(5) An assignment of "the contract" or of "all my rights under the contract" or an assignment in similar general terms is an assignment of rights and unless the language or the circumstances (as in an assignment for security) indicate the contrary, it is a delegation of performance of the duties of the assignor and its acceptance by the assignee constitutes a promise by the assignee to perform those duties. This promise is enforceable by either the assignor or the other party to the original contract.
(6) The other party may treat any assignment which delegates performance as creating reasonable grounds for insecurity and may without prejudice to his or her rights against the assignor demand assurances from the assignee (Code Section 11-2-609).

§ 11-2-301. General obligations of parties
The obligation of the seller is to transfer and deliver and that of the buyer is to accept and pay in accordance with the contract.

§ 11-2-302. Unconscionable contract or clause
(1) If the court as a matter of law finds the contract or any clause of the contract to have been unconscionable at the time it was made the court may refuse to enforce the contract, or it may enforce the remainder of the contract without the unconscionable clause, or it may so limit the application of any unconscionable clause as to avoid any unconscionable result.
(2) When it is claimed or appears to the court that the contract or any clause thereof may be unconscionable the parties shall be afforded a reasonable opportunity to present evidence as to its commercial setting, purpose, and effect to aid the court in making the determination.

§ 11-2-303. Allocation or division of risks
Where this article allocates a risk or a burden as between the parties "unless otherwise agreed," the agreement may not only shift the allocation but may also divide the risk or burden.

§ 11-2-304. Price payable in money, goods, realty, or otherwise
(1) The price can be made payable in money or otherwise. If it is payable in whole or in part in goods each party is a seller of the goods which he is to transfer.
(2) Even though all or part of the price is payable in an interest in realty the transfer of the goods and the seller's obligations with reference to them are subject to this article, but not the transfer of the interest in realty or the transferor's obligations in connection therewith.

§ 11-2-305. Open price term
(1) The parties if they so intend can conclude a contract for sale even though the price is not settled. In such a case the price is a reasonable price at the time for delivery if:
(a) Nothing is said as to price; or
(b) The price is left to be agreed by the parties and they fail to agree; or
(c) The price is to be fixed in terms of some agreed market or other standard as set or recorded by a third person or agency and it is not so set or recorded.
(2) A price to be fixed by the seller or by the buyer means a price for him to fix in good faith.
(3) When a price left to be fixed otherwise than by agreement of the parties fails to be fixed through fault of one party the other may at his option treat the contract as canceled or himself fix a reasonable price.
(4) Where, however, the parties intend not to be bound unless the price be fixed or agreed and it is not fixed or agreed there is no contract. In such a case the buyer must return any goods already received or if unable so to do must pay their reasonable value at the time of delivery and the seller must return any portion of the price paid on account.

§ 11-2-306. Output, requirements, and exclusive dealings
(1) A term which measures the quantity by the output of the seller or the requirements of the buyer means such actual output or requirements as may occur in good faith, except that no quantity unreasonably disproportionate to any stated estimate or in the absence of a stated estimate to any normal or otherwise comparable prior output or requirements may be tendered or demanded.
(2) A lawful agreement by either the seller or the buyer for exclusive dealing in the kind of goods concerned imposes unless otherwise agreed an obligation by the seller to use best efforts to supply the goods and by the buyer to use best efforts to promote their sale.

§ 11-2-307. Delivery in single lot or several lots
Unless otherwise agreed all goods called for by a contract for sale must be tendered in a single delivery and payment is due only on such tender but where

the circumstances give either party the right to make or demand delivery in lots the price if it can be apportioned may be demanded for each lot.

§ 11-2-308. Absence of specified place for delivery

Unless otherwise agreed:

(a) The place for delivery of goods is the seller's place of business or if he has none his residence; but

(b) In a contract for sale of identified goods which to the knowledge of the parties at the time of contracting are in some other place, that place is the place for their delivery; and

(c) Documents of title may be delivered through customary banking channels.

§ 11-2-309. Absence of specific time provisions; notice of termination

(1) The time for shipment or delivery or any other action under a contract if not provided in this article or agreed upon shall be a reasonable time.

(2) Where the contract provides for successive performances but is indefinite in duration it is valid for a reasonable time but unless otherwise agreed may be terminated at any time by either party.

(3) Termination of a contract by one party except on the happening of an agreed event requires that reasonable notification be received by the other party and an agreement dispensing with notification is invalid if its operation would be unconscionable.

§ 11-2-310. Open time for payment or running of credit; authority to ship under reservation

Unless otherwise agreed:

(a) Payment is due at the time and place at which the buyer is to receive the goods even though the place of shipment is the place of delivery; and

(b) If the seller is authorized to send the goods he or she may ship them under reservation, and may tender the documents of title, but the buyer may inspect the goods after their arrival before payment is due unless such inspection is inconsistent with the terms of the contract (Code Section 11-2-513); and

(c) If delivery is authorized and made by way of documents of title otherwise than by subsection (b) of this Code section then payment is due regardless of where the goods are to be received (i) at the time and place at which the buyer is to receive delivery of the tangible documents or (ii) at the time the buyer is to receive delivery of the electronic documents and at the seller's place of business or if none, the seller's residence; and

(d) Where the seller is required or authorized to ship the goods on credit the credit period runs from the time of shipment but post-dating the invoice or delaying its dispatch will correspondingly delay the starting of the credit period.

§ 11-2-311. Options and cooperation respecting performance

(1) An agreement for sale which is otherwise sufficiently definite (subsection (3) of Code Section 11-2-204) to be a contract is not made invalid by the fact that it leaves particulars of performance to be specified by one of the parties. Any such specification must be made in good faith and within limits set by commercial reasonableness.

(2) Unless otherwise agreed specifications relating to assortment of goods are at the buyer's option and except as otherwise provided in subsections (1)(c) and (3) of Code Section 11-2-319 specifications or arrangements relating to shipment are at the seller's option.

(3) Where such specification would materially affect the other party's performance but is not seasonably made or where one party's cooperation is necessary to the agreed performance of the other but is not seasonably forthcoming, the other party in addition to all other remedies:

(a) Is excused for any resulting delay in his own performance; and

(b) May also either proceed to perform in any reasonable manner or after the time for a material part of his own performance treat the failure to specify or to cooperate as a breach by failure to deliver or accept the goods.

§ 11-2-312. Warranty of title and against infringement; buyer's obligation against infringement

(1) Subject to subsection (2) of this Code section there is in a contract for sale a warranty by the seller that:

(a) The title conveyed shall be good, and its transfer rightful; and

(b) The goods shall be delivered free from any security interest or other lien or encumbrance of which the buyer at the time of contracting has no knowledge.

(2) A warranty under subsection (1) of this Code section will be excluded or modified only by specific language or by circumstances which give the buyer reason to know that the person selling does not claim title in himself or that he is purporting to sell only such right or title as he or a third person may have.

(3) Unless otherwise agreed a seller who is a merchant regularly dealing in goods of the kind warrants that the goods shall be delivered free of the rightful claim of any third person by way of infringement or the like but a buyer who furnishes specifications to the seller must hold the seller harmless against any such claim which arises out of compliance with the specifications.

§ 11-2-313. Express warranties by affirmation, promise, description, sample

(1) Express warranties by the seller are created as follows:

(a) Any affirmation of fact or promise made by the seller to the buyer which relates to the goods and becomes part of the basis of the bargain creates an express warranty that the goods shall conform to the affirmation or promise.

(b) Any description of the goods which is made part of the basis of the bargain creates an express warranty that the goods shall conform to the description.

(c) Any sample or model which is made part of the basis of the bargain creates an express warranty that the whole of the goods shall conform to the sample or model.

(2) It is not necessary to the creation of an express warranty that the seller use formal words such as "warrant" or "guarantee" or that he have a specific intention to make a warranty, but an affirmation merely of the value of the goods or a statement purporting to be merely the seller's opinion or commendation of the goods does not create a warranty.

§ 11-2-314. Implied warranty: merchantability; usage of trade

(1) Unless excluded or modified (Code Section 11-2-316), a warranty that the goods shall be merchantable is implied in a contract for their sale if the seller is a merchant with respect to goods of that kind. Under this Code section the serving for value of food or drink to be consumed either on the premises or elsewhere is a sale.

(2) Goods to be merchantable must be at least such as:

(a) Pass without objection in the trade under the contract description; and

(b) In the case of fungible goods, are of fair average quality within the description; and

(c) Are fit for the ordinary purposes for which such goods are used; and

(d) Run, within the variations permitted by the agreement, of even kind, quality, and quantity within each unit and among all units involved; and

(e) Are adequately contained, packaged, and labeled as the agreement may require; and

(f) Conform to the promises or affirmations of fact made on the container or label if any.

(3) Unless excluded or modified (Code Section 11-2-316) other implied warranties may arise from course of dealing or usage of trade.

§ 11-2-315. Implied warranty: fitness for particular purpose

Where the seller at the time of contracting has reason to know any particular purpose for which the goods are required and that the buyer is relying on the seller's skill or judgment to select or furnish suitable goods, there is unless excluded or modified under Code Section 11-2-316 an implied warranty that the goods shall be fit for such purpose.

§ 11-2-316. Exclusion or modification of warranties

(1) Words or conduct relevant to the creation of an express warranty and words or conduct tending to negate or limit warranty shall be construed wherever reasonable as consistent with each other; but subject to the provisions of this article on parol or extrinsic evidence (Code Section 11-2-202) negation or limitation is inoperative to the extent that such construction is unreasonable.

(2) Subject to subsection (3) of this Code section, to exclude or modify the implied warranty of merchantability or any part of it the language must mention merchantability and in case of a writing must be conspicuous, and to exclude or modify any implied warranty of fitness the exclusion must be by a writing and conspicuous. Language to exclude all implied warranties of fitness is sufficient if it states, for example, that "There are no warranties which extend beyond the description on the face hereof."

(3) Notwithstanding subsection (2) of this Code section:

(a) Unless the circumstances indicate otherwise, all implied warranties are excluded by expressions like "as is," "with all faults," or other language which in common understanding calls the buyer's attention to the exclusion of warranties and makes plain that there is no implied warranty; and

(b) When the buyer before entering into the contract has examined the goods or the sample or model as fully as he desired or has refused to examine the goods there is no implied warranty with regard to defects which an examination ought in the circumstances to have revealed to him; and

(c) An implied warranty can also be excluded or modified by course of dealing or course of performance or usage of trade; and

(d) With respect to the sale of cattle, hogs, and sheep by a licensed auction company or by an agent, there shall be no implied warranty by said auction company or agent that the cattle, hogs, and sheep are free from disease; provided, however, that the provisions of this paragraph shall not be applicable to brucellosis reactor cattle detected at an official state laboratory within 30 days following the date of sale.

(4) Remedies for breach of warranty can be limited in accordance with the provisions of this article on liquidation or limitation of damages and on contractual modification of remedy (Code Sections 11-2-718 and 11-2-719).

(5) The implied warranty of merchantability under Code Section 11-2-314 and the implied warranty of fitness for a particular purpose under Code Section 11-2-315 shall not be applicable to the procurement, processing, storage, distribution, or use of whole human blood, blood plasma, blood products, blood derivatives, or other human tissue or organs for the purpose of injecting, transfusing, incorporating, or transplanting any of them into the human body. The injection, transfusion, or other transfer of blood, blood plasma, blood products, or blood derivatives and the transplanting or other transfer of any tissue, bones, or organs into or unto the human body shall not be considered, for the purpose of this article, commodities subject to sale or barter, but shall be considered as medical services.

§ 11-2-317. Cumulation and conflict of warranties express or implied

Warranties whether express or implied shall be construed as consistent with each other and as cumulative, but if such construction is unreasonable the intention of the parties shall determine which warranty is dominant. In ascertaining that intention the following rules apply:

(a) Exact or technical specifications displace an inconsistent sample or model or general language of description.

(b) A sample from an existing bulk displaces inconsistent general language of description.

(c) Express warranties displace inconsistent implied warranties other than an implied warranty of fitness for a particular purpose.

§ 11-2-318. Third party beneficiaries of warranties express or implied

A seller's warranty whether express or implied extends to any natural person who is in the family or household of his buyer or who is a guest in his home if it is reasonable to expect that such person may use, consume, or be affected by the goods and who is injured in person by breach of the warranty. A seller may not exclude or limit the operation of this Code section.

§ 11-2-319. F.O.B. and F.A.S. terms

(1) Unless otherwise agreed the term F.O.B. (which means "free on board") at a named place, even though used only in connection with the stated price, is a delivery term under which:

(a) When the term is F.O.B. the place of shipment, the seller must at that place ship the goods in the manner provided in this article (Code Section 11-2-504) and bear the expense and risk of putting them into the possession of the carrier; or

(b) When the term is F.O.B. the place of destination, the seller must at his own expense and risk transport the goods to that place and there tender delivery of them in the manner provided in this article (Code Section 11-2-503);

(c) When under either paragraph (a) or (b) of this subsection the term is also F.O.B. vessel, car, or other vehicle, the seller must in addition at his own expense and risk load the goods on board. If the term is F.O.B. vessel the buyer must name the vessel and in an appropriate case the seller must comply with the provisions of this article on the form of bill of lading (Code Section 11-2-323).

(2) Unless otherwise agreed the term F.A.S. vessel (which means "free alongside") at a named port, even though used only in connection with the stated price, is a delivery term under which the seller must:

(a) At his own expense and risk deliver the goods alongside the vessel in the manner usual in that port or on a dock designated and provided by the buyer; and

(b) Obtain and tender a receipt for the goods in exchange for which the carrier is under a duty to issue a bill of lading.

(3) Unless otherwise agreed in any case falling within subsection (1)(a) or (c) or subsection (2) of this Code section the buyer must seasonably give any needed instructions for making delivery, including when the term is F.A.S. or F.O.B. the loading berth of the vessel and in an appropriate case its name and sailing date. The seller may treat the failure of needed instructions as a failure of cooperation under this article (Code Section 11-2-311). He may also at his option move the goods in any reasonable manner preparatory to delivery or shipment.

(4) Under the term F.O.B. vessel or F.A.S. unless otherwise agreed the buyer must make payment against tender of the required documents and the seller may not tender nor the buyer demand delivery of the goods in substitution for the documents.

§ 11-2-320. C.I.F. and C. & F. terms

(1) The term C.I.F. means that the price includes in a lump sum the cost of the goods and the insurance and freight to the named destination. The term C. & F. or C.F. means that the price so includes cost and freight to the named destination.

(2) Unless otherwise agreed and even though used only in connection with the stated price and destination, the term C.I.F. destination or its equivalent requires the seller at his own expense and risk to:

(a) Put the goods into the possession of a carrier at the port for shipment and obtain a negotiable bill or bills of lading covering the entire transportation to the named destination; and

(b) Load the goods and obtain a receipt from the carrier (which may be contained in the bill of lading) showing that the freight has been paid or provided for; and

(c) Obtain a policy or certificate of insurance, including any war risk insurance, of a kind and on terms then current at the port of shipment in the usual amount, in the currency of the contract, shown to cover the same goods covered by the bill of lading and providing for payment of loss to the order of the buyer or for the account of whom it may concern; but the seller may add to the price the amount of the premium for any such war risk insurance; and

(d) Prepare an invoice of the goods and procure any other documents required to effect shipment or to comply with the contract; and

(e) Forward and tender with commercial promptness all the documents in due form and with any endorsement necessary to perfect the buyer's rights.

(3) Unless otherwise agreed the term C. & F. or its equivalent has the same effect and imposes upon the seller the same obligations and risks as a C.I.F. term except the obligation as to insurance.

(4) Under the term C.I.F. or C. & F. unless otherwise agreed the buyer must make payment against tender of the required documents and the seller may not tender nor the buyer demand delivery of the goods in substitution for the documents.

§ 11-2-321. C.I.F. or C. & F.: "net landed weights"; "payment on arrival"; warranty of condition on arrival

Under a contract containing a term C.I.F. or C. & F.:

(1) Where the price is based on or is to be adjusted according to "net landed weights," "delivered weights," "out turn" quantity or quality, or the like, unless otherwise agreed the seller must reasonably estimate the price. The payment due on tender of the documents called for by the contract is the amount so estimated, but after final adjustment of the price a settlement must be made with commercial promptness.

(2) An agreement described in subsection (1) of this Code section or any warranty of quality or condition of the goods on arrival places upon the seller the risk of ordinary deterioration, shrinkage, and the like in transportation but has no effect on the place or time of identification to the contract for sale or delivery or on the passing of the risk of loss.

(3) Unless otherwise agreed where the contract provides for payment on or after arrival of the goods the seller must before payment allow such preliminary inspection as is feasible; but if the goods

are lost delivery of the documents and payment are due when the goods should have arrived.

§ 11-2-322. Delivery "ex-ship."
(1) Unless otherwise agreed a term for delivery of goods "ex-ship" (which means from the carrying vessel) or in equivalent language is not restricted to a particular ship and requires delivery from a ship which has reached a place at the named port of destination where goods of the kind are usually discharged.
(2) Under such a term unless otherwise agreed:
(a) The seller must discharge all liens arising out of the carriage and furnish the buyer with a direction which puts the carrier under a duty to deliver the goods; and
(b) The risk of loss does not pass to the buyer until the goods leave the ship's tackle or are otherwise properly unloaded.

§ 11-2-323. Form of bill of lading required in overseas shipment; "overseas."
(1) Where the contract contemplates overseas shipment and contains a term C.I.F. or C. & F. or F.O.B. vessel, the seller unless otherwise agreed shall obtain a negotiable bill of lading stating that the goods have been loaded in board or, in the case of a term C.I.F. or C. & F., received for shipment.
(2) Where in a case within subsection (1) of this Code section a tangible bill of lading has been issued in a set of parts, unless otherwise agreed if the documents are not to be sent from abroad the buyer may demand tender of the full set; otherwise only one part of the bill of lading need be tendered. Even if the agreement expressly requires a full set:
(a) Due tender of a single part is acceptable within the provisions of this article on cure of improper delivery (subsection (1) of Code Section 11-2-508); and
(b) Even though the full set is demanded, if the documents are sent from abroad the person tendering an incomplete set may nevertheless require payment upon furnishing an indemnity which the buyer in good faith deems adequate.
(3) A shipment by water or by air or a contract contemplating such shipment is "overseas" insofar as by usage of trade or agreement it is subject to the commercial, financing, or shipping practices characteristic of international deep water commerce.

§ 11-2-324. "No arrival, no sale" term
Under a term "no arrival, no sale" or terms of like meaning, unless otherwise agreed:
(a) The seller must properly ship conforming goods and if they arrive by any means he must tender them on arrival but he assumes no obligation that the goods will arrive unless he has caused the nonarrival; and
(b) Where without fault of the seller the goods are in part lost or have so deteriorated as no longer to conform to the contract or arrive after the contract time, the buyer may proceed as if there had been casualty to identified goods (Code Section 11-2-613).

§ 11-2-325. "Letter of credit" term; "confirmed credit."
(1) Failure of the buyer seasonably to furnish an agreed letter of credit is a breach of the contract for sale.
(2) The delivery to seller of a proper letter of credit suspends the buyer's obligation to pay. If the letter of credit is dishonored, the seller may on seasonable notification to the buyer require payment directly from him.
(3) Unless otherwise agreed the term "letter of credit" or "banker's credit" in a contract for sale means an irrevocable credit issued by a financing agency of good repute and, where the shipment is overseas, of good international repute. The term "confirmed credit" means that the credit must also carry the direct obligation of such an agency which does business in the seller's financial market.

§ 11-2-326. Sale on approval and sale or return; rights of creditors.
(1) Unless otherwise agreed, if delivered goods may be returned by the buyer even though they conform to the contract, the transaction is:
(a) A "sale on approval" if the goods are delivered primarily for use; and
(b) A "sale or return" if the goods are delivered primarily for resale.
(2) Goods held on approval are not subject to the claims of the buyer's creditors until acceptance; goods held on sale or return are subject to such claims while in the buyer's possession.
(3) Any "or return" term of a contract for sale is to be treated as a separate contract for sale within the statute of frauds section of this article (Code Section 11-2-201) and as contradicting the sale aspect of the contract within the provisions of this article on parol or extrinsic evidence (Code Section 11-2-202).

§ 11-2-327. Special incidents of sale on approval and sale or return
(1) Under a sale on approval unless otherwise agreed:
(a) Although the goods are identified to the contract the risk of loss and the title do not pass to the buyer until acceptance; and
(b) Use of the goods consistent with the purpose of trial is not acceptance but failure seasonably to notify the seller of election to return the goods is acceptance, and if the goods conform to the contract acceptance of any part is acceptance of the whole; and
(c) After due notification of election to return, the return is at the seller's risk and expense but a merchant buyer must follow any reasonable instructions.
(2) Under a sale or return unless otherwise agreed:
(a) The option to return extends to the whole or any commercial unit of the goods while in substantially their original condition, but must be exercised seasonably; and
(b) The return is at the buyer's risk and expense.

§ 11-2-328. Sale by auction
(1) In a sale by auction if goods are put up in lots each lot is the subject of a separate sale.
(2) A sale by auction is complete when the auctioneer so announces by the fall of the hammer or in other customary manner. Where a bid is made while the

hammer is falling in acceptance of a prior bid the auctioneer may in his discretion reopen the bidding or declare the goods sold under the bid on which the hammer was falling. In sales by auction the auctioneer shall be considered agent of both parties so far as to dispense with any further memorandum in writing than his own entries.
(3) Such a sale is with reserve unless the goods are in explicit terms put up without reserve. In an auction with reserve the auctioneer may withdraw the goods at any time until he announces completion of the sale. In an auction without reserve, after the auctioneer calls for bids on an article or lot, that article or lot cannot be withdrawn unless no bid is made within a reasonable time. In either case a bidder may retract his bid until the auctioneer's announcement of completion of the sale, but a bidder's retraction does not revive any previous bid.
(4) If the auctioneer knowingly receives a bid on the seller's behalf or the seller makes or procures such a bid, and notice has not been given that liberty for such bidding is reserved, the buyer may at his option avoid the sale or take the goods at the price of the last good faith bid prior to the completion of the sale. This subsection shall not apply to any bid at a forced sale.

§ 11-2-401. Passing of title; reservation for security; limited application of this Code section

Each provision of this article with regard to the rights, obligations, and remedies of the seller, the buyer, purchasers, or other third parties applies irrespective of title to the goods except where the provision refers to such title. Insofar as situations are not covered by the other provisions of this article and matters concerning title become material the following rules apply:

(1) Title to goods cannot pass under a contract for sale prior to their identification to the contract (Code Section 11-2-501), and unless otherwise explicitly agreed the buyer acquires by their identification a special property as limited by this title. Any retention or reservation by the seller of the title (property) in goods shipped or delivered to the buyer is limited in effect to a reservation of a security interest. Subject to these provisions and to the provisions of the article on secured transactions (Article 9 of this title), title to goods passes from the seller to the buyer in any manner and on any conditions explicitly agreed on by the parties.

(2) Unless otherwise explicitly agreed title passes to the buyer at the time and place at which the seller completes his or her performance with reference to the physical delivery of the goods, despite any reservation of a security interest and even though a document of title is to be delivered at a different time or place; and in particular and despite any reservation of a security interest by the bill of lading:

(a) If the contract requires or authorizes the seller to send the goods to the buyer but does not require him or her to deliver them at destination, title passes to the buyer at the time and place of shipment; but

(b) If the contract requires delivery at destination, title passes on tender there.

(3) Unless otherwise explicitly agreed where delivery is to be made without moving the goods:

(a) If the seller is to deliver a tangible document of title, title passes at the time when and the place where he or she delivers such documents and if the seller is to deliver an electronic document of title, title passes when the seller delivers the document; or

(b) If the goods are at the time of contracting already identified and no documents of title are to be delivered, title passes at the time and place of contracting.

(4) A rejection or other refusal by the buyer to receive or retain the goods, whether or not justified, or a justified revocation of acceptance revests title to the goods in the seller. Such revesting occurs by operation of law and is not a "sale."

§ 11-2-402. Rights of seller's creditors against sold goods

(1) Except as provided in subsections (2) and (3) of this Code section, rights of unsecured creditors of the seller with respect to goods which have been identified to a contract for sale are subject to the buyer's rights to recover the goods under this article (Code Sections 11-2-502 and 11-2-716).
(2) A creditor of the seller may treat a sale or an identification of goods to a contract for sale as void if as against him a retention of possession by the seller is fraudulent under any rule of law of the state where the goods are situated, except that retention of possession in good faith and current course of trade by a merchant-seller for a commercially reasonable time after a sale or identification is not fraudulent.
(3) Nothing in this article shall be deemed to impair the rights of creditors of the seller:

(a) Under the provisions of the article on secured transactions (Article 9 of this title); or

(b) Where identification to the contract or delivery is made not in current course of trade but in satisfaction of or as security for a preexisting claim for money, security, or the like and is made under circumstances which under any rule of law of the state where the goods are situated would apart from this article constitute the transaction a fraudulent transfer or voidable preference.

§ 11-2-403. Power to transfer; good faith purchase of goods; "entrusting."

(1) A purchaser of goods acquires all title which his transferor had or had power to transfer except that a purchaser of a limited interest acquires rights only to the extent of the interest purchased. A person with voidable title has power to transfer a good title to a good faith purchaser for value. When goods have been delivered under a transaction of purchase the purchaser has such power even though:

(a) The transferor was deceived as to the identity of the purchaser; or

(b) The delivery was in exchange for a check which is later dishonored; or

(c) It was agreed that the transaction was to be a "cash sale"; or

(d) The delivery was procured through fraud punishable as larcenous under the criminal law.

(2) Any entrusting of possession of goods to a merchant who deals in goods of that kind gives him power to transfer all rights of the entruster to a buyer in ordinary course of business.

(3) "Entrusting" includes any delivery and any acquiescence in retention of possession regardless of any condition expressed between the parties to the delivery or acquiescence and regardless of whether the procurement of the entrusting or the possessor's disposition of the goods have been such as to be larcenous under the criminal law.
(4) The rights of other purchasers of goods and of lien creditors are governed by the articles on secured transactions (Article 9 of this title), bulk transfers (Article 6 of this title), and documents of title (Article 7 of this title).

§ 11-2-501. Insurable interest in goods; manner of identification of goods
(1) The buyer obtains a special property and an insurable interest in goods by identification of existing goods as goods to which the contract refers even though the goods so identified are nonconforming and he has an option to return or reject them. Such identification can be made at any time and in any manner explicitly agreed to by the parties. In the absence of explicit agreement identification occurs:
(a) When the contract is made if it is for the sale of goods already existing and identified;
(b) If the contract is for the sale of future goods other than those described in paragraph (c) of this subsection, when goods are shipped, marked, or otherwise designated by the seller as goods to which the contract refers;
(c) When the crops are planted or otherwise become growing crops or the young are conceived if the contract is for the sale of unborn young to be born within 12 months after contracting or for the sale of crops to be harvested within 12 months or the next normal harvest season after contracting whichever is longer.
(2) The seller retains an insurable interest in goods so long as title to or any security interest in the goods remains in him and where the identification is by the seller alone he may until default or insolvency or notification to the buyer that the identification is final substitute other goods for those identified.
(3) Nothing in this Code section impairs any insurable interest recognized under any other statute or rule of law.

§ 11-2-502. Buyer's right to goods on seller's insolvency
(1) Subject to subsections (2) and (3) of this Code section and even though the goods have not been shipped a buyer who has paid a part or all of the price of goods in which the buyer has a special property under the provisions of Code Section 11-2-501 may on making and keeping good a tender of any unpaid portion of their price recover them from the seller if:
(a) In the case of goods bought for personal, family, or household purposes, the seller repudiates or fails to deliver as required by the contract; or
(b) In all cases, the seller becomes insolvent within ten days after receipt of the first installment on their price.
(2) The buyer's right to recover the goods under paragraph (a) of subsection (1) of this Code section vests upon acquisition of a special property, even if the seller had not then repudiated or failed to deliver.
(3) If the identification creating the buyer's special property has been made by the buyer he or she acquires the right to recover the goods only if they conform to the contract for sale.

§ 11-2-503. Manner of seller's tender of delivery
(1) Tender of delivery requires that the seller put and hold conforming goods at the buyer's disposition and give the buyer any notification reasonably necessary to enable him to take delivery. The manner, time, and place for tender are determined by the agreement and this article, and in particular:
(a) Tender must be at a reasonable hour, and if it is of goods they must be kept available for the period reasonably necessary to enable the buyer to take possession; but
(b) Unless otherwise agreed the buyer must furnish facilities reasonably suited to the receipt of the goods.
(2) Where the case is within Code Section 11-2-504 respecting shipment tender requires that the seller comply with its provisions.
(3) Where the seller is required to deliver at a particular destination tender requires that he comply with subsection (1) of this Code section and also in any appropriate case tender documents as described in subsections (4) and (5) of this Code section.
(4) Where goods are in the possession of a bailee and are to be delivered without being moved:
(a) Tender requires that the seller either tender a negotiable document of title covering such goods or procure acknowledgment by the bailee of the buyer's right to possession of the goods; but
(b) Tender to the buyer of a nonnegotiable document of title or of a record directing the bailee to deliver is sufficient tender unless the buyer seasonably objects, and except as otherwise provided in Article 9 of this title receipt by the bailee of notification of the buyer's rights fixes those rights as against the bailee and all third persons; but risk of loss of the goods and of any failure by the bailee to honor the nonnegotiable document of title or to obey the direction remains on the seller until the buyer has had a reasonable time to present the document or direction, and a refusal by the bailee to honor the document or to obey the direction defeats the tender.
(5) Where the contract requires the seller to deliver documents:
(a) He or she shall tender all such documents
(b) Tender through customary banking channels is sufficient and dishonor of a draft accompanying or associated with the documents constitutes nonacceptance or rejection.

§ 11-2-504. Shipment by seller
Where the seller is required or authorized to send the goods to the buyer and the contract does not require him to deliver them at a particular destination, then unless otherwise agreed he must:
(a) Put the goods in the possession of such a carrier and make such a contract for their transportation as may be reasonable having regard to the nature of the goods and other circumstances of the case; and
(b) Obtain and promptly deliver or tender in due form any document necessary to enable the buyer to

obtain possession of the goods or otherwise required by the agreement or by usage of trade; and

(c) Promptly notify the buyer of the shipment. Failure to notify the buyer under paragraph (c) of this Code section or to make a proper contract under paragraph (a) of this Code section is a ground for rejection only if material delay or loss ensues.

§ 11-2-505. eller's shipment under reservation

(1) Where the seller has identified goods to the contract by or before shipment:

(a) His or her procurement of a negotiable bill of lading to his or her own order or otherwise reserves in him or her a security interest in the goods. His or her procurement of the bill to the order of a financing agency or of the buyer indicates in addition only the seller's expectation of transferring that interest to the person named.

(b) A nonnegotiable bill of lading to himself or herself or his or her nominee reserves possession of the goods as security but except in a case of conditional delivery (subsection (2) of Code Section 11-2-507) a nonnegotiable bill of lading naming the buyer as consignee reserves no security interest even though the seller retains possession or control of the bill of lading.

(2) When shipment by the seller with reservation of a security interest is in violation of the contract for sale it constitutes an improper contract for transportation within Code Section 11-2-504 but impairs neither the rights given to the buyer by shipment and identification of the goods to the contract nor the seller's powers as a holder of a negotiable document of title.

§ 11-2-506. Rights of financing agency

(1) A financing agency by paying or purchasing for value a draft which relates to a shipment of goods acquires to the extent of the payment or purchase and in addition to its own rights under the draft and any document of title securing it any rights of the shipper in the goods including the right to stop delivery and the shipper's right to have the draft honored by the buyer.

(2) The right to reimbursement of a financing agency which has in good faith honored or purchased the draft under commitment to or authority from the buyer is not impaired by subsequent discovery of defects with reference to any relevant document which was apparently regular.

§ 11-2-507. Effect of seller's tender; delivery on condition

(1) Tender of delivery is a condition to the buyer's duty to accept the goods and, unless otherwise agreed, to his duty to pay for them. Tender entitles the seller to acceptance of the goods and to payment according to the contract.

(2) Where payment is due and demanded on the delivery to the buyer of goods or documents of title, his right as against the seller to retain or dispose of them is conditional upon his making the payment due.

§ 11-2-508. Cure by seller of improper tender or delivery; replacement

(1) Where any tender or delivery by the seller is rejected because nonconforming and the time for performance has not yet expired, the seller may seasonably notify the buyer of his intention to cure and may then within the contract time make a conforming delivery.

(2) Where the buyer rejects a nonconforming tender which the seller had reasonable grounds to believe would be acceptable with or without money allowance the seller may if he seasonably notifies the buyer have a further reasonable time to substitute a conforming tender.

§ 11-2-509. Risk of loss in the absence of breach

(1) Where the contract requires or authorizes the seller to ship the goods by carrier:

(a) If it does not require him to deliver them at a particular destination, the risk of loss passes to the buyer when the goods are duly delivered to the carrier even though the shipment is under reservation (Code Section 11-2-505); but

(b) If it does require him to deliver them at a particular destination and the goods are there duly tendered while in the possession of the carrier, the risk of loss passes to the buyer when the goods are there duly so tendered as to enable the buyer to take delivery.

(2) Where the goods are held by a bailee to be delivered without being moved, the risk of loss passes to the buyer:

(a) On his or her receipt of possession or control of a negotiable document of title covering the goods; or

(b) On acknowledgment by the bailee of the buyer's right to possession of the goods; or

(c) After his or her receipt of possession or control of a nonnegotiable document of title or other direction to deliver in a record, as provided in subsection (4)(b) of Code Section 11-2-503.

(3) In any case not within subsection (1) or (2) of this Code section, the risk of loss passes to the buyer on his receipt of the goods if the seller is a merchant; otherwise the risk passes to the buyer on tender of delivery.

(4) The provisions of this Code section are subject to contrary agreement of the parties and to the provisions of this article on sale on approval (Code Section 11-2-327) and on effect of breach on risk of loss (Code Section 11-2-510).

§ 11-2-510. Effect of breach on risk of loss

(1) Where a tender or delivery of goods so fails to conform to the contract as to give a right of rejection the risk of their loss remains on the seller until cure or acceptance.

(2) Where the buyer rightfully revokes acceptance he may to the extent of any deficiency in his effective insurance coverage treat the risk of loss as having rested on the seller from the beginning.

(3) Where the buyer as to conforming goods already identified to the contract for sale repudiates or is otherwise in breach before risk of their loss has passed to him, the seller may to the extent of any deficiency in his effective insurance coverage treat

the risk of loss as resting on the buyer for a commercially reasonable time.

§ 11-2-511. Tender of payment by buyer; payment by check

(1) Unless otherwise agreed tender of payment is a condition to the seller's duty to tender and complete any delivery.
(2) Tender of payment is sufficient when made by any means or in any manner current in the ordinary course of business unless the seller demands payment in legal tender and gives any extension of time reasonably necessary to procure it.
(3) Subject to the provisions of this title on the effect of an instrument on an obligation, payment by check is conditional and is defeated as between the parties by dishonor of the check on due presentment.

§ 11-2-512. Payment by buyer before inspection

(1) Where the contract requires payment before inspection nonconformity of the goods does not excuse the buyer from so making payment unless:
(a) The nonconformity appears without inspection; or
(b) Despite tender of the required documents the circumstances would justify injunction against honor under the provisions of this title (Code Section 11-5-109).
(2) Payment pursuant to subsection (1) of this Code section does not constitute an acceptance of goods or impair the buyer's right to inspect or any of his remedies.

§ 11-2-513. Buyer's right to inspection of goods

(1) Unless otherwise agreed and subject to subsection (3) of this Code section, where goods are tendered or delivered or identified to the contract for sale, the buyer has a right before payment or acceptance to inspect them at any reasonable place and time and in any reasonable manner. When the seller is required or authorized to send the goods to the buyer, the inspection may be after their arrival.
(2) Expenses of inspection must be borne by the buyer but may be recovered from the seller if the goods do not conform and are rejected.
(3) Unless otherwise agreed and subject to the provisions of this article on C.I.F. contracts (subsection (3) of Code Section 11-2-321), the buyer is not entitled to inspect the goods before payment of the price when the contract provides:
(a) For delivery "C.O.D." or on other like terms; or
(b) For payment against documents of title, except where such payment is due only after the goods are to become available for inspection.
(4) A place or method of inspection fixed by the parties is presumed to be exclusive but unless otherwise expressly agreed it does not postpone identification or shift the place for delivery or for passing the risk of loss. If compliance becomes impossible, inspection shall be as provided in this Code section unless the place or method fixed was clearly intended as an indispensable condition failure of which avoids the contract.

§ 11-2-514. When documents deliverable on acceptance; when on payment

Unless otherwise agreed documents against which a draft is drawn are to be delivered to the drawee on acceptance of the draft if it is payable more than three days after presentment; otherwise, only on payment.

§ 11-2-515. Preserving evidence of goods in dispute

In furtherance of the adjustment of any claim or dispute:
(a) Either party on reasonable notification to the other and for the purpose of ascertaining the facts and preserving evidence has the right to inspect, test, and sample the goods including such of them as may be in the possession or control of the other; and
(b) The parties may agree to a third party inspection or survey to determine the conformity or condition of the goods and may agree that the findings shall be binding upon them in any subsequent litigation or adjustment.

§ 11-2-601. Buyer's rights on improper delivery

Subject to the provisions of this article on breach in installment contracts (Code Section 11-2-612) and unless otherwise agreed under the Code sections on contractual limitations of remedy (Code Sections 11-2-718 and 11-2-719), if the goods or the tender of delivery fail in any respect to conform to the contract, the buyer may:
(a) Reject the whole; or
(b) Accept the whole; or
(c) Accept any commercial unit or units and reject the rest.

§ 11-2-602. Manner and effect of rightful rejection

(1) Rejection of goods must be within a reasonable time after their delivery or tender. It is ineffective unless the buyer seasonably notifies the seller.
(2) Subject to the provisions of Code Sections 11-2-603 and 11-2-604 on rejected goods:
(a) After rejection any exercise of ownership by the buyer with respect to any commercial unit is wrongful as against the seller; and
(b) If the buyer has before rejection taken physical possession of goods in which he does not have a security interest under the provisions of this article (subsection (3) of Code Section 11-2-711), he is under a duty after rejection to hold them with reasonable care at the seller's disposition for a time sufficient to permit the seller to remove them; but
(c) The buyer has no further obligations with regard to goods rightfully rejected.
(3) The seller's rights with respect to goods wrongfully rejected are governed by the provisions of this article on seller's remedies in general (Code Section 11-2-703).

§ 11-2-603. Merchant buyer's duties as to rightfully rejected goods

(1) Subject to any security interest in the buyer (subsection (3) of Code Section 11-2-711), when the seller has no agent or place of business at the market of rejection a merchant buyer is under a duty after

rejection of goods in his possession or control to follow any reasonable instructions received from the seller with respect to the goods and in the absence of such instructions to make reasonable efforts to sell them for the seller's account if they are perishable or threaten to decline in value speedily. Instructions are not reasonable if on demand indemnity for expenses is not forthcoming.
(2) When the buyer sells goods under subsection (1) of this Code section, he is entitled to reimbursement from the seller or out of the proceeds for reasonable expenses of caring for and selling them, and if the expenses include no selling commission then to such commission as is usual in the trade or if there is none to a reasonable sum not exceeding 10 percent on the gross proceeds.
(3) In complying with this Code section the buyer is held only to good faith and good faith conduct hereunder is neither acceptance nor conversion nor the basis of an action for damages.

§ 11-2-604. Buyer's options as to salvage of rightfully rejected goods
Subject to the provisions of Code Section 11-2-603 on perishables if the seller gives no instructions within a reasonable time after notification of rejection the buyer may store the rejected goods for the seller's account or reship them to him or resell them for the seller's account with reimbursement as provided in Code Section 11-2-603. Such action is not acceptance or conversion.

§ 11-2-605. Waiver of buyer's objections by failure to particularize
(1) The buyer's failure to state in connection with rejection a particular defect which is ascertainable by reasonable inspection precludes him from relying on the unstated defect to justify rejection or to establish breach:
(a) Where the seller could have cured it if stated seasonably; or
(b) Between merchants when the seller has after rejection made a request in writing for a full and final written statement of all defects on which the buyer proposes to rely.
(2) Payment against documents made without reservation of rights precludes recovery of the payment for defects apparent in the documents.

§ 11-2-606. What constitutes acceptance of goods
(1) Acceptance of goods occurs when the buyer:
(a) After a reasonable opportunity to inspect the goods signifies to the seller that the goods are conforming or that he will take or retain them in spite of their nonconformity; or
(b) Fails to make an effective rejection (subsection (1) of Code Section 11-2-602), but such acceptance does not occur until the buyer has had a reasonable opportunity to inspect them; or
(c) Does any act inconsistent with the seller's ownership; but if such act is wrongful as against the seller it is an acceptance only if ratified by him.
(2) Acceptance of a part of any commercial unit is acceptance of that entire unit.

§ 11-2-607. Effect of acceptance; notice of breach; burden of establishing breach after acceptance; notice of claim or litigation to person answerable over
(1) The buyer must pay at the contract rate for any goods accepted.
(2) Acceptance of goods by the buyer precludes rejection of the goods accepted and if made with knowledge of a nonconformity cannot be revoked because of it unless the acceptance was on the reasonable assumption that the nonconformity would be seasonably cured but acceptance does not of itself impair any other remedy provided by this article for nonconformity.
(3) Where a tender has been accepted:
(a) The buyer must within a reasonable time after he discovers or should have discovered any breach notify the seller of breach or be barred from any remedy; and
(b) If the claim is one for infringement or the like (subsection (3) of Code Section 11-2-312) and the buyer is sued as a result of such a breach he must so notify the seller within a reasonable time after he receives notice of the litigation or be barred from any remedy over for liability established by the litigation.
(4) The burden is on the buyer to establish any breach with respect to the goods accepted.
(5) Where the buyer is sued for breach of a warranty or other obligation for which his seller is answerable over:
(a) He may give his seller written notice of the litigation. If the notice states that the seller may come in and defend and that if the seller does not do so he will be bound in any action against him by his buyer by any determination of fact common to the two litigations, then unless the seller after seasonable receipt of the notice does come in and defend he is so bound.
(b) If the claim is one for infringement or the like (subsection (3) of Code Section 11-2-312) the original seller may demand in writing that his buyer turn over to him control of the litigation including settlement or else be barred from any remedy over and if he also agrees to bear all expense and to satisfy any adverse judgment, then unless the buyer after seasonable receipt of the demand does turn over control the buyer is so barred.
(6) The provisions of subsections (3), (4), and (5) of this Code section apply to any obligation of a buyer to hold the seller harmless against infringement or the like (subsection (3) of Code Section 11-2-312).

§ 11-2-608. Revocation of acceptance in whole or in part
(1) The buyer may revoke his acceptance of a lot or commercial unit whose nonconformity substantially impairs its value to him if he has accepted it:
(a) On the reasonable assumption that its nonconformity would be cured and it has not been seasonably cured; or
(b) Without discovery of such nonconformity if his acceptance was reasonably induced either by the difficulty of discovery before acceptance or by the seller's assurances.
(2) Revocation of acceptance must occur within a reasonable time after the buyer discovers or should

have discovered the ground for it and before any substantial change in condition of the goods which is not caused by their own defects. It is not effective until the buyer notifies the seller of it.
(3) A buyer who so revokes has the same rights and duties with regard to the goods involved as if he had rejected them.

§ 11-2-609. Right to adequate assurance of performance
(1) A contract for sale imposes an obligation on each party that the other's expectation of receiving due performance will not be impaired. When reasonable grounds for insecurity arise with respect to the performance of either party the other may in writing demand adequate assurance of due performance and until he receives such assurance may if commercially reasonable suspend any performance for which he has not already received the agreed return.
(2) Between merchants the reasonableness of grounds for insecurity and the adequacy of any assurance offered shall be determined according to commercial standards.
(3) Acceptance of any improper delivery or payment does not prejudice the aggrieved party's right to demand adequate assurance of future performance.
(4) After receipt of a justified demand failure to provide within a reasonable time not exceeding 30 days such assurance of due performance as is adequate under the circumstances of the particular case is a repudiation of the contract.

§ 11-2-610. Anticipatory repudiation
When either party repudiates the contract with respect to a performance not yet due the loss of which will substantially impair the value of the contract to the other, the aggrieved party may:
(a) For a commercially reasonable time await performance by the repudiating party; or
(b) Resort to any remedy for breach (Code Section 11-2-703 or Code Section 11-2-711), even though he has notified the repudiating party that he would await the latter's performance and has urged retraction; and
(c) In either case suspend his own performance or proceed in accordance with the provisions of this article on the seller's right to identify goods to the contract notwithstanding breach or to salvage unfinished goods (Code Section 11-2-704).

§ 11-2-611. Retraction of anticipatory repudiation
(1) Until the repudiating party's next performance is due he can retract his repudiation unless the aggrieved party has since the repudiation canceled or materially changed his position or otherwise indicated that he considers the repudiation final.
(2) Retraction may be by any method which clearly indicates to the aggrieved party that the repudiating party intends to perform, but must include any assurance justifiably demanded under the provisions of this article (Code Section 11-2-609).
(3) Retraction reinstates the repudiating party's rights under the contract with due excuse and allowance to the aggrieved party for any delay occasioned by the repudiation.

§ 11-2-612. "Installment contract"; breach
(1) An "installment contract" is one which requires or authorizes the delivery of goods in separate lots to be separately accepted, even though the contract contains a clause "each delivery is a separate contract" or its equivalent.
(2) The buyer may reject any installment which is nonconforming if the nonconformity substantially impairs the value of that installment and cannot be cured or if the nonconformity is a defect in the required documents; but if the nonconformity does not fall within subsection (3) of this Code section and the seller gives adequate assurance of its cure the buyer must accept that installment.
(3) Whenever nonconformity or default with respect to one or more installments substantially impairs the value of the whole contract there is a breach of the whole. But the aggrieved party reinstates the contract if he accepts a nonconforming installment without seasonably notifying of cancellation or if he brings an action with respect only to past installments or demands performance as to future installments.

§ 11-2-613. Casualty to identified goods
Where the contract requires for its performance goods identified when the contract is made, and the goods suffer casualty without fault of either party before the risk of loss passes to the buyer, or in a proper case under a "no arrival, no sale" term (Code Section 11-2-324) then:
(a) If the loss is total the contract is avoided; and
(b) If the loss is partial or the goods have so deteriorated as no longer to conform to the contract the buyer may nevertheless demand inspection and at his option either treat the contract as avoided or accept the goods with due allowance from the contract price for the deterioration or the deficiency in quantity but without further right against the seller.

§ 11-2-614. Substituted performance
(1) Where without fault of either party the agreed berthing, loading, or unloading facilities fail or an agreed type of carrier becomes unavailable or the agreed manner of delivery otherwise becomes commercially impracticable but a commercially reasonable substitute is available, such substitute performance must be tendered and accepted.
(2) If the agreed means or manner of payment fails because of domestic or foreign governmental regulation, the seller may withhold or stop delivery unless the buyer provides a means or manner of payment which is commercially a substantial equivalent. If delivery has already been taken, payment by the means or in the manner provided by the regulation discharges the buyer's obligation unless the regulation is discriminatory, oppressive, or predatory.

§ 11-2-615. Excuse by failure of presupposed conditions
Except so far as a seller may have assumed a greater obligation and subject to Code Section 11-2-614 on substituted performance:
(a) Delay in delivery or nondelivery in whole or in part by a seller who complies with paragraphs (b) and

(c) of this Code section is not a breach of his duty under a contract for sale if performance as agreed has been made impracticable by the occurrence of a contingency the nonoccurrence of which was a basic assumption on which the contract was made or by compliance in good faith with any applicable foreign or domestic governmental regulation or order whether or not it later proves to be invalid.

(b) Where the clauses mentioned in paragraph (a) of this Code section affect only a part of the seller's capacity to perform, he must allocate production and deliveries among his customers but may at his option include regular customers not then under contract as well as his own requirements for further manufacture. He may so allocate in any manner which is fair and reasonable.

(c) The seller must notify the buyer seasonably that there will be delay or nondelivery and, when allocation is required under paragraph (b) of this Code section, of the estimated quota thus made available for the buyer.

§ 11-2-616. Procedure on notice claiming excuse

(1) Where the buyer receives notification of a material or indefinite delay or an allocation justified under Code Section 11-2-615 he may by written notification to the seller as to any delivery concerned, and where the prospective deficiency substantially impairs the value of the whole contract under the provisions of this article relating to breach of installment contracts (Code Section 11-2-612), then also as to the whole:

(a) Terminate and thereby discharge any unexecuted portion of the contract; or

(b) Modify the contract by agreeing to take his available quota in substitution.

(2) If after receipt of such notification from the seller the buyer fails so to modify the contract within a reasonable time not exceeding 30 days the contract lapses with respect to any deliveries affected.

(3) The provisions of this Code section may not be negated by agreement except insofar as the seller has assumed a greater obligation under Code Section 11-2-615.

§ 11-2-701. Remedies for breach of collateral contracts not impaired

Remedies for breach of any obligation or promise collateral or ancillary to a contract for sale are not impaired by the provisions of this article.

§ 11-2-702. Seller's remedies on discovery of buyer's insolvency

(1) Where the seller discovers the buyer to be insolvent he may refuse delivery except for cash including payment for all goods theretofore delivered under the contract, and stop delivery under this article (Code Section 11-2-705).

(2) Where the seller discovers that the buyer has received goods on credit while insolvent he may reclaim the goods upon demand made within ten days after the receipt, but if misrepresentation of solvency has been made to the particular seller in writing within three months before delivery the ten-day limitation does not apply. Except as provided in this subsection the seller may not base a right to reclaim goods on the buyer's fraudulent or innocent misrepresentation of solvency or of intent to pay.

(3) The seller's right to reclaim under subsection (2) of this Code section is subject to the rights of a buyer in ordinary course or other good faith purchaser or lien creditor under this article (Code Section 11-2-403). Successful reclamation of goods excludes all other remedies with respect to them.

§ 11-2-703. Seller's remedies in general

Where the buyer wrongfully rejects or revokes acceptance of goods or fails to make a payment due on or before delivery or repudiates with respect to a part or the whole, then with respect to any goods directly affected and, if the breach is of the whole contract (Code Section 11-2-612), then also with respect to the whole undelivered balance, the aggrieved seller may:

(a) Withhold delivery of such goods;

(b) Stop delivery by any bailee as hereafter provided (Code Section 11-2-705);

(c) Proceed under Code Section 11-2-704 respecting goods still unidentified to the contract;

(d) Resell and recover damages as hereafter provided (Code Section 11-2-706);

(e) Recover damages for nonacceptance (Code Section 11-2-708) or in a proper case the price (Code Section 11-2-709);

(f) Cancel.

§ 11-2-704. Seller's right to identify goods to the contract notwithstanding breach or to salvage unfinished goods

(1) An aggrieved seller under Code Section 11-2-703 may:

(a) Identify to the contract conforming goods not already identified if at the time he learned of the breach they are in his possession or control;

(b) Treat as the subject of resale goods which have demonstrably been intended for the particular contract even though those goods are unfinished.

(2) Where the goods are unfinished an aggrieved seller may in the exercise of reasonable commercial judgment for the purposes of avoiding loss and of effective realization either complete the manufacture and wholly identify the goods to the contract or cease manufacture and resell for scrap or salvage value or proceed in any other reasonable manner.

§ 11-2-705. Seller's stoppage of delivery in transit or otherwise

(1) The seller may stop delivery of goods in the possession of a carrier or other bailee when he discovers the buyer to be insolvent (Code Section 11-2-702) and may stop delivery of carload, truckload, planeload, or larger shipments of express or freight when the buyer repudiates or fails to make a payment due before delivery or if for any other reason the seller has a right to withhold or reclaim the goods.

(2) As against such buyer the seller may stop delivery until:

(a) Receipt of the goods by the buyer; or

(b) Acknowledgment to the buyer by any bailee of the goods except a carrier that the bailee holds the goods for the buyer; or

(c) Such acknowledgment to the buyer by a carrier by reshipment or as a warehouse; or

(d) Negotiation to the buyer of any negotiable document of title covering the goods.

(3) (a) To stop delivery the seller shall so notify as to enable the bailee by reasonable diligence to prevent delivery of the goods.

(b) After such notification the bailee shall hold and deliver the goods according to the directions of the seller but the seller is liable to the bailee for any ensuing charges or damages.

(c) If a negotiable document of title has been issued for goods the bailee is not obliged to obey a notification to stop until surrender of possession or control of the document.

(d) A carrier who has issued a nonnegotiable bill of lading is not obliged to obey a notification to stop received from a person other than the consignor.

§ 11-2-706. Seller's resale including contract for resale

(1) Under the conditions stated in Code Section 11-2-703 on seller's remedies, the seller may resell the goods concerned or the undelivered balance thereof. Where the resale is made in good faith and in a commercially reasonable manner the seller may recover the difference between the resale price and the contract price together with any incidental damages allowed under the provisions of this article (Code Section 11-2-710), but less expenses saved in consequence of the buyer's breach.

(2) Except as otherwise provided in subsection (3) of this Code section or unless otherwise agreed resale may be at public or private sale including sale by way of one or more contracts to sell or of identification to an existing contract of the seller. Sale may be as a unit or in parcels and at any time and place and on any terms but every aspect of the sale including the method, manner, time, place, and terms must be commercially reasonable. The resale must be reasonably identified as referring to the broken contract, but it is not necessary that the goods be in existence or that any or all of them have been identified to the contract before the breach.

(3) Where the resale is at private sale the seller must give the buyer reasonable notification of his intention to resell.

(4) Where the resale is at public sale:

(a) Only identified goods can be sold except where there is a recognized market for a public sale of futures in goods of the kind; and

(b) It must be made at a usual place or market for public sale if one is reasonably available and except in the case of goods which are perishable or threaten to decline in value speedily the seller must give the buyer reasonable notice of the time and place of the resale; and

(c) If the goods are not to be within the view of those attending the sale the notification of sale must state the place where the goods are located and provide for their reasonable inspection by prospective bidders; and

(d) The seller may buy.

(5) A purchaser who buys in good faith at a resale takes the goods free of any rights of the original buyer even though the seller fails to comply with one or more of the requirements of this Code section.

(6) The seller is not accountable to the buyer for any profit made on any resale. A person in the position of a seller (Code Section 11-2-707) or a buyer who has rightfully rejected or justifiably revoked acceptance must account for any excess over the amount of his security interest, as hereinafter defined (subsection (3) of Code Section 11-2-711).

§ 11-2-707. "Person in the position of a seller."

(1) A "person in the position of a seller" includes as against a principal an agent who has paid or become responsible for the price of goods on behalf of his principal or anyone who otherwise holds a security interest or other right in goods similar to that of a seller.

(2) A person in the position of a seller may as provided in this article withhold or stop delivery (Code Section 11-2-705) and resell (Code Section 11-2-706) and recover incidental damages (Code Section 11-2-710).

§ 11-2-708. Seller's damages for nonacceptance or repudiation

(1) Subject to subsection (2) of this Code section and to the provisions of this article with respect to proof of market price (Code Section 11-2-723), the measure of damages for nonacceptance or repudiation by the buyer is the difference between the market price at the time and place for tender and the unpaid contract price together with any incidental damages provided in this article (Code Section 11-2-710), but less expenses saved in consequence of the buyer's breach.

(2) If the measure of damages provided in subsection (1) of this Code section is inadequate to put the seller in as good a position as performance would have done then the measure of damages is the profit (including reasonable overhead) which the seller would have made from full performance by the buyer, together with any incidental damages provided in this article (Code Section 11-2-710), due allowance for costs reasonably incurred and due credit for payments or proceeds of resale.

§ 11-2-709. Action for the price

(1) When the buyer fails to pay the price as it becomes due the seller may recover, together with any incidental damages under Code Section 11-2-710, the price:

(a) Of goods accepted or of conforming goods lost or damaged within a commercially reasonable time after risk of their loss has passed to the buyer; and

(b) Of goods identified to the contract if the seller is unable after reasonable effort to resell them at a reasonable price or the circumstances reasonably indicate that such effort will be unavailing.

(2) Where the seller sues for the price he must hold for the buyer any goods which have been identified to the contract and are still in his control except that if resale becomes possible he may resell them at any time prior to the collection of the judgment. The net proceeds of any such resale must be credited to the buyer and payment of the judgment entitles him to any goods not resold.

(3) After the buyer has wrongfully rejected or revoked acceptance of the goods or has failed to make a payment due or has repudiated (Code Section 11-2-610), a seller who is held not entitled to the price under this Code section shall nevertheless be awarded damages for nonacceptance under Code Section 11-2-708.

§ 11-2-710. Seller's incidental damages
Incidental damages to an aggrieved seller include any commercially reasonable charges, expenses, or commissions incurred in stopping delivery, in the transportation, care, and custody of goods after the buyer's breach, in connection with return or resale of the goods or otherwise resulting from the breach.

§ 11-2-711. Buyer's remedies in general; buyer's security interest in rejected goods
(1) Where the seller fails to make delivery or repudiates or the buyer rightfully rejects or justifiably revokes acceptance then with respect to any goods involved, and with respect to the whole if the breach goes to the whole contract (Code Section 11-2-612), the buyer may cancel and whether or not he has done so may in addition to recovering so much of the price as has been paid:
(a) "Cover" and have damages under Code Section 11-2-712 as to all the goods affected whether or not they have been identified to the contract; or
(b) Recover damages for nondelivery as provided in this article (Code Section 11-2-713).
(2) Where the seller fails to deliver or repudiates the buyer may also:
(a) If the goods have been identified recover them as provided in this article (Code Section 11-2-502); or
(b) In a proper case obtain specific performance or replevy the goods as provided in this article (Code Section 11-2-716).
(3) On rightful rejection or justifiable revocation of acceptance a buyer has a security interest in goods in his possession or control for any payments made on their price and any expenses reasonably incurred in their inspection, receipt, transportation, care, and custody and may hold such goods and resell them in like manner as an aggrieved seller (Code Section 11-2-706).

§ 11-2-712. "Cover"; buyer's procurement of substitute goods
(1) After a breach within Code Section 11-2-711 the buyer may "cover" by making in good faith and without unreasonable delay any reasonable purchase of or contract to purchase goods in substitution for those due from the seller.
(2) The buyer may recover from the seller as damages the difference between the cost of cover and the contract price together with any incidental or consequential damages as hereinafter defined (Code Section 11-2-715), but less expenses saved in consequence of the seller's breach.
(3) Failure of the buyer to effect cover within this Code section does not bar him from any other remedy.

§ 11-2-713. Buyer's damages for nondelivery or repudiation
(1) Subject to the provisions of this article with respect to proof of market price (Code Section 11-2-723), the measure of damages for nondelivery or repudiation by the seller is the difference between the market price at the time when the buyer learned of the breach and the contract price together with any incidental and consequential damages provided in this article (Code Section 11-2-715), but less expenses saved in consequence of the seller's breach.
(2) Market price is to be determined as of the place for tender or, in cases of rejection after arrival or revocation of acceptance, as of the place of arrival.

§ 11-2-714. Buyer's damages for breach in regard to accepted goods
(1) Where the buyer has accepted goods and given notification (subsection (3) of Code Section 11-2-607) he may recover as damages for any nonconformity of tender the loss resulting in the ordinary course of events from the seller's breach as determined in any manner which is reasonable.
(2) The measure of damages for breach of warranty is the difference at the time and place of acceptance between the value of the goods accepted and the value they would have had if they had been as warranted, unless special circumstances show proximate damages of a different amount.
(3) In a proper case any incidental and consequential damages under Code Section 11-2-715 may also be recovered.

§ 11-2-715. Buyer's incidental and consequential damages
(1) Incidental damages resulting from the seller's breach include expenses reasonably incurred in inspection, receipt, transportation, and care and custody of goods rightfully rejected, any commercially reasonable charges, expenses, or commissions in connection with effecting cover, and any other reasonable expense incident to the delay or other breach.
(2) Consequential damages resulting from the seller's breach include:
(a) Any loss resulting from general or particular requirements and needs of which the seller at the time of contracting had reason to know and which could not reasonably be prevented by cover or otherwise; and
(b) Injury to person or property proximately resulting from any breach of warranty.

§ 11-2-716. Buyer's right to specific performance or replevin
(1) Specific performance may be decreed where the goods are unique or in other proper circumstances.
(2) The decree for specific performance may include such terms and conditions as to payment of the price, damages, or other relief as the court may deem just.
(3) The buyer has a right of replevin for goods identified to the contract if after reasonable effort the buyer is unable to effect cover for such goods or the circumstances reasonably indicate that such effort will be unavailing or if the goods have been shipped under reservation and satisfaction of the security interest in them has been made or tendered. In the case of goods bought for personal, family, or

household purposes, the buyer's right of replevin vests upon acquisition of a special property, even if the seller had not then repudiated or failed to deliver.

§ 11-2-717. Deduction of damages from the price
The buyer on notifying the seller of his intention to do so may deduct all or any part of the damages resulting from any breach of the contract from any part of the price still due under the same contract.

§ 11-2-718. Liquidation or limitation of damages; deposits
(1) Damages for breach by either party may be liquidated in the agreement but only at an amount which is reasonable in the light of the anticipated or actual harm caused by the breach, the difficulties of proof of loss, and the inconvenience or nonfeasibility of otherwise obtaining an adequate remedy. A term fixing unreasonably large liquidated damages is void as a penalty.
(2) Where the seller justifiably withholds delivery of goods because of the buyer's breach, the buyer is entitled to restitution of any amount by which the sum of his payments exceeds:
(a) The amount to which the seller is entitled by virtue of terms liquidating the seller's damages in accordance with subsection (1) of this Code section; or
(b) In the absence of such terms, 20 percent of the value of the total performance for which the buyer is obligated under the contract or $500.00, whichever is smaller.
(3) The buyer's right to restitution under subsection (2) of this Code section is subject to offset to the extent that the seller establishes:
(a) A right to recover damages under the provisions of this article other than subsection (1) of this Code section; and
(b) The amount or value of any benefits received by the buyer directly or indirectly by reason of the contract.
(4) Where a seller has received payment in goods their reasonable value or the proceeds of their resale shall be treated as payments for the purposes of subsection (2) of this Code section; but if the seller has notice of the buyer's breach before reselling goods received in part performance, his resale is subject to the conditions laid down in this article on resale by an aggrieved seller (Code Section 11-2-706).

§ 11-2-719. Contractual modification or limitation of remedy
(1) Subject to the provisions of subsections (2) and (3) of this Code section and of Code Section 11-2-718 on liquidation and limitation of damages:
(a) The agreement may provide for remedies in addition to or in substitution for those provided in this article and may limit or alter the measure of damages recoverable under this article, as by limiting the buyer's remedies to return of the goods and repayment of the price or to repair and replacement of nonconforming goods or parts; and
(b) Resort to a remedy as provided is optional unless the remedy is expressly agreed to be exclusive, in which case it is the sole remedy.
(2) Where circumstances cause an exclusive or limited remedy to fail of its essential purpose, remedy may be had as provided in this title.
(3) Consequential damages may be limited or excluded unless the limitation or exclusion is unconscionable. Limitation of consequential damages for injury to the person in the case of consumer goods is prima facie unconscionable but limitation of damages where the loss is commercial is not.

§ 11-2-720. Effect of "cancellation" or "rescission" on claims for antecedent breach
Unless the contrary intention clearly appears, expressions of "cancellation" or "rescission" of the contract or the like shall not be construed as a renunciation or discharge of any claim in damages for an antecedent breach.

§ 11-2-721. Remedies for fraud
Remedies for material misrepresentation or fraud include all remedies available under this article for nonfraudulent breach. Neither rescission or a claim for rescission of the contract for sale nor rejection or return of the goods shall bar or be deemed inconsistent with a claim for damages or other remedy.

§ 11-2-722. Who can sue third parties for injury to goods
Where a third party so deals with goods which have been identified to a contract for sale as to cause actionable injury to a party to that contract:
(a) A right of action against the third party is in either party to the contract for sale who has title to or a security interest or a special property or an insurable interest in the goods; and if the goods have been destroyed or converted a right of action is also in the party who either bore the risk of loss under the contract for sale or has since the injury assumed that risk as against the other;
(b) If at the time of the injury the party plaintiff did not bear the risk of loss as against the other party to the contract for sale and there is no arrangement between them for disposition of the recovery, his suit or settlement is, subject to his own interest, as a fiduciary for the other party to the contract;
(c) Either party may with the consent of the other sue for the benefit of whom it may concern.

§ 11-2-723. Proof of market price: time and place
(1) If an action based on anticipatory repudiation comes to trial before the time for performance with respect to some or all of the goods, any damages based on market price (Code Section 11-2-708 or Code Section 11-2-713) shall be determined according to the price of such goods prevailing at the time when the aggrieved party learned of the repudiation.
(2) If evidence of a price prevailing at the times or places described in this article is not readily available the price prevailing within any reasonable time before or after the time described or at any other place which in commercial judgment or under usage of trade would serve as a reasonable substitute for the one described may be used, making any proper

allowance for the cost of transporting the goods to or from such other place.
(3) Evidence of a relevant price prevailing at a time or place other than the one described in this article offered by one party is not admissible unless and until he has given the other party such notice as the court finds sufficient to prevent unfair surprise.

§ 11-2-724. Admissibility of market quotations
Whenever the prevailing price or value of any goods regularly bought and sold in any established commodity market is in issue, reports in official publications or trade journals or in newspapers or periodicals of general circulation published as the reports of such market shall be admissible in evidence. The circumstances of the preparation of such a report may be shown to affect its weight but not its admissibility.

§ 11-2-725. Statute of limitations in contracts for sale
(1) An action for breach of any contract for sale must be commenced within four years after the cause of action has accrued. By the original agreement the parties may reduce the period of limitation to not less than one year but may not extend it.
(2) A cause of action accrues when the breach occurs, regardless of the aggrieved party's lack of knowledge of the breach. A breach of warranty occurs when tender of delivery is made, except that where a warranty explicitly extends to future performance of the goods and discovery of the breach must await the time of such performance the cause of action accrues when the breach is or should have been discovered.
(3) Where an action commenced within the time limited by subsection (1) of this Code section is so terminated as to leave available a remedy by another action for the same breach such other action may be commenced after the expiration of the time limited and within six months after the termination of the first action unless the termination resulted from voluntary discontinuance or from dismissal for failure or neglect to prosecute.
(4) This Code section does not alter the law on tolling of the statute of limitations nor does it apply to causes of action which have accrued before January 1, 1964.

ARICLE 9

§ 11-9-101. Short title.
This article may be cited as "Uniform Commercial Code -- Secured Transactions."

§ 11-9-102. Definitions and index of definitions.
(a) *Article 9 definitions.* As used in this article, the term:
(1) "Accession" means goods that are physically united with other goods in such a manner that the identity of the original goods is not lost.
(2) "Account," except as used in "account for," means a right to payment of a monetary obligation, whether or not earned by performance, (i) for property that has been or is to be sold, leased, licensed, assigned, or otherwise disposed of, (ii) for services rendered or to be rendered, (iii) for a policy of insurance issued or to be issued, (iv) for a secondary obligation incurred or to be incurred, (v) for energy provided or to be provided, (vi) for the use or hire of a vessel under a charter or other contract, (vii) arising out of the use of a credit or charge card or information contained on or for use with the card, or (viii) as winnings in a lottery or other game of chance operated or sponsored by a state, governmental unit of a state, or person licensed or authorized to operate the game by a state or governmental unit of a state. The term includes health care insurance receivables. The term does not include (i) rights to payment evidenced by chattel paper or an instrument, (ii) commercial tort claims, (iii) deposit accounts, (iv) investment property, (v) letter of credit rights or letters of credit, or (vi) rights to payment for money or funds advanced or sold, other than rights arising out of the use of a credit or charge card or information contained on or for use with the card.
(3) "Account debtor" means a person obligated on an account, chattel paper, or general intangible. The term does not include persons obligated to pay a negotiable instrument, even if the instrument constitutes part of chattel paper.
(4) "Accounting," except as used in "accounting for," means a record:
(A) Authenticated by a secured party;
(B) Indicating the aggregate unpaid secured obligations as of a date not more than 35 days earlier or 35 days later than the date of the record; and
(C) Identifying the components of the obligations in reasonable detail.
(5) "Agricultural lien" means an interest in farm products:
(A) Which secures payment or performance of an obligation for:
(i) Goods or services furnished in connection with a debtor's farming operation; or
(ii) Rent on real property leased by a debtor in connection with its farming operation;
(B) Which is created by statute in favor of a person that:
(i) In the ordinary course of its business furnished goods or services to a debtor in connection with a debtor's farming operation; or
(ii) Leased real property to a debtor in connection with the debtor's farming operation; and
(C) Whose effectiveness does not depend on the person's possession of the personal property.
(6) "As-extracted collateral" means:
(A) Oil, gas, or other minerals that are subject to a security interest that:
(i) Is created by a debtor having an interest in the minerals before extraction; and
(ii) Attaches to the minerals as extracted; or
(B) Accounts arising out of the sale at the wellhead or minehead of oil, gas, or other minerals in which the debtor had an interest before extraction.
(7) "Authenticate" means:
(A) To sign; or
(B) To execute or otherwise adopt a symbol, or encrypt or similarly process a record in whole or in part, with the present intent of the authenticating

person to identify the person and adopt or accept a record.

(8) "Authority" means the Georgia Superior Court Clerks' Cooperative Authority.

(9) "Bank" means an organization that is engaged in the business of banking. The term includes savings banks, savings and loan associations, credit unions, and trust companies.

(10) "Cash proceeds" means proceeds that are money, checks, deposit accounts, or the like.

(11) "Certificate of title" means a certificate of title with respect to which a statute provides for the security interest in question to be indicated on the certificate as a condition or result of the security interest's obtaining priority over the rights of a lien creditor with respect to the collateral.

(12) "Chattel paper" means a record or records that evidence both a monetary obligation and a security interest in specific goods, a security interest in specific goods and software used in the goods, a lease of specific goods, or a lease of specific goods and license of software used in the goods. As used in this paragraph, "monetary obligation" means a monetary obligation secured by the goods or owed under a lease of the goods and includes a monetary obligation with respect to software used in the goods. The term does not include:

(A) Charters or other contracts involving the use or hire of a vessel; or

(B) Records that evidence a right to payment arising out of the use of a credit or charge card or information contained on or for use with the card. If a transaction is evidenced by records that include an instrument or series of instruments, the group of records taken together constitutes chattel paper.

(13) "Collateral" means the property subject to a security interest or agricultural lien. The term includes:

(A) Proceeds to which a security interest attaches;

(B) Accounts, chattel paper, payment intangibles, and promissory notes that have been sold; and

(C) Goods that are the subject of a consignment.

(14) "Commercial tort claim" means a claim arising in tort with respect to which:

(A) The claimant is an organization; or

(B) The claimant is an individual and the claim:

(i) Arose in the course of the claimant's business or profession; and

(ii) Does not include damages arising out of personal injury to or the death of an individual.

(15) "Commodity account" means an account maintained by a commodity intermediary in which a commodity contract is carried for a commodity customer.

(16) "Commodity contract" means a commodity futures contract, an option on a commodity futures contract, a commodity option, or another contract if the contract or option is:

(A) Traded on or subject to the rules of a board of trade that has been designated as a contract market for such a contract pursuant to federal commodities laws; or

(B) Traded on a foreign commodity board of trade, exchange, or market and is carried on the books of a commodity intermediary for a commodity customer.

(17) "Commodity customer" means a person for which a commodity intermediary carries a commodity contract on its books.

(18) "Commodity intermediary" means a person that:

(A) Is registered as a futures commission merchant under federal commodities law; or

(B) In the ordinary course of its business provides clearance or settlement services for a board of trade that has been designated as a contract market pursuant to federal commodities law.

(19) "Communicate" means:

(A) To send a written or other tangible record;

(B) To transmit a record by any means agreed upon by the persons sending and receiving the record; or

(C) In the case of transmission of a record to or by a filing office or the authority, to transmit a record by any means prescribed by filing office rule.

(20) "Consignee" means a merchant to which goods are delivered in a consignment.

(21) "Consignment" means a transaction, regardless of its form, in which a person delivers goods to a merchant for the purpose of sale and:

(A) The merchant:

(i) Deals in goods of that kind under a name other than the name of the person making delivery;

(ii) Is not an auctioneer; and

(iii) Is not generally known by its creditors to be substantially engaged in selling the goods of others;

(B) With respect to each delivery, the aggregate value of the goods is $1,000.00 or more at the time of delivery;

(C) The goods are not consumer goods immediately before delivery; and

(D) The transaction does not create a security interest that secures an obligation.

(22) "Consignor" means a person that delivers goods to a consignee in a consignment.

(23) "Consumer debtor" means a debtor in a consumer transaction.

(24) "Consumer goods" means goods that are used or bought for use primarily for personal, family, or household purposes.

(25) "Consumer goods transaction" means a consumer transaction in which:

(A) An individual incurs an obligation primarily for personal, family, or household purposes; and

(B) A security interest in consumer goods secures the obligation.

(26) "Consumer obligor" means an obligor who is an individual and who incurred the obligation as part of a transaction entered into primarily for personal, family, or household purposes.

(27) "Consumer transaction" means a transaction in which (i) an individual incurs an obligation primarily for personal, family, or household purposes, (ii) a security interest secures the obligation, and (iii) the collateral is held or acquired primarily for personal, family, or household purposes. The term includes consumer goods transactions.

(28) "Continuation statement" means an amendment of a financing statement which:

(A) Identifies, by its file number, the initial financing statement to which it relates; and

(B) Indicates that it is a continuation statement for, or that it is filed to continue the effectiveness of, the identified financing statement.

(29) "Debtor" means:

(A) A person having an interest, other than a security interest or other lien, in the collateral, whether or not the person is an obligor;

(B) A seller of accounts, chattel paper, payment intangibles, or promissory notes; or

(C) A consignee.

(30) "Deposit account" means a demand, time, savings, passbook, or similar account maintained with a bank. The term does not include investment property or accounts evidenced by an instrument.

(31) "Document" means a document of title or a receipt of the type described in subsection (2) of Code Section 11-7-201.

(32) "Electronic chattel paper" means chattel paper evidenced by a record or records consisting of information stored in an electronic medium.

(33) "Encumbrance" means a right, other than an ownership interest, in real property. The term includes mortgages and other liens on real property.

(34) "Equipment" means goods other than inventory, farm products, or consumer goods.

(35) "Farm products" means goods, other than standing timber, with respect to which the debtor is engaged in a farming operation and which are:

(A) Crops grown, growing, or to be grown, including:

(i) Crops produced on trees, vines, and bushes; and

(ii) Aquatic goods produced in aquacultural operations;

(B) Livestock, born or unborn, including aquatic goods produced in aquacultural operations;

(C) Supplies used or produced in a farming operation; or

(D) Products of crops or livestock in their unmanufactured states.

(36) "Farming operation" means raising, cultivating, propagating, fattening, grazing, or any other farming, livestock, or aquacultural operation.

(37) "File number" means the number assigned to an initial financing statement pursuant to subsection (a) of Code Section 11-9-519.

(38) "Filing office" means an office designated in Code Section 11-9-501 as the place to file a financing statement.

(39) "Filing office rule" means a rule adopted pursuant to Code Section 11-9-526.

(40) "Financing statement" means a record or records composed of an initial financing statement and any filed record relating to the initial financing statement.

(41) "Fixture filing" means the filing of a financing statement covering goods that are or are to become fixtures and satisfying subsections (a) and (b) of Code Section 11-9-502. The term includes the filing of a financing statement covering goods of a transmitting utility which are or are to become fixtures.

(42) "Fixtures" means goods that have become so related to particular real property that an interest in them arises under real property law.

(43) "General intangible" means any personal property, including things in action, other than accounts, chattel paper, commercial tort claims, deposit accounts, documents, goods, instruments, investment property, letter of credit rights, letters of credit, money, and oil, gas, or other minerals before extraction. The term includes payment intangibles and software.

(44) "Good faith" means honesty in fact and the observance of reasonable commercial standards of fair dealing.

(45) "Goods" means all things that are movable when a security interest attaches. The term includes (i) fixtures, (ii) standing timber that is to be cut and removed under a conveyance or contract for sale, (iii) the unborn young of animals, and (iv) crops grown, growing, or to be grown, even if the crops are produced on trees, vines, or bushes. The term also includes a computer program embedded in goods and any supporting information provided in connection with a transaction relating to the program if (i) the program is associated with the goods in such a manner that it customarily is considered part of the goods, or (ii) by becoming the owner of the goods, a person acquires a right to use the program in connection with the goods. The term does not include a computer program embedded in goods that consist solely of the medium in which the program is embedded. The term also does not include accounts, chattel paper, commercial tort claims, deposit accounts, documents, general intangibles, instruments, investment property, letter of credit rights, letters of credit, money, or oil, gas, or other minerals before extraction.

(46) "Governmental unit" means a subdivision, agency, department, county, parish, municipality, or other unit of the government of the United States, a state, or a foreign country. The term includes an organization having a separate corporate existence if the organization is eligible to issue debt on which interest is exempt from income taxation under the laws of the United States.

(47) "Health care insurance receivable" means an interest in or claim under a policy of insurance which is a right to payment of a monetary obligation for health care goods or services provided or to be provided.

(48) "Instrument" means a negotiable instrument or any other writing that evidences a right to the payment of a monetary obligation, is not itself a security agreement or lease, and is of a type that in ordinary course of business is transferred by delivery with any necessary indorsement or assignment. The term does not include (i) investment property, (ii) letters of credit, or (iii) writings that evidence a right to payment arising out of the use of a credit or charge card or information contained on or for use with the card.

(49) "Inventory" means goods, other than farm products, which:

(A) Are leased by a person as lessor;

(B) Are held by a person for sale or lease or to be furnished under a contract of service;

(C) Are furnished by a person under a contract of service; or

(D) Consist of raw materials, work in process, or materials used or consumed in a business.

(50) "Investment property" means a security, whether certificated or uncertificated, security entitlement, securities account, commodity contract, or commodity account.

(51) "Jurisdiction of organization," with respect to a registered organization, means the jurisdiction under whose law the organization is organized.

(52) "Letter of credit right" means a right to payment or performance under a letter of credit, whether or not the beneficiary has demanded or is at the time entitled to demand payment or performance. The term does not include the right of a beneficiary to demand payment or performance under a letter of credit.

(53) "Lien creditor" means:

(A) A creditor that has acquired a lien on the property involved by attachment, levy, or the like;

(B) An assignee for benefit of creditors from the time of assignment;

(C) A trustee in bankruptcy from the date of the filing of the petition; or

(D) A receiver in equity from the time of appointment.

(54) "Mortgage" means a consensual interest in real property, including fixtures, which secures payment or performance of an obligation. The term includes a deed to secure debt.

(55) "New debtor" means a person that becomes bound as debtor under subsection (d) of Code Section 11-9-203 by a security agreement previously entered into by another person.

(56) "New value" means (i) money, (ii) money's worth in property, services, or new credit, or (iii) release by a transferee of an interest in property previously transferred to the transferee. The term does not include an obligation substituted for another obligation.

(57) "Noncash proceeds" means proceeds other than cash proceeds.

(58) "Obligor" means a person that, with respect to an obligation secured by a security interest in or an agricultural lien on the collateral, (i) owes payment or other performance of the obligation, (ii) has provided property other than the collateral to secure payment or other performance of the obligation, or (iii) is otherwise accountable in whole or in part for payment or other performance of the obligation. The term does not include issuers or nominated persons under a letter of credit.

(59) "Original debtor," except as used in subsection (c) of Code Section 11-9-310, means a person that, as debtor, entered into a security agreement to which a new debtor has become bound under subsection (d) of Code Section 11-9-203.

(60) "Payment intangible" means a general intangible under which the account debtor's principal obligation is a monetary obligation.

(61) "Person related to," with respect to an individual, means:

(A) The spouse of the individual;

(B) A brother, brother-in-law, sister, or sister-in-law of the individual;

(C) An ancestor or lineal descendant of the individual or the individual's spouse; or

(D) Any other relative, by blood or marriage, of the individual or the individual's spouse who shares the same home with the individual.

(62) "Person related to," with respect to an organization, means:

(A) A person directly or indirectly controlling, controlled by, or under common control with the organization;

(B) An officer or director of, or a person performing similar functions with respect to, the organization;

(C) An officer or director of, or a person performing similar functions with respect to, a person described in subparagraph (A) of this paragraph;

(D) The spouse of an individual described in subparagraph (A), (B), or (C) of this paragraph; or

(E) An individual who is related by blood or marriage to an individual described in subparagraph (A), (B), (C), or (D) of this paragraph and shares the same home with the individual.

(63) "Proceeds," except as used in subsection (d) of Code Section 11-9-609, means the following property:

(A) Whatever is acquired upon the sale, lease, license, exchange, or other disposition of collateral;

(B) Whatever is collected on, or distributed on account of, collateral;

(C) Rights arising out of collateral;

(D) To the extent of the value of collateral, claims arising out of the loss, nonconformity, or interference with the use of, defects or infringement of rights in, or damage to the collateral; or

(E) To the extent of the value of collateral and to the extent payable to the debtor or the secured party, insurance payable by reason of the loss or nonconformity of, defects or infringement of rights in, or damage to the collateral.

(64) "Promissory note" means an instrument that evidences a promise to pay a monetary obligation, does not evidence an order to pay, and does not contain an acknowledgment by a bank that the bank has received for deposit a sum of money or funds.

(65) "Proposal" means a record authenticated by a secured party which includes the terms on which the secured party is willing to accept collateral in full or partial satisfaction of the obligation it secures pursuant to Code Sections 11-9-620, 11-9-621, and 11-9-622.

(66) "Public finance transaction" means a secured transaction in connection with which:

(A) Debt securities are issued;

(B) All or a portion of the securities issued have an initial stated maturity of at least five years; and

(C) The debtor, obligor, secured party, account debtor or other person obligated on collateral, assignor or assignee of a secured obligation, or assignor or assignee of a security interest is a state or a governmental unit of a state.

(67) "Pursuant to commitment," with respect to an advance made or other value given by a secured party, means pursuant to the secured party's obligation, whether or not a subsequent event of default or other event not within the secured party's control has relieved or may relieve the secured party from its obligation.

(68) "Record," except as used in "for record," "of record," "record or legal title," and "record owner," means information that is inscribed on a tangible medium or which is stored in an electronic or other medium and is retrievable in perceivable form.

(69) "Registered organization" means an organization organized solely under the law of a single state or the United States and as to which the state or the United States must maintain a public record showing the organization to have been organized.

(70) "Secondary obligor" means an obligor to the extent that:

(A) The obligor's obligation is secondary; or

(B) The obligor has a right of recourse with respect to an obligation secured by collateral against the debtor, another obligor, or property of either.

(71) "Secured party" means:

(A) A person in whose favor a security interest is created or provided for under a security agreement, whether or not any obligation to be secured is outstanding;

(B) A person that holds an agricultural lien;

(C) A consignor;

(D) A person to which accounts, chattel paper, payment intangibles, or promissory notes have been sold;

(E) A trustee, indenture trustee, agent, collateral agent, or other representative in whose favor a security interest or agricultural lien is created or provided for; or

(F) A person that holds a security interest arising under Code Section 11-2-401, 11-2-505, or subsection (3) of Code Section 11-2-711, subsection (5) of Code Section 11-2A-508, Code Section 11-4-210, or Code Section 11-5-118.

(72) "Security agreement" means an agreement that creates or provides for a security interest.

(73) "Send," in connection with a record or notification, means:

(A) To deposit in the mail, deliver for transmission, or transmit by any other usual means of communication, with postage or cost of transmission provided for, addressed to any address reasonable under the circumstances; or

(B) To cause the record or notification to be received within the time that it would have been received if properly sent under subparagraph (A) of this paragraph.

(74) "Software" means a computer program and any supporting information provided in connection with a transaction relating to the program. The term does not include a computer program that is included in the definition of goods.

(75) "State" means a state of the United States, the District of Columbia, Puerto Rico, the United States Virgin Islands, or any territory or insular possession subject to the jurisdiction of the United States.

(76) "Supporting obligation" means a letter of credit right or secondary obligation that supports the payment or performance of an account, chattel paper, a document, a general intangible, an instrument, or investment property.

(77) "Tangible chattel paper" means chattel paper evidenced by a record or records consisting of information that is inscribed on a tangible medium.

(78) "Termination statement" means an amendment of a financing statement which:

(A) Identifies, by its file number, the initial financing statement to which it relates; and

(B) Indicates either that it is a termination statement or that the identified financing statement is no longer effective.

(79) "Transmitting utility" means a person primarily engaged in the business of:

(A) Operating a railroad, subway, street railway, or trolley bus;

(B) Transmitting communications electrically, electromagnetically, or by light;

(C) Transmitting goods by pipeline or sewer; or

(D) Transmitting or producing and transmitting electricity, steam, gas, or water.

(b) *Definitions in other articles.* "Control" as provided in Code Section 11-7-106 and the following definitions in other articles apply to this article:

"Applicant." Code Section 11-5-102.
"Beneficiary." Code Section 11-5-102.
"Broker." Code Section 11-8-102.
"Certificated security." Code Section 11-8-102.
"Check." Code Section 11-3-104.
"Clearing corporation." Code Section 11-8-102.
"Contract for sale." Code Section 11-2-106.
"Customer." Code Section 11-4-104.
"Entitlement holder." Code Section 11-8-102.
"Financial asset." Code Section 11-8-102.
"Holder in due course." Code Section 11-3-302.
"Issuer" (with respect to a letter of credit or letter of credit right). Code Section 11-5-102.
"Issuer" (with respect to a security). Code Section 11-8-201.
"Issuer" (with respect to documents of title). Code Section 11-7-102.
"Lease." Code Section 11-2A-103.
"Lease agreement." Code Section 11-2A-103.
"Lease contract." Code Section 11-2A-103.
"Leasehold interest." Code Section 11-2A-103.
"Lessee." Code Section 11-2A-103.
"Lessee in ordinary course of business." Code Section 11-2A-103.
"Lessor." Code Section 11-2A-103.
"Lessor's residual interest." Code Section 11-2A-103.
"Letter of credit." Code Section 11-5-102.
"Merchant." Code Section 11-2-104.
"Negotiable instrument." Code Section 11-3-104.
"Nominated person." Code Section 11-5-102.
"Note." Code Section 11-3-104.
"Proceeds of a letter of credit." Code Section 11-5-114.
"Prove." Code Section 11-3-103.
"Sale." Code Section 11-2-106.
"Securities account." Code Section 11-8-501.
"Securities intermediary." Code Section 11-8-102.
"Security." Code Section 11-8-102.
"Security certificate." Code Section 11-8-102.
"Security entitlement." Code Section 11-8-102.
"Uncertificated security." Code Section 11-8-102.

(c) *Article 1 definitions and principles.* Article 1 of this title contains general definitions and principles of construction and interpretation applicable throughout this article.

§ 11-9-103. Purchase money security interest; application of payments; burden of establishing.
(a) *Definitions.* As used in this Code section, the term:
(1) "Purchase money collateral" means goods or software that secures a purchase money obligation incurred with respect to that collateral.
(2) "Purchase money obligation" means an obligation of an obligor incurred as all or part of the price of the collateral or for value given to enable the debtor to acquire rights in or the use of the collateral if the value is in fact so used.
(b) *Purchase money security interest in goods.* A security interest in goods is a purchase money security interest:
(1) To the extent that the goods are purchase money collateral with respect to that security interest;
(2) If the security interest is in inventory that is or was purchase money collateral, also to the extent that the security interest secures a purchase money obligation incurred with respect to other inventory in which the secured party holds or held a purchase money security interest; and
(3) Also to the extent that the security interest secures a purchase money obligation incurred with respect to software in which the secured party holds or held a purchase money security interest.
(c) *Purchase money security interest in software.* A security interest in software is a purchase money security interest to the extent that the security interest also secures a purchase money obligation incurred with respect to goods in which the secured party holds or held a purchase money security interest if:
(1) The debtor acquired its interest in the software in an integrated transaction in which it acquired an interest in the goods; and
(2) The debtor acquired its interest in the software for the principal purpose of using the software in the goods.
(d) *Consignor's inventory purchase money security interest.* The security interest of a consignor in goods that are the subject of a consignment is a purchase money security interest in inventory.
(e) *Application of payment in nonconsumer goods transaction.* In a transaction other than a consumer goods transaction, if the extent to which a security interest is a purchase money security interest depends on the application of a payment to a particular obligation, the payment must be applied:
(1) In accordance with any reasonable method of application to which the parties agree;
(2) In the absence of the parties' agreement to a reasonable method, in accordance with any intention of the obligor manifested at or before the time of payment; or
(3) In the absence of an agreement to a reasonable method and a timely manifestation of the obligor's intention, in the following order:
(A) To obligations that are not secured; and
(B) If more than one obligation is secured, to obligations secured by purchase money security interests in the order in which those obligations were incurred.
(f) *No loss of status of purchase money security interest in nonconsumer goods transaction.* In a transaction other than a consumer goods transaction, a purchase money security interest does not lose its status as such, even if:
(1) The purchase money collateral also secures an obligation that is not a purchase money obligation;
(2) Collateral that is not purchase money collateral also secures the purchase money obligation; or
(3) The purchase money obligation has been renewed, refinanced, consolidated, or restructured.
(g) *Burden of proof in nonconsumer goods transaction.* In a transaction other than a consumer goods transaction, a secured party claiming a purchase money security interest has the burden of establishing the extent to which the security interest is a purchase money security interest.
(h) *Nonconsumer goods transactions; no inference.* The limitation of the rules in subsections (e), (f), and (g) of this Code section to transactions other than consumer goods transactions is intended to leave to the court the determination of the applicable rules in consumer goods transactions. The court may not infer from that limitation the nature of the applicable rule in consumer goods transactions and may continue to apply established approaches.

§ 11-9-104. Control of deposit account.
(a) *Requirements for control.* A secured party has control of a deposit account if:
(1) The secured party is the bank with which the deposit account is maintained;
(2) The debtor, secured party, and bank have agreed in an authenticated record that the bank will comply with instructions originated by the secured party directing disposition of the funds in the deposit account without further consent by the debtor; or
(3) The secured party becomes the bank's customer with respect to the deposit account.
(b) *Debtor's right to direct disposition.* A secured party that has satisfied subsection (a) of this Code section has control, even if the debtor retains the right to direct the disposition of funds from the deposit account.

§ 11-9-105. Control of electronic chattel paper.
A secured party has control of electronic chattel paper if the record or records comprising the chattel paper are created, stored, and assigned in such a manner that:
(1) A single authoritative copy of the record or records exists which is unique, identifiable, and, except as otherwise provided in paragraphs (4), (5), and (6) of this Code section, unalterable;
(2) The authoritative copy identifies the secured party as the assignee of the record or records;
(3) The authoritative copy is communicated to and maintained by the secured party or its designated custodian;
(4) Copies or revisions that add or change an identified assignee of the authoritative copy can be made only with the participation of the secured party;
(5) Each copy of the authoritative copy and any copy

of a copy is readily identifiable as a copy that is not the authoritative copy; and

(6) Any revision of the authoritative copy is readily identifiable as an authorized or unauthorized revision.

§ 11-9-106. Control of investment property.

(a) *Control under Code Section 11-8-106.* A person has control of a certificated security, uncertificated security, or security entitlement as provided in Code Section 11-8-106.

(b) *Control of commodity contract.* A secured party has control of a commodity contract if:

(1) The secured party is the commodity intermediary with which the commodity contract is carried; or

(2) The commodity customer, secured party, and commodity intermediary have agreed that the commodity intermediary will apply any value distributed on account of the commodity contract as directed by the secured party without further consent by the commodity customer.

(c) *Effect of control of securities account or commodity account.* A secured party having control of all security entitlements or commodity contracts carried in a securities account or commodity account has control over the securities account or commodity account.

§ 11-9-107. Control of letter of credit right.

A secured party has control of a letter of credit right to the extent of any right to payment or performance by the issuer or any nominated person if the issuer or nominated person has consented to an assignment of proceeds of the letter of credit under subsection (c) of Code Section 11-5-114 or otherwise applicable law or practice.

§ 11-9-108. Sufficiency of description.

(a) *Sufficiency of description.* Except as otherwise provided in subsections (c), (d), and (e) of this Code section, a description of personal or real property is sufficient, whether or not it is specific, if it reasonably identifies what is described.

(b) *Examples of reasonable identification.* Except as otherwise provided in subsection (d) of this Code section, a description of collateral reasonably identifies the collateral if it identifies the collateral by:

(1) Specific listing;

(2)Category;

(3) Except as otherwise provided in subsection (e) of this Code section, a type of collateral defined in this title;

(4)Quantity;

(5) Computational or allocational formula or procedure; or

(6) Except as otherwise provided in subsection (c) of this Code section, any other method, if the identity of the collateral is objectively determinable.

(c) *Supergeneric description not sufficient.* A description of collateral as "all the debtor's assets" or "all the debtor's personal property" or using words of similar import does not reasonably identify the collateral.

(d) *Investment property.* Except as otherwise provided in subsection (e) of this Code section, a description of a security entitlement, securities account, or commodity account is sufficient if it describes:

(1) The collateral by those terms or as investment property; or

(2) The underlying financial asset or commodity contract.

(e) *When description by type insufficient.* A description only by type of collateral defined in this title is an insufficient description of:

(1) A commercial tort claim; or

(2) In a consumer transaction, consumer goods, a security entitlement, a securities account, or a commodity account.

[redacted]

[redacted]

UCC FINANCING STATEMENT

FOLLOW INSTRUCTIONS

A. NAME & PHONE OF CONTACT AT FILER (optional)

B. E-MAIL CONTACT AT FILER (optional)

C. SEND ACKNOWLEDGMENT TO: (Name and Address)

THE ABOVE SPACE IS FOR FILING OFFICE USE ONLY

1. DEBTOR'S NAME: Provide only one Debtor name (1a or 1b) (use exact, full name; do not omit, modify, or abbreviate any part of the Debtor's name); if any part of the Individual Debtor's name will not fit in line 1b, leave all of item 1 blank, check here ☐ and provide the Individual Debtor information in item 10 of the Financing Statement Addendum (Form UCC1Ad)

1a. ORGANIZATION'S NAME				
OR 1b. INDIVIDUAL'S SURNAME	FIRST PERSONAL NAME	ADDITIONAL NAME(S)/INITIAL(S)		SUFFIX
1c. MAILING ADDRESS	CITY	STATE	POSTAL CODE	COUNTRY

2. DEBTOR'S NAME: Provide only one Debtor name (2a or 2b) (use exact, full name; do not omit, modify, or abbreviate any part of the Debtor's name); if any part of the Individual Debtor's name will not fit in line 2b, leave all of item 2 blank, check here ☐ and provide the Individual Debtor information in item 10 of the Financing Statement Addendum (Form UCC1Ad)

2a. ORGANIZATION'S NAME				
OR 2b. INDIVIDUAL'S SURNAME	FIRST PERSONAL NAME	ADDITIONAL NAME(S)/INITIAL(S)		SUFFIX
2c. MAILING ADDRESS	CITY	STATE	POSTAL CODE	COUNTRY

3. SECURED PARTY'S NAME (or NAME of ASSIGNEE of ASSIGNOR SECURED PARTY): Provide only one Secured Party name (3a or 3b)

3a. ORGANIZATION'S NAME				
OR 3b. INDIVIDUAL'S SURNAME	FIRST PERSONAL NAME	ADDITIONAL NAME(S)/INITIAL(S)		SUFFIX
3c. MAILING ADDRESS	CITY	STATE	POSTAL CODE	COUNTRY

4. COLLATERAL: This financing statement covers the following collateral:

5. Check only if applicable and check only one box: Collateral is ☐ held in a Trust (see UCC1Ad, item 17 and Instructions) ☐ being administered by a Decedent's Personal Representative

6a. Check only if applicable and check only one box:
☐ Public-Finance Transaction ☐ Manufactured-Home Transaction ☐ A Debtor is a Transmitting Utility

6b. Check only if applicable and check only one box:
☐ Agricultural Lien ☐ Non-UCC Filing

7. ALTERNATIVE DESIGNATION (if applicable): ☐ Lessee/Lessor ☐ Consignee/Consignor ☐ Seller/Buyer ☐ Bailee/Bailor ☐ Licensee/Licensor

8. OPTIONAL FILER REFERENCE DATA:

FILING OFFICE COPY — UCC FINANCING STATEMENT (Form UCC1) (Rev. 04/20/11) International Association of Commercial Administrators (IACA)

BOOK______________

PAGE______________

GWINNETT SUPERIOR COURT
TRADE NAME REGISTRATION

PERSONALLY APPEARED THE UNDERSIGNED WHO ON OATH DEPOSES AND SAYS

THAT:

*____
(name of proprietor or corporate name if corporation)

*____
(address of proprietor or parent corporation)

and
*____
(name of second proprietor or corporation if any)

*____
(address)

IS/ARE DOING BUSINESS IN GWINNETT COUNTY, GEORGIA UNDER THE NAME OF:

TRADENAME:*______________________________________

ADDRESS:*____
(tradename address in______________________ County)

and that the nature of the business to be carried on at such address is

*____

*______________________________
(signature of person making declaration)

SWORN TO AND SUBSCRIBED BEFORE

ME THIS_______ DAY OF_______________, 20____

____
NOTARY PUBLIC OR DEPUTY CLERK

FEES Due at Time or Registration

$161.00 FILING FEE TO CLERK SUPERIOR COURT (CASH, ATTORNEY CHECK OR CERTIFIED FUNDS ONLY)
$40.00 PUBLICATION FEE TO GWINNETT DAILY POST (CHECK OR MONEY ORDER ONLY)

FORM 30

Control No. 07019395

STATE OF GEORGIA

Secretary of State

Corporations Division
315 West Tower
#2 Martin Luther King, Jr. Dr.
Atlanta, Georgia 30334-1530

CERTIFICATE OF ORGANIZATION

I, **Karen C Handel**, the Secretary of State and the Corporations Commissioner of the State of Georgia, hereby certify under the seal of my office that

STUART HUDSON ENTERPRISES, LLC
a Domestic Limited Liability Company

has been duly organized under the laws of the State of Georgia on **03/05/2007** by the filing of articles of organization in the Office of the Secretary of State and by the paying of fees as provided by Title 14 of the Official Code of Georgia Annotated.

WITNESS my hand and official seal of the City of Atlanta and the State of Georgia on March 5, 2007

Karen C Handel
Secretary of State

Control No: 07019385
Date Filed: 03/06/2007 05:35 PM
Karen C Handel
Secretary of State

March 05, 2007

ARTICLES OF ORGANIZATION
FOR GEORGIA LIMITED LIABILITY COMPANY

The name of the Limited Liability Company is:
Stuart Hudson Enterprises, LLC

Filer name, address and phone number:
Robert Douglas Lenhardt
220 College Avenue , Suite 314
Athens, GA 30601
(706) 369-5433

The principal mailing address of the Limited Liability Company is:
400 Timber Creek Drive
Athens, GA 30605

The Registered Agent is:
Daniel Stuart Simmons
400 Timber Creek Drive
Athens, GA 30605
County: Clarke

The name and address of each organizer(s) are:

Daniel Stuart Simmons	Jason Ellis
400 Timber Creek Drive	1283 E. Broad Street
Athens, GA 30605	Athens, GA 30601

The optional provisions are:
No optional provisions.

IN WITNESS WHEREOF, the undersigned has executed these Articles of Organization on the date set forth below.

Signature(s):	**Date:**
Attorney-in-Fact, Robert Douglas Lenhardt	March 05, 2007

Index

Made in United States
Orlando, FL
04 November 2026

90200398R00207